MANAGING METALS PRICE RISK

MANAGING METALS PRICE RISK

UBS
Union Bank of Switzerland

RISK
PUBLICATIONS

Published by Risk Publications
104–112 Marylebone Lane
London W1M 5FU
Tel +44 (0)171 487 5326; fax +44 (0)171 486 0879

ISBN 1 899332 80 4 - Hardback
ISBN 1 899332 85 5 - Softback

Editor: Robert Jameson
Desk Editor: Laurie Donaldson
Production Editor: Miles Smith-Morris

Printed and bound in Great Britain by Bookcraft (Bath) Ltd,
Midsomer Norton.
Covers printed by Grange Press, Southwick.

PREFACE

This book brings together current thinking on how to measure and manage price risk in the metals markets. We have grouped the chapters into three main sections, each dealing with a key theme in advanced risk management.

The first section describes risk management instruments, using selected metals markets to demonstrate the structure and application of tools such as swaps, options and futures contracts. As well as making clear why certain instruments are more useful (and used) in some markets than others, the four chapters in this section provide plenty of detailed, practical examples.

The second section looks at the controversial question of why a metals corporation might choose to build a risk management strategy. What types of price risk should a corporation seek to manage in order to create shareholder value? How should a firm set about devising and implementing its risk management strategy? This section also explores variation in the "risk appetite" of different *kinds* of metals corporation.

The third section of the book explores themes in metals risk analysis and derivative valuation. Readers of these chapters will grasp more clearly the contrasting ways in which researchers try to understand price formation and price volatility in the short-term and longer term metals markets. Other issues dealt with here include how to adapt the classic Black–Scholes approach to option valuation to the metals markets, and how to understand the different mix of supply and demand fundamentals that inform long-term prices in each of the metals markets.

It is the interaction of these three themes – instrument structure, corporate goals, and market analysis and modelling – that makes metals risk management such a challenging and interesting field. We hope that this book will provide a point of reference in this rapidly growing, and increasingly complex, market.

John Bishop

Senior Vice President of Commodities Trading, Sales and Risk Management

Union Bank of Switzerland

July 1997

CONTENTS

KEY THEMES IN METALS PRICE RISK MANAGEMENT

Throughout this book special panels introduce key concepts and themes and describe worked examples:

AUTHORS

Celso Brunetti is a PhD student in the Department of Economics, Queen Mary and Westfield College, University of London. He obtained his laurea from the Catholic University in Milan, and an MEcon from Bocconi University, Milan. His thesis topic was modelling financial market volatility.

Oliver Frankel is vice president in Goldman Sachs' Currency and Commodity Strategies group. His responsibilities include risk management of the metals desk, modelling metals risk, and derivative pricing and hedging. He also offers risk advisory services to the bank's clients. Before joining Goldman Sachs in 1993, Oliver was the head of US interest rate options trading at a commercial bank, and during his career he has also consulted with the US Department of Defense on Operations Research and Economics (1985) and the Strategic Defense Initiative (1986). He has a PhD in system science from UCLA (1988) and an MA in mathematics from Cambridge University.

Christopher L. Gilbert is Professor of Applied Econometrics and Head of the Economics Graduate School, Queen Mary and Westfield College, University of London. He obtained his doctorate from Oxford University, and also studies at the London School of Economics. Christopher has written extensively on commodity markets and on futures. His recent work includes a study of the effects of fund activity on coffee and cocoa futures, a study of long-term trends in metals price volatility, and a study on the implications of the Sumitomo affair for UK futures regulation.

Chris Harris graduated in metallurgy and materials science at Cambridge University, where he completed his PhD in fracture metallurgy. Prior to BZW, he headed derivative trading divisions in cross currencies (AIG Trading) and metals (Gerald Metals). At BZW, he has headed metal derivative trading and commodity marketing. Chris now works in quantitative analysis. He has written and presented many articles covering the different aspects of metal prices and metal markets.

David L. Mengle is a vice president at JP Morgan Securities Inc in New York, as well as adjunct associate professor of finance at the Fordham University Graduate School of Business. He is also editor and primary contributor to *The JP Morgan/Arthur Andersen Guide to Corporate Risk Management.* Prior to joining Morgan in 1991, David was an economist with the Federal Reserve Bank of Richmond. He holds a BA from The Citadel and a PhD in economics from the University of California, Los Angeles.

Mark Nicholls is a staff writer at *Risk* magazine. He is responsible for reporting on risk management and regulation in the commodities markets, as well as covering the full range of derivatives issues. He holds a degree in politics from Durham University and a masters in European politics from the London School of Economics.

David Quarmby is a vice president of Chase Manhattan Bank in the Global Commodities division, based in London. He is responsible for marketing metals risk management and commodity finance for Europe, Africa and the Middle East. Prior to this, David had worked for a UK merchant bank and a London Metal Exchange ring-dealing member. He holds a BA in economics from the University of East Anglia, Norwich.

Jud Roderick is head of commodity derivatives at FirstDerivatives, a division of the First National Bank of Southern Africa. Over the past three years, he has built up a base metals desk, focused on marketing metal derivatives to Southern African corporates. Jud's previous risk management experience includes four years with Australian Airlines in the position of treasurer, operations, responsible for the management of the airline's interest rate, foreign exchange and jet fuel exposures. Prior to that, he worked with The Australian Wheat Board and, in this role, was involved with the execution and monitoring of the Board's active grain futures hedging programme on the Chicago Board of Trade. Jud has a Bec Hons from the University of Western Australia.

Jon Serbin undertakes global capital management and planning for Morgan Stanley, Dean Witter and Discover & Co in New York City. Prior to joining the capital planning and treasury group, he was in the equity research department covering the banking industry. Before joining

Morgan Stanley, Jon was a vice president of Multinational Strategies Inc, an associate of MIT's International Financial Services Research Centre and a research associate at the Harvard Business School. He did his undergraduate studies in government at Harvard College and graduate work in finance at MIT's Sloan School of Management.

Andy Smith has been precious metals analyst at Union Bank of Switzerland since 1988. As such, he is responsible for forecasts of, and research into, gold, silver and platinum group metals for commodities risk management and the bank as a whole. Andy's move into financial services followed a scenic route: a spell at British Petroleum (as a senior economist in corporate strategy) and a sojourn at Consolidated Gold Fields (as a group economist). These were preceded by six years at Her Majesty's pleasure, in the UK civil service (with four years in HM Treasury, latterly as economic adviser). He is a graduate of Reading University and holds a masters degree in economics from the London School of Economics.

Gilles P. Teyssiere is a lecturer in the Department of Economics, Queen Mary and Westfield College, University of London. He obtained his doctorate from the University of Marseilles, and also studied at the European University Institute, Florence. He works on applied econometric modelling problems associated with large datasets, and in particular on nonparametric and semiparametric estimation in financial markets and also in labour markets.

Jason A. Tudor is senior options dealer at Metallgesellschaft Ltd, the largest ring-dealing member of the London Metal Exchange (LME), and the only ring dealer to make markets in every LME futures and options contract. Previously, he spent three years as manager of MG's overseas office. Jason joined MG in 1990, after graduating from Cambridge University with a degree in engineering and management studies.

Peter Tufano is an associate professor of business administration at Harvard Business School. His research focuses on the corporate uses of financial engineering for managing risk. His recent research on risk management practices in the gold mining industry has been published in the *Journal of Finance* and shared the Smith-Breeden prize for the best article in the journal in 1996. Peter teaches MBA and executive education courses on the subject of corporate financial engineering, and published the book *Cases in Financial Engineering* with his colleagues Scott Mason, Robert C. Merton and Andre Perold. He received his AB, MBA and PhD degrees from Harvard University.

RISK MANAGEMENT INSTRUMENTS AND THE METALS MARKETS

1

Precious Metals Swaps and Forwards

Andy Smith
UBS

This chapter examines how the instruments and strategies most commonly used for managing the price risk of precious metals relate to the underlying structure of the markets. We begin by looking at how the gold forward and swap markets mirror the "repo" market in financial securities. Both markets are driven by a "simultaneous spot sale and forward purchase, thereby financing a long position".[1] We survey the range of forward-based risk management instruments now available to end-users, highlighting their advantages and disadvantages, and conclude by analysing the motivation of the central banks and other market participants.

The gold repo market

Lending inventories of precious metals is as old as the hills. Indeed, pawnbroking may be the second oldest profession. Jargon, of course, varies – the lender can be variously "funding an inventory", or undertaking "collateralised borrowing" – but the principles remain the same. They translate into the ability of the holder of an asset to borrow funds at less than market interest rates; or, similarly, to earn a return by lending surplus stock. This ability is, in turn, the crucial feature of risk management in all the world's "second-hand" stockholding markets, such as those for currencies, equities, bonds and gold. It distinguishes these financial markets from pure commodity markets, where above-ground stocks are normally only a fraction of new flows. This availability of metal liquidity fuels the gold repo market, or pawn shop, as illustrated in Figure 1.

When a commercial bank is sold gold forward by a mining company (seeking to hedge its price exposure), the bank borrows gold from a central bank, sells it in the market and deposits the dollar receipts at dollar-denominated Libor. The commercial bank eventually pays the miner the forward gold price (spot price plus contango or "swap rate") out of the Libor dollar interest. The residual – the difference between the revenue that can be raised simply by depositing funds at Libor, and the price of gold in the forward markets – is the gold "lease rate", the central bank's return for lending gold.

At the close of the hedge, the gold delivered by the mining corporation is effectively put back into the central bank vault. The key to this kind of transaction is that the gold market is reliably in "contango" – where spot prices are lower than forward or future prices (see Panel 3). If the market were regularly in "backwardation" – where spot prices are at a premium to forward prices – the gold repo market would not exist.

The central bank may decide to swap, rather than deposit, its gold. As shown in Figure 1, this involves selling the gold for dollars and agreeing to buy back the gold at the dollar spot price plus contango. In effect, the buyer of the gold has lent dollars to the central bank at Libor minus the

1. Gold forward sale funded by a gold swap

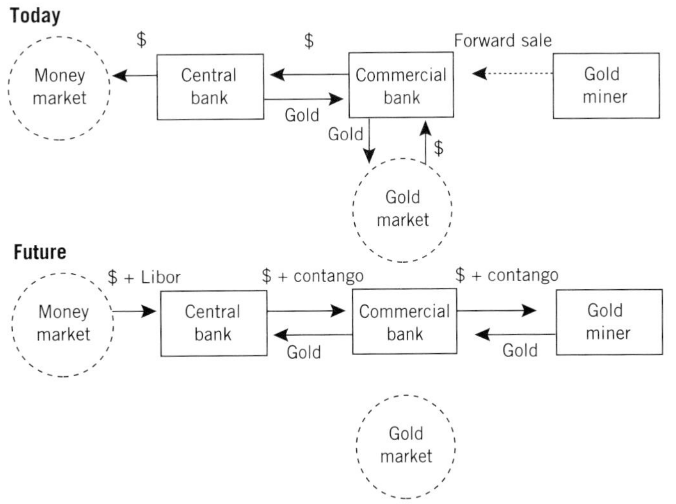

PANEL 1

COMPARING FINANCIAL REPO AND GOLD SWAP MARKETS

Repo market feature	Comparable gold swap market feature
Term repo: sale and repurchase of security at maturity	**Fixed forward sale:** sale of gold at an agreed maturity
Open repo: open-ended repurchase, or repurchase closed at the discretion of either party	**Spot-deferred sale:** forward sale contract without a pre-defined delivery date
Tri-party repo: delivery of collateral to an agreed third party	**Swap, loco London at the Bank of England:** swap with gold held and priced for delivery in London
Duration of repos: "from overnight out to one year, with even longer maturities possible"; the "duration of most trades tends to be inside three months"[1]	"Half of the metal made available by central banks to the London market has an initial life of no more than three months"[2]
Returns: "lenders are typically looking at less than 50 basis points as their fee for making US Treasury bills available to borrowers"[1]	Average three-month lease rate since 1982: 100bp
Maturity mismatch: "most match books worthy of the name are deliberately mismatched"[1] to exploit short-term interest rate movements and anticipated changes in the supply and demand for the security	Given the long maturity of some of the forward sale programmes ... there is considerable maturity mismatch in the market, and this itself is a source of instability"[2]
Loans or swaps: "issues such as dividend and voting rights" mean lending, while retaining ownership "is the preferred transaction structure" in equity markets[3]	One-third of central bank loans are swaps, two-thirds are in the form of deposits

1 UBS, *Investor Guide to the International Repo Market*, August 1995.
2 Bank of England, London Central Banking Conference, November 1995.
3 *Financial Times*, March 1996.

gold lease rate. The attraction for the central bank, apart from avoiding the counterparty risk of unsecured gold deposits, is the reduction in borrowing cost below Libor.

The gold repo market and security repo market are essentially similar. However, there are three important differences of degree:

❑ bond repos are an integral part of central bank monetary policy, whereas most gold swaps/deposits are discretionary, with no policy implications or motivation. Of course, the main activity of the borrower or short seller in the bond market is not to produce bonds; in gold, the *raison d'être* of mining companies which sell gold forward is to mine gold;

❑ almost all large central banks are active in securities repos, whereas most large central banks still do not lend gold. Indeed, the main reason gold is not a pure "cost of carry market", with contango exactly equal to Libor, is that only a minority of central banks take advantage of the arbitrage opportunity to sell now and buy back later; and

❑ securities repo markets enjoy the safety net of "lenders of last resort" – eg, the Federal Reserve Bank (Fed) offers a bond "line" to primary dealers. The gold swap market, on the other hand, has no such comfort (although the nascent gold lease-rate options market could be viewed as a synthetic lender of last resort).

One indication of the size of the gold swap market (unlike in the foreign exchange market, the Bank for International Settlements (BIS) carries out no formal survey), is the demand side of business – predominantly forward selling by gold producers. Estimates by Gold Fields Mineral Services suggest a growth compatible with that of micro-chips, from a couple of hundred tonnes in the late 1980s to almost 2,000 tonnes in 1996 (equivalent to one year's global mine production). Matching the physical growth in the gold swaps market is an ever-increasing variety of sophisticated hedge products, from the first 30-tonne gold loan in the late 1980s to the wide variety of structures described in this chapter. Roles in the gold swap market have blurred, with mining companies acting like commercial banks in taking positions on money market and gold interest rates, and with central banks adopting the guise of producers, taking advantage of the forward market to sell some of their reserves.

The limits to growth of the gold swap market are to be found in the central bank community - the source of most borrowed gold - and in the ingenuity of the interbank market in teasing out more official gold liquidity. Thanks to the generosity of past taxpayers, 20 years' worth of mine supply sits in a readily lendable form in official vaults, distanced from its former monetary role. In principle, this makes it available to be lent at very low lease rates. In practice, however, ensuring a smooth supply response to hedgers' demands to borrow gold is more difficult. Multilateral organisations such as the International Monetary Fund (IMF) do not lend; only one central bank with reserves of over 1,000 tonnes of gold reserves currently lends. Estimates suggest that, out of the total 35,000 tonnes of official gold, only those banks that hold around 7,000 tonnes are active, and it is they that lend or swap the 2,000 tonnes in the current market.

Does this suggest scope for growth, or a likelihood of bottlenecks? A long-term drift up in the lease rate implies, predictably, that a higher reward is required to tempt more gold out of official vaults. The brevity of squeezes in the gold lease market - as in the November 1995 squeeze described in Panel 2 (overleaf), when short lease rates moved above money market rates, creating a two-day backwardation - suggests a flexibility in gold lending which should reassure gold hedgers.

Indeed, whether it be the mining company locking in forward prices for their future output, or the gold fabricator taking the price risk out of his working capital, gold borrowing costs should remain well below the cost of money. With a more or less permanent premium on forward prices, gold mining companies enjoy - in a sense - a unique public subsidy. Ask any copper, or for that matter platinum, producer what they would give for such a hedging privilege.

Metal price risk products

PLAIN FORWARDS

All precious metal forward prices are calculated using precious metal swap rates. These are a function of supply/demand (lending/borrowing) for the underlying metal and of money market interest rates. Therefore, if there is excess demand for metal borrowing, swap rates will be

2. Cumulative mine forward sales and gold lease rate

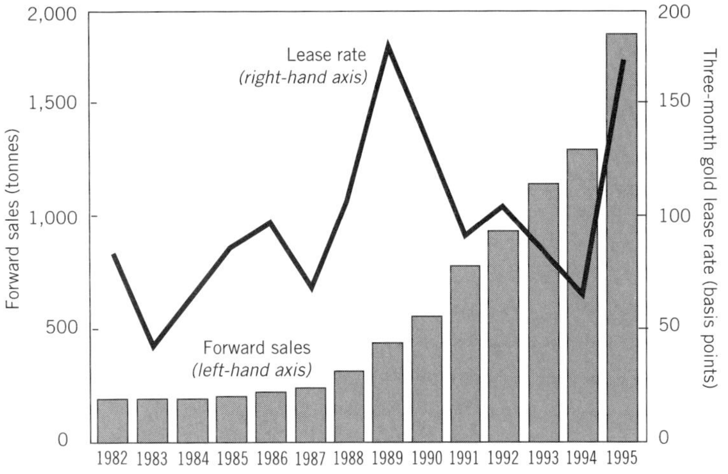

Source: GFMS (forward sales, by kind permission), UBS (lease rates)

3. Libor, gold contango and lease rate

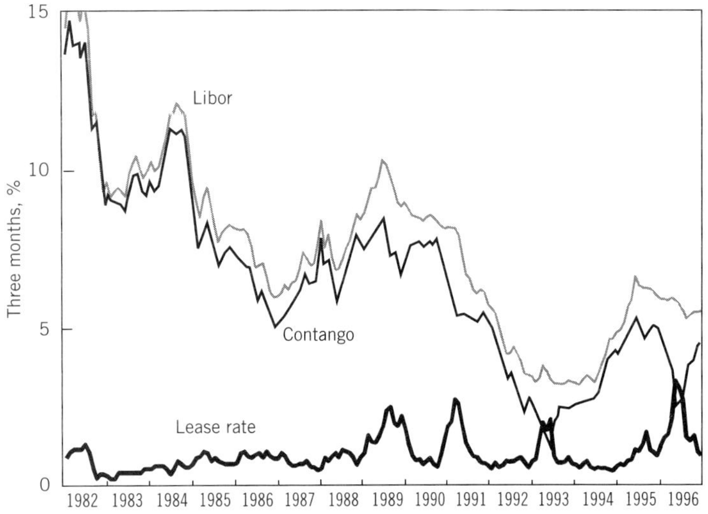

quoted lower (swappers will be asked to pay less to buy their gold back in the future). In turn, the spread between the metal swap and the money market rate will widen, which will mean that the cost of borrowing metal will increase. Figure 3 clarifies the relationship between dollar interest rates (Libor) and the gold swap rate (contango), while showing the difference between the two - the gold lease rate. Therefore:

$Metal lease rate = Libor *minus* $Metal swap rate (contango)

All forward/swap transactions are based on a common market standard. Gold traded must conform to the "good delivery" standard stipulated by the London Bullion Market Association (LBMA); that is, gold must be of a minimum of 995 fineness, with gold bars being within a stipu-

PANEL 2

THE NOVEMBER 1995 GOLD SQUEEZE

On November 28 and 29, 1995, the gold market moved into backwardation; prices up to two months forward fell below the spot price, and gold lease rates rose above dollar interest rates (this spike is illustrated in the figure). The squeeze in gold liquidity was concentrated at the short-dated end of the borrowing spectrum, where most business is done, leaving longer-dated lease rates relatively unmoved. Consequently, the gold lease rate yield curve (12-month rates minus one-month rates) inverted for several weeks – itself an unusual (although not unique) event.

Short-term gold lease rates were pushed to these unusual levels quite simply because gold borrowing exceeded gold lending. While the lack of transparency in the gold swap market led to a search for scapegoats, many players took active parts in the squeeze. These included:

- gold mining companies, especially from South Africa and Australia, which had completed around 300 tonnes of extra hedging (forward sales) since August 1995. This amounted to 60% of South Africa's annual output, and represented an increase of about a third of the normal borrowing over a three-month period;
- central banks, which may have been active selling gold forward out of reserves; and
- some interbank players, which may have been forced into borrowing to cover positions unusually exposed by the lease-rate spike.

The lending response to this "bunching" of borrowing was slow. The reasons for this are twofold: many traditional central bank lenders had already increased their lending limits in response to the rise in the lease rate in the first quarter of 1995 – increasing them twice in a calendar year is bureaucratically difficult; and private investor deposits of gold with the interbank market are now too small to make it feasible to access substantial new private lending.

However, the "demand side" of the market responded quite quickly to the allure of higher gold lease rates. At 600bp, these were some 500bp above the historical norm. Producer borrowing was choked off and the market reverted to contango (indeed some producers took advantage of the fall in forward prices to buy back forward sales and realise a trading profit). November 1995 was, therefore, a case of famine turning to feast.

Gold lease rates, 1995–96

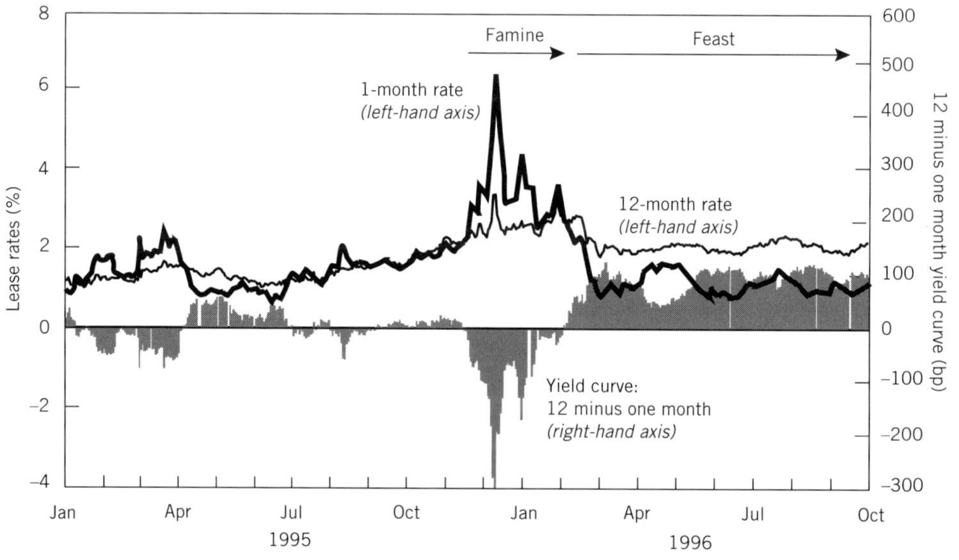

lated weight range around 400 ounces and carrying a stamp from an approved smelter and assayer. In fact, gold which fails to meet these requirements can be traded, but refining and upgrading costs would be factored into the (higher) gold swap rate quoted. Traditionally, precious metal forwards are traded either "loco" (location) London or Zurich, although banks can quote for alternative locations by factoring a discount/premium into the London/Zurich quote.

Gold lending supply originates mainly from institutional sources (central banks), although this is augmented by private investors, speculators, scrap sources and, in certain market situations, by producer buy-backs of forward sales. (It makes sense to "buy back" forward sales previously contracted at spot price + X for spot price + Y, when Y is less than X and profit for X – Y can be realised.) A fall in swap rates (gold contango) might cause such a switch in producer behaviour (see Panel 2). Gold borrowing demand comes primarily from gold producers and physical buyers (such as the jewellery, electronics and dental industries).

Plain forwards (or "outright" forwards) are utilised by both ends of the hedging spectrum in precious metals: the producer and the consumer.

Producers often hedge the future physical production from their mines by matching the production schedule to a strip of plain forward sales (see Panel 2). The hedging offers important operational advantages:

- by selling future gold production at a locked-in price, often several years ahead, producers realise a significant compound premium over the spot price; and
- it allows better cashflow and investment planning, stabilises income flow and can improve budgeted revenue.

On the debit side of the hedging debate, however, mining companies risk suffering an opportunity loss if the spot gold price rallies above the forward sale price. When the bullion market turns bullish, grassroots pressure from shareholders may deter mining companies from hedging.

Gold fabricators, principally the gold jewellery industry, would ideally match their buying of precious metal raw material with their fabrication requirements. These requirements tend to peak at certain times of the year, such as prior to Christmas and the Indian wedding season. However, instead of waiting until the metal is needed and risking an adverse spot price movement (higher), the jewellery industry buys gold at levels that they deem attractive on a plain forward basis – with delivery dates that match their requirements. This avoids the cost of holding gold and having to fund the dollar payment.

Speculators often use plain forward transactions to close out their position prior to maturity, thus avoiding any physical metal transfers or dollar funding requirements. Until the speculator closes out the transaction, they run the risk of adverse movements in gold price and forward rates.

A variant of the forward sale used by producers is the "fee-based forward" structure. This permits the producer to sell to a forward date, fixing both the spot price and US interest rate, but floating the gold lease rate. Producers can use this structure to exploit movements in the gold lease rate. For example, if they believe lease rates will be lower on a three-month rolling basis, this structure would fit their requirements better than locking in the lease rate for the life of the hedging transaction. The producer will pay the lease "fee" at the end of each floating period and reset the gold borrowing rate for a further period.

FORWARD/FORWARD

Precious metal forward/forward transactions are similar in structure to transactions in the interest rate market. The standard transaction is the forward/forward precious metal swap, utilised by market makers and clients alike. For example, a market maker might contract to enter into a swap at some specified future date. The pricing of a forward/forward gold swap is calculated using the dollar "forward rate agreement" (FRA) for the relevant period and the pricing of the relevant standard gold swaps.

Market makers can use forward/forward transactions to flatten unwanted liquidity mismatches – say, too much borrowing one year out, too much lending five years out – in their forward book, or to manage house positions in either future precious metal lease rates or in dollar interest rates.

Producers can use this type of transaction to "roll forward" deals that will mature at some point in the future. This extends the maturity of the deal and pushes forward the date on which the producer will have to deliver the physical metal.

Precious metal forward/forward transactions have recently evolved to incorporate deposits and leases. As such, they provide increased flexibility to two groups of precious metal participants: not just borrowers of leased metal, but also the main lenders, the central banks. For example, official lenders can take advantage of higher longer-term gold deposit (lease) rates irrespective of whether they have gold deposits maturing (coming due for repayment by the commercial bank) at that stage. They do this by requesting forward/forward deposit rates from the commercial bank counterparties they are permitted to deal with.

PANEL 3

COMPARISON OF RISK MANAGEMENT TECHNIQUES IN GOLD, PLATINUM AND SILVER

Gold

If the secret of the property market is "location", the key to understanding how the nature of risk management in the gold market differs from that of other precious metals is "liquidity". The ability of gold hedgers (through interbank market intermediaries) to borrow gold cheaply from stockholders (mainly central banks) means the forward price structure of gold forms an almost textbook "cost of carry" pattern. This is a positive contango, with forward prices above the spot price by almost the full extent of market interest rates. It is "almost", because the difference between market rates and contango is the return charged by the central bank for lending gold.

In other precious metals, large holders of stock are conspicuous by their absence. Most central banks disposed of their monetary silver reserves a century ago. Platinum has never enjoyed the status of an official reserve asset; silver and platinum stocks are, therefore, more widely dispersed in private hands and are consequently less accessible than gold. Buyers of these "white metals" (especially the tiny platinum market) are often willing to pay an "insurance premium" to the seller for the comfort of immediate delivery. In the jargon of forward markets, this means a "backwardation": spot prices trade at a premium to forward prices.

Since the cost of borrowing metal is the difference between market (dollar) interest rates and contango, a backwardation (sometimes called negative contango) means lease rates are above market rates. Recent movements in precious metal lease rates reflect these very different underlying price structures. For most of 1995, platinum was in huge backwardation – lease rate above Libor – reflecting production difficulties at the world's second-largest supplier, Impala. Without a ready pool of metal to draw upon, Impala's extra borrowing to meet contract commitments, and that by other market players, pushed platinum lease rates to almost double figures. Even in the extraordinary squeeze of November 1995, gold lease rates (on a three-month basis) failed to clear market rates (Fig. A).

The implication of this for risk management is that gold hedgers enjoy a reliable premium on forward over spot prices; "squeezes" are almost unknown. Therefore, forward-selling structures tend to be much more popular in gold. These are often accompanied by gold put option purchases, which are relatively cheaply priced on forward prices above current prices. Of course, selling forward in a backwardated market, like platinum in

A. Precious metal lease rates, 1995–96

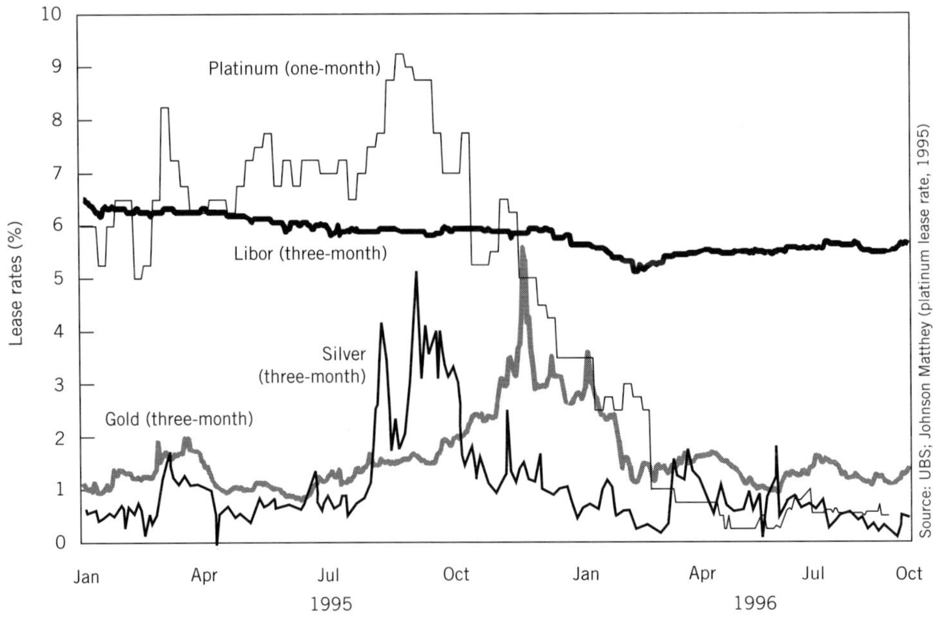

1995, may still make sense; but the hedger must expect the price to fall faster than the rate implied by the discount of forward to spot prices. The steeper the backwardation, the riskier this proposition must seem.

Platinum

Platinum producers, therefore, tend to use "man-made" (as opposed to market-made) risk management methods, in the shape of annual contracts with major buyers (like car manufacturers buying platinum group metals, such as platinum, palladium and rhodium, for anti-emission catalysts). These arrangements rarely involve commercial bank intermediaries, but are negotiated directly between the buyer and seller. The concentration of buyers and sellers (South African and Russian producers; Japanese trading houses and global car manufacturers, respectively) make the logistics of contract negotiation much more straightforward than in either the gold or silver markets. Contract prices are often related to some moving average of market values, which smoothes out wilder swings in spot prices. Contracts may also include "minimum purchase" commitments by the buyer, which provide the seller with greater certainty in price and volume. (In the case of Russian/Japanese contracts, Japanese trading house buyers, in the interests of maintaining goodwill with Russian suppliers, often commit to buy a mix of platinum metals which may not suit their immediate customer requirements.) Contracts may only cover a proportion (albeit large) of total metal production, leaving scope for some sales into what the mining company hopes will be a bullish spot market.

Silver

Silver hedging remains something of an enigma. While gold mining companies hedge around one year's worth of production, silver producers hedge only one to two month's worth, on average. Only a small part of this difference is explained by the (theoretically) less reliable contango in the silver market. Most producers refrain from hedging because their silver is produced very largely (84%) as a by-product of base metals and gold production. Consequently, silver is regarded as a bonus, something which covers the smelting costs of primary, base-metal treatment. Thus, it may seem hardly worth arranging price protection.

The implications for risk management of having liquidity "on tap" are perhaps best illustrated by the contrast between gold and copper prices and lease rates over the last 10 years (Fig. B). While the price and lease rates of gold remained comparatively stable, those of copper (like platinum, there are no reliable holders of large marketable stocks) varied enormously. These huge swings from backwardation to contango indicate that copper producers tend to favour the flexibility of options hedging structures over the contango-dependent forward sale.

B. Gold and copper prices and lease rates

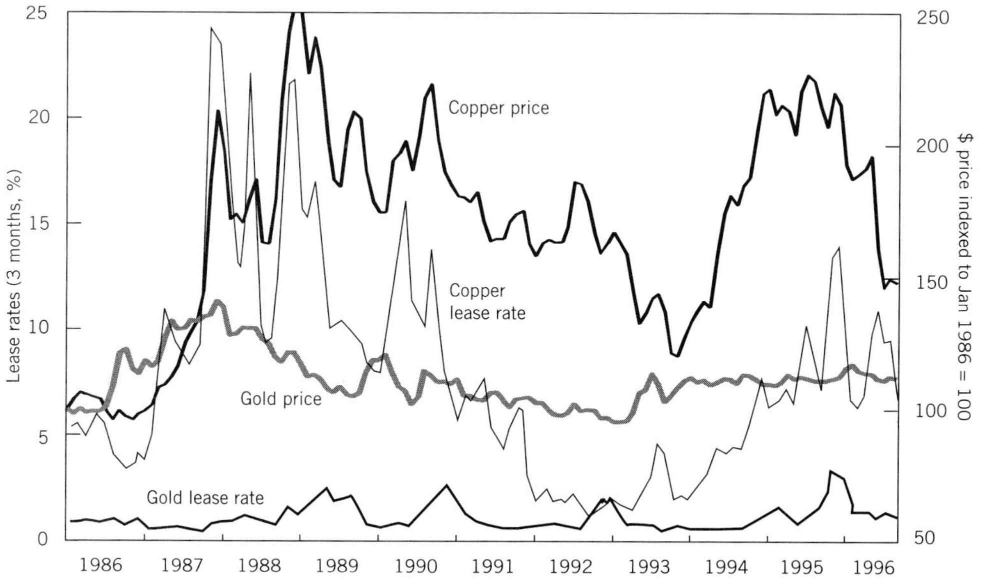

PANEL 4

FORWARD/FORWARD GOLD DEPOSIT TRANSACTION

Often a shortage of gold at the turn of the year can cause the gold deposit or lease rate (ie, the rate of interest paid for gold deposited) to increase substantially, especially in the period out to three months. With deposit rates, say, increasing from 1.00% to 2.50%, central bank X is of the opinion that these levels are not sustainable. However, suppose the earliest its gold deposits are due for repayment is in one month. To take advantage of what it sees as a spike in rates, it requests a forward/forward deposit rate of "one month against four months", and is quoted a deposit rate of 1.95%. Central bank X, therefore, achieves a rate substantially above its expected three-month rate in one month's time. The risk the central bank takes is that the deposit rate for that period in one month's time could, in fact, exceed 1.95%.

PANEL 5

SPOT-DEFERRED FORWARDS FOR A GOLD PRODUCER UNDER THREE INTEREST RATE ENVIRONMENTS

Basis spot: $380/oz

Scenario	Motive	Gold forward rate (%)	Gold forward price in 12 months ($)
Fixed forward price using current 12-month gold swap/forward rate	The producer believes that dollar interest rates will not rise over the next 12 months	4.00	395.41
Continually rolling forward on a spot-deferred basis using overnight rates (but rates do not rise)	The producer believes that overnight dollar interest rates may rise during the course of the next 12 months	3.90	395.234
Continually rolling forward on deferred basis until dollar interest rates rise in six months' time, at which time the producer locks away the higher rates for the second six months	The producer believes that overnight dollar interest rates may rise during the course of the next 12 months	3.90 (first six months) 4.50 (second six months)	395.355

SPOT-DEFERRED FORWARD

A deferred forward is a forward contract without a pre-defined delivery date. While the pricing of a plain forward will be based on the known gold swap rate to maturity, the deferred forward will be calculated on a rolling basis using the shorter-dated rates requested by the client. These rates can be of varying tenors, from overnight to one year or longer. As each shorter-dated forward matures, it is rolled for a further period; therefore, no settlement is required until the customer's chosen maturity date.

Using deferred forwards introduces an extra element of market risk. Since the final maturity date is unknown, it is not possible to fix the interest components until maturity. This gives rise to an exposure to floating dollar and gold lease interest rates. Often, such instruments are used by producers which believe that dollar interest rates are expected to rise in the future (see Panel 5). The producer will roll spot sales on a deferred (floating) basis until dollar rates have risen, giving the producer a more attractive contango (swap rate) to lock in until maturity.

LEASE RATE OPTIONS

Lease rate options, a recent innovation, were first developed for Australian gold producers in 1995. They are now gradually being adopted by the producer community worldwide and by some central banks. Unlike most financial markets, there is limited information on the volatility of

PANEL 6

CHOOSING THE CORRECT FORWARD INSTRUMENT: A COMPARISON[1]

Plain (fixed) forward

Best-use application

- when dollar interest rates are comparatively high and may fall during the life of the contract
- when gold borrowing costs are low (contango /swap rate is high) and could rise

Advantages

- guaranteed contango through contract
- no active management required
- can be unwound before delivery
- can exploit view on dollar rates and gold borrowing rates

Disadvantages

- fixed delivery date
- opportunity loss if spot price at maturity exceeds contracted forward price, if gold borrowing costs fall or dollar rates rise
- settlement payable only on maturity

Fee-based (floating gold rate) forward

Best-use application

- when dollar interest rates are comparatively high and may fall during the life of the contract
- when gold borrowing costs are high (contango/ swap rate low) and could fall

Advantages

- guaranteed, although only partly known, contango through contract
- minimal management
- can be unwound before delivery
- can exploit view that gold borrowing costs may fall, and short-dated gold borrowing costs tend to be lower than long-dated ones

Disadvantages

- fixed delivery date
- opportunity loss if spot price at maturity exceeds contracted forward price, or if dollar rates rise
- cash adjustment payable by hedger if gold borrowing costs rise
- final contango known only at maturity

Spot-deferred forward

Best-use application

- if the physical delivery of metal could be a problem
- when dollar rates may increase and gold borrowing costs may fall during the life of the contract

Advantages

- guaranteed, but unknown, contango through contract
- minimal management
- can be unwound before delivery
- no fixed delivery date, flexibility which can reduce the opportunity loss if the spot price exceeds the forward price

gold lease rates, especially for long-dated transactions. Table 1 provides an indication for rates up to one year during the 1990s. One should note the extreme volatility in the shorter-dated rates, where most central bank lending is concentrated.

Using lease rate options enables the producer to borrow at a specific fixed rate on a quarterly basis for a period of several years. This fixed rate is set lower than the existing market rate, which the producer achieves by issuing lease rate put options at the specified fixed rate. If the producer issues a large enough quantity of puts, a zero-cost structure (ie, a hedge requiring no upfront premium) can be constructed.

The structure works as follows: on a quarterly basis, if the lease rate, Libor minus "GOFO mean" (the Reuters page quoting gold swap rates), exceeds 1.50%, the producer borrows metal at 1.50%. If rates fall below 1.50%, the bank has the right, but not the obligation, to exercise the 1.50% put options against the producer. These are financially settled and are based on the difference between the strike price of the put option and the Libor minus GOFO (swap) rate.

A variation on this theme is the forward/forward lease rate option. Here, the producer specifies a strike level for a lease rate at which it is prepared to borrow metal on a forward/forward basis. The bank then calculates the price in basis points by offering a call option at the specified strike rate. At the start date of the transaction, if lease rates are in excess of the strike price (calculated from Libor minus GOFO mean), the pro-

Table 1. Gold lease rate volatilities, 1990–96 (%)

	Lease rate			
	One-month	Three-month	Six-month	12-month
Average volatility	144	102	88	83
High volatility	401	188	167	157
Low volatility	43	44	33	34

(60-day standard deviations of daily percentage changes)

Disadvantages
❑ settlement payable only on maturity
❑ bank may request delivery, but only after a reasonable notice period
❑ more regular renewal periods increase the cost of deferral and shorten the delivery notice period

Participating forward (forward contract with attached call option)
Best-use application
❑ if the opportunity loss of upside in the spot price is a major concern
❑ periods of high price volatility
❑ when dollar rates may fall and gold borrowing costs may rise during the contract
Advantages
❑ loss of price upside potential minimised by call option, exercised if spot exceeds option strike price on maturity
❑ minimal management
❑ can be unwound before delivery
❑ ability to lock in higher prices as spot price rises (not available with option "min-max" products)
Disadvantages
❑ settlement payable only on maturity
❑ fixed delivery date
❑ if option is exercised, slightly more management attention is required
❑ no contango is paid out; the contango is used to buy the call option
❑ if, on maturity, the spot exceeds the contract price but the call option is out of the money, the option expires worthless and the premium (contango) is lost
❑ opportunity loss if gold borrowing costs fall or dollar rates rise; both reduce funds available to buy options

Pre-paid or advanced premium forward/ swap (forward contract with contango payable in advance)
Best-use application
❑ early in a new project, matching contango receipts with cashflow requirements
❑ when dollar rates may fall or gold borrowing costs may rise during the contract
Advantages
❑ minimal management
❑ can be unwound before delivery
❑ contango (partly) payable before delivery
Disadvantages
❑ fixed delivery date
❑ opportunity loss if spot exceeds contract price at maturity
❑ opportunity loss if gold borrowing costs fall or dollar rates rise
❑ premium charged for up-front payment, reducing contango in later years

1 Adapted with kind permission from Jessica Cross, 1994, *The Derivatives Revolution*, Rosendale Press.

ducer gains the right, but not the obligation, to borrow at the gold lease implied by the option strike price.

PLAIN VANILLA SWAPS
A precious metal swap transaction is a spot sale/purchase of metal with a simultaneous purchase/sale of metal at a specified date in the future. The interest cost associated with this method of financing is reflected in the forward price of the gold swap (ie, the saving on Libor is the gold swap rate). Swaps are the most common form of precious metal forward product, quoted from a tenor of overnight to an interbank tenor of five years, with some producers dealing in excess of this tenor. The standard quantity of gold involved in a gold swap is one tonne of metal,[2] although quantities can vary from a couple of thousand ounces to amounts in excess of 100,000oz.

Gold swaps allow market participants to use their bullion reserves to raise currency (cash), or to invest the money in return for interest. Raising cash via gold swaps cuts costs for participants, which otherwise would have to approach the money markets for funding at rates of Libor or higher. Swaps can also be linked to zero-cost option structures, which protect asset values if the price of gold falls during the life of the swap.

LOCATION SWAPS
A gold swap can also facilitate the transfer of gold between locations. As the counterparty bank incorporates the cost of shipment of gold into the gold swap rate, an official institution can move gold to a market (such as London or Zurich) where it can be utilised more easily, without paying an up-front fee. For example, a bank might buy gold loco South America and then arrange for repayment in six months at the client's account at the Bank of England. This

means that the client's gold can, in future, be employed for standard bullion market operations – removing the disadvantage of an unusual location.

PRE-PAID SWAPS

A pre-paid forward works in the same way as a plain forward, with one major difference. Instead of funds flowing between the parties on maturity, the fixed leg of the transaction is set at a discount to the prevailing forward price and the mining company receives an up-front cash sum. On the maturity date, the contract can either be settled through physical delivery of the metal, or cash settled (as would be the case against the floating rate).

A producer is most likely to enter a pre-paid swap as a method of raising finance against future production (Panels 8 and 9 overleaf). The advantage of such a strategy is that the producer can raise financing off balance sheet (the financial institution advances funds to the client, with the proceeds secured by the future delivery of the metal). In certain jurisdictions, there may be some additional tax and accounting treatment benefits. An additional advantage is that the structure embeds both a loan and a hedge of future gold production.

The main players in precious metal price hedging

PRODUCERS

Metal producers are a natural customer for commodity forward and swap transactions. Advances in mining and geological techniques have made it possible for mining companies to estimate, with a certain degree of comfort, the future quantities and costs of extracting metal. Mining companies naturally concentrate their technical and management skills on cost control and technical efficiency. Their revenue stream, however, is subject to the vagaries of the markets. With the vast sums required to finance a mining operation, both lenders and shareholders require a degree of certainty of earnings stream before investments will be made.

The most certain method of guaranteeing revenues, and hence financial viability, is to lock in a fixed price today for the sale of the commodity in the future. In the case of a "deliverable" commodity (such as gold bullion), arranging forward sales with physical delivery on maturity is the most efficient and cost-free strategy. Unlike options, forwards incur no up-front premiums. The only cost associated with forwards/swaps is the "opportunity cost" of not being able to sell the metal at a higher spot price, should prices be higher than the fixed forward price on maturity.

On the other hand, a producer of "non-deliverable" material (of which base metals are a good example) will most likely use swaps rather than forwards. This enables the producer to match revenues from the delivery of material to smelters, with forward cover. Generally, a smelter will pay the producer for the metal content of their concentrate by averaging the cash price over a pre-defined quotation period (QP). The producer can fix this price with a financial instrument. The financial institution will pay the pre-agreed fixed price to the producer, but will not require physical delivery of the contract; the producer will pay or receive the difference between the fixed price and the price of replacing the physical delivery in the cash market.

PANEL 7

GOLD SWAP

Gold swaps take a variety of forms. In this example, we describe a transaction between a commercial bank and a central bank that wishes to convert some of its gold into currency (cash) without disturbing the market by selling gold into it.

Example

Market spot rate gold $383 per oz
Market gold swap rate 12-month 4–4.3%

When the swaps are due, the counterparties can either renew the agreement at the going gold interest rates and spot prices, or simply end the contract.

Spot date: September 1996

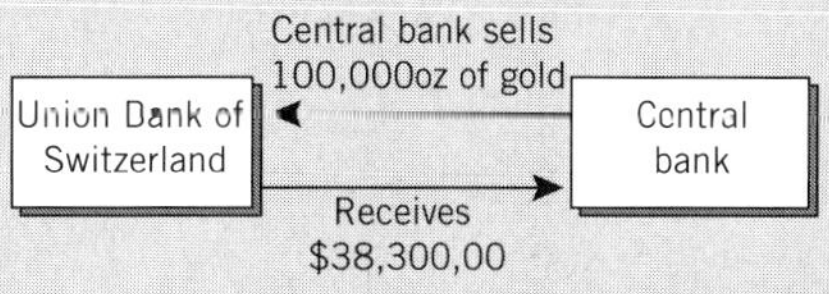

Maturity date: September 1997

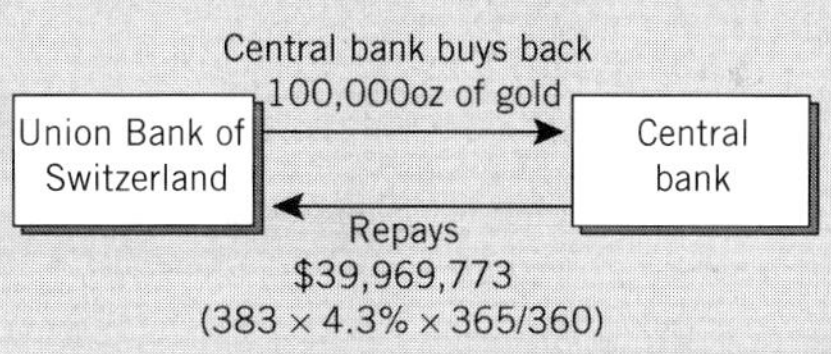

PANEL 8

PRE-PAID FORWARD/SWAP TRANSACTION

ABC mining company wishes to develop a new shaft, which will produce 100,000oz of gold each quarter for the next two years. Before commencing mining operations, it must spend $150 million to build a processing plant. To raise the necessary funds, ABC enters into a pre-paid forward with XYZ Bank, which will generate the $150 million immediately.

The structure of the transaction is as follows: ABC agrees to deliver to XYZ 50,000oz of gold every quarter for the next three years. In lieu of ABC receiving the forward price on each of the maturity dates, XYZ pays them up-front the discounted forward price on spot value, eg $380.05 for Q2 delivery against a forward price of $394.40 (see Table A). ABC can use the money advanced to them for the construction of the processing plant. ABC is free to sell the balance of its production as it sees fit.

A. Pre-paid gold swap

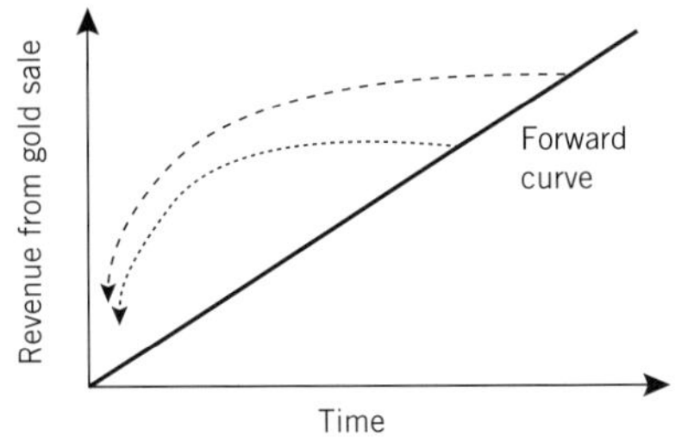

Table A

Maturity	Forward price ($/oz)	Discounted forward price ($/oz)	Quantity (oz)	XYZ pays to ABC ($)
Q1	391.35	382.70	50,000	19,135,000
Q2	394.40	380.05	50,000	19,002,500
Q3	398.70	378.60	50,000	18,930,000
Q4	402.40	376.40	50,000	18,820,000
Q5	406.30	374.10	50,000	18,705,000
Q6	410.15	371.85	50,000	18,592,500
Q7	414.00	369.30	50,000	18,465,000
Q8	417.90	366.55	50,000	18,327,500

PANEL 9

REFINANCING CASE STUDY

In September 1996, Ashanti Goldfields announced a $40 million deal with UBS and Dresdner Bank to refinance $28 million of high-coupon debt and make available $12 million of expansion capital for its Cluff Zimbabwe operations.

Financing was structured as a seven-year pre-paid forward gold sale, with good delivery of gold underwritten by the Ashanti parent (thus defraying the performance risk of Cluff itself). In other words, as group treasurer Mona Caesar Addo put it, this was "an advance payment for future deliveries of gold ... We were looking for something better than a conventional gold loan which, even for borrowers of the highest standing, rarely extends beyond a five-year term. The advantages of this facility will enable the Zimbabwe facility to prioritise its cashflow for investment in the mine."

At the start of this arrangement, some $20 million was immediately drawn down, the rest to be drawn down in tranches. Gold deliveries will start after 18 months. The present value of gold shipments discounted at Libor (plus margin) equals the loan amount. Interest rate cost savings compared with a conventional loan amount to $1 million.

FINANCIAL INSTITUTIONS

Commercial banks play an integral role as the intermediary between the producer and the financial markets. This occurs in two significant ways: as credit intermediaries; and as financial engineers, which reshape standard market products to the individual needs of producers.

As credit intermediaries, banks provide the bridge between central bank lenders and mining company borrowers. It is unreasonable to expect central banks to deal directly with a range of mining companies; they have neither the expertise nor the desire to assess the creditworthiness of such corporations. Rather, central banks are far more comfortable dealing with large commercial banks which, in turn, have the ability to spread

PANEL 10

METAL LOAN AND HEDGING STRUCTURES

A joint venture between a state-owned mine company and an international mining conglomerate in a remote desert area discovered surprisingly high quantities of gold in the waste products from the mine. A feasibility study found that extraction was economic, but only just: costs for leaching the gold from the tailings were marginally below the gold price. UBS proposed a transaction that would fund their capital installation costs and secure future gold prices. For a quarter of the gold extracted from the tailings over the next four years, UBS offered a three-year gold loan at rates below Libor. The company paid back the loan by sending monthly gold shipments to UBS' own precious metals processing company, Argor Heraeus SA, in Mendrisio, Switzerland. The remaining three-quarters of production were hedged using options and forwards: 50% with a plain forward and 50% with a floor-price option structure that ensured a minimum price for the gold produced. The premium payments for the floor structure were met by the sale of a call option, giving the producer a zero-cost collar (or "min-max" option).

The joint venture benefited from both low-cost funding for the initial infrastructure investment, and from contango-enhanced prices (ie, sales made at a price above the spot price) for most of the hedged gold production.

exposure across a group of mining houses. For a fee – the bid/offer spreads in quoted rates – the commercial bank brings together lenders and borrowers that would otherwise never meet.

In their capacity as financial engineers, banks play a necessary intermediary role between producers and the professional markets. Generally, the professional markets (such as futures exchanges) provide excellent liquidity in financial products, but are hindered by the need to standardise financial instruments. The banking intermediary provides a valuable service, by repackaging those financial tools into more user-friendly structures, which mirror the exact financial risks faced by individual mining companies. Effectively, the financial institution is absorbing the financial risk the producer would face by dealing in standardised products which do not meet their exact risk management needs.

CENTRAL BANKS

It is important to consider why central banks bother to lend gold. After all, while repo operations in security markets have implications for monetary policy, dealings in gold no longer have any such ramifications. In addition, while the $67 billion or so earned annually on their collective $1.3 trillion of foreign currency reserves is naturally a major concern, surely the mere $250 million earned every year by those central banks that do lend/swap their gold is of marginal importance?

How can one account for the inexorable growth in official gold lending and swapping? There are a couple of possible explanations. Even a few basis points of interest helps "keep the wolf from the door" – in the case of central banks, it is the finance ministry baying for the adoption of a strict profit and loss (P&L) approach to reserve asset management. By showing some return, albeit small, on an otherwise inert asset, central bankers prove that gold can at least provide a symbolic contribution to its keep (storage, opportunity costs, etc). Of course, the lower market rates are, the more significant these symbolic few basis points of gold interest can be (the lower the opportunity cost of hoarding gold).

In some instances, swapping gold (borrowing secured by gold) is the only way nations can raise dollars in a crisis. Many such cases in the emerging market have been well publicised, while those involving "Western" central banks (which may be more substantial) usually receive less attention.

It follows that central bank lending/swapping is not readily increased by higher gold lease rates.

4. Official gold lending in context, 1995

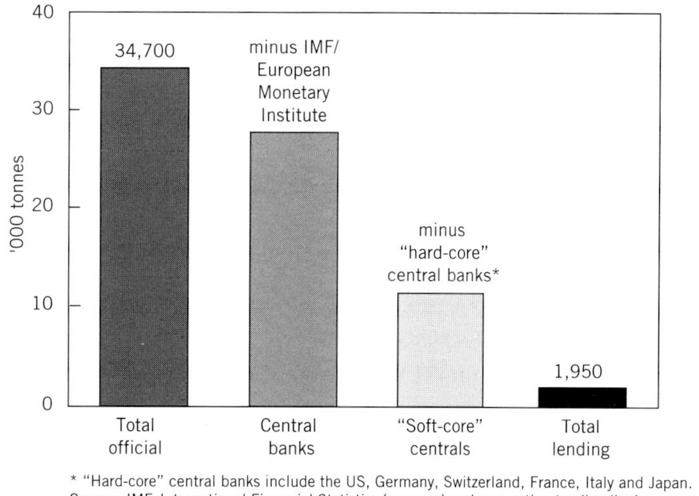

* "Hard-core" central banks include the US, Germany, Switzerland, France, Italy and Japan.
Source: IMF *International Financial Statistics* (reserves) and own estimates (lending).

5. Gold lease rate and Fed gold holdings

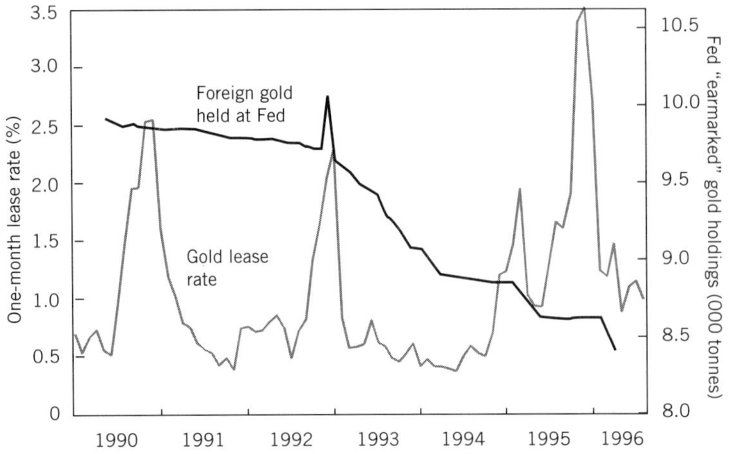

This "lumpiness" in gold lending supply is compounded by the fact that bureaucratic timetables rarely synchronise with market opportunities. For example, once a central bank has decided to increase its gold lending limits in a given year, it may find it bureaucratically difficult to raise them again during the same year, regardless of the gold lease rate. At the very least, there is an unpredictable lag between higher gold lease rates and the response of the central bank. One indication of this "delayed reaction" is the movement of foreign-owned official gold out of the custody of the Fed in recent years (to be upgraded and located in the London market, ready for swapping/lending). While the reaction time seems to be getting shorter, spikes in the lease rate still take a while to excite the withdrawal of gold.

Indeed, especially sharp spikes in the gold lease rate can stimulate a perverse short-term official reaction: higher rates on gold can be interpreted as bringing higher risk, which may be unwelcome in what has come to be regarded as a low-risk, low-return activity. In the short term, some central banks may even withdraw gold deposits from the interbank market, until the dust (and, alas for them, the lease rate) settles.

Consequently, surges of gold borrowing (such as the bunching of mine forward sales described in Panel 2) can meet an essentially passive short-term central bank response. The effect of this is that gold lease rates shoot higher. However, the fact that these squeezes are so rare implies that there is medium- to longer-term flexibility in gold lending. In the last two years at least, another 10 central banks have begun to lend gold, while a further 10 have increased their lending limits.

How long can gold producers, fabricators and short sellers rely on the availability of cheap gold finance? How long can they escape paying the insurance premiums for spot delivery (backwardation), which are often faced in other commodity markets? Considering the three issues below may help us to answer these questions.

European Monetary Union It is claimed that, once a committee (members of a single European central bank) manages Europe's 14,000 tonnes of gold, less will be lent – simply because the bigger the committee, the slower the decision-making process. There is something in this argument; after all, the debate over whether the IMF should mobilise even a tiny fraction of its gold is still exercising members, a decade after it began. The change to gold lending supply, however, need not be as dramatic as this implies.

For one thing, no one really knows how much European gold will be pooled under the auspices of the single European central bank, or what the arrangements for the "unpooled" portion of national gold reserves will be. For another, most of the big official holders of gold in Europe do not lend gold anyway.

Transfer of official gold from "West" to "East" It is hard to find evidence for the widely held proposition that emerging-nation central banks will buy the gold sold by developed-country central banks. There is, however, one implication often overlooked by adherents to this view – emerging nations are now significantly more aggressive in their gold mobilisation policies than Western nations (see Figure 6). Therefore, to the extent that there was any transfer of gold from the "old world" to the "new world", a larger proportion of global gold reserves is likely to be lent.

Silver lining It is unlikely that gold will face the exact fate of silver – sold off by central banks, over a relatively small number of years, once its monetary role had ceased. Gold stock holding is likely to remain in relatively few (official) hands for a generation or two to come. The logistics of lending gold will remain favourable – commercial banks seeking central bank counterparties, rather than calling on peasant farmers in India to lend their private hoards, for example. At the same time, a completely passive strategy of holding gold will most likely be a luxury very few central banks will either be able to afford, or care to choose, over the next few decades, as more pragmatic managers take over reserve mobilisation responsibility.

It is now 26 years since gold was pensioned off from its monetary day job (the gold backing

6. Distribution of gold reserves and lending, at end-1995

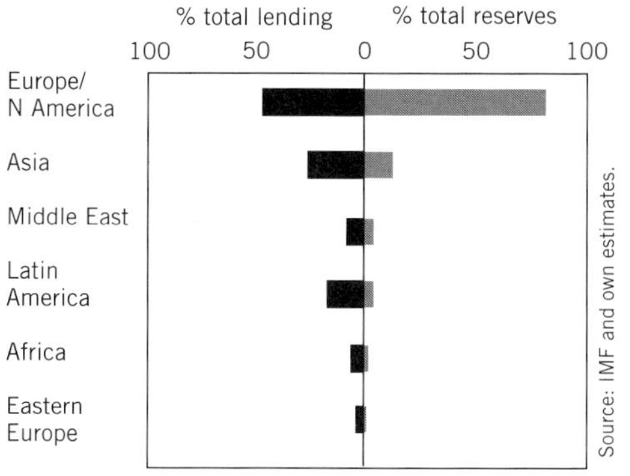

7. Gold lease rate and imports into six major centres, 1995–96

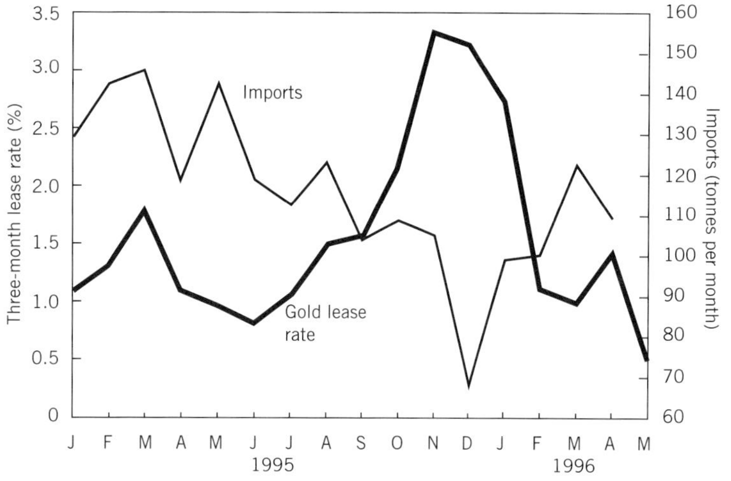

of the dollar), and it seems that it will be readily lent (on a part-time basis) to the commercial interbank market for some time to come.

CONSUMERS

One of the more deeply ingrained global traditions of the gold market is the warehousing of metal near the point of final demand. Whether it be in the Middle East, Singapore, Hong Kong, Taiwan, parts of South America or now India, it is through these 150–200 tonnes or so of "consignment stocks" (placed in the safekeeping of local banks – the arteries of the market) that supplying Swiss or American bullion banks can access the myriad of small local buyers.

Local bank borrowers of gold may not "fix" the price of their gold for up to one or two months, enjoying interest-free gold loans. In return, bullion banks enjoy payments in kind:

❑ other banking business (such as foreign exchange);

❑ savings in the back-office and transport costs, instead of making multiple gold shipments; and

❑ the "flow" business in gold; turnover is crucial to all gold operations in an increasingly competitive industry, particularly so if the bullion bank also runs a high fixed-cost refinery.

As long as the measurable cost – the gold lease rate foregone – is low (say 50bp), bullion banks have been content (if not happy) to pump gold into consignment. Disturb the delicate trade-off between tangible cost and intangible benefit, however, and the arteries tend to harden. It is probably no coincidence that the sharp rise in lease rates at the end of 1995 saw a correspondingly sharp fall in imports into six main gold centres (Singapore, Dubai, Hong Kong, Taiwan, Turkey and Japan – see Figure 7). This was also at a time when final demand in the regions they serve was, supposedly, holding up well. One explanation for this is that imports were "supply constrained": bullion banks were reluctant to lend freely the gold which they had to borrow at lease rates near 6%. Therefore, local consignments were run down to meet local demand and were not readily replenished.

Bullion banks react differently to high gold lease rates, depending both on the regional split of their physical business and on whether their physical operation is a separate profit centre. But, if lease rates are high, most examine much more closely which local banks actually turn over the consignment. For example, the underlying economics of the consignment business (the break-even relationship between bar premium – say, loco Dubai over Zurich – and turnover, as shown in Figure 8 overleaf) are much more obvious when the lease rate is 3%. Suppose, for instance, that competitive pressures fix the premium that bullion banks can charge customers at about 20 cents/oz – at 3% lease rates, a consignment must, therefore, turn over an improbable six times to break even with borrowing costs. Alternatively, at the same 3% lease rates, if turnover is fixed by local demand conditions at twice per month, the premium would have to rise to around an impossible 50 cents/oz.

A special case in this context is Italy, where about half of the consignments with local banks are in the form of normal gold loans – here higher lease rates can be partly passed on. Slightly higher gold borrowing charges would still be more attractive to Italian fabricators than borrowing at an even higher lira interest rate to buy gold, which would expose them to price risk. Aside from this exception, the question of increasing bar premiums (and what that might do to final gold demand) is largely academic; bullion bank margins would simply be squeezed a little more.

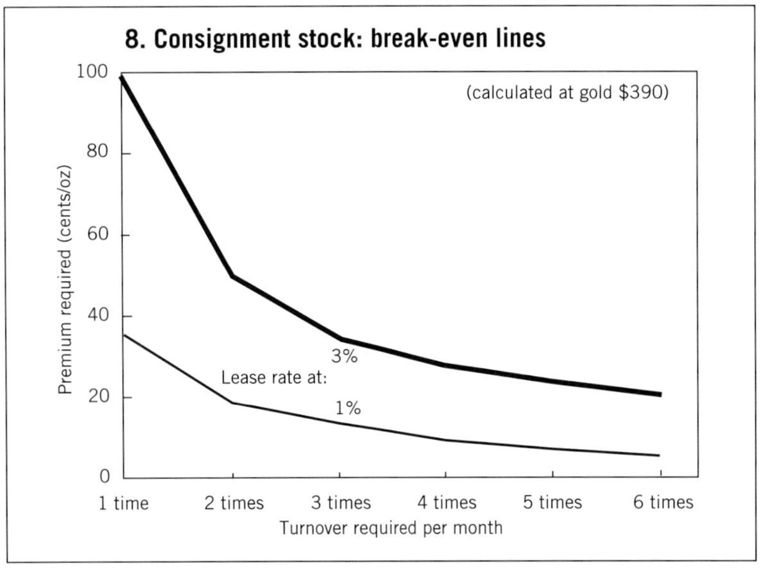

It is, in fact, the refinery stage of the physical gold pipeline which suffers the unkindest cuts if gold lease rates rise. To avoid price risk while ore from a mine is being treated, the refiner normally borrows gold from a commercial bank (sometimes another division of the bank owning the refinery), sells the bullion to raise cash to pay the miner for his ore, and then repays the commercial bank refined gold (plus borrowing costs) once treatment is completed. With the chronic excess capacity that affected refinery margins at that time, a couple of weeks' spike in lease rates late in 1995 (see Panel 2) wiped out the profits that many refiners had made for the whole year up to that point.

The exposure of a refinery to higher gold borrowing costs can be readily appreciated by the potential response of the industry:

❑ refining operations might be accelerated to reduce gold borrowing periods, even though the cutting edge of refining technology is already widely in place; and

❑ funding charges might be separately itemised in contracts, rather than losing them under the rubric of "treatment charges". But it seems doubtful that placing such funding charges in the "shop window" will make the client (the producer) any less selective a buyer.

In reality, under higher lease rates, even lower refining margins would have to be accepted. Much of the current excess refining capacity, and a good deal of planned capacity, is partly government owned, protected by political priorities from economic realities. Refiners without state patronage, a large, established network of clients, or the lifebelt of a profitable global bullion operation, could even collapse.

1 *UBS,* Investor Guide to the International Repo Market, *August 1995.*

2 *Being 32,151 troy ounces.*

2

Precious Metals OTC Options

David Mengle
JP Morgan

Financial risk management involves either trading a risk one does not want to bear for a risk one prefers, paying another firm to assume a risk one does not want to bear, or consciously deciding to bear a given risk. A precious metals producer, for example, might pursue its risk management objectives by giving up exposure to an unfavourable price outcome in return for sacrificing the potential benefit of a favourable outcome. Forward contracts, futures or swaps – described in Chapters 1 and 3 – offer an appropriate solution in such cases. Others might prefer to "insure" against adverse outcomes, while retaining the ability to benefit from favourable price movements, by paying another firm to assume the downside risks. Options are the appropriate solution for these producers.

This chapter has two main objectives:

❑ to explore in more detail, using a series of examples, the circumstances in which precious metals producers and other market participants might want to use options; and

❑ to investigate some characteristics of options that metals risk managers should understand. In particular, we will look at the factors that affect the value of an option, and explain how dealers dynamically hedge the value of their options portfolios.

The over-the-counter options market: overview

It is difficult to gauge the size of the market in privately negotiated, or over-the-counter (OTC), precious metals options. A survey conducted by the Bank for International Settlements in March 1995, shown in Table 1, indicates that the notional value of OTC gold options, which represent contract amounts but not amounts at risk, totalled approximately $59 billion. This is 40% of the total notional value of OTC gold contracts outstanding. Table 1 also shows the notional value of exchange-traded gold options outstanding as of the same date, which is only about 20% of the notional amount of OTC gold options outstanding. OTC gold options constitute approximately 54% of all outstanding OTC commodity options, but only about 1% of the OTC options market as a whole – because the market as a whole is dominated by interest rate and foreign exchange options. Similar figures are not available for other precious metals.

Liquidity is an important aspect of options markets because it enables dealers to hedge their positions. Anecdotal evidence suggests that liquidity in the gold market is generally high, that

Table 1. Notional contract amounts outstanding, March 1995, $ billion

GOLD DERIVATIVES CONTRACTS		NOTIONAL
OTC contracts		
Forwards and swaps		88.3
OTC options		58.9
Bought	30.6	
Sold	28.3	
Total OTC contracts		**147.3**
Exchange-traded contracts		
Futures		11.7
Bought	5.3	
Sold	6.4	
Options		11.3
Bought	8.2	
Sold	14.0	
Total exchange-traded contracts		**34.0**
ALL OTC DERIVATIVES CONTRACTS		
Currency contracts		13,095
Options	1,957	
Interest rate contracts		26,645
Options	3,548	
Equity contracts		579
Options	527	
Commodity contracts		318
Options	109	
Total OTC options	6,141	
Total OTC derivatives contracts		**40,637**

Source: Bank for International Settlements, *Central Bank Survey of Foreign Exchange and Derivatives Market Activity*, Basle, May 1996.

PANEL 1

AN OPTIONS PRIMER

An option contract gives its buyer (also called the *holder*) the right, but not the obligation, to transact at an agreed price (*strike* or *exercise* price) at some time in the future. The buyer must pay a fee (*premium*) for this right and the contract has a specified expiration date (*maturity* or *expiry*). While the buyer of an option has purchased a right, the seller (also caller the *writer*) has assumed an obligation to perform according to the contract terms if the option is exercised.

The option can take two forms: a *call option* is an option to buy, and a *put option* is an option to sell. The advantage of options over swaps or forwards is that they give buyers the desired protection, while potentially allowing them to benefit from a favourable movement in the underlying price; the premium is the price of this advantage. If put options with consecutive expiry dates are strung together, the result is called a *floor*; if call options are strung together, the result is a *cap*. Some options, known as *American* options, can be exercised at any time before expiry; others, known as *European* options, can only be exercised at expiry.

When an option is exercised, there are two different ways to settle the obligation. One is *physical* (or *bullion*) *delivery*, in which one party delivers the underlying metal in return for the strike price. The other is *cash* (or *financial*) *settlement* in which one party pays the other the cash difference between the market price and the strike price; no physical delivery takes place.

The left side of Figure 1 in the main text shows the payoff at expiry from an uncovered put option. (An uncovered option is simply an option viewed in isolation, disregarding any offsetting physical or financial position.) The solid line shows the payoff to the buyer of the put. Until gold falls to $350, the put is *out of the money*, because there is no benefit to exercise. When gold falls below $350, say to $345, the put is *in the money* and the result will depend on whether the contract involves bullion delivery or financial settlement. In the case of bullion delivery, the option writer must buy from the option holder the underlying gold for $350 per ounce; the holder can buy the gold in the market for $345 per ounce, deliver it and benefit by $2 per ounce (net of the $3 premium). Under financial settlement, the option seller simply pays the option buyer the $5 per ounce difference between the market price and the strike price; again, the net benefit is $2 per ounce.

The dashed line shows the mirror-image payoff from the point of view of the option seller; the seller receives a premium of $3 per ounce, and is not obligated to perform until gold reaches $350. When gold is less than $350 and the buyer exercises the option, the seller must either buy gold at the strike price (physical settlement) or pay the difference between the strike price and the current gold price (financial settlement).

silver is significantly less liquid, and that platinum and palladium are much less liquid still. Lower liquidity leads to higher price volatility but hampers dealers' ability to provide options that could protect against such volatility. Reasons for the low liquidity and high volatility in the silver market include:

❑ the small size of the underlying market relative to that of the gold market (estimates by Gold Fields Mineral Services suggest that in 1996 the dollar value of the supply of gold was over 10 times that of the supply of silver);

❑ silver is produced largely as a by-product of other metals such as gold, copper, lead or zinc. It follows that silver production is sometimes influenced more by demand for the primary metals than by demand for silver. Inventories are often insufficient to dampen price fluctuations if silver supply increases during periods of reduced demand, or decreases during periods of increased demand;

❑ industrial demand has a relatively greater importance for silver than for gold; consequently, silver is more prone to fluctuations in industrial activity, and economic cycles in general, than gold.

In contrast with silver, platinum and palladium are often mined as primary metals. Like the silver market, however, the underlying platinum and palladium markets are small (relative to the gold market), and industrial demand is of crucial importance. Again, the result is low liquidity and high volatility.

Using precious metals options

The examples in this section illustrate how precious metals options can help metals producers and other market participants to manage the financial risks they face.

EXAMPLE 1: PROTECTING AGAINST FALLING GOLD PRICES

A gold producer, ABC Co, projects that, if gold maintains its current price level of $358 per ounce, it will be able to service its debts, meet its operational spending needs, and keep current investment plans on track. ABC Co needs to guard against the consequences of the gold price falling below the level assumed in the firm's business plan.

One possible solution is to sell a forward contract on gold. Here, the producer locks in a specific gold price by selling the gold forward at the forward price quoted by a dealer. But if ABC Co wishes to benefit from an increase in the gold price while insuring against the negative consequences of a price fall, purchasing a put option on gold might be the more appropriate solution. The solid line in the left-hand diagram in Figure 1 shows payoff (net of premium) for the put option for a strike price of $350 per ounce and an up-front premium of $3 per ounce. On the exercise date the producer will receive a payment from the dealer equal to either:

- zero, or
- the difference between the strike price and the current price of gold, if the price of gold is less than the strike price.

The result, shown for 100,000 ounces of gold in the right-hand diagram of Figure 1, is that the producer has insured against gold dropping below the $350 strike price, net of the $3 premium. In order to obtain this price insurance, while maintaining the ability to benefit from a rise in price, ABC Co incurs two costs. One is the premium paid for the option. The other cost results from the risk that the dealer might default if ABC Co exercises the option; in other words, the producer has taken on a contingent credit risk. Options and other derivatives do not make risks disappear but they do allow users choice over which risks they shed, which risks they retain and which risks they actively assume.

If the producer desires protection over a longer period, say two years, put options can be linked together into a *gold price floor*, consisting of a series of put options on the gold price, struck at a desired floor level. The floor buyer pays an up-front premium equal to the combined premiums of each individual put option over the two-year period. In return, at each expiry date, the seller pays the difference between the strike price and the price prevailing on that day (if the difference is a positive figure). As with the single period put, the effective price received will be equal to the floor strike, but in this case it will be net of the up-front premium amortised over two years. The floor strike can be a single price, constant over the life of the put, or it can increase with the forward rate; the latter alternative generally involves a lower premium (see next section).

An *average price* option, commonly called an *Asian option*, is a variation on the put or floor. Here the strike price at exercise is compared, not with the price prevailing on the exercise date but, instead, with the average price prevailing during a specified period prior to expiry. An Asian option might be an appropriate solution for a producer that sells its output steadily over the exercise period. The more volatile the price of gold, the larger the potential divergence between the average price (the real price exposure) and the price on the day of expiry (the payout from an ordinary European-style option). Of course, the more volatile markets seem likely to become, the more such producers are drawn to Asian-style options. Another attraction is that the premium on an Asian option is typically lower than that on an otherwise similar European

1. Put option on gold

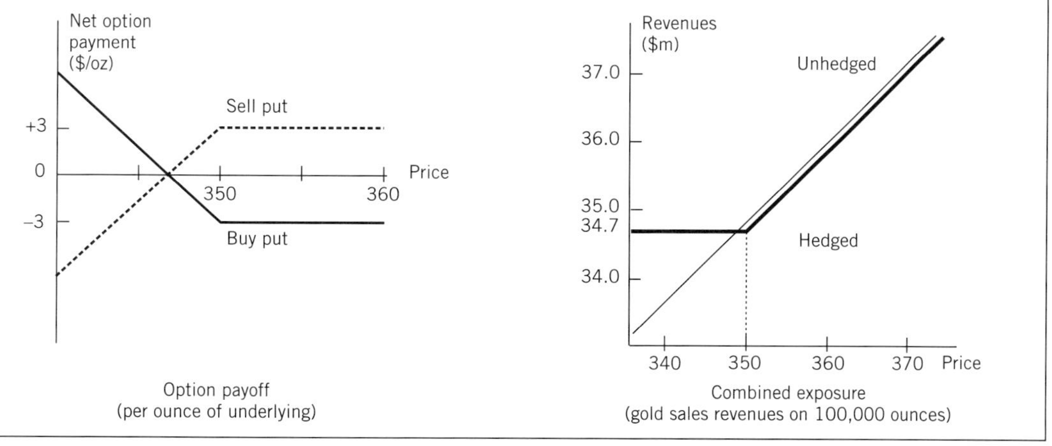

2. Min-max option on gold

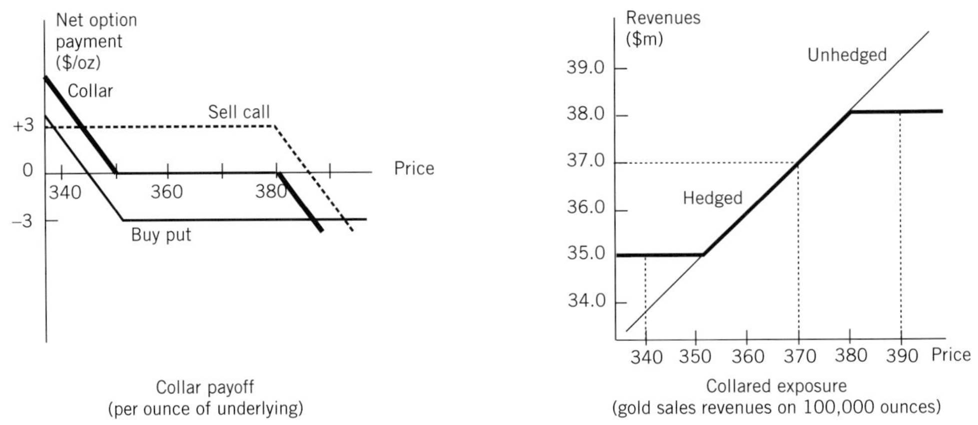

option, the reason being that average prices tend to be less volatile than prices prevailing on a single day (we explain the link between volatility and option premium in the next section).

EXAMPLE 2: REDUCING THE COST OF INSURING AGAINST PRICE RISK

Suppose the same producer, ABC Co, becomes uncomfortable with the size of the option premium quoted by dealers. A strategy known as a gold "collar", or *min-max* option, occupies the middle ground between locking in a price with a forward and insuring with options. This strategy involves subsidising the cost of the put option position (the hedge position) by selling selected call options; in effect, insurance against the market price falling is paid for by "selling" some potential upside benefit.

The left-hand diagram of Figure 2 shows how a min-max works. ABC buys puts struck at $350 on 100,000 ounces for $3 per ounce, as in the previous example. At the same time it sells calls struck at $380 on the same underlying amount, also for $3 per ounce. The premium received for the calls equals the premium paid for the puts, with a zero net premium. On the expiry date, if gold falls below $350, ABC will receive a payment that will compensate it for the amount by which gold fell below $350 on the underlying amount. If gold rises above $380, however, ABC will pay the amount by which gold rose above $380. The resulting risk profile is shown in the right-hand diagram of Figure 2. ABC has bought protection against low prices by selling the benefit of high prices, but the producer will benefit from price appreciation up to the $380 call strike.

3. Participating collar

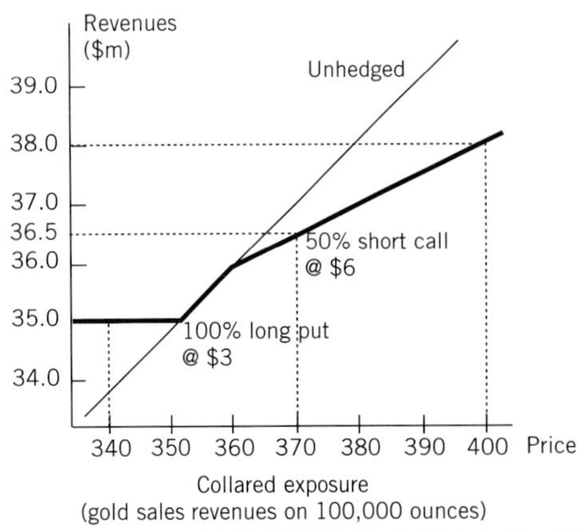

A variation on the collar is a *participating collar*; a participation is any option bought or sold on less than the entire underlying amount. In Figure 3, for example, ABC Co buys puts struck at $350 on the entire underlying 100,000 ounces as before, but sells calls struck at $360, at a premium of $6 per ounce, on half the underlying amount. The net premium is still zero but the payoff profile has changed. As before, if gold falls below the put strike to $340, for example, ABC will receive a payment of $10 per ounce to keep the lower price limit of $350. If the price rises above $360, however, ABC will have to pay the difference between the current price and $360 on 50,000 ounces.

In contrast with the standard collar, the participating collar enables ABC Co to retain some upside potential while still paying no explicit premium. Whether the participating collar makes the producer better off than a standard collar will depend on the increase in the gold price. If it only rose to $370, for example, ABC Co's net sales revenues are $37 million under the standard collar and $36.5 million under the participating collar. At any price above $400, ABC's revenue is capped at $380 with the standard collar but rises above $380 with the participating collar.

EXAMPLE 3: REVENUE ENHANCEMENT

Consider the position of a central bank that would like to earn extra revenue by selling European call options on some of its gold stocks. The bank has decided it is willing to part with the gold at the strike price if the options end up in the money.

The diagram on the left of Figure 4 shows the payoff profile of the short option position struck at \$360 and carrying a premium of \$6. If the price at expiry is at or below the \$360 strike price, the writer of the call makes no payment and keeps the entire premium. If gold finishes above \$360, however, the call will be exercised against the central bank, which will give up the difference between the current price and the strike price.

The price of gold could theoretically rise to infinity, so if we look at the option position in isolation there is no inherent limit to the losses on the contract. As the central bank also holds the underlying asset, however, its option position is "covered". That is, the bank can simply deliver the underlying gold (or sell the gold in the market and pay the option buyer the difference between the market price and the strike price) if the option is exercised. The resulting exposure is shown in the right-hand diagram of Figure 4. If gold rises above the strike, the covered option writer's benefit from selling the underlying gold is capped at the strike price plus the premium received. If gold remains at or falls below the strike price, then the bank keeps the premium and the gold; the premium income offsets somewhat the decline in the value of the gold.

Note that the exposure profile of the combined long gold and short call positions is equivalent to that of a short put position. The downside risk is similar to that of the unhedged gold position, but it is enhanced by the option premium income. The upside, however, has been sold in return for the premium. Moreover, in contrast to a purchased option, a written option carries no credit risk once the premium has been received.

EXAMPLE 4: SYNTHETIC STRATEGIES

Example 3 above suggests that option positions and cash positions can generally be combined to form other types of contract. Such *synthetic* positions might be useful in the event that a particular contract is wanted but not available or, more probably, as a means of carrying out arbitrage between different contracts or market views. Panel 2 (overleaf) demonstrates how one might evaluate alternative synthetic strategies.

Consider, for example, the combination of a short forward position and a long call position, struck at the forward price. The resulting exposure, shown on the left-hand diagram of Figure 5 (overleaf), is a synthetic long put. Below the strike price, the increase in value of the short forward is offset somewhat by the amount of the premium paid. As the price rises above the strike price, however, the increasing payment on the call option completely offsets the decreasing value of the forward.

Similarly, a long put position and short call position struck at the same price combine to form a synthetic short forward position. Assuming that:

- both are struck at \$360,
- the call premium received is \$6, and
- the put premium paid is \$4,

then the implied forward price locked in is \$362. For example, if the put option is exercised when gold is \$355, the buyer can sell gold for \$360 which, when combined with the net premium of \$2, gives a net price of \$362. Alternatively, if the call option is exercised on the writer when gold is \$368, the put expires worthless; the option writer is obliged to sell gold for \$360 and the net

4. Writing covered calls

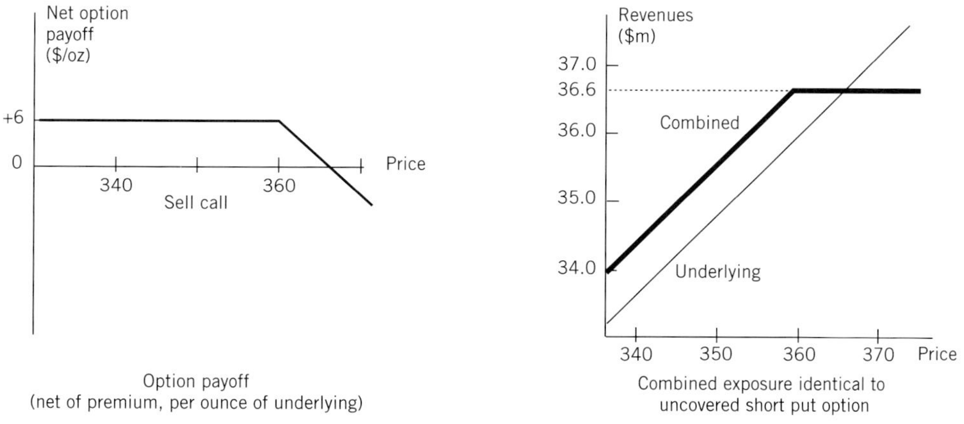

PANEL 2

COMPARING STRATEGIES

Once the decision to hedge has been taken, the issue becomes one of how to hedge. Choosing between forwards, swaps and options is only the beginning; a firm also faces a choice between standard options and synthetic options. The appropriate solution will depend on management's perception of the shareholders' desired risk profile, on the firm's view regarding future prices, and on the cost of the alternatives.

The figure compares three hedging strategies, assuming a gold spot price of $360 and a forward price of $365:

- selling gold forward at $365;
- purchasing put options struck at $350 for a premium of $3 per ounce;
- selling forward and purchasing call options struck at $380 for a premium of $3 per ounce – that is, a synthetic (long) put option struck at $380.

Comparison of strategies

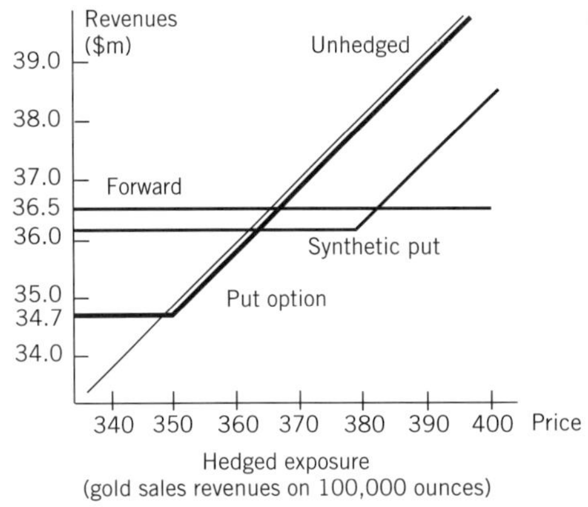

Selling the gold forward locks in a price of $365. The strategy is most appropriate to a "bearish" market because it will perform best if prices end up falling or if spot prices remain unchanged so that "contango" (forward prices greater than spot prices) is earned.

Purchasing put options places a floor of $347 (the strike price net of the premium) on the gold price received, while reducing revenues by the amount of the premium at prices at or above the strike. It will work best if the firm wishes to maintain maximum upside potential while protecting against a drop in price. The lower the strike price, the lower the put premium, so the firm faces a trade-off between cost of protection and the price at which the downside protection should kick in.

Finally, the synthetic put locks in the forward price net of the premium, but allows for upside movement once the price rises above $380. It is likely to appeal to firms that are bearish about the market but wish to maintain upside potential in case prices rise instead. The higher the strike price, the lower the call premium, so the firm faces a trade-off between cost of protection and the price at which the upside benefit should kick in.

premium again gives a net price of $362. Any significant differences between the forward prices quoted in the market and the forward prices implied in synthetic forwards give rise to arbitrage opportunities, which quickly disappear as market participants rush to profit from them.

One example of a synthetic hedging strategy used for project finance is the South African gold producer Johannesburg Consolidated Investment's (JCI) Western Areas mine, described in more detail in Chapter 5. In the transaction, JCI sold forward 8½ years of production and at the same time bought call options on 55% of the output. The net result was a synthetic participating

5. Synthetic positions

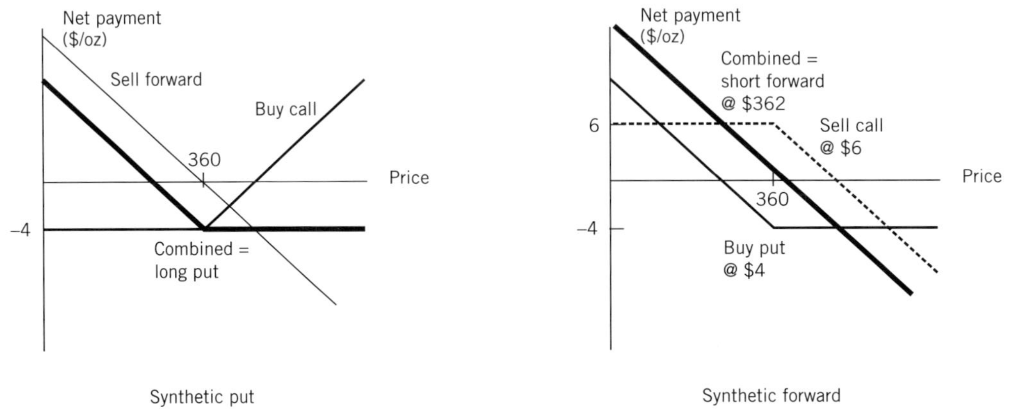

put that provided full downside protection and 55% participation in price increases.

EXAMPLE 5: HEDGING EMBEDDED CURRENCY RISK

Gold is generally priced in US dollars on the world markets. Producers and investors based outside the US may consequently be exposed to currency risk along with gold price risk.

Figure 6 shows how price risks and currency risks can either reinforce or offset each other. It assumes that:

- ❑ the producer in our examples, ABC Co, is based in Canada;
- ❑ it has both a long gold position and a long US dollar (ie, short Canadian dollar) position because revenues are in US dollars;
- ❑ costs are in Canadian dollars; and
- ❑ exchange rate is 1.35C$/US$.

ABC Co benefits:

- ❑ when the price of gold rises;
- ❑ when the Canadian dollar falls against the US dollar; or
- ❑ when both of these things happen.

The lower left quadrant of Figure 6 shows the worst situation, in which gold falls and the Canadian dollar rises. In the upper left and lower right quadrants, a favourable move can offset an unfavourable move. Finally, in the upper right quadrant gold rises and the Canadian dollar falls – two positive outcomes.

When ABC Co hedges the gold price by purchasing a put option, it protects itself against the two outcomes in the two lower quadrants. This, however, leaves open the possibility in the upper left quadrant – that currency depreciation erodes the gains in price. Figure 7 shows the potential effect of US dollar depreciation on the firm's Canadian dollar revenues from a sale of 100,000 ounces (assuming a gold price of $360).

One solution is to hedge the currency risk with a currency option, specifically a US dollar put option (which is equivalent to a Canadian dollar call). In Figure 7, the put is struck at 1.35 C$/US$ and carries a premium of 0.85% of the underlying notional amount (C$413,000). If the US dollar falls below C$1.35, the producer can exercise the option and will have the right to convert US$36.0 million into C$48.6 million, which provides a net value of C$48.2 million.

Currency options can also be used with synthetic strategies. In the case of the Western Areas example, mentioned above and described in Chapter 5, the forward contracts and call options were denominated in South African rand.

6. Interaction of gold price and currency exchange rates

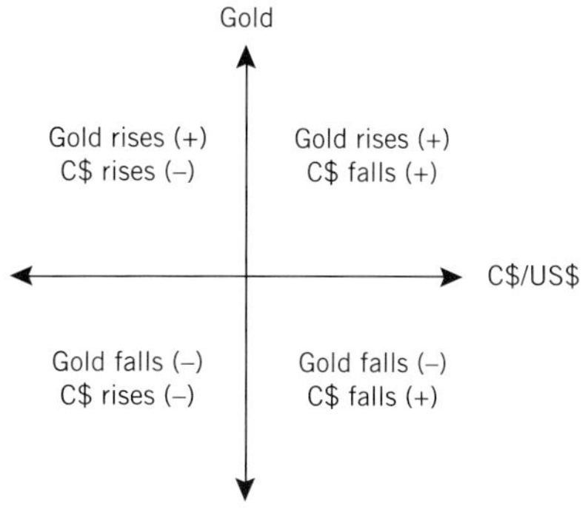

7. Hedging currency exposure

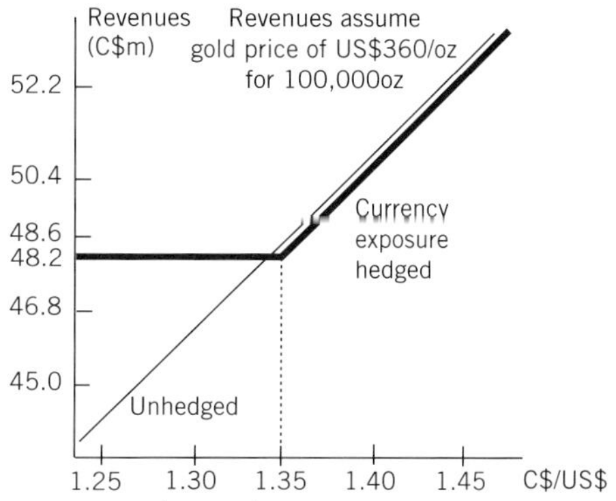

US$ put (C$ call) premium is 0.85% of C$48.6m notional amount

Normally, rand depreciation translates directly into an increase in the rand price of gold, but locking in a rand price using a forward contract subjected Western Areas to a currency exposure. The call options eliminated the currency exposure on 55% of the output, but the remaining output was exposed to rand depreciation. The solution was to hedge the exposed output with dollar calls (rand puts), which restored the ability of Western Areas to benefit from nominal price increases in gold brought about by rand depreciation against the US dollar.

EXAMPLE 6: EXOTIC OPTIONS

If a producer is uncomfortable with the cost of insuring against US dollar depreciation, the interaction of gold prices and exchange rates, as illustrated in Figure 6, might allow for less expensive solutions. For example, hedging the gold price with a put option provides protection even in the lower right quadrant, even though US dollar appreciation might offset gold price depreciation. If ABC Co hedges the currency risk, it will be protected even in the upper left quadrant, in which gold price appreciation offsets the US dollar depreciation. Hedging both gold price and currency risks might thus provide protection even when it is not needed. This involves paying premiums on both the gold put and the US dollar put. Exotic options, which include payoff features that are more complex than those found in standard options, might in this case be an appropriate solution.

One form of exotic option is a *barrier option* – an option that can either activate (knock-in) or extinguish itself (knock-out) if a reference price passes a predetermined barrier level. For example, the dealer could sell ABC Co a knock-out put option on gold, which provides protection against a fall in the gold price but also extinguishes (knocks out) if the Canadian dollar falls below a specified level. ABC Co is still protected in the lower left quadrant, but the option knocks out at some level in the lower right quadrant. The advantage of the *knock-out option* over the standard put option is that the knock-out option should carry a lower premium because the possibility of knocking out means a lower probability of the option being exercised.

One drawback of a knock-out option, however, arises from currency volatility during the period prior to expiry. It is possible that the Canadian dollar might fall and knock out the option, and then rise again before expiry; the option might not be there when it is needed. An alternative is a *knock-in option*, which activates if the Canadian dollar rises above a stated level. Another kind of exotic option suited to this problem is a *currency-denominated put*, which provides protection against gold falling below a specified strike denominated in Canadian dollars.

The applications of exotic options described here all take advantage of the correlation between prices and exchange rates. As the gold price on one hand and the Canadian/US dollar exchange rate on the other are not perfectly correlated, the two might to some degree offset each other. The lower (or more negative) the correlation, the greater the potential offset and the lower the combined volatility, both of which lead to a lower premium.

8. Buying volatility: straddle payoff per ounce of silver

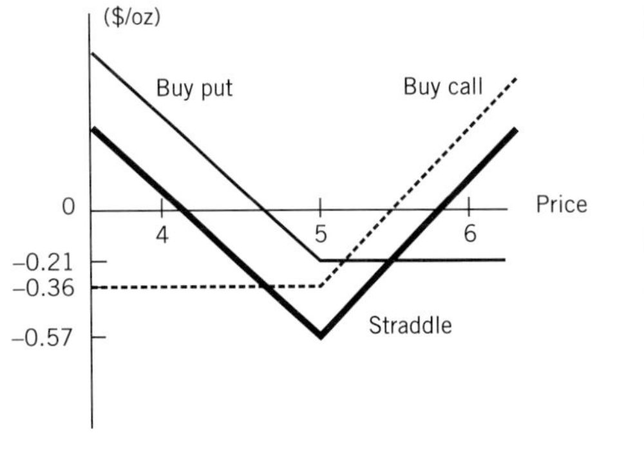

EXAMPLE 7: BUYING VOLATILITY

For reasons we discussed at the beginning of this chapter, the price volatility of silver is often twice that of gold. Consequently, investors are sometimes attracted to contracts linked to the volatility of silver. For example, an investor, PQR Fund, believes that the volatility of the silver price is likely to increase over the next month and that a major price movement is likely, either up or down. To act on this view, PQR could enter the *long option straddle* shown in Figure 8. Buying such a straddle involves buying a call and a put, both struck at the same price; the buyer profits from increased volatility. If the price stays at the strike price, the investor's loss is limited to the combined call and put premium of \$0.57. If the price either rises or falls by more than \$0.57, the investor can profit. As PQR Fund will benefit from a movement in prices either up or down, it is said to be "long volatility". Similarly, if PQR Fund *sells* a straddle by going short both a call and a put, it profits from the price not moving much from the strike; thus it is "short volatility".

Pricing and valuing options

The value of any financial instrument, be it a security, forward, swap, or option, is the present value of expected cashflows. Estimating the value of options – and hedging option positions – is more complex than estimating the value of cash instruments, forwards or swaps. But the complex mathematical models used by dealers are based on simple principles that by themselves explain most of what affects option prices. Understanding these principles helps risk managers appreciate the risks and benefits of options, without obliging them to enter into the details of the pricing models.

The reasons for the greater complexity of options lie in their distinguishing characteristics, which are:

❑ *"Optionality"* It is up to the holder of an option to exercise the option. It is uncertain whether or (for an American option) when the option will be exercised, and the ability to delay the decision to exercise is valuable to the holder.

❑ *Asymmetry of payoff* At expiry an in-the-money option can take an unlimited number of values, but an out-of-the-money option can only take a zero value.

❑ *Non-linearity* The relationship between market movements and option values is not constant. For example, the effect of a $2 increase in the price of gold on the value of an option is not simply twice the effect of a $1 increase.

These characteristics affect how one estimates the expected cashflows from an option.

INTRINSIC VALUE AND TIME VALUE

Figure 9 shows the payoff for a long call and a long put option if they are exercised immediately; the payoff is known as the *intrinsic value* of an option. When a call option is in the money, the intrinsic value is equal to the current underlying price minus the strike price; when it is at the money or out of the money, the intrinsic value is zero. Similarly, when a put option is in the money, intrinsic value is equal to the strike price minus the underlying price; otherwise it is zero.

The choice of "underlying price" varies according to the type of option. For a European option, the buyer and seller are primarily concerned with prices that will prevail at the option's expiry; thus the relevant underlying price prior to expiry is the forward price. In contrast, an American option can be exercised at any time prior to expiry; thus the relevant underlying price is either the spot price or the forward price, whichever gives the larger intrinsic value.

At expiry, the value of an option is equal to intrinsic value. But prior to expiry, the value of an option is normally greater than intrinsic value. There are two reasons. First, "optionality" has value unless an option is either deep in or out of the money. And second, cost of carry is relevant. For example, a dealer that writes a call option hedges by holding some quantity of the underlying gold (discussed below); the interest on the cash borrowed to finance the gold purchase is higher than the lease rate that can be earned lending out the gold prior to exercise. In contrast, a dealer that writes a put option hedges by selling short some quantity of the underlying gold; the cash taken in when shorting the gold can be reinvested at a rate higher than the lease rate on the gold borrowed to sell short.

The resulting difference between the option's total value and its intrinsic value is known as *time value*. Time value is generally positive, that is, an option's value is generally greater than its intrinsic value. For an American option, time value is always positive. But for a European put that is deep in the money, time value can be negative. The reason is that, prior to having to pay the strike price when the put expires, the writer can earn interest on the amount of the strike price. For an American put, time value is always positive.

Figure 10 (overleaf) shows values for an in-the-money call and an out-of-the-money put, both as functions of the underlying price of gold. The straight lines show intrinsic value, the curved lines show total value; the vertical distance between the intrinsic value line and the price curve at a given underlying price is the time value at that price. Consider the option value if the underlying price is $354, for example. Three months before expiry ($t = 90$), the call has a value of $11, even though intrinsic value is only $4; time value is consequently $7. By 10 days before expiry, total option value has declined to $5 even though intrinsic value is still $4; time value is now $1. For the put option, intrinsic value is

9. Intrinsic values for options

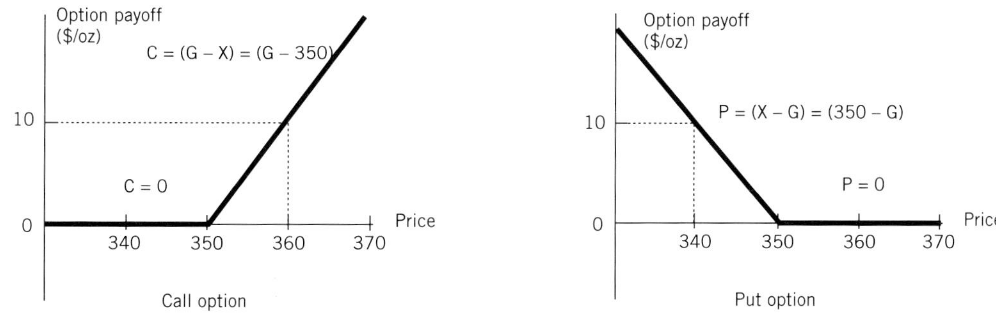

G = price of gold (prior to maturity, the forward price)
X = strike price = $350
C = value of call = max (G – X,0)
P = value of put = max (X – G,0)

10. Intrinsic value and time value

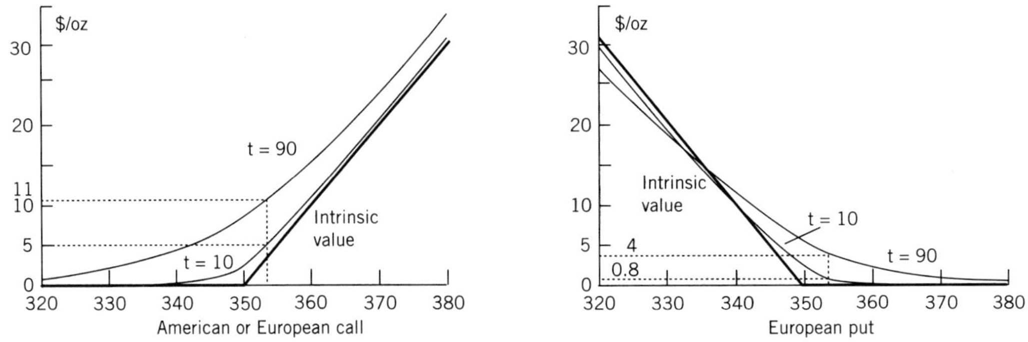

Price of gold = $354; strike price = $350; t = time to maturity (days); volatility = 10%

zero when the underlying price is $354, yet the value of the option three months prior to expiry is $4; in this case the value of the option consists entirely of time value. As the options near expiry, the line depicting the value of the option converges more and more closely with the line charting the intrinsic value. Note that time value is negative when the European put is deep in the money.

FACTORS AFFECTING THE VALUE OF AN OPTION

Five main factors influence the value of an option. They are:

❑ *The price of the underlying asset* As the value of the underlying asset increases, a call option will either move closer to being in the money or will go deeper into the money. For a put option, the opposite is true: as the underlying price increases the put will approach being out of the money or will go deeper out of the money. Consequently, as Figure 10 shows, as the value of the underlying increases, the value of a call option increases and the value of a put option decreases.

The rate at which the value of an option changes in response to a one-unit change in the value of the underlying – that is, the slope (or first derivative) of the price curves shown in Figure 10 – is known as the delta of an option. (Table 2 provides an at-a-glance summary of the meaning of this and the other "Greeks".)

The delta for an out-of-the-money call option is relatively low and approaches zero as the call goes deeply out of the money, or as it approaches expiry. For an in-the-money call, the delta is relatively high and approaches one (because of the one-for-one relationship between underlying and intrinsic value) as the call goes more deeply into the money or approaches expiry. The opposite is true of the delta of the put option, which has a negative value because its value declines as the underlying price rises. A common intuitive interpretation of delta is that it is a measure of the probability of an option expiring in the money.

As Figure 10 shows, the delta of an option changes as the price of the underlying changes; the only exception is at expiry, when an option's value coincides with its intrinsic value so that delta is either zero or one. The rate of change of the slope in response to a change in the underlying (that is, the second derivative or curvature of the price curve) is known as the gamma of the option. A high gamma, which is found when an option is at the money, means that delta changes a large amount in response to a change in the underlying variable; high gamma shows up as the most "convex" section of the curve. Conversely, a low or zero gamma, which is found when an option is either deep in or out of the money, means the price curve is nearly linear; that is, delta changes very little as the underlying price changes.

Since delta can be interpreted as a measure of the probability of a call finishing in the money, it

Table 2. What influences the value of an option?

Delta	δ	The change in value of an option in response to a change in the underlying price. Positive for calls, negative for puts
Gamma	γ	The change in the delta of an option in response to a change in the underlying price
Theta	θ	The change in value of an option for a given passage of time; time decay. Always negative
Kappa	κ	The change in value of an option in response to a change in volatility; commonly known as *vega*. Always positive
Rho	ρ	The change in value of an option for a given change in the discount rate

provides a measure of how much of the underlying asset must be bought or sold to hedge an option. As gamma measures the change in delta as the underlying price changes, it measures the additional amount that must be bought or sold to maintain the hedge as the underlying price changes further.

❑ *Strike price* Generally, the higher the strike price, the lower the value of a call option; for a put option, raising the strike price increases the value of the option. Raising the strike price of a call option either "raises the bar" the underlying price must hurdle over in order to go into the money, or makes it easier for an in-the-money call to go out of the money. The opposite is true for a put option.

❑ *The time remaining to expiry* As we discussed above, the longer (shorter) the time remaining to expiry, the greater (smaller) the chance that the option will go into the money. The measure of time decay, known as *theta*, describes the change in option value with respect to time; specifically, the passage of one day. Each passing day means some loss of value, so theta is always negative. The effect of time also shows up in Figure 10 as the shifting out of the price curve as time to expiry increases. Theta tends to be low for long-dated options because each passing day means only a small loss of value, but as the option nears expiry the loss of another day becomes increasingly critical. Time decay is most pronounced for at-the-money options which could go either way just before expiry; for in-the-money and out-of-the-money options, in contrast, there is less decay prior to expiry as change becomes less likely.

❑ *The volatility of the underlying asset* The variability of the price of the underlying asset is known as *volatility*; Panel 3 (overleaf) describes two different but commonly used concepts of volatility and how they are measured. Higher volatility means a higher option price. The reason is that a more volatile underlying price can, by definition, take a wider range of values. The greater range of values increases the number and size of probable in-the-money outcomes, with positive payouts, as well as the number of out-of-the-money outcomes, with zero payouts. As the out-of-the-money payouts are zero (rather than negative), the average expected value of the possible outcomes inevitably rises. The measure of the effect of volatility, called *kappa* or *vega*, describes the change in option value as volatility increases, and it is positive for both call and put options. Just like the time-to-maturity effect, increased volatility shifts any curve illustrating the whole option price away and up from the curve showing the option's intrinsic value – ie, it increases the time value of an option.

❑ *The interest rate used to discount the underlying asset* The buyer of a call pays the strike price at exercise; higher interest rates mean higher earnings on the invested strike price during the period preceding exercise. The buyer of a put option receives the strike price at exercise; higher interest rates mean higher foregone earnings during the period preceding exercise. Alternatively, one can view the effect of interest rates in terms of hedge costs to the seller as mentioned above. Either way, the measure of the effect of interest rates, known as *rho*, is positive for calls and negative for puts. In practice, the relevant rate when pricing gold options is the *gold forward rate*, which is the difference between the funding cost and the gold lease rate.

ESTIMATING THE VALUE OF AN OPTION

The following discussion concentrates on valuing European options – American options are slightly more complex. It also focuses on valuing call options, although the same principles apply to put options.

Three main factors are needed to value an option:

❑ the probability that an option will expire in the money;

❑ the expected value of the underlying price if the option expires in the money;

❑ the discount rate used to estimate the present value of expected in-the-money cashflows. In contrast with options on other underlying assets, for precious metals the discount rate takes account of the lease rate used to finance metals inventories as well as the rate on borrowed funds.

These three factors are then applied to the formula for the value of a call option at expiry:

$$C = \max(G - X, 0)$$

that is, the option value (C) is equal to the greater of

❑ the difference between the underlying price (G) at expiry and the strike price (X); or

❑ zero.

If the option expires out of the money, expected cashflows will be zero; thus we need concentrate only on in-the-money cashflows and determine their likelihood. If the option expires in the money, the option will be worth $G - X$. To

PANEL 3

WHAT IS VOLATILITY?

There are two concepts of volatility in common use.

Historical volatility measures the dispersion of the price of the underlying asset about its average level over a period in the past. It is generally measured as the standard deviation of price movements:

$$\sigma = \sqrt{\sum_{t=1}^{n} \frac{(R_t - \mu)^2}{n-1}}$$

where:

$$R_t = \ln\left(\frac{P_{t+1}}{P_t}\right),$$

the percentage change in prices from period t.
μ = mean of R_t
P_t = underlying price in period t
n = number of periods in historical period.

The number of periods chosen is a matter of judgment; so is the length of period t (daily, biweekly, monthly). The formula can also be modified to place more weight on most recent observations. Historical volatility measures the average variability during some period in the past. To value an option, however, it is preferable to estimate volatility expected in the future, over the life of the option. Historical volatility is the appropriate measure only if one expects past trends to continue.

Implied volatility attempts to solve this problem by providing an estimate of the volatility implied in the market prices that dealers are quoting for options. As this volatility is only one component of the price of an option, it cannot be observed directly, but must be derived using option pricing models. The Figure shows how this works.

When pricing an option, the user inputs the underlying price, the strike price, the maturity, the interest rate, and an *estimate* of volatility (often the historical volatility) of the underlying; the output of the model is the option premium. This does not correspond to the information available, however: volatility is not directly observable, except in the form of historical volatility, but option premium is observable in any liquid market. Consequently, the user can input the market premium of the option instead of the volatility estimate, along with the other variables, and the model will then output an estimate of volatility. This is the implied volatility, which measures the volatility implied by the current price given the values of the other variables.

Implied volatility

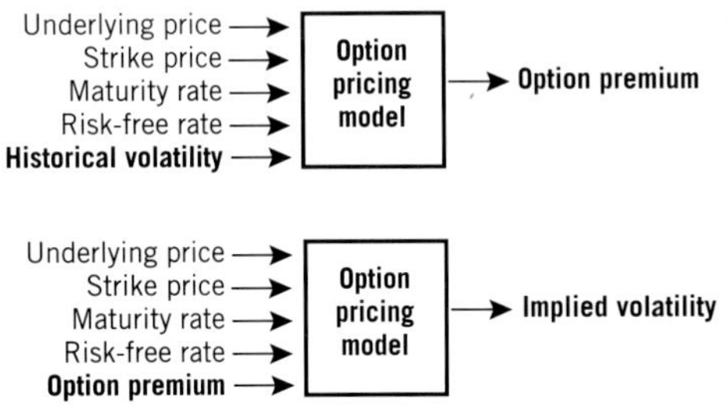

Option traders can use implied volatilities to decide whether an option is cheap or expensive by comparing one option's implied volatility with others in the market; the relationship between volatility and premium is positive, so a low implied volatility relative to other options might signal an underpriced option. Implied volatility can also help compare options between time periods. For example, in order to determine whether options this week are "cheaper" than they were a week ago, it is necessary to adjust for changes in the underlying price and the passage of time; if implied volatility is lower after adjusting the other factors it is reasonable to conclude that options have indeed become cheaper. Finally, implied volatilities aid comparisons between options on the same underlying but with different strike prices. If they are priced correctly relative to one another they should have the same implied volatility.

Traders can also compare implied volatilities for various options with historical volatilities, or with those predicted by econometric or statistical models. The trader might buy options with implied volatilities that are significantly low compared with historical volatilities, for example. In practice, however, it is still a matter of judgment as to when historical or implied volatilities are appropriate. Both have their place in dealers' and end-users' toolkits. It should also be borne in mind that implied volatilities derived from an inappropriate model will be misleading. An example is the use of a European-style option model to determine the implied volatility of an American-style option.

Chapter 8 of this book compares advanced techniques for measuring price volatilities in the base metals markets.

turn $G - X$ into an expected value, it is necessary to multiply it by the probability that the option will expire in the money. Finally, because expiry is at some time in the future, the expected value must be discounted to the present. The result is the following formula:

$$C = p(G_T > X) * D * [E(G_T | G_T > X) - X]$$

where
G_T = gold price at the option's expiry
$p(G_T > X)$ = probability that the underlying price exceeds the strike price
$E(G_T | G_T > X)$ = expected value of the underlying price, given that the option expires in the money
D = discount factor used to estimate the present value.

The value of a call option is equal to the expected difference between the gold price and the strike price on expiry, discounted and multiplied by the probability that the option will expire in the money. All option pricing and valuation models attempt to estimate this value.

PRICING AND VALUATION MODELS

Option pricing and valuation models fall into three general categories:

❑ The first, known as *closed-form solutions* or *analytic solutions*, estimate the present value of expected in-the-money cashflows - that is, the option value - from the variables mentioned above, namely the value of the underlying, the strike price, time to expiry, discount rate and volatility. The best known closed-form solution is the Black–Scholes model (eg, Hull 1997). The Black–Scholes model, discussed further in Chapter 9, is normally sufficient for modelling European options, but must be modified to value American options. Closed-form solutions are not always available for exotic options.

❑ *Numerical solutions* approximate the value of an option by means of computations. A commonly used numerical technique is the *binomial tree*, which traces various paths the underlying price can take and then calculates option values corresponding to the different price outcomes. Again, these values are the present values of expected in-the-money cashflows - that is, the averages of all the different option values under different price scenarios, weighted by their probability of occurring. An advantage of numerical methods is that they can be easily tailored to the characteristics of an individual option; they are particularly useful when the holder must decide whether to exercise the options prior to maturity. A disadvantage is that they may require extensive computational resources to take account of the huge number of paths the underlying price could take.

❑ A final category is simulation (usually *Monte Carlo simulation*), which calculates the value of an option from a sample of randomly generated price scenarios. Simulation is often used for options that are resistant to either closed-form or numerical solutions. It is particularly useful for path-dependent options, for which the payoff depends on the history of the underlying price prior to maturity.

Hedging options

Hedging options involves the same complexities as pricing and valuing them. The essential difficulty is that when an option is written it is uncertain whether it will be exercised at maturity. If writers hedge the short option by buying or selling the underlying position, they will not know until maturity whether the hedge position will be needed to offset the obligation to perform on the option.

In most of the examples in the earlier part of this chapter, the options were automatically hedged because the producers were "naturally long" the underlying gold. Even the central bank that sells calls does so covered by its long gold position. The end-users buy or sell the options with terms tailored to match the timing of the underlying cashflows, using strategies in which the option gains or losses beyond the strike price are matched by offsetting gains or losses on the underlying. All these are examples of *static hedging strategies*, because they involve putting a hedge in place and leaving it there. Most corporate hedging strategies are static strategies.

There are some circumstances, however, in which *dynamic hedging*, involving frequent adjustments to a hedge, might be preferable. One example is a rolling hedge as shown in Table 3 (overleaf), in which a producer adjusts a gold floor in order to lock in gains when the underly-

Table 3. Rolling hedge

Time to maturity (days)	Forward price ($/oz)	Strike price ($/oz)	Premium ($/oz)	Net outlay ($/oz)
180	350	350	(5.7018)	(5.7018)
120	360	350	2.3956	
120	360	360	(5.3367)	(2.9411)
90	370	360	1.4825	
90	370	370	(4.4398)	(2.9573)
Net				(11.6002)

ing position moves in the firm's favour. Imagine, for example, that the forward price of gold is $350 per ounce and that a producer buys at-the-money six-month puts on 100,000 ounces struck at $350. With a premium of $5.70 per ounce, the producer has guaranteed a minimum price of $344.30 per ounce. Suppose that after two months the forward price rises to $360. The gain on the underlying position is $10 per ounce, and the producer could lock in a net gain by selling the original hedge for $2.40 per ounce and buying an at-the-money put, struck at the new price, for $5.34 per ounce. Finally, if the forward price rises a further $10 per ounce after another month, the producer can sell the old put for $1.48 and buy a new put, struck at the new price of $370, for $4.44, for a net outlay of $2.96. At the end, the producer has paid a net premium of $11.60, so the effective price floor for the remaining 90 days of the option is $358.40.

Although option end-users might sometimes benefit from dynamic hedging strategies, dealers in the precious metals markets must hedge dynamically, because most of their clients take positions against the market moving in one particular direction (ie, down). For example, imagine that a dealer sells a European put option on 100,000 ounces of gold struck at $350; if the put is in the money at expiration, the dealer will be obliged to buy 100,000 ounces from the option holder at the strike price. The dealer can hedge this position in three ways:

- selling short 100,000 ounces of gold. However, if the put option finishes out of the money, the money the dealer made by selling the put option might well not be enough to cover any loss on this short sale;
- taking an offsetting position with another client. But in a "one-way" market, it will probably be difficult for the dealer to find an opposite position; or
- hedging dynamically, using the strategies we discuss below.

The simplest form of dynamic hedge is a *stop-loss strategy*, by means of which the seller of an option commits itself to buying or selling the underlying asset when the price passes a designated level. For example, the dealer in the example above could specify that it will sell short the underlying amount when the price goes below $350 and buy it back when it goes above that sum. This strategy means that the dealer is likely to have the appropriate hedge in place when it is needed. The disadvantage is that, because it involves buying or selling the entire underlying amount, differences between bid and offer prices could quickly make the strategy costly if the price fluctuates in and out of the money prior to maturity.

An alternative to this simple stop-loss strategy is to draw up a schedule of successive stop-loss purchases or sales, to be made as underlying prices rise or fall further. The problem then becomes to determine the size of the stop-loss transactions. In practice, as an option goes into the money and delta approaches one (or as an option goes out of the money and delta approaches zero) the dealer will hold or short a proportion (rather than the full amount) of the underlying in anticipation of exercise (or non-exercise). Using this strategy, known as *delta hedging*, a dealer effectively immunises the value of its option portfolio against small movements in the underlying price by repeatedly adjusting the hedge amount.

For example, imagine that a dealer writes a put option on gold. It hedges that potential long position by selling the underlying asset short, and the amount sold would be equal to delta (the hedge ratio) times the underlying position. If the price falls after the initial sale, delta becomes greater (in absolute value), so the dealer sells more of the underlying to conform with the new, higher hedge ratio. If the price rises, the dealer buys back some of the underlying. Because delta is equal to minus 1 only if the option is deep in the money, the dealer holds the entire underlying short position only when it is reasonably certain that the option will be exercised.

Similarly, when a dealer writes a call option it takes on a potential short position in the form of an obligation to sell at the strike price if exercised. It delta hedges by buying the underlying asset and buys more to maintain the hedge as the price (and delta) rises and sells as price (and delta) falls. Note that, as mentioned above, cost of carry becomes significant as the option goes in the money.

A dealer normally uses the opposite strategy when buying options. A long put-option position, for example, is damaged by a rising price, so the dealer hedges by taking a long position in the underlying equal to the hedge ratio suggested by the option delta. If the price rises, the dealer sells to conform to the lower delta; if the price falls, the dealer buys to conform to the higher delta.

In practice, several factors make delta hedging more complex than described so far. Firstly, the value of delta changes as expiry approaches, so adjustments might be necessary even if the underlying price does not change. Secondly, delta will be affected initially by the choice of volatility measure (historical or implied) that is fed into the model, and subsequently by changes in volatility. Thirdly, when an option is at the money or nearly so, the increasingly critical uncertainty of whether exercise will occur shows up in an unstable delta, especially just before expiry. Finally, buying and selling the underlying means paying away the bid/offer spread; it is here that the illiquidity of some precious metals markets can cause complications. The dealer consequently faces a trade-off between accuracy and cost, both of which increase with the frequency of adjustment of the hedge. And when markets become more volatile, spreads widen and the costs of hedging increase even further.

Delta hedging has little effect on the market price for gold as long as there is symmetry between the delta hedging of long and short positions. As discussed above, however, in the precious metals markets most end-users are option buyers, which means that dealers mostly have to delta hedge short option positions. If most delta hedging is for short option positions, the above description of delta hedging suggests that hedgers are doing the exact opposite of what traders normally do – they are selling as prices fall and buying as prices rise. This feature of option hedging by dealers leads to suggestions that delta hedging in practice is destabilising to markets, in that it accentuates price movements instead of dampening them. This is discussed further in Panel 4 (overleaf).

Managing options

In 1993, the Group of Thirty (G30) released its study, *Derivatives: Practices and Principles*, containing recommendations on risk management practices for derivatives dealers and end-users. The recommendations are not necessarily intended to be applied literally, but are rather a source of ideas for adapting the experience of some firms to particular situations. The study describes four main categories of risk related to using derivatives:

- *Market risk* Uncertainty related to the change in value or liquidity of a portfolio of financial instruments resulting from changes in the financial markets;
- *Credit risk* Degree of uncertainty of the ability of the counterparties to fulfil their legal obligations;
- *Operational risk* Uncertainty related to losses resulting from inadequate systems or controls, human error, or management failure; and
- *Legal risk* Uncertainty arising from the possibility that a contract might not be enforceable.

This concluding section suggests some questions that will help a firm define the management structure most appropriate to its situation.

MANAGEMENT AND ORGANISATION

Successful risk management programmes are characterised by the active support and involvement of senior management; without support from the highest level risk management controls are vulnerable to failure precisely at the time they are needed most. In most firms, it is the responsibility of senior management to develop risk management policies and for the board of directors to assess the results.

The G30 group recommends that a firm establish an independent risk management function. This does not necessarily mean creating a new department or hiring new people; rather, it means that a firm's risk management process should be made more independent by separating decision management (initiation and implementation) from decision control (approval and monitoring). For example, those whose job it is to take risks should not also be allowed to decide whether those risks are within acceptable limits; the failure of Barings Bank in 1995, in which the head trader of a dealing room was also responsible for the back office, demonstrates this. In most firms, controller, audit, and financial planning departments have the necessary independence from the risk-taking units to be able to assume some share of risk-monitoring responsibilities.

VALUATION AND MARKET RISK

The G30 group emphasises the importance of marking contracts to market in order to monitor the performance and the continued appropriateness of a hedge. The appropriate level of investment in valuation capabilities is an important matter for most firms. Firms that are frequent users of options and other derivatives might find it worthwhile to buy or develop computer packages for valuing contracts. Others might find it sufficient to obtain values from dealers; a common practice is to obtain valuations from several dealers simultaneously. Alternatively, there are consulting firms that specialise in providing independent valuations. As computing costs fall and models become more efficient, more firms will find it cost effective to have their own pricing models. Other relevant questions include how often to value contracts (daily, monthly, quar-

PANEL 4

IS DELTA HEDGING DESTABILISING?

As mentioned in the main text, delta hedging of short options positions involves buying in rising markets and selling in falling markets. The concern is that widespread delta hedging by dealers might, although it is intended to reduce individual dealers' risks, end up accentuating swings in markets. The extreme case is the regulatory "systemic risk" nightmare, in which delta hedging by dealers leads to "positive feedback loops". In other words, hedging activity by dealers grows large relative to overall market liquidity, resulting in amplified market swings and market crises.

In fact, concern with positive feedback loops need not be confined to options hedging. One could find the same thing if, for example, market participants were to place stop-loss orders to sell as prices fall below a certain level; indeed, a series of stop-loss orders at successively lower prices would resemble delta hedging even more closely.

Returning to options, two points should be made about delta hedging. Firstly, few would deny that it is an effective risk management tool in normal markets, which is what dealers face most of the time. Secondly, dealers are well aware of the limits of delta hedging outside of normal market conditions, when volatility suddenly jumps higher. That is why dealers place limits on positions to be hedged, both in terms of size and of maturity; indeed, it would be self-defeating for dealers to allow their hedge positions to grow so large that adjusting them could move the market significantly. In addition, dealers engage in "stress testing" their options portfolios to determine how the positions would behave if liquidity were to dry up, or under other unusual market conditions. Based on the results of stress tests, they might arrange for additional sources of liquidity, or adopt additional limits. As a general matter, then, concerns that delta hedging could be destabilising seem to be based on an implicit assumption of mechanistic behaviour by traders regardless of market conditions, an assumption that overlooks the crucial role of judgement and of experience in risk management.

The almost universal use of delta hedging by dealers suggests that it provides significant benefits. One is to create a "common currency", in which all contracts can be expressed in terms of the underlying asset. The result is to make individual contract liquidity less important than overall market liquidity. It is, therefore, possible to hedge relatively illiquid contracts with a reasonable degree of precision, as long as there is a liquid underlying market.

The second benefit of delta hedging is to allow for the gradual adjustment of hedge positions under normal markets. Contrast delta hedging with two alternatives – a stop-loss hedging strategy, and not hedging at all. In a stop-loss hedging strategy for a short put option, for example, the dealer sells short the entire underlying amount as the option goes in the money, and buys it all back if it goes out of the money; transacting in the entire underlying amount has more potential market impact than does transacting in incremental delta adjustments. The other alternative, keeping an unhedged position, also involves selling the underlying when the option is exercised; again, the large block is more likely to move the underlying market than would incremental adjustments to the delta.

terly) and how to value the underlying assets and compare the results with the value of the hedge.

Market risk management involves three things:

- ❑ assembling position and market data and translating them into a common measure;
- ❑ estimating the sensitivity of a portfolio of assets and contracts to changes in underlying market variables; and
- ❑ determining whether the resulting exposure to market movements falls within acceptable limits (here it is important to include the offsetting risks of the underlying hedged assets).

A commonly used measure of market risk is *value-at-risk* (VAR), which is the maximum expected loss of value resulting from an adverse market movement under normal market conditions. It always specifies a confidence level, that is, a probability that an observed loss will not be greater than the value at risk. Many firms use a 95% confidence level, in which losses are not expected to exceed the value at risk more than once every 20 days. Value at risk also specifies an unwind period, which is the number of days required to unwind (or fully hedge) a losing position without undue loss of liquidity.[1]

Many financial firms use VAR to aggregate risks in different businesses into a single risk measure. JP Morgan, for example, bases its daily "4:15 Report", a one-page summary of all the firm's market risks produced each day at 4:15pm and distributed to senior management, on VAR measures. Further, value at risk provides a useful way to specify position limits for risk takers. Each business specifies limits for its risk takers, and the firm in turn decides how much risk it will allow for all businesses combined. These limits are all described in terms of VAR.

For non-financial corporations, one problem with VAR is that it was designed for instruments that are marked to market, whereas many corporations are concerned with cashflows that are not marked to market. To remedy this problem, some researchers are developing "cashflow at risk" measures that estimate the vulnerability of cashflows to market movements.

When using VAR, it is easier to measure market risk than to assemble the relevant data in a timely and accurate manner. Firstly, it is necessary to assemble data on both derivatives contracts and on values of underlying assets, often from different systems, and to ensure that they are reported in a common language. Secondly, it is important to verify the accuracy of the data, especially on recent transactions. Finally, the resulting risk measures must be updated to reflect changes in the data. In gathering market data and turning them into usable and meaningful market risk information, users face a continual trade-off between being "approximately right" and "precisely wrong".

CREDIT RISK

As mentioned in the examples given in the earlier section of this chapter, a firm that buys an option contract is exposed to the risk of default by the dealer. If the dealer defaults, the hedge that the firm thought it had in place disappears and the firm has to replace the hedge. Similarly, a firm that sells an option creates a credit exposure for the buyer. Indeed, the measure of credit risk used by virtually all derivatives dealers is the replacement cost of in-the-money contracts.

Credit enhancement is often necessary in order to make possible a transaction that may make sense from a strategic viewpoint but might exceed a corporation's available lines of credit with the dealer. A gold producer wishing to enter into a min-max contract, for example, presents a credit exposure to the dealer on the call component: if gold prices rise above the cap level in the min-max, the dealer incurs a loss if the producer defaults, so the dealer might insist on some form of credit enhancement to offset the credit risk.

The producer could go to a bank, for example, and obtain a guarantee or letter of credit, in which the bank agrees to compensate the dealer in the event of default by the producer. Alternatively, the producer could post collateral on the positive value of the call; if the producer defaults, the collateral is available to offset the loss. Finally, the dealer could periodically mark the option to market and the producer pay any positive amount to the dealer; this is analogous to margin accounts on futures exchanges.

An important way to reduce credit risk is by means of a netting agreement – a legally binding agreement that a portfolio of contracts with a counterparty can be treated as having one net value, rather than each contract being treated as free-standing. One form of netting takes place at the settlement level, in which obligations are netted across transactions falling on the same day. The more important form of netting from the point of view of credit risk, however, is close-out netting, which occurs in bankruptcy. Close-out netting prevents a bankruptcy liquidator from choosing which contracts he will enforce against the counterparty and which ones he will cancel, and instead nets in-the-money contracts against out-of-the-money contracts. Bankruptcy laws in many countries do not recognise close-out netting, however, so credit risk can vary between jurisdictions.

An important part of the credit risk management function is to ensure that transactions are properly documented. Master agreements, which extend across contracts and underlying risks, can standardise the documentation process. The most commonly used master agreement is the International Swaps and Derivatives Association (ISDA) Master Agreement. Its risk-reducing features include:

- ❑ reducing uncertainty by specifying events of default and what happens when one or more of the events occurs;
- ❑ reducing settlement risk by allowing payments to be netted against each other; and
- ❑ reducing credit exposure by committing the parties to close-out netting where it is enforceable.

OPERATIONAL CONTROLS

Each company should design operational controls in a manner appropriate to its type and level of option activity. Relevant considerations include:

❑ who determines hedging policies?

❑ who is permitted to enter into options transactions, and for what amounts?

❑ does your firm also have a procedure for verifying the authority of your counterparty to enter into options contracts?

❑ how does your firm evaluate the performance of hedges?

❑ are there independent checks on transactions, including independent reporting relationships and dual signatures?

INFORMATION DISCLOSURE

Disclosure is an important element of a hedging strategy because it alerts the public, including both shareholders and analysts, to what the company is trying to do.

❑ Disclosure helps outline how corporate management views its risks and how it intends to implement its view of the firm's appropriate risk profile.

❑ It helps the reader to understand the company's goals.

❑ It helps dispel confusion that could arise regarding why the firm is using derivatives. For example, disclosure can help the public distinguish between hedging and speculative uses of derivatives.

❑ It can also help clear up potential misinterpretation of reported versus economic results when, for example, the underlying instrument is carried at historical cost while the hedging contract is marked to market.

As with other aspects of risk management, disclosure should be tailored to fit a firm's particular circumstances and level of activity. The following give some ideas on what type of information might help clarify a firm's objectives.

❑ The company's view of its appropriate risk profile. For example, should a company be exposed directly to precious metal prices, or to the performance of its managers?

❑ The underlying risks to be hedged.

❑ The types of contract used to hedge the underlying risk.

❑ The hedging strategy a firm plans to use. Relevant considerations include whether to adjust the hedge as market conditions change, or whether to leave it in place.

❑ The risk profile that results from the hedge. This might include a description both of risks shed and of risks taken on, as well as of how the result is consistent with the overall corporate strategy.

❑ Potential differences between economic results and reported results. As mentioned above, careful disclosure of corporate objectives and the accounting environment could help the public "see through" reported results to the actual results the company is trying to accomplish.

It should be emphasised that disclosure involves its own risks, including the possibility that the public will misinterpret the information. The solution is not failure to disclose, which is an even more risky strategy, but rather to disclose as carefully and candidly as possible.

1 *A readily available VAR methodology and data set is JP Morgan's RiskMetrics, which can run on its accompanying software package, FourFifteen, as well as on other commercially available packages. Morgan followed up in April 1997 with CreditMetrics, which applies VAR methodology to the measurement of credit risk.*

BIBLIOGRAPHY

Cross, J., 1994, *New Frontiers in Gold: The Derivatives Revolution*, London: Rosendale Press.

Galitz, L., 1995, *Financial Engineering*, Burr Ridge, Illinois: Irwin.

Hull, J., 1997, *Options, Futures and Other Derivatives*, 3rd ed, Upper Saddle River, New Jersey: Prentice-Hall.

Risk, 1997, *The JP Morgan/Arthur Andersen Guide to Corporate Risk Management*, London: Risk Publications.

Risk, 1997, *Financial Risk and the Corporate Treasury: New Developments in Strategy and Control*, London: Risk Publications.

Smithson, C., C. Smith, and S. Wilford, 1995, *Managing Financial Risk*, Burr Ridge, Illinois: Irwin.

3

Exchange-Based Metals Markets

Jason A. Tudor
Metallgesellschaft Limited

This chapter surveys the exchange-based metals markets, with a special focus on base metals contracts and their use as risk management instruments. We begin with a short history of how exchanges developed, relating this to some key differences between the two principal modern metals exchanges in terms of contract type and trading arrangements. This in turn links into a discussion of some recent events in the market, including the Sumitomo affair and its implications.

Risk managers not only have to decide between competing exchanges, but also whether they would be best served on the exchanges or by negotiating an over-the-counter (OTC) contract with a bank or some other party. We therefore compare the strengths and weaknesses of OTC and exchange contracts, with an eye to the kinds of "basis risk" that can be incurred when using standardised contracts. The chapter concludes with a look at new contracts and other key developments on the world's metal exchanges.

Development of trading on exchanges

Market trading has been a feature of larger towns and cities for thousands of years. As shipping routes became established, the largest centres of trading were naturally the major ports. Chicago, home of the oldest structured commodity exchange, the Chicago Board of Trade (CBOT), owes its prominence to its accessibility as a railway hub. As the grades and sizes of many diverse commodities became standardised, it became common to buy and sell "sight unseen", and merchants in trading centres in the developed nations began to trade "arrivals", that is, buying and selling material or produce that had yet to arrive in the specified location. If the quality of the delivery turned out to be unacceptable, arbitration was routinely used to settle any dispute. In time, standardised futures contracts were developed to prevent such problems and generate trading liquidity.

ORIGINS OF TRADING IN LONDON

Historically, Europe's main trading cities were the ports of London, Rotterdam, Hamburg and Antwerp. London became, and remains, the recognised trading centre, although the physical import and export of goods is now centred on continental European and other British ports. By the early 19th century, metal merchants in London had begun to congregate in the Jerusalem Coffee House, off Cornhill. Eventually, in 1876, the London Metal Exchange Company (LME) was established, somewhat later than the Baltic Exchange, the Liverpool Cotton Exchange and the CBOT. The advent of telegraphic communications at that time allowed vessels to communicate their positions, thus removing the uncertainty of arrival times, so that, from inception, the exchange could trade in days rather than months. Another LME practice that has stood the test of time is the rolling "three months date" – the forward date in which trading liquidity is concentrated. Although this was the approximate shipping time of Chilean copper (the only deliverable copper at that time) to Europe, the habit of trading three months forward was not formalised on the exchange until 1888.

Business expanded rapidly, and the sheer number of merchants led to the establishment of ring trading. In those days, a chalk circle was simply drawn on the floor; the padded leather seats were to come later! In 1882, the Exchange moved to its first purpose-built home in Whittington Avenue, Leadenhall Market. For the next century or so, metal specifications were updated and new contracts were launched, but the methods of conducting business on a principal-to-principal basis hardly changed. Then, as now, trading activity was concentrated in two on-exchange sessions, with complementary inter-office dealings during the day. The LME retained its unique status as a cash and forwards market: profits and losses do not become payable until the "prompt date".

By 1985, the year of the tin crisis, strong pressure had grown for the LME to reform its unusual structure. The crisis and the Financial Services Act of 1986 significantly changed the LME's operations and dealings. The dual structure of board, responsible for administration and the health of the exchange, and committee, responsible for rules and contract specifications, was abolished to make way for a unitary management board of mixed composition, representing ring-dealing members and the metals trade itself.

A clearing system was finally introduced so that member firms could deal with one another free of creditworthiness concerns. Whereas American practice was for an exchange to set up its own clearing and guaranteeing organisation, the LME appointed the International Commodities Clearing House (ICCH). Compulsory margining of members' positions – a feature of trading we discuss below – greatly improved the security of both members' and clients' business. The ICCH began life as the London Produce Clearing House, and was superseded in June 1991 by the London Clearing House.

In addition, new requirements for members to report large positions have allowed the LME executive to monitor the market, and to take steps if necessary. Recent years have seen the imposition of a number of backwardation limits (limits to the premium of nearby or spot prices over the prices of further forward contracts), particularly for copper.

The last decade has seen extraordinary growth in LME volume: turnover in 1996 exceeded $2 trillion. Although recent years have seen a levelling off in the number of contracts traded, further increases are likely, as more companies recognise the benefits of hedging. In addition, the market's improving liquidity and regulatory regime should attract further investment fund business.

1. LME contract volumes (base 1987 = 100)

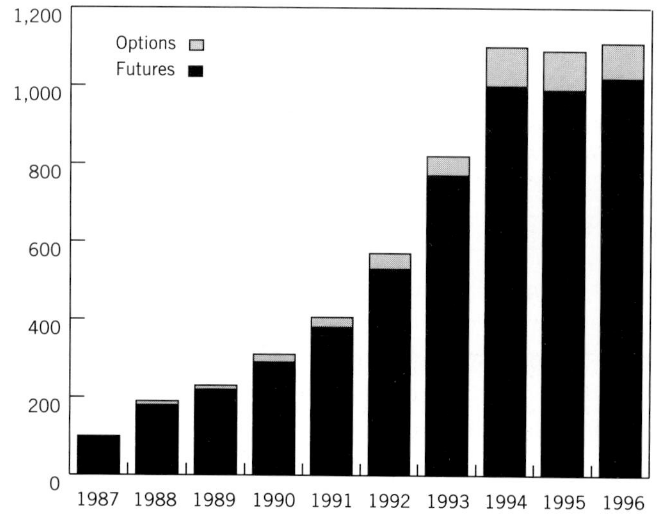

ORIGINS OF TRADING IN NEW YORK

In 1872, a group of Manhattan dairy merchants established the Butter and Cheese Exchange of New York, in an attempt to improve the efficiency of their chaotic local markets. After the addition of other commodities, including eggs, groceries and poultry, the exchange's name was changed in 1882 to the New York Mercantile Exchange (Nymex). This body benefited from the consolidation of regional American exchanges, which accelerated in the early 20th century as communications and transport facilities improved.

In 1883, seven years after the London Metal Exchange Company was established, the New York Metal Exchange was incorporated. This entity gave way to the National Metal Exchange, which eventually joined with the Rubber Exchange of New York, the National Raw Silk Exchange and the New York Hide Exchange to create the commodity exchange known as Comex. This merged body opened for business in 1933, offering trading in six commodities: copper, silver, tin, hides, rubber and silk. The next 40 years saw only intermittent growth, as trading was affected by World War II and the Korean conflict. At one time or another, every commodity listed on the exchange was subjected to government controls, allocations, price ceilings or other disruptions. Indeed, the private ownership of gold was forbidden until December 31, 1974.

Comex left its original home in Broad Street in 1977 for the Commodities Exchange Center (CEC) in New York's World Trade Center. After many years as close neighbours, Nymex and Comex merged on August 3, 1994 to create the world's largest physical commodity futures exchange.

Comex, responsible for 95% of the metals contracts traded under the newly merged body, has struggled during the past decade. An aluminium contract was launched and soon withered while, in copper, the LME consolidated its pre-eminence over the competing Comex contract by allowing metal to be delivered into registered warehouses in the US. Comex should benefit from the superior marketing skills of its new partner; Nymex energy contracts have been extremely successful.

RECENT GROWTH IN TRADING

The last decade has seen an unprecedented rise in metals trading volumes, both for exchange-traded and OTC products. OTC volumes are, of course, difficult to compute with any accuracy but, in the wake of the Sumitomo scandal that sent copper prices crashing in June 1996 (see Panel 2), estimates for outstanding LME-based Asian-style copper options for calendar 1997

2. Comex contract volumes (base 1987 = 100)

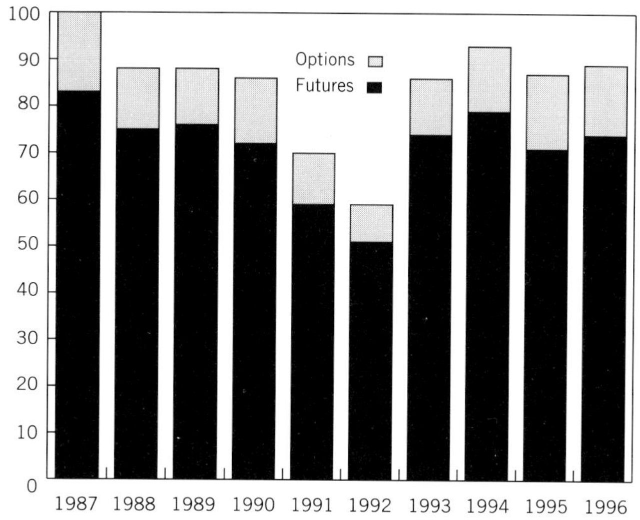

PANEL 1

MAJOR METAL EXCHANGES OF THE WORLD

The table below lists the metals traded on the world's most important exchanges, and the maximum forward availability of futures and options contracts for each metal.

Outside of Nymex pit trading times, platinum, copper, gold and silver are also available on the Nymex Access electronic trading system.

There are many other exchanges with metals contracts of less global significance, including the Kuala Lumpur Commodity Exchange (tin), the Shanghai Metal Exchange (all LME metals except aluminium alloy) and numerous small bullion-based exchanges, such as the Istanbul Gold Exchange. Such contracts trade in fairly small volumes, and are usually listed in the appropriate local currency.

Exchange/metals traded	Futures	Options	Units
London Metal Exchange (LME)			
Copper A Grade	27 months	27 months	US$/tonne
Aluminium High Grade	27 months	27 months	US$/tonne
Aluminium Alloy	15 months	15 months	US$/tonne
Zinc Special High Grade	27 months	27 months	US$/tonne
Nickel	27 months	27 months	US$/tonne
Lead	15 months	15 months	US$/tonne
Tin	15 months	15 months	US$/tonne
New York Mercantile Exchange (Nymex Division)			
Platinum	15 months	9 months	US$/oz
Palladium	15 months	Not traded	US$/oz
New York Mercantile Exchange (Comex Division)			
Copper High Grade	24 months	24 months	US¢/lb.
Gold	60 months	24 months	US$/oz.
Silver	60 months	24 months	US¢/oz.
Tokyo Commodity Exchange (Tocom)			
Gold	12 months	Not traded	¥/g
Silver	12 months	Not traded	¥/10g
Platinum	12 months	Not traded	¥/g
Palladium	12 months	Not traded	¥/g
Aluminium (from April 1997)	12 months	Not traded	¥/kg

PANEL 2

THE SUMITOMO AFFAIR – A CHRONOLOGY

Mark Nicholls, Risk

On June 13, 1996, after months of extreme volatility in the copper markets, Sumitomo Corporation announced that it had sacked its chief copper trader, Yasuo Hamanaka, for a series of unauthorised trades that were ultimately to cost the Japanese trading giant over $2.6 billion. With Hamanaka pleading guilty to fraud charges in Toyko on February 17, 1997, the opportunity was lost for the courts to examine the details behind the scandal. And, while no evidence had come to light by the time of the trial, it is estimated that Hamanaka's unauthorised trades went back to the mid-1980s.

The first sign that things were amiss at Sumitomo came in November 1991 when Hamanaka wrote to David Threlkeld, a major US-based copper trader, asking him to confirm fictitious trades. Threlkeld informed the London Metal Exchange (LME), which in turn asked its regulator, the Securities and Investments Board (SIB), to investigate. SIB and LME officials met with Hamanaka to discuss the letter. He claimed that the request involved moving trades into different accounting periods for tax reasons. No further action was taken. Around this time, the International Wrought Copper Council (IWCC) expressed its concern to the LME at what it saw as distortions in the copper market.

In September 1993, the LME placed a $5/tonne limit to the daily backwardation (the premium paid for spot or nearby dates) to ease a squeeze on the market. This squeeze was attributed by traders to Hamanaka's trading strategy. Hamanaka's exact strategy, and the intentions behind it, remain unclear. However, from 1993, he began buying up physical stocks of copper in an effort to support its price at levels which bore no relation to the metal's fundamentals. Later, he was to sell huge quantities of in-the-money put options. The premiums earned were used to continue to support copper, so that the options would remain unexercised.

In response to further concerns from the IWCC, the LME investigated the market in November 1995. LME chief executive David King obtained information on client positions and credit lines, and discovered that Sumitomo had extensive physical holdings of copper, as well as numerous credit lines at LME member firms. The following month, UK regulators began an investigation.

Around December and January, Hamanaka was buying physical copper to support the price of around $3,000 per tonne. A number of major hedge funds, including George Soros' huge Quantum fund, were selling against his position, believing copper to be hugely overpriced. The price of copper dipped, dropping to around $2,500 in February. However, by mid-May, using

were as high as 6 million tonnes. The ongoing hedging needs of the providers of OTC products such as these contributed to the boom in on-exchange futures and options trading.

3. Exchange-traded metals turnover, 1996 ($bn)

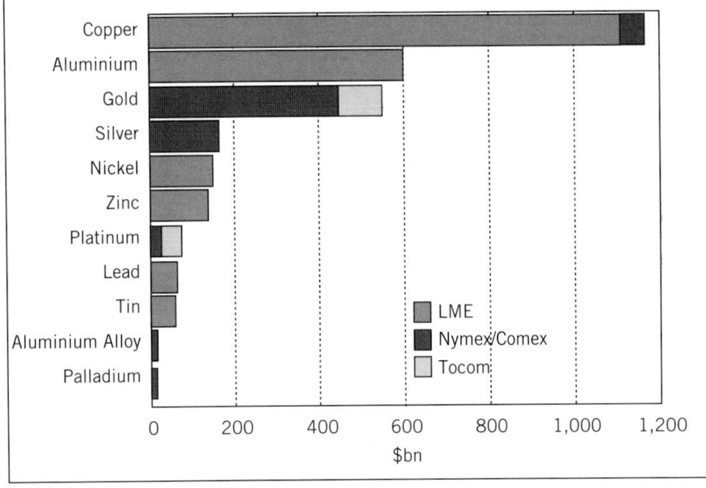

At the same time, the improved liquidity of base metals has attracted investment funds that previously confined their metals exposure to gold and silver contracts on Comex. Thus, while the LME is still very much a trade-driven rather than a speculator-driven market, investment activity now accounts for perhaps 20% of turnover. The emergence of low interest rates in the early 1990s encouraged fund managers to turn their attentions away from laggard equities and low-yielding bonds, and search for a new "asset class", the prices of which were negatively correlated with both of these traditional investment vehicles. As any rise in interest rates would have a negative effect on bond prices, and was expected to have the same effect on equities, it became clear that an inflation or interest rate hedge was required. Gold had fulfilled this role for investors for many years, but the gold market was in persistent contango and clearly trading

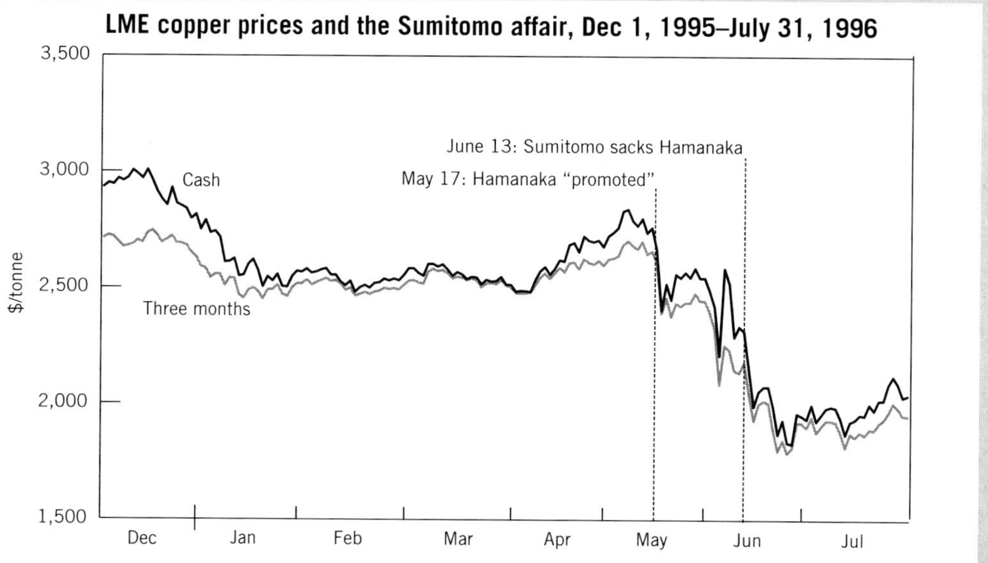

cash borrowed fraudulently from Sumitomo, Hamanaka had fought the price back up to $2,800 per tonne.

Despite the investigations by the regulators in the UK and US, it was the discovery of irregularities by an accounts clerk at Sumitomo that blew the whistle on Hamanaka. On May 17, he was "promoted" from his post as chief trader. Unsupported by Hamanaka, copper prices began their fall (see Figure). Late on June 5, Sumitomo found the evidence of his unauthorised trading. Between May 30 and June 17, the cash copper price plummeted from $2,586 to $1,990.

On June 13, 1996, Sumitomo announced that it had sacked Hamanaka, and reported losses of $1.8 billion on a series of unauthorised trades. In September, Sumitomo revised the figure to $2.6 billion as Hamanaka's loss-making long position was gradually unwound.

On June 19, despite the continued "orderly running" of the market, the LME asked the SIB to conduct a review of the metals markets (see Panel 3). On October 22, four months after Sumitomo fired Hamanaka, their former star trader was arrested in Toyko and charged with forging documents authorising trades. He was later charged with the more serious offence of fraud. On February 25, 1997, Sumitomo's chairman, Tomiichi Akiyama, resigned, taking responsibility for the lack of management oversight that led to the losses.

"sideways" in the medium term. For fund managers, switching from precious metals contracts to the increasingly liquid base metals contracts required only a small mental jump, and this led to unprecedented buying of base metals futures for investment purposes in late 1993 and early 1994.

The liquidity in the markets that made this possible was rooted in the deregulation of the global financial services industry during the 1980s, led by the US and the UK. Deregulation led to massive increases in trading volumes in almost every commodity. At the same time, the removal of traditional practices, such as fixed commission rates, led to intense competition for business. As the costs of transacting business fell ever lower, greatly helped by computerisation, so volumes increased, creating a "virtuous circle" of increasing liquidity and turnover in commodity trading that has lasted for 10 years or so.

For competing exchanges, establishing a lead early on in this global process proved crucial in determining the success or failure of a contract. Turnover and liquidity create their own markets. For example, copper business has thrived on the LME, while the less liquid Comex equivalent continues to struggle.

Contract structure and margining

LME FORWARD/FUTURES CONTRACTS

Technically, LME contracts are forward contracts rather than futures contracts; that is, profits and losses are not realised until the prompt date matures. This unusual feature is extremely useful for corporate hedgers in terms of cashflow: it allows them to match payments associated with the hedge to the underlying payments for the physical product. This does not mean that the exchange itself is exposed to fluctuations in contract prices. Instead, the LME members authorised to issue contracts effectively act as buffers

PANEL 3

"IT COULDN'T HAPPEN HERE" – REGULATION ON THE LME AND COMEX

Mark Nicholls, Risk

In the aftermath of Sumitomo's $2.6 billion losses on the copper markets, the workings of the London metal markets were subject to intense scrutiny. Regulation and trading practices on the London Metal Exchange (LME) came under particularly heavy fire from the US. Comex, the metals division of the New York Mercantile Exchange, lists a rival copper contract, and Nymex executives were vocal critics of what they characterised as the overly lax system of controls at the LME.

Ultimately, a lack of internal controls at Sumitomo allowed head copper trader Yasuo Hamanaka to carry out unauthorised trades for up to 10 years (see Panel 2). In addition, as Sumitomo Corp was not an LME member, it did not fall within the exchange's regulatory purview. Instead, its trading on the LME was carried out through regulated LME brokers.

Nonetheless, Nymex officials argued that the regulation of their exchange would have made a similar scandal impossible. Indeed, they noted that, in 1993, Hamanaka ceased using the Comex copper contract, allegedly favouring the lighter controls on the LME.

The differences between regulation on Comex and the LME stem from the fact that the latter considers itself an "industrial" exchange, organised around the needs of its commercial users to a greater extent than many other futures markets. Only some 20–25% of trades are carried out for investment purposes – the remainder are initiated for hedging purposes by industrial end-users or producers.

Two of the main differences between trading on the two exchanges – non-cash clearing and historical price carries (known to the LME as NMPTs, or non-market price transactions) – stem from this distinction. Both of these features are said to have facilitated Hamanaka's manipulation. Comex, in common with most futures exchanges, runs a system of cash clearing. As on the LME, initial margin – either cash or collateral such as bank guarantees – is paid to the clearing house when a contract is entered into. On a daily basis, both exchanges mark contracts to market by calculating the daily variation margin – the difference between the current and the previous day's closing price.

Comex, unlike the LME, then requires that these variation margins are paid immediately in cash by those with losing positions to those with gaining positions, via the clearing house. In contrast, on the LME, profits and losses on positions are not realised until expiry. Variation margins can instead be collateralised, in the same way as initial margins. With some justification, the LME says that this system of non-cash clearing suits its industrial users. It matches the cashflow from the hedge to that of the trade in the physical metal, and requires less credit to finance the position.

The LME also allows the controversial practice of historical price carries (HPCs). Here, on expiry, a customer's forward position is rolled over at its original price for an additional period. Profits or losses are not realised so, on a loss making position, the clearing member effectively provides the customer with credit for the loss. Strict rules govern the use

or intermediaries, granting margin credit lines to their customers and depositing margin on their behalf at the London Clearing House on a daily or intra-daily basis.

Provided the marked-to-market value of their overall cash and forward positions falls within their credit line, larger clients are unlikely to be asked by their brokers to make any margin payment. Should their overall position exceed the agreed credit limit, variation margin is required. As a result of this structure, clients do not need even to be a member of the LME, although many are Associate Trade Members, which ensures that they have a voice in the running of the exchange.

The Sumitomo scandal has resulted in much negative press for the LME, and demands for changes to the way it conducts its business (see also Panel 3). Comex, one of the most vociferous interested parties, has demanded that the LME adopt the kind of cash clearing and compulsory daily margining of all clients described below. However, surveys show that users of the LME are against such changes.

Before the British currency was floated in July 1972, LME contracts were denominated in pounds sterling. Since then, all contracts have gradually moved over to US dollar pricing. Any new contracts will almost certainly follow recent history by trading in dollars from the outset.

of HPCs, relating to approval from the customer's board, although poor internal management could allow traders to conceal losses by way of HPCs. This practice, again, is a response to industrial needs, allowing customers to extend a hedge to allow for late delivery due to shipping delays, for example.

Differences also exist between Comex and the LME as regards transparency and position controls. Comex is an open-outcry pit trading exchange. All contracts are traded in the pit, with all bids, offers and transacted prices visible to the market. In contrast, the LME has two types of trading. Two ring trading (open-outcry) sessions are held daily; each consists of two five-minute rings for each metal in rotation, followed by a kerb-trading period when all metals can be traded. In addition, inter-office trading takes place 24 hours a day. These are private, bilateral contracts, accounting for around 75% of the LME's business, including all options trading. With no obligation for dealers to reveal the prices at which inter-office trades are transacted, transparency is significantly lower than in open-outcry trading.

Large position reporting requirements are stricter at US exchanges than in the UK. At Comex, all the positions of all clearing members are monitored daily. Non-member clients with large positions are also obliged to report weekly to the Commodity Futures Trading Commission, thus avoiding the possibility of customers avoiding scrutiny by spreading their business among several brokers. Comex also imposes a system of position limits for both clearing members and customers.

Uniquely among UK exchanges, the LME does have a system of voluntary position monitoring, where each broker reports large positions privately to the chief executive. About 95% of such positions are reported. However, the LME has no position limits, and presently has little power – short of imposing backwardation limits – to intervene if it believes manipulation is taking place.

Generally speaking, it is fair to say that US exchanges are more closely regulated than their UK competitors, with US regulatory bodies adopting a more hands-on approach. However, the LME did call in its regulator, the Securities and Investments Board (SIB), to review the exchange and the metal markets in the wake of Sumitomo's losses. While generally endorsing the running of the LME, the SIB review, published in December 1996, called for enhanced market monitoring, particularly of large positions, improved transparency in inter-office and options trading, tighter controls over, and greater transparency, of the LME's metal warehouses, which are used for the delivery of physical metals, and changes to the LME's governance to avoid conflicts of interest. Notably, the review found that neither non-cash clearing nor HPCs posed any systemic risk and, given the support of the exchange's users, should be maintained. The LME agreed to implement the changes recommended over the course of 1997.

The pressure on the LME to change its workings and regulation as little as possible is very strong. Between 1988 and 1995, turnover increased some 700%, and around 95% of all on-exchange copper trading worldwide takes place at the LME. In the aftermath of the Sumitomo debacle, confidence in the LME remained strong among its industrial users and, ultimately, the LME provides liquidity in copper trading that Comex cannot currently match. However, as its critics point out, while light regulation may prove a boon in the short-term, repeated scandals can quickly destroy confidence in a market.

FUTURES CONTRACTS AT OTHER EXCHANGES

Other futures exchanges worldwide operate on the basis of compulsory margining; all market participants must post good-faith deposits through clearing members of the relevant exchange. As soon as any company buys or sells a futures contract, it must deposit with its clearing member an amount of money that the exchange determines is sufficient to cover any one-day price move; this is known as "initial margin". Should the market move adversely, additional "variation margin" is calculated and paid on a daily basis.

Comex, for example, operates this system of cash clearing and daily margining. While helping to maintain market integrity, the paper trail created by the ensuing daily payments and receipts inevitably adds to the costs of transacting business. It is important to note that Comex itself is the counterparty to every trade.

As an additional safeguard, New York Mercantile Exchange/Comex clearing members contribute to a pool of funds, known as a "guaranty fund", that can be used if a member or customer of the exchange defaults on its obligation after the customer's own clearing member and the exchange itself have already contributed funds. So far, it has not been necessary to use this fund.

Contracts are usually denominated in US dollars or the respective local currency.

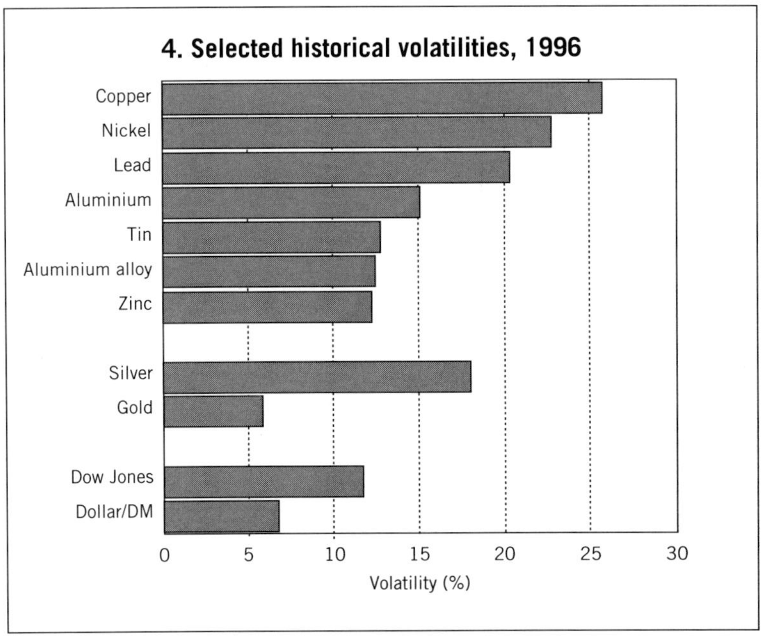

OPTIONS CONTRACTS ON THE EXCHANGES

All exchange-based options contracts refer directly to the underlying futures market on the same exchange (ie they give the right, but not the obligation, to buy or sell a particular futures contract). The volatility of each commodity determines the relative cost of the options. If traded volatilities are very high, a nickel producer may choose to sell futures rather than buy seemingly expensive put options. Alternatively, it could sell call options; however, this strategy, while producing revenue up-front, does not protect the producer from a drastic fall in the nickel price.

Like other commodities, the volatility of metals prices is quite high compared with financial instruments, as Figure 4 illustrates. Gold, historically a store of value, is the exception. As described in Chapter 1, central bank stocks prevent the emergence of all but the tamest backwardation, and steady governmental sales have kept price rallies in check. In trading terms, gold is in many ways more akin to a currency than a commodity.

LME OPTIONS CONTRACTS

In practice, traditional LME options are European style, in that exercise takes place on a specific day – the first Wednesday of each month. Such options are exercised into the underlying forward contract, the prompt date of which is the third Wednesday in the month. American-style early exercise is possible but pointless, as profits cannot be realised until the prompt date.

LME TAPOs (Traded Average Price Options), however, are financially settled. These Asian-style contracts were launched for copper and aluminium in February 1997, and may be extended to cover other LME metals in due course. Declaration or abandonment is automatic, and determined by the relationship between the option's strike price and the average settlement price for the metal and month in question. Declaration results in two offsetting futures contracts, with the second business day of the following month as prompt date.

As an example, imagine a copper producer has purchased 1,000 tonnes of a July $2,000 TAPO put. Should the average copper settlement price for July turn out to be higher than $2,000, this option would be worthless and abandoned. However, with an average settlement price of, say, $1,920, the following two futures positions would be allocated to the producer:

- ❑ Short 1,000 tonnes of copper at $2,000 (the strike price); and
- ❑ Long 1,000 tonnes of copper at $1,920 (the average settlement price for July).

The prompt or value date for both positions would be the second business day in August, when the producer's hedging profits could be taken. Of course, the writer of this option would be allocated equal and opposite positions to the taker.

OPTIONS CONTRACTS AT OTHER EXCHANGES

All other exchange-traded options are exercised into the underlying futures contract. They are American-style, allowing exercise at any time before expiry. Although early exercise rarely makes sense, it does allow profits to be realised immediately if an offsetting futures position is in place. For example, if a call option is purchased and the underlying futures price rises steeply, the option can be exercised, giving the holder a long futures position at the option strike price. By instigating an offsetting short futures position either before or after exercise, profits can be crystallised.

However, if the option has a significant period left to run, it would be wiser to wait and see whether the futures price moves back below the strike price. In this case, the short futures position, instigated at a higher level than the strike price, could be closed out by means of a long futures position, effected at a level below the option strike price.

Of course, the simplest way to realise profits in this case would be to sell the call option, but this may not be profitable if the underlying market has only risen late in the option's life. Also, traded option volatilities may have fallen, reducing the option's value.

EXCHANGE CONTRACTS AS PRICE REFERENCES

In many cases, particularly where no suitable exchange contract exists, buyers and sellers of physical commodities agree off-exchange forward deals at some negotiated fixed price. Unfortunately, should market prices change significantly before delivery, one of the parties may attempt to renegotiate their "firm" commitment on this forward deal. A more satisfactory method of conducting such business is to agree on a reference price and then negotiate a physical premium, which takes into account product quality, delivery details and pricing options. Unlike a fixed price deal, the underlying commodity price does not need to be continually checked to ensure that neither party has a built-in advantage. Ideally, the reference price should be an exchange-traded product.

While such a technique is not necessary for the spot or cash market, it offers valuable protection for companies trading many months or years forward. The separation of the base or reference price from the premium paid for physical delivery allows long-term deals to be struck with a higher degree of confidence, as the incentive to renegotiate a contract due to an unfavourable price change is removed.

For example, one of the most important physical pricing benchmarks for aluminium is the CIF Japan premium. In this case, the reference price is normally the LME cash settlement price. A Japanese trading house requiring 1,000 tonnes of aluminium per month for the next year may ask five or more suppliers for their premium offer. Without the need to keep one eye on the underlying reference price, both sides can discuss this premium and finer details such as delivery options. Either before or after agreeing the CIF Japan premium, both parties can convert their physical premium trade to a fixed outright price by locking in the appropriate tonnage in the underlying exchange-based market.

PHYSICAL DELIVERY

As well as providing daily reference prices and the ability to hedge price risk, an important role of any metal exchange is to be the physical customer of last resort. In other words, in times of ample supply, metal can be sold on the exchange and delivered into an appropriate registered warehouse. Alternatively, in times of physical tightness, metal can be bought and removed from one of these warehouses. A number of shapes and sizes of metal are acceptable for delivery, which helps to ensure adequate trading liquidity. However, as the exact specification is at the "seller's option", a buyer of material will almost certainly have to pay a premium for a specific warehouse location, origin, shape or size.

As discussed above, physical trades are normally conducted between producers, merchants and consumers by adding a premium for physical delivery (or a discount in the case of off-grade material) to the LME or other reference price. Such contracts normally allow some flexibility in shipping and pricing periods, unlike rigid exchange-based contracts. In the case of the LME, only 1% or so of forward contracts result in physical delivery or "off-take"; nevertheless, this link to the "real world" ensures that exchange prices remain in line with the true balance of supply and demand in the physical market.

EFPS

Nymex and other commodity exchanges worldwide allow parties to make physical deliveries through a facility known as an Exchange of Futures for Physical (EFP). By means of an EFP, a buyer or seller in a cash market transaction may exchange a futures position for a physical position of approximately equal quantity. EFPs may be used to initiate, terminate or transfer a futures position:

❑ *Initiating a futures position* A physical deal between two counterparties can be "booked out" and replaced by a pair of equal and opposite long and short futures contracts.

❑ *Terminating a futures position* Two users that are long and short of the same futures contract can agree to liquidate the futures positions and substitute a cash market transaction.

❑ *Transferring a futures position* If one party has a long futures position and another has a physical holding, these positions can be switched between the two parties. This is effected with equal and opposite cash and futures transactions.

EFPs are offered by exchanges as a means of increasing the flexibility of exchange-traded futures contracts, by allowing pricing to be separated from supply arrangements. Practical uses include:

❑ *Delivery flexibility* Market participants can choose their physical counterparty and select a mutually convenient date, location and quality;

❑ *Round-the-clock trading* An out-of-hours physical deal transacted simultaneously with an EFP has the effect of allowing futures trading even when the exchange is closed; and

❑ *Simultaneous transactions* A trader could close out a futures hedge position and separately enter into a physical transaction. An EFP allows both legs to be transacted simultaneously, eliminating the risk of an adverse price move in the intervening period.

The availability of EFPs also reduces the risk of "squeezes" in the market, in that a short futures position can be closed out by making a physical delivery outside the market. For example, the silver market showed considerable signs of stress between August 1979 and March 1980. The Hunt brothers were the most public participants in a scheme to drive the Comex silver price ever higher, by insisting that they would take delivery of the long positions they had established on the exchange. EFPs made the situation of market participants with short positions in the market more tolerable, as silver which would not normally qualify as "good delivery" under a futures contract could still be delivered by means of an exchange for futures.

Key trading and hedging strategies

In recent years, techniques and terminology common in other markets have become widespread in the metals business. Some of the jargon serves only to complicate what are in reality quite straightforward strategies. Apart from those involving exotic options – still a rarity in the metals markets – most strategies are simple combinations of "plain vanilla" futures and options contracts. In this section we look at some simple options strategies, a classic strategy to take advantage of a particular market condition, and a more complex strategy appropriate for "intermediate hedgers" – ie, hedgers that have to cope with both inflows and outflows of metal.

COLLARS

Options allow companies to manage their price risks while at the same time benefiting from any favourable price changes. When used to protect a company's cashflow in a difficult market environment – for example, the revenues of a high-cost metals producer at a time of low prices – they are often regarded as a kind of insurance.

Many companies recognise the flexibility that options provide, but far fewer are willing to pay the premiums involved. To mitigate this, the "min-max" or "costless collar" strategy was devised. This strategy involves the purchase of one option and the sale of another option of equal value. In this way, a producer would finance the purchase of a put option with the sale of a call option, while a consumer would finance the purchase of a call option with the sale of a put option. The client effectively sets minimum and maximum price levels for its metal intake or sales – hence the min-max moniker.

More generally, a collar consists of a cap (call option) and a floor (put option), one of which partly finances the other. The costless collar is simply a special case where the two premiums are equal. Variations on this theme are endless; the maturities and quantities involved may be deliberately mismatched, particularly if the client only wants to offset part of the cost of the options that it wishes to buy. Of course, by selling an option the client leaves itself vulnerable to substantial opportunity costs if the market moves far in the "wrong" direction. The risk/reward ratio of such a strategy must be fully understood.

SYNTHETIC OPTIONS

Many trading strategies can be replicated with combinations of standard futures and options products, with minor differences in profit and loss profiles. For example, instead of buying a put option, a producer could sell forward and simultaneously buy a call option, creating a "synthetic put". Normally, the option premiums involved would be embedded in the forward sale price, removing the need for any up-front payment.

Some hedgers may try to "beat the market" by selling forward into a market rally, and buying the calls on the next market dip; great care should be taken to ensure that the options are eventually purchased! Alternatively, if a simple forward sale were in place, and the underlying price had fallen significantly since this position had been initiated, the sale could be protected by the purchase of a call option that guarantees hedging "surpluses".

FORWARD PRICE STRUCTURE

Opportunities sometimes arise from the forward structure of the market. Although contangos and backwardations are inextricably linked to the more actively traded nearby contracts, with further forward prices tending to move at a somewhat slower speed, canny traders learn to recognise and trade against price curves that seem to be excessively steep. In some markets, such borrowing and lending operations are referred to as "curve-locks" (see Panel 4). The simplest strategy is to "borrow" metal at a sizeable contango. This involves purchasing metal with a nearby prompt date, and simultaneously selling metal with a forward prompt date, at times when the price of the latter is higher. There is little chance of large losses occurring, as any con-

PANEL 4

FORWARD PRICE STRUCTURES: AN EXAMPLE IN ALUMINIUM

In September and October 1996, a rapid downturn in the three-month aluminium price was only partially reflected in aluminium prices for dates further into the future – a classic "curve-lock" opportunity. A number of producers decided to lock in the healthy contango that had emerged between the nearby dates and the forward price of aluminium in "calendar 1998" (ie, the strip of forward contracts accounting for the 12 months of 1998). They did so in the expectation that the spread between the nearby and further forward prices would eventually narrow, allowing them to take a profit. They implemented the curve-lock by "borrowing" metal: simultaneously establishing a nearby long position and a forward short position.

Over the following few months, the three-months aluminium price rose strongly, allowing the first leg of this "carry" trade to be unwound at a substantial profit. This surplus was then deferred to the desired hedging period, 1998, increasing the price of the original forward short position. In this way, the producers achieved a forward sale in excess of $1,800. By the end of January 1997, when these producers had completed their hedging programme, selling by less sophisticated producers had helped to transform the forward market into a small backwardation! A representative numerical example of this strategy is set out below:

October 1, 1996

- Buy 12,000 tonnes prompt February 19, 1997 at $1,380.
- Sell 1,000 tonnes per month 1998 (prompt the third Wednesday in each month) at $1,534, locking in a contango of $154.
- Leave an order to replace this carry trade with a forward sale of $1,800 or better for calendar 1998.

January 24, 1997

- Liquidate February 19, 1997 position at the market price of $1,628.
- Roll the February 1997 profits of $248 per tonne into 1998, increasing the forward sale price by $268 ($248 plus interest at 6% per annum), achieving a final 1998 sale price for 1,000 tonnes per month of $1,802 ($1,534 plus $268).

tango is limited to the cost of finance, warehouse rent and insurance. If the nearby leg of such a "carry" is allowed to become prompt, then the warrants are "taken up". That is, the borrower actually pays for the metal that it has bought (the first leg of the carry that it initiated) and bearer warrants are delivered to the purchaser's broker for safekeeping. These warrants may have some intrinsic value if the location and/or brand specified is (or becomes) in demand.

Alternatively, consider the case of a lead market in substantial backwardation. A lead recycling organisation might choose to lend forward lead in anticipation of a narrowing backwardation, or indeed a change to a contango market structure. Should this happen, the position could be "borrowed back" and profits taken. Alternatively, lead could be delivered onto LME warrant in settlement of the short position; however, substantial costs may be incurred if the nearest LME registered warehouse is not conveniently situated. Anyone undertaking such an operation must be confident that material will be available prior to the short position's prompt date, as backwardations can be severe.

STRATEGY FOR INTERMEDIATE HEDGERS

Metal producers and end-users, who are primarily concerned with the direction of movements in metals prices, can hedge their exposures with simple futures or options products. A refiner's position is not so straightforward, as it is exposed to changes in price differentials between the metals concentrates it purchases to feed into the refining plant, and the refined metal that it has to sell at a later date. The refiners' profitability is determined by its management of this considerable price risk, and this is discussed in detail in Panel 5 (overleaf). The arguments used in Panel 5 are equally valid for recycling companies, whose stocks of scrap have some intrinsic value, and fabricators, whose purchase and sale prices are both linked to exchange-traded prices.

OTC versus exchange-based strategies

The key advantage of OTC contracts is that they can be fully customised to suit a client's individual requirements, whereas exchange-based contracts have to be standardised in order to promote price transparency and market liquidity. However, OTC deals have two particular disadvantages.

PANEL 5

REFINER HEDGING

If the price curve for any metal were level, then devising a hedge for a refiner would be a trivial matter. A short hedge against the intrinsic value of metal contained in concentrate stocks could be unwound at a suitable time after the metal had been refined – ideally timed to coincide with the pricing period relating to the sale of this refined metal. In reality, metals prices exhibit either a contango or backwardation structure, and occasionally a combination of these two effects.

The simplified examples below, for a copper refiner, make clear the hedging process and the effect of different market structures.

As Table 1 shows, the hedging results in a $10 per tonne surplus (the original "cash to three months" contango). The refiner is fully protected against adverse price moves.

As Table 2 shows, hedging results in a $40 per tonne deficit (the original cash to three months backwardation). However, the cash price has fallen by $120, so the hedge was certainly justified. In effect, the refiner was obliged to pay a fee to a market in backwardation for his price risk management. Although "paying a backwardation" may be painful, it does not provide a valid argument against hedging, as changes in the outright metal price can dwarf any backwardation. Rather, other risk management strategies, perhaps involving options, should be investigated.

Table 1. Contango market

Timing	Physical trades	LME prices	LME trades
March	Buy 1,000 tonnes basis spot at $2,000	Cash $2,000 three months $2,010	Sell 1,000 tonnes three months at $2,010
June	Sell 1,000 tonnes basis spot at $1,920	Cash $1,920 three months $1,935	Buy 1,000 tonnes cash at $1,920
Result	*Down $80,000*		*Up $90,000*

Table 2. Backwardation market

Timing	Physical trades	LME prices	LME trades
March	Buy 1,000 tonnes basis spot at $2,360	Cash $2,360 three months $2,320	Sell 1,000 tonnes three months at $2,320
June	Sell 1,000 tonnes basis spot at $2,240	Cash $2,240 three months $2,210	Buy 1,000 tonnes cash at $2,240
Result	*Down $120,000*		*Up $80,000*

Firstly, as OTC trades exist outside the scope of any contract clearing mechanism, there is a risk that the counterparty will fail to fulfil its side of the contract. As many OTC deals extend for two or more years, this risk may increase within the term of the deal. Secondly, OTC trades may be difficult to unwind, particularly if the deal structure is somewhat exotic, without paying a significant profit margin to the provider.

In the case of base metals, the most successful OTC product has been the Asian, or average rate, option. In the case of copper, producers worldwide sell most of their output at prices based on the monthly LME settlement price, plus a physical premium dependent on shape, quality and location, so monthly Asian options have been widely used to hedge this price exposure. Over the last 10 years, copper producers have preferred to use OTC Asian options rather than exchange-based European-style options. This prompted the LME to introduce TAPOs for copper and aluminium as clearable contracts in February 1997. This is an excellent example of how a highly competitive market environment can lead to the emergence of a product that is simple to understand and (reasonably) straightforward to price, and of how an exchange must constantly evolve to meet the needs and demands of its many users. The listing of monthly Asian-style options, a worldwide first for any exchange, will afford greater market and price transparency for this kind of contract.

Readers might wonder why much of the last decade's growth in the provision of OTC price

PANEL 6

OTC VERSUS EXCHANGE-BASED MARKETS: KEY DIFFERENCES

	Exchange-based markets	OTC markets
Marketplace	Centralised	Disparate
Instruments	Standardised	Customised
Counterparty	Clearing house	Provider
Regulation	Full	Partial
Margining	Yes[1]	No
Market participants	All	Many
Ease of offset	Routine	Difficult
Dealing costs	Known	Unpredictable
Liquidity	Good	Uncertain
Transparency	Excellent	Poor
Product range	Narrow	Infinite
Product lead time	Long	Short

Glancing at this table, the reader may wonder why a company would bother to engage in OTC trades, with their associated costs. Firstly, the fact that OTC products have become more standardised over the last few years has tended to mitigate some of the disadvantages listed above (eg price transparency). Secondly, the advantage to a company of having a tailor-made risk management product can often outweigh the disadvantages. Thirdly, many companies intend to let their risk management contracts run to maturity and settlement, which to some extent negates the transparency and liquidity advantages of exchange-traded contracts.

1 Regarding margins, note that LME member firms authorised to issue LME contracts routinely offer lines of credit to cover their larger customers' marked-to-market losses, where they exist. Variation margin is charged on forward losses above this amount. See main text for a fuller explanation of margining.

protection has been supplied by newer entrants to the base metals markets, rather than companies with a longer history of trading base metals (eg, ring-dealing exchange members). This is largely due to the counterparty risks mentioned above: the big investment banks have brought billion-dollar-plus balance sheets to the table as security for large clients. In turn, the banks were able to hedge most of their price and volatility risks using listed LME futures and options contracts – although some basis risk (see below) remained. The listing of TAPOs has now removed much of the inherent basis risk for the key Asian options market, while increasing the range of price providers and greatly reducing the threat of counterparty risk.

Basis risk

Basis risk is the risk that the value or price of the chosen hedging vehicle does not move in line with that of the underlying exposure. Examples include:

- ❑ calendar basis risk;
- ❑ locational basis risk; and
- ❑ product basis risk.

As discussed above, the banks that provide Asian-style base metals options expose themselves to a form of calendar basis risk, simply because the price underlying the bought and sold Asian contract – an average settlement price over a certain period – is not in itself a liquid tradable instrument (with the recent exception of the LME TAPO contracts). Hence, the provider can find itself juggling with a futures hedge in the middle of a month that has a value which has become somewhat divorced from the price exposure being managed.

The simplest form of calendar risk occurs when an exchange-traded product is used to hedge a longer-term exposure. Significant "rollover risk" can then be encountered. Increasingly, market users are loath to assume this risk themselves and prefer to enter into OTC trades with creditworthy institutions, which then manage this risk themselves. To the extent that the contracts fall within the maturity of the relevant exchange-traded product, they can easily be converted into exchange-based, clearable trades for extra security. Because many contracts on the metals exchanges are offered with maturities and liquidities that extend relatively far into the future (see Panel 1), rollover risk is less of an issue than in the energy markets.

In the case of refined metals, locational risk is often minimal, as physical premiums for specific locations are small relative to the value of the metal; nevertheless, these premiums can alter rapidly in times of economic flux or changes in the tax structure. In other markets, for instance crude oil, higher storage costs and oligopolistic practices mean that some locational prices show poor correlation to the relevant exchange-traded product.

Whereas crude oil is traded in numerous grades, the relative ease with which high metal purities are achieved tends to limit the number of metal grades traded. In addition, very pure or off-grade metal is normally traded at a premium or discount to the only available exchange-traded grade, whereas the crude oil hedger has a variety of exchange products at his/her disposal. Hence, product basis risk occurs most in the metal markets when the material being hedged is of very low purity, or is scrap.

Recent market events

In this section, we look at two specific market events that highlight some of the special risks of the metal markets, and which have a particular relevance for the market in exchange-traded risk management instruments. The first example illustrates the risks that can arise out of the structure of the underlying metals markets, while the second underlines the market risks that can arise out of the actions of major market participants in any commodity market.

THE BULL RUN, 1994

After a peak in the three-month price of almost $3,200 in June 1988, aluminium entered into a sustained bear market that lasted until Christmas 1993. During this period, the Soviet Union broke up, leading to massive dumping of aluminium onto the world market. One of the fastest ways to realise hard currency from such a valuable commodity was to deliver metal onto warrant in an LME warehouse. In fact, LME warehouse stocks rocketed from just over 41,000 tonnes in April 1988 to a peak of 2.66 million tonnes in June 1994. Such was the rate of deliveries that external storage was authorised by the exchange for the first time in its history.

As the world moved into recession, it became clear that the price of aluminium would continue to fall, to the detriment of all producers, unless production was cut back. American producers were naturally worried that any OPEC-like cartel would lead to expensive anti-trust litigation, so the US Government was deliberately involved in the creation of the worldwide Memorandum of Understanding, signed on March 1, 1994, in which the participants agreed to cut production by up to 10% for a period of two years. The "MOU" was signed by six major aluminium-producing areas: the US, Canada, Russia, the European Union, Norway and Australia.

Widespread rumours of these temporary shutdowns prompted the unprecedented buying of aluminium by investment funds, particularly in the first quarter of 1994; the three months price rose from a nadir of $1,035 on November 5, 1993 to over $1,300 by early February 1994. The beginning of the year is traditionally a time for funds to make asset allocation decisions, and a profitable start to any year often leads to an increase in the size of the trading positions that are being held. Confirmation in March that the MOU had indeed been signed was therefore the trigger for a fresh bout of buying, which soon spilled over into the rest of the base metals complex. Aluminium finally peaked at $2,195 on January 24, 1995.

Nickel prices also rose strongly, and producers were happy to continue selling at prices based on the monthly average settlement price, particularly as this allowed them to benefit from any backwardation that should emerge in the price structure of nickel in the cash to three months period (ie, between the spot price and the price of the three-month futures contract). In order to reassure their consumer customers, however, producers offered them price ceilings of between $9,000 and $13,000. Of course, this exposed the producers themselves to a price risk. Not wishing to miss out on any price spike beyond the level of the ceilings they had offered, a number of major producers simply purchased LME call options to cover these price caps. Most of these options were purchased in July and August 1994, when the three-month price was in the $6,000–6,500 range, with maturities spread evenly through 1995.

When purchased, these options were a long way out of the money and, at about $30 per tonne, cost just 0.5% of the underlying nickel price. As the market rose, however, dealers that had sold these options had to buy increasing amounts of nickel futures to cover their potential liabilities; this was exacerbated by a rise in traded volatilities for 1995 maturities, from 25% to over 40%. This buying pushed an illiquid market ever higher, until the price began to move through the relevant strike prices, before the three months price finally peaked at $10,500 in January 1995. As the market fell, the long futures positions initiated to protect the call options became unnecessary, and were sold, putting further downward pressure on the price. The subsequent collapse saw three-month nickel trade as low as $6,800, within just five weeks of its pinnacle.

THE RADR DEAL, 1993

In the summer of 1993, years before the scandal described in Panel 2 of this chapter, Sumitomo Corporation and Winchester Commodities transacted the most controversial deal in the history of the LME, code-named RADR. Details of this transaction have only recently entered the public domain. Documentation reportedly stressed "the total need for secrecy" and explained the "core strategy of control of pricing spreads". RADR, a collection of nearly 100 separate trades, allowed Sumitomo to take a massive bet on the price of copper rising. One part of the deal involved Sumitomo buying over 1 million tonnes of long-dated call options, with prompt dates in 1995. Independent analysis of this deal conservatively suggests that Winchester profited to the tune of $40 million; Winchester insists that the RADR structure was designed to hedge Sumitomo's physical copper requirements for two or more years forward.

Sumitomo's positions were held at Credit Lyonnais Rouse (CLR), Winchester's clearing broker. CLR received clearing fees and was also entitled to a share of 20% in any of Winchester's profits (or losses). With the cash copper market tightening, the LME imposed a backwardation limit of $5 per day on September 8, 1993, and warned CLR to reduce the outstanding position. RADR documents apparently stated that "it is imperative that we support the price of three months copper at $1,950", but Sumitomo was forced to liquidate its position nine days later, on September 17.

The LME issued a statement which included this segment: "CLR accepts that the situation could have been interpreted as involving an undue influence over the market. However, CLR took no action because it was satisfied that no such undue influence was or would be exercised." Bizarrely, the LME accepted a payment of £100,000 from CLR, as a contribution to the exchange's costs. This was a quite insignificant sum compared with the fees and profits being generated.

In a further effort to drive copper prices higher, RADR II was conceived in September 1993. This deal was never implemented in the markets, but independent analysis of its mechanics suggested that the pricing of some long-dated options within the strategy would have been "unfair" to Sumitomo; "excess" profits of about $50 million would have been generated for other parties involved in the deal. Instead of implementing RADR II, Sumitomo sold a large tranche of put options to raise enough cash to pay for the original RADR losses. Investigations into this affair rumbled on into 1997, leading to the raiding of various properties, including offshore companies in Guernsey.

Exchanges and the future

NEW CONTRACTS

Two of the most interesting exchange-based metals trading vehicles to be launched in 1997 are TAPOs on the London Metal Exchange, and yen-denominated aluminium futures on the Tokyo Commodity Exchange (Tocom). Initially, copper and aluminium TAPOs will be traded, followed by the other LME metals should this kind of contract raise sufficient interest. As discussed earlier, TAPOs are perfectly suited to clients whose pricing methods relate to the monthly average settlement price for the base metal in question.

The Tocom launch is a bolder initiative that will serve to increase the transparency of the Asian aluminium market, providing "overnight" liquidity and reflecting the strength or weakness of the local market more accurately than the global LME price. It remains to be seen whether the volume and open interest will grow to more than a fraction of those of the comparable LME contract. It should be noted that, initially at least, the costs of transacting business on Tocom will be much higher. Tocom intends to launch other base metals contracts, although this will clearly depend on the success of the aluminium contract.

The most recently launched metal contract is Aluminium Alloy, which has traded on the LME since October 1992. (Between June and October of that year, Metallgesellschaft Limited operated a "grey market" in alloy; all trades in this period were automatically registered as official LME contracts in October.) Although the volumes traded remain small, there was also substantial resistance to the (ultimately) successful High Grade Aluminium contract when it was launched in 1978.

Which metal will the next new exchange contract be based on? One of the candidates is stainless steel, although more research needs to be undertaken to ascertain whether sufficient liquidity could be achieved. Although stainless steel is a colossal global market, the sheer number of grades, shapes and sizes means that creating a futures contract specification is very difficult. If one particular specification of stainless steel were chosen as a benchmark, liquidity would be poor, as substantial basis risk would exist for any company attempting to hedge metal of a different specification. On the other hand, if a number of specifications were deliverable against a new stainless steel futures contract, the price might be unrepresentative for some of these specifications. The imposition of fixed price differentials between grades is a possible solution but, as demands change, these premiums or discounts would become increasingly unrepresentative. It may be necessary for the more flexible OTC market to start providing risk management contracts, before a tighter exchange-traded contract can be launched.

When we look at the statistics on open interest provided by metals exchanges worldwide, it is clear that the majority of open positions are of short-term maturities; about 60% of cleared LME positions are concentrated between the immediate cash market and three months forward. However, in the OTC markets, gold, aluminium and copper routinely trade three or more years forward, although bid/offer spreads degenerate (ie, become much wider and more unpredictable) beyond this tenor. As OTC liquidity for far forward dates gradually improves, exchanges with a strong interest in these metals may investigate extending forward their contracts. The difficulty here is to ensure that liquidity is sufficient to prevent market participants manipulating the prices of the contracts for these lesser-traded dates.

CUSTOMISED HEDGING PROGRAMMES

An aluminium producer might be exposed to energy prices, interest rates and exchange rates, as well as the price of aluminium. Until recently, companies tended to identify these price risks on an individual basis, and hedge them separately. The next explosion in trading volumes could be driven by a new breed of instrument, cross-market derivatives, so called because the payout of each customised derivative is dependent on more than one underlying instrument. Examples would include an aluminium put option, the strike price of which is dependent on the price of electricity (electricity futures are traded on Nymex), and an interest rate swap with payments linked to the price of gold.

As discussed in detail in Chapter 4, the beauty of such integrated hedges is that the overall cost of risk management is lower, as the prices of each component are only partially correlated to each other. In fact, the less related the exposures, the more cost effective the integrated hedge will be. As this hedging technique employs customised OTC derivatives, it is not practical to actively trade in and out of the position; rather, an integrated hedge should be constructed to protect long-term, predictable exposures. The immediate significance of this kind of contract for the exchanges is that the providers of such hedging strategies (primarily major banks and energy companies) will use the relevant exchange-traded contracts to manage their positions.

SPAN MARGINING AT THE LME

In an earlier section of this chapter, we discussed the margining system used on the LME. Although the simplicity of the credit system makes its implementation straightforward, it is rather crude, as it ignores both market volatility and sensitivity to price movements. These deficiencies become even more obvious if a member's portfolio of open positions includes options as well as futures.

In August 1997, the LCH will begin to margin cleared LME trades using a new system called SPAN (Standard Portfolio Analysis of Risk), in line with other LCH clearable products and many exchanges worldwide. With this more sophisticated system, originally devised by the Chicago Mercantile Exchange, the total initial margin requirement is calculated by estimating the risk of an entire portfolio of contracts, rather than by summing the estimated risks of each individual contract. Variation margin is then simply calculated on the basis of daily price moves. Despite such improved risk measurement, average initial margin requirements across clearing members were reduced by 16% in LCH test modelling.

At the heart of SPAN is a pricing model that undertakes a series of "what if" calculations, analysing a portfolio under a variety of different market scenarios. The aim is to calculate an initial margin sufficient to cover the maximum likely cost of closing out a defaulting member's position. This model assesses the impact of changes in futures prices and implied volatilities, and the worst-case result of this stress test is deemed the "scanning risk" (see also Panel 7). In addition, the risk inherent in mismatched long and short positions is catered for with an "inter-prompt spread charge". Furthermore, if the risk between prompt dates increases beyond the normal parameters, perhaps as the result of the emergence of a severe backwardation, SPAN also provides for the inclusion of an additional "prompt month charge".

The final stage in the SPAN analysis relates to the "short option minimum charge". Short far-out-of-the-money options positions may show zero or minimal risk under the scanning system. In these cases, SPAN requires a minimum charge for each net short option position, reflecting the true cost of closing out the position. Normally, the total initial margin requirement is the sum of scanning risk, inter-prompt spread charges and prompt month charges. However, should this sum be lower than the short option minimum charge, then the initial margin requirement is simply the short option minimum charge.

Clearing members are expected to use the SPAN methodology to calculate the margins they require from clients, where appropriate. It should be noted that the success of SPAN depends on the clearing house and the exchange setting suitable parameters for each of the initial margin components detailed above. In rapidly moving markets, these parameters can be changed in the middle of the working day, leading to intra-day margin calls.[1]

ELECTRONIC TRADING

Most of the world's major exchanges were set up before cheap and reliable computer technology became available, and therefore trading is conducted by open outcry (in a pit or ring). However, as volumes and liquidity increase, the need for a physical exchange diminishes, and a "virtual exchange" of computer terminals becomes a viable prospect. Cheap global communications mean that the transparency afforded by open outcry can also be duplicated. Cost pressures will increase the pace of change, as new electronic exchanges could easily win significant market share on the basis of extremely low dealing costs. Over time, computing costs decrease, while the cost of maintaining a floor dealing team tends only to increase!

In fact, many of the most successful of the 50 or so automated execution systems worldwide are extensions of floor-traded contracts, enabling almost round-the-clock trading. Two widely accepted systems are Globex, set up to attract overseas business to the Chicago exchanges, and Nymex Access, introduced in 1993. As well as energy products, Access allows participants to trade in copper, gold, silver and platinum contracts outside the US business day.

PANEL 7

EXPLANATION OF SPAN SCANNING RISK

SPAN methodology is used to calculate the initial margin requirement of a portfolio by calculating the worst-case loss that would occur under 16 pre-defined scenarios, listed below. The clearing body and the relevant exchange set a "worst probable" day-to-day range (ie, the largest probable difference between successive closing prices) for each commodity. The size of this range will depend on that commodity's historical volatility. A worst probable one-day change in implied volatilities is also set.

1	Futures Unchanged	Volatility Up
2	Futures Unchanged	Volatility Down
3	Futures Up 1/3 Range	Volatility Up
4	Futures Up 1/3 Range	Volatility Down
5	Futures Down 1/3 Range	Volatility Up
6	Futures Down 1/3 Range	Volatility Down
7	Futures Up 2/3 Range	Volatility Up
8	Futures Up 2/3 Range	Volatility Down
9	Futures Down 2/3 Range	Volatility Up
10	Futures Down 2/3 Range	Volatility Down
11	Futures Up 3/3 Range	Volatility Up
12	Futures Up 3/3 Range	Volatility Down
13	Futures Down 3/3 Range	Volatility Up
14	Futures Down 3/3 Range	Volatility Down
15	Futures Up Extreme Move	
16	Futures Down Extreme Move	

For example, if a worst probable day-to-day range of $120 is set, a 3/3 Up move would describe a $120 rise, while a 1/3 Down move would signify a $40 fall in price. Similarly, if a worst probable volatility change of 15% is set, and the current volatility is 20%, Up and Down moves would signify volatilities of 23% (20×0.15) and 17% (20×0.85), respectively.

The last two scenarios above use a move of twice the normal scanning range, but only 35% of the value is used so that these scenarios do not always dominate the other 14, reflecting the fact that such a large move is unlikely. These last two scenarios evaluate the risk of options which are some way out of the money, and which would not be assessed other than by the "short option minimum charge".

1 *In the wake of the Sumitomo affair, intraday margin calls were made by the LME on a number of occasions in May and June 1996. This was due to copper's extreme and unprecedented price volatility, although the corresponding fall in the aluminium price led to some additional margin calls on that metal as well. On June 6, the initial margin for copper was doubled, from $200 to $400, and on June 17 it was raised further to $600 per tonne, one-third of the contract value. On June 21, the LCH reported record copper margin deposits of $3.5 billion.*

4

Cross-Market Risk Management and Commodity-Linked Finance

David Quarmby
The Chase Manhattan Bank

The first part of this chapter discusses what is meant by "cross-market risk" and explores ways in which an integrated approach to risk management can lead to substantially reduced hedging costs. Adopting a fully integrated approach to risk management involves netting exposures and using portfolio theory to avoid the inefficiency of over-hedging.

The second part of the chapter defines commodity-linked finance and examines a number of techniques that combine commodity hedging with financing. Commodity-linked finance arguably always has a "cross-market" component, because it references markets other than the money markets to determine the eventual cost of finance.

This chapter does not offer an exhaustive overview of current integrated hedging and commodity-linked finance techniques. Rather, it aims to give examples of cross-market hedging and finance with respect to metals, focusing mainly on base metals.

Cross-market risk management

CENTRALISING RISK MANAGEMENT

In the simplest analysis, a manufacturer engages in at least two markets: the input market, where it buys its raw material, and the output market, where it sells its finished product. Naturally, throughout its normal business, a firm will usually transact in many subsets of these markets. Each subset market has its own characteristic risks, which often arise out of circumstances beyond the firm's control. For instance, a firm will necessarily inherit a foreign exchange risk by trading beyond its domestic market, an interest rate risk from a cash financing or deposit requirement, and a commodity price risk where it consumes or produces a physical commodity. These external risks leave companies exposed to price shocks, which can damage current operating performance and push vulnerable or highly leveraged companies into bankruptcy.

Traditionally, market risks have been managed individually, as they arise. The separate treatment of risk means that sometimes even market risks of the same type are managed from within different business units of the same firm. This can lead to duplication of hedging. For example, a purchasing department could decide to buy forward part of its commodity requirement (either by agreeing fixed prices with the supplier or by buying forward exchange contracts) while the sales department simultaneously decides to sell forward a similar quantity of its commodity production, again either by selling fixed price or by selling forward exchange contracts. It is clearly more efficient if the company nets its overall commodity price risk. Netting allows greater price transparency and avoids paying bid–ask spreads or clearing fees (where they exist) by eliminating situations where the company buys and sells forward exchange contracts at the same time. The centralisation of risk management has been adopted by many companies worldwide, and is now common practice when dealing with foreign exchange, money market and, increasingly, commodity market price exposures.

However, even when a company decides to net its price exposures to the same market, if it has exposures to two or more markets it may still be guilty of over-hedging (see Panel 1). Once a centralised netting approach has been adopted, the next logical step is for a firm to take advantage of the synergies across different markets by utilising a new generation of cross-market hedging tools. A cross-market risk is simply a simultaneous price exposure to two or more markets. These markets can be financial, such as the foreign exchange or interest rate markets, or physical such as the oil or aluminium commodity

PANEL 1

OVER-HEDGING IN THE COPPER MARKET

A UK manufacturing group consumes significant amounts of US dollar-denominated copper semi-finished goods, the prices of which are linked to the LME copper price. It decides to purchase call options to protect itself against the possibility of higher copper prices and/or a sterling depreciation. If the current cost of copper is £1,300 per tonne, the treasury may decide to purchase a US dollar call/sterling put struck at $1.68. Meanwhile, the purchasing department may decide to protect against higher copper prices by purchasing a copper call option struck at $2,184 per tonne. By means of this strategy, the manufacturer has protected itself against higher sterling copper prices, but it has paid two premiums.

The options combine to produce a copper hedge struck at £1,300 (ie, 2,184/1.68). However, the firm would be over-hedged when either the pound strengthens and the copper price rises, or the pound weakens and the copper price falls. For example, if the pound rose to 1.84 against the dollar, and the copper price rose to $2,300, then the sterling base price to the UK manufacturer for its copper goods would have fallen by £50 to £1,250 (2,300/1.84), yet it would still be receiving $116 per tonne under the copper call option hedge (2,300 – 2,184). The company is overhedged to the extent that it receives payment under its hedging programme when the actual physical cost of its copper input has fallen. The table illustrates the scenarios in which the copper company is potentially over-hedged and could receive payment unnecessarily:

	Copper price	
	Decrease	**Increase**
+ £	No hedge payment	Over-hedged
vs		
– $	Over-hedged	Hedge payment

If the firm had chosen to purchase a "cross-market" sterling copper call option instead, it would have made only one sterling premium payment. This option premium payment it likely to be higher than either of the two (copper and foreign exchange) option hedges separately, but a good deal cheaper than the two options combined. The cross-market hedge premium is cheaper, because it does not pay out unless the sterling price of copper has increased. While it is always pleasant to receive a windfall profit from one of the options, it is more efficient to pay a lower premium at the outset and be assured of a known maximum sterling copper price.

markets. Cross-market risk management is the use of hedging techniques that pull together these disparate risks and allow the manipulation of an overall price exposure. Cross-market hedging helps companies control the joint impact of exposures on underlying profitability.

Cross-market risk management is more efficient because it allows a firm to take advantage of the fact that prices in different markets rarely move together (ie, they are uncorrelated). Essentially, when markets exhibit some degree of independence from each other it is unlikely that they will all move in the same direction at precisely the same time and with the same velocity. Correlation effects enable firms to take advantage of a fundamental concept in financial analysis – portfolio theory – to lower their risk management costs.

PORTFOLIO THEORY

Portfolio theory simply states that the variance of the return on a collection of assets will nearly always be less than the variance of the return on any subset of the portfolio. In other words, a movement in the price of one asset in a portfolio is likely to be offset, to some extent, by a movement in the price of another asset. The average return on the portfolio will, therefore, be less volatile than the return on any one of its individual members.

In the investment world, the portfolio effect is usually illustrated with reference to the overall return for a group of equities. Here, however, we shall consider a portfolio of commodity and financial price risks. Suppose a firm consumes 1,000 metric tonnes of aluminium per month. The firm also generates ¥1.8 billion from the sale of goods in Japan – but it must repatriate the yen in US dollars. Over the period January 1994–June 1995, the firm would on average have suffered, as the price of aluminium rose at an average annual rate of 2.6% per month, while the average dollar value of the yen rose at an average 1.6% per month. The volatility of aluminium over this period was about 21.9%, while that of the yen/dollar exchange rate was 10.9%.

It is tempting to suggest that the volatility of this portfolio of risks is simply the sum of the volatilities of the aluminium price and the yen/dollar exchange rate, or 21.9% + 10.9% per year. However, this figure would over-estimate the portfolio's volatility as it does not take into account the likelihood that a change in the price of aluminium will be partly offset by a change in the yen/dollar exchange rate. In fact, throughout January 1994–June 1995, in only one out of 18 months did a rise in the value of the dollar coincide with an increase in the price of aluminium. Likewise, in only three months was there both a dollar depreciation against the yen and an increase in the price of aluminium.

These facts suggest that movements in the exchange rate and the aluminium price are largely uncorrelated; the estimated correlation co-efficient between the two prices confirms this, as it is approximately zero.

An appropriate estimate of the volatility of the portfolio must take into account the extent to which the prices move together. In general, the less positively correlated the exchange rate and the aluminium price, the smaller the volatility of the portfolio. The precise formula that represents this relationship makes this clear:

$$\text{Volatility of portfolio} = \sqrt{\begin{aligned}&W^2_{ali}(\text{volatility of aluminium prices})^2 + \\ &W^2_{¥/\$}(\text{volatility of ¥ / \$})^2 + \\ &W_{ali}W_{¥/\$}(\text{covariance of aluminium and ¥ / \$})\end{aligned}}$$

In this equation, W_{ali} represents the proportion of the portfolio representing the dollar value of aluminium, and $W_{¥/\$}$ represents the proportion of the portfolio representing the dollar value of the yen.

The covariance term is simply the correlation between volatilities of the members of the portfolio, scaled by the volatilities themselves:

$$\begin{gathered}\text{Covariance of ali and ¥/\$} = \\ (\text{volatility of ali}) \times (\text{volatility of ¥/\$}) \times \\ (\text{correlation between ali and ¥/\$})\end{gathered}$$

In the example above, given recent aluminium prices, exchange rates, the firm's exposure to the yen/dollar exchange rate and the price of aluminium are very roughly equal, so that $W_{ali} = W_{¥/\$} = 1/2$. Given these "weights", and the volatilities for the prices themselves, the volatility of the portfolio is given by:

$$\text{Volatility of portfolio} = \sqrt{\begin{aligned}&\left(\tfrac{1}{2}\right)^2(21.9\%)^2 + \left(\tfrac{1}{2}\right)^2(10.9\%)^2 + \\ &\tfrac{1}{2} \times \tfrac{1}{2} \times (\text{covariance of ali and ¥ / \$})\end{aligned}}$$

Note that the smaller the correlation between the asset prices, the smaller the volatility of the entire portfolio.

THE APPLICATION OF CROSS-MARKET HEDGING

Given the theoretical advantages outlined above, and the simple practical applications that are described in detail in Panels 2, 3 and 5, it seems fair to ask why cross-market hedging is not already the norm among major international corporations with significant exposures to the metals markets.

There are a number of reasons for this. Perhaps the most important is the practical consideration we mentioned at the beginning of this chapter: in many firms, a purchasing department manages commodity price risks, the treasury manages foreign exchange risks and the finance department takes decisions on interest rate exposures. It can be difficult to bring their hedging strategies together. Cross-market hedging involving metals demands close, ongoing co-operation between the operations departments (the traditional hedgers of commodity price risk) and the treasury. In particular, the operations departments need to provide the treasury with detailed technical information concerning their activity and the structure of the commodity markets in which they are dealing.

A firm may also wish to actively manage cross-market hedges and may feel it must fully understand the correlations between its various market exposures. Yet measuring correlation risk can be a fairly difficult and time-consuming task. If company policy requires that all hedges are independently marked to market on a daily basis, it may not be willing to continually reprice its hedge(s).

A further consideration is that a different set of legal documents may govern over-the-counter (OTC) hedges, or a firm's internal controls may be uncomfortable with non-exchange hedging. Most cross-market instruments are, almost by definition, OTC rather than as exchange-traded contracts, because exchanges do not usually quote a wide range of currencies, or anything other than European- or Asian-style option exercises. Hedging instruments traded OTC usually incorporate bespoke features that make them difficult to price and trade quickly. Nevertheless, the formal exchange contract is still used to provide a transparent and independent price source to serve as indisputable reference prices for the cross-market hedge's component parts. Note the relative benefits of hedging both "on" and "off" exchanges are compared in more detail in Chapter 3.

It is important to consider these practical problems when implementing cross-market hedges, but they do not negate the fundamental benefit of

PANEL 2

FOREIGN EXCHANGE HEDGING: ZINC PTY'S US DOLLAR/AUSTRALIAN DOLLAR OPTION WITH A ZINC KNOCK-OUT

Zinc Pty is an imaginary Australian low-cost zinc producer. Its operational costs are set in Australian dollars, whereas the revenues from its output of zinc are in US dollars. The company is keen to hedge its foreign exchange exposure over a one-year time horizon using an option-based strategy. It does not wish to protect itself against lower zinc prices, because it forecasts stable prices, and because it regards its position as a low-cost producer as a natural hedge.

The traditional hedge would be to purchase a series of European-style Australian dollar call/US dollar put options, which would place a limit on the mining company's exposure to a weakening US dollar.

The management of Zinc Pty, while concerned about its foreign exchange position, are unhappy with the premium cost of this traditional strategy. They decide to try to reduce the hedging cost by exploiting the firm's exposure to zinc prices. As a producer, the firm naturally benefits from a rise in the price of zinc, but suffers reduced US dollar revenues should the price of zinc fall.

The firm therefore decides to add a "knock-out" feature to the foreign exchange option in order to reduce the premium cost. A standard currency knock-out option would eliminate the hedge if the US dollar strengthened beyond a specified trigger level against the Australian dollar, the idea being that, if the US dollar strengthened to a given point, the hedge would become unnecessary and could therefore be eliminated. However, a zinc trigger level may be used instead to construct a cross-market knock-out hedge. Should the price of zinc rise and the zinc trigger level be breached, the currency option would automatically be terminated, leaving the firm's Australian dollar/US dollar exposure unhedged. In these circumstances the higher zinc price would be beneficial to Zinc Pty, increasing its US dollar revenues.

The reduction in premium for the knock-out relative to the traditional European-style foreign exchange option will depend on three things:

- the zinc trigger level;
- the volatility of zinc prices; and
- the correlation between the price movements of zinc and the Australian dollar/US dollar exchange rate.

In general, the more volatile the zinc price, the lower the currency option price (because there is a greater chance of the option contract being knocked out). The more positive the correlation between zinc and Australian dollar/US dollar prices, the greater the likelihood that the price of zinc will reach the trigger while the option is in the money – again, reducing the currency option's premium.

The table below compares the price of an Australian dollar call/US dollar put with that of an identical option without a zinc knock-out. It also charts the effect of different correlation scenarios on the price of the knock-out option. Note that the correlation between the changes in the Australian dollar/US dollar exchange rate and the changes in zinc prices determines the extent of the savings to Zinc Pty.

The setting of the zinc trigger level is the key to determining the overall effectiveness of the hedge. If the option contract is terminated, then the unhedged currency risk needs to be fully offset by the gain in the US dollar revenues from the higher zinc prices.

Premium savings from inclusion of knock-out in Zink Pty's foreign exchange option, 12-month maturity

Strike price	Price of European option	Cost of option including knock-out –30%	0%	+30%
0.76	0.0259	0.0136	0.0104	0.0073
0.78	0.0173	0.0094	0.0070	0.0046
0.80	0.0109	0.0062	0.0044	0.0027
0.82	0.0066	0.0038	0.0026	0.0015

integration: the use of the portfolio effect in hedging significantly reduces hedging costs without reducing the overall level of protection.

INDIRECT CROSS-MARKET RISKS: THE ELECTRICITY POWER SUPPLY CONTRACT

Sometimes a company will face a multitude of risks arising from a business relationship with one large, very important, customer. This may require a cross-market hedge, and we will look at some of the issues this raises by developing the example of how to hedge the financial exposure caused by power pricing contracts that are indexed to the price of Deutschmark aluminium.

Around the world, energy-intensive aluminium smelters are often attracted to contracts offered by their power suppliers that directly link power prices to the price of aluminium. In effect, the smelters use these contracts to shift some of their aluminium price risk onto the electricity provider at an attractive price. For instance, when the price of aluminium settles above the agreed power supply contract's reference price, the power supply invoice increases by an amount equivalent to the settlement price less the agreed power supply reference price multiplied by the agreed leverage factor (usually expressed in terms of a notional aluminium tonnage). It is often argued that, because the rate charged under the indexation moves in the same direction as the price of aluminium, the smelter's costs relate more closely to its underlying sales revenue and profitability.

If we assume that a German electricity producer, Elec GmbH, fixes its power supply reference price at DM2,800 per tonne on a notional volume of 200,000 tonnes per year, then a settlement price of DM3,000 would result in additional income to Elec GmbH of DM200 per tonne or DM40 million per annum. Expressed on a quarterly basis, the notional amount of aluminium would be 50,000 tonnes and result in an incremental income to Elec GmbH of DM10 million. If, on the other hand, the aluminium price settles at the current cash price of DM2,720, Elec GmbH would receive a shortfall on its power contract of DM80 per tonne, a total loss of DM16 million for the year.

The above aluminium-indexed power contract gives Elec GmbH a profit and loss profile equivalent to an outright physical purchase of 200,000 tonnes of aluminium metal at the agreed DM2,800 reference price and sold at the equivalent of the average quarterly settlement price for cash London Metal Exchange (LME) aluminium metal. Although Elec GmbH never actually pays for or takes delivery of aluminium, the exposure exists every year until the power supply contract expires, or the power reference price is renegotiated.

The annual 200,000 tonnes of aluminium price risk transferred to Elec GmbH by the aluminium-linked power supply contract can be mitigated by hedging. In order to remove its exposure to lower aluminium prices, Elec GmbH is able to enter into a cash-settled aluminium forward sale at the same fixed price, notional volume and maturity as the aluminium-indexed power contract.

By entering into an aluminium forward sale hedge, Elec GmbH commits itself to a Deutschmark cash-settled contract that fixes a price for a notional volume of aluminium at the agreed maturity date. In order to settle this agreed fixed price against the market, Elec GmbH will have to select in agreement with its hedging counterparty a reference price for settlement. For Elec GmbH, it is important that the basis for settlement is the same as the one used in the aluminium-linked power contract. In this case, Elec GmbH has referenced the official second ring LME cash settlement price for Deutschmark aluminium in both the supply and the hedging contracts. This figure is widely available and serves as a common basis for price determination throughout the metals industry. In order to remove any basis risk, Elec GmbH will also fix a quarterly settled average price for both the hedge and the supply contract.

Having effected a forward sale hedge to match its power supply contract reference price, Elec GmbH receives any shortfall in the aluminium settlement price below the hedge's DM2,800 agreed fixed forward sales price. A settlement price of DM2,500 would, therefore, result in a payment of DM300 per tonne to Elec GmbH.

By entering into a forward sale hedge, Elec GmbH also agrees to pay to the hedging bank any LME price settlement above the agreed fixed forward sales price. Assuming that Elec GmbH has obtained a fixed forward sales price of DM2,800, and the average official settlement of LME aluminium was DM3,000, Elec GmbH would be liable to pay DM200 per tonne.

The payment and receipt of these cash amounts maintains a price of DM2,800. Should the settlement price actually equal the fixed forward sales price of DM2,800, no payment will be made either to or by Elec GmbH. At all other LME settlement prices a payment will be made to equate the settlement price with the fixed forward sales price.

An aluminium forward sale effectively extinguishes Elec GmbH's "long" position in aluminium so that it is compensated for a shortfall in income resulting from a settlement below the power supply reference price.

The forward sale described above removes all the price risk associated with the aluminium power indexation. The symmetry of the power contract reference price (DM2,800) and the DM2,800 forward sale price ensures that Elec GmbH will always achieve its budgeted price per megawatt (MW) return.

However, unless the power contract and the

PANEL 3

INTEREST RATE HEDGING: CABLE INC'S LIBOR CAP WITH A COPPER KNOCK-OUT

Cable Inc is a US company that purchases large quantities of copper to manufacture cable products. The corporation finances its need for working capital by borrowing at a fixed rate of interest. To the extent that the price of copper and the rate of interest tend to rise together, their impact on the firm's bottom line is negative; to the extent that they fall together the impact is positive. More interestingly, to the extent that interest rates and copper prices tend to move in opposite directions, the impact of each individual price on the firm's results is neutralised. In other words, there is a natural hedge effect whenever this inverse relationship exists.

If this firm were to purchase a conventional interest rate hedge, such as an interest rate cap, the firm would be buying protection against interest rate movements without regard to copper prices. In this case, even when the movements in interest rates and copper prices tend to neutralise each other, the firm would receive a windfall profit from the interest rate cap. This may again seem positive but, in fact, the company would simply have spent money for protection it did not need.

An alternative might be for the company to choose a hedging structure that could tailor the protection more closely to its cost function: an interest rate cap with a payoff that is contingent on the price level of copper. One way to create such a hedge is through a copper-linked Libor cap. The payoff of this structure is the higher of spot interest rates minus the cap strike, but only when copper prices are in excess of the barrier level set in the cap. The hedge compensates Cable Inc only when it is exposed to an upward interest rate movement in a higher copper price environment.

As the payoff profile of this hedge depends on the copper price, the cost of the option will, once again, be less than one that is independent of the performance of this market.

The performance of the standard Libor cap provides an interest rate hedge when copper prices are low. Under these circumstances, Cable Inc is well able to fund higher interest costs due to its higher profitability.

The standard cap payout contrasts with that of the copper-linked cap. This instrument produces a similar payout to that of the standard cap when copper prices are above the agreed trigger level. At all other copper prices, interest rates are the market rates then prevailing.

A. Libor cap linked to copper

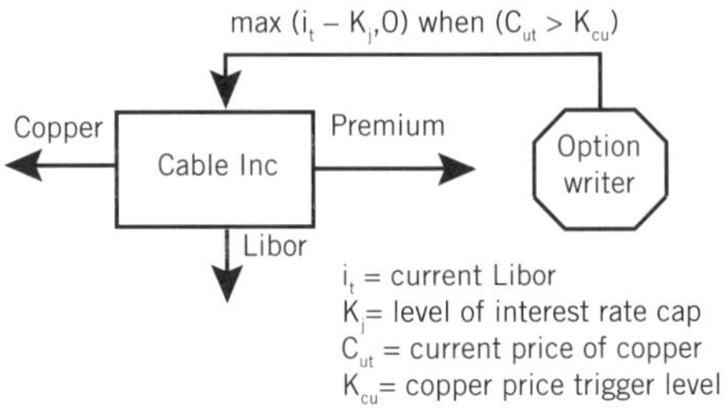

The institution selling the option, the option writer, receives an option premium and agrees to pay Cable Inc the difference between the interest rate cap K_l and the prevailing level of Libor i_t when Libor is greater than the cap's strike price. The option writer is only committed to make the payments, however, if the price of the copper price C_{ut} is greater than the copper price trigger level K_{cu}.

forward sale hedge are agreed together, it is unlikely that the forward sale price will equal the power supply reference price. The forward sale price is a function of the forward curves of the LME aluminium and US dollar/Deutschmark markets at the time the hedge is implemented, while the power supply contract is a separately negotiated bilateral contract.

Elec GmbH will, therefore, probably incur a mismatch between the fixed forward sale price and the power supply reference price. Entering into a Deutschmark aluminium forward sale will remove Elec GmbH's aluminium exposure, but at the same time it would lock in either a profit or a loss (see Panel 4).

The above analysis illustrates the crucial importance of the power contract reference price with respect to the forward sale price of aluminium in domestic currency. If the power contract is negotiated simultaneously with the hedging forward sale, Elec GmbH may be able to mitigate all its aluminium price exposure and avoid losses. If it is not, it will have to devise a strategy to handle the mismatch.

Commodity-linked finance

Commodity-linked finance can be defined as debt where the principal and/or interest repay-

PANEL 4

ELEC GMBH'S HEDGE STRATEGY: TWO SCENARIOS

SCENARIO 1

Suppose that Elec GmbH negotiates an aluminium-indexed power contract with a reference price of DM2,600 and is able to fix the forward sale price of aluminium at DM2,800. In this scenario, Elec GmbH has locked in a DM200 per tonne profit by removing its aluminium price exposure.

If, for example, the aluminium price settled at DM2,400 per tonne, Elec GmbH would incur a shortfall of DM200 on its power supply contract, but would receive a payment of DM400 on its forward sale hedge. The net result would be DM200 profit. Similarly, if the market price settled at DM3,000, Elec GmbH would receive a windfall gain on its aluminium power contract equivalent to DM400 per tonne, but would only be obliged to pay DM200 away on the forward sale hedge. The net result would again be DM200 profit.

Elec GmbH could alter the price of the forward hedge by reducing it from DM2,800 to DM2,600 and take an up-front profit on the contract. Alternatively, Elec GmbH may not wish to show an instant profit, but may rather wish to participate in higher aluminium prices above DM2,600. This could be achieved by the purchase of aluminium call options, whose premium is paid for by the profit on the hedging contract.

SCENARIO 2

On the other hand, suppose that Elec GmbH has again agreed a power contract with a reference price of DM2,600, but by selling in the forward market it can only obtain a price of DM2,400. Under these circumstances, Elec GmbH locks in a DM200 loss by hedging. Elec GmbH does, however, have a known fixed price for its aluminium exposure. An unhedged position could easily lead to substantial losses if, for instance, the aluminium market were to drop towards its recent historic lows of just over DM1,800 per tonne.

In our example, this loss of DM200 per tonne represents a total annual loss of DM40 million (200 per tonne multiplied by 200,000). Of course, this loss must be seen in the context of the extra revenue generated by having a captive energy-intensive customer. This loss is, in fact, a subsidy to the smelter. The subsidy, in the form of a power pricing contract, is as real as a cash investment, or tax subsidy, in the building of the smelter itself. Elec GmbH has agreed to pay DM40 million over the forward price of aluminium, for 200,000 tonnes of aluminium annually for the power contract's life.

Elec GmbH could decide to enhance the forward hedge from DM2,400 to DM2,600 with an off-market forward sale. This enhancement would require Elec GmbH to pay an up-front adjustment. Elec GmbH may attempt to balance this by increasing its megawatt power charge to cover the payment necessary to enhance the forward sale price to a DM2,600 off-market forward sale, or simply view it as an investment in the smelter plant.

ments are in some way linked to commodity prices. The cost of a conventional loan is ordinarily determined by money market interest rates (such as US dollar rates) alone. A commodity-linked loan will typically incur a rate of interest that varies according to the settlement of a given commodity price. For instance, a typical quarterly settled three-month US dollar Libor-based loan could be overlaid with a quarterly settled copper swap. On the interest due date, the borrower pays an amount dependent on both the three-month US dollar interest rate fixing and the cash copper price settlement.

On the other hand, debt can be linked solely to a commodity price by fixing, and thereby eliminating, the money interest rate element at the start of the transaction (with a US dollar swap or similar). Furthermore, if the US dollar rate has been fixed and the notional value of the commodity swap is equal to the notional amount of the loan, then the borrower can be said to have entered into a commodity loan (as opposed to a commodity-linked loan). A commodity loan will have a leverage of 100%. That is to say, the US dollar value of the loan is equal to the notional amount of the commodity indexation. A commodity-linked loan may have a commodity indexation that is either greater or smaller than the value of the loan.

The most common example of a commodity loan remains the gold loan discussed below. Commodity-linked finance provides a natural hedge against variations in a company's inherent input/output market price risk. A company that requires metal as an input to its finished product would usually elect to pay a fixed price on the commodity swap in order to offset price rises. By agreeing to a fixed price, the company pays a lower rate of interest when metal prices rise because the commodity swap has a cash-positive payout. Of course, payment of a fixed price also means that, if the metal price falls, the company will be obliged to pay a higher rate of interest on the loan (although this would probably be offset by lower input costs and higher profits). Similarly, a metal producer, such as a mine, would look to receive a fixed price under the commodity swap and thereby pay a lower interest rate if prices fall, and a higher rate as prices rise.

In times of extreme volatility, the interest rate on the loan might become zero or even negative – because the payment due under the commodity swap has equalled or exceeded the interest amount due for that period. The borrower would then enjoy a cash payment on the "interest due" date.

THE EVOLUTION OF COMMODITY-LINKED FINANCE

The origins of commodity-linked finance can be traced back to the gold loans of the early 1980s. Encouraged by a relatively high gold price, mining development flourished in Australia and the Western US. However, much of this gold exploration and production came from new companies that had limited access to traditional sources of finance. Together with the bullion dealers and commercial and investment banks, these smaller mining companies pioneered the use of gold loans to fund their mine development.

In the then prevailing economic environment (US interest rates rose towards 20%), gold interest rates (or the gold "lease" rates) stood at a mere 2%.[1]

These attractive rates of finance meant that soon many larger mining companies began to take an interest in gold loans with lengthening maturities. In response, banks with project finance capabilities in their mining departments and bullion operations became increasingly active. Bullion banks sought to satisfy this demand for gold by attracting central bank bullion deposits and they began to find themselves in a mediating role between the central banks, commodity exchanges and mining companies.

As described in Chapter 1 of this book, central banks are by far the largest single primary source of gold bullion (with an estimated 35,000 tonnes). These banks are, however, generally unable to lend gold directly to mining companies, either because of legal restrictions or, more commonly, an unwillingness to evaluate and take on such risks. Nevertheless, central banks are usually able to lend gold in the form of a deposit to a creditworthy intermediary bank, which can in turn lend it to the producers. Central bank deposits with bullion banks tend to range between one month and several years (although most commonly up to one year), but intermediary banks can match loans more closely to the life of the project being financed (deals of 10 years and beyond are not uncommon).

BASE METALS FINANCING: BACKGROUND

Whether a company produces base metals, precious metals or a combination of these, most metals producers face a similar cost/revenue structure when developing mining projects. There are usually:

- ❑ large capital outflows as the mine is being built;
- ❑ once the mine is operative, enormous quantities of ore may need to be processed in order to retrieve a relatively small amount of metal; but
- ❑ as the ore-body becomes more exposed, proportionally greater quantities of metal can be extracted.

It follows that significant cashflow is required to keep the project viable for, say, its first two or three years. While traditional loans can provide much of the initial capital, additional sources of finance, such as forward sales, are used as the project starts to produce and has a more certain output profile.

The capital requirement of sizeable projects for copper and aluminium in Latin America, China and elsewhere has led to an increased interest in metals-linked debt. As a result, the methods and skills developed in gold finance have gradually been transferred to project finance for other metals and minerals. Examples of new projects and estimated capital requirements include the Argentine Bajo de la Alumbrera mine ($870 million), and the Chilean projects El Abra ($1 billion) and Collahuasi ($1.5 billion).

Although the basic techniques for providing base metal- (and other commodity-) linked finance are the same, there are important differences in the underlying markets. In particular, the base metals market is subject to periods of great volatility, caused by a mismatch in the structure of the world market. The demand for base metals is very much linked to world GDP

PANEL 5

BASKET HEDGING: CAR CORP'S METALS BASKET HEDGE

Car Corp is a US vehicle manufacturer that requires a variety of different metals to construct its end product. Some of them are hedgeable; others are not. Like many high value-added companies, Car Corp used to regard hedging its input costs as a low priority but, as competition increased, many of its models became fiercely price competitive with other vehicle manufacturer's cars. Car Corp found it was unable to raise prices when metals prices increased, and so began to look at ways of protecting itself.

Even so, Car Corp considered its aluminium price exposure to be the only metal price risk worth hedging. It considered hedging each of the other metals separately, but concluded that it would not be cost effective: the amounts involved were too small to hedge individually. A metals index, however, overcomes this problem by gathering together all the non-aluminium hedgeable metals (eg, nickel and copper) to form a critical mass.

Furthermore, it will also be in the interests of Car Corp to include its entire exposure of hedgeable metals in the index in order to reduce the index's correlation component. The index would include all the metals consumed by the company in a predetermined ratio. The metal indexation typically uses a monthly average settlement price to determine the index's floating price. The floating price is thereby built up from a variety of individual metals prices, which combine to make up one notional index unit.

In the following example, Car Corp decides that metals prices currently represent good value and are likely to rise in the near future. The decision is taken to continue to hedge its aluminium price exposure, but also to hedge its non-aluminium metal consumption two years forward with a metals basket call option. After researching its input market, Car Corp concludes that it is exposed to the following metals with the attached US dollar weightings:

Platinum	30%	$460/oz
Zinc	15%	$1,250/mt
Copper	30%	$2,150/mt
Nickel	10%	$7,764/mt
Lead	15%	$670/mt
Total	**100%**	

Taken together with their relevant forward prices, the weighted base metal basket price is calculated at $64 per unit. In contrast, the price for each individual call option would be $110 per unit.

Car Corp may yet decide that this price is still too high, and may choose to sell a floor option against the index and hedge itself with a metal basket min-max or collar option.

At the end of each monthly reference period, the arithmetic average of each metal settlement price is multiplied by its weight and compared with the index strike price. It receives a cash compensation equivalent to the metals index price, less the strike price, multiplied by the notional index units hedged.

If Car Corp did not purchase its components in US dollars – for instance if it was a European-based car manufacturer with a foreign exchange requirement – it could denominate the option in a currency other than US dollars, or even use a hybrid instrument such as a foreign exchange knock-out.

growth and infrastructure investment, which leads to significant and rapid fluctuations in demand. Yet, the supply of base metals is relatively inelastic: the long lead times in commissioning new smelter capacity can lead to acute supply shortages and bottlenecks, although a smelter's high fixed costs and relatively low marginal costs mean that there is always an incentive to overproduce metal.

In contrast to this extreme short-term cash volatility, far forward prices are subject to much lower levels of volatility. Forward price stability is a function of long-run price equilibrium; the market is able to adjust supply to match demand. High cash prices and shortages of metal will eventually result in the commissioning of new smelters, and hence a lower price. On the other hand, consistently low cash prices and dumping at below cost eventually leads to smelter bankruptcies and reduced supply, and thereby raises prices.

When producers are trying to implement hedges, one of the most difficult problems they face is the relative lack of liquidity in the base metals markets relative to the bullion markets. Hedges have to be placed with care and may not be easy to exit.

WHY LINK FINANCING TO BASE METALS PRICES?

Given the volatility in base metals prices, managing the revenue stream of a mining company by protecting against price falls can help to enhance investor value by reducing earnings volatility. This is particularly important in the cyclical base metals industry - otherwise earnings are at the mercy of the peaks and troughs of the world's business cycle. The prolonged period of low base metals prices from 1991 to 1994 resulted in unacceptably low rates of return for many producers. A smelter's (unhedged) risk profile is subject to the high volatility of the metals cash market, as opposed to the much lower volatility of the far forward metals markets.

A producer with a secured revenue stream is considered a higher credit by banks. A better credit rating means that a company can take on more debt at lower rates - and use its scarce equity capital for other projects. In effect, hedging allows companies to attract lenders that are willing to accept a lower rate of return (for increased security) than equity providers.

A carefully structured and timed hedging programme will also allow metals companies to take advantage of the structure of forward prices in markets they know well. For example, in periods of prolonged low cash prices, an integrated hedging and financing package may look attractive for a producer. The loan can unlock the unrealised value of the metal forward curve by indexing much higher forward prices. A metal-linked interest rate will reference prices that are much closer to the long-run sustainable metals price, rather than the depressed cash price.

Integrated hedging and finance can be particularly well suited to borrowers located in underdeveloped capital markets. (Borrowers in OECD countries are often driven by other factors, such as preferential tax treatment.) The covenants associated with pre-export finance and project finance may also be less restrictive if hedging is included. The hedge removes some of the project's economic risk and enhances the deal's creditworthiness.

Hedging may also enable the producer to develop more projects. To take a simple example of an integrated zinc mine/smelter: in a traditional project finance, a zinc smelter may be able to borrow at $1,100 per tonne, even though the cash value of zinc is more than $1,300 per tonne. The lending bank assumes a low zinc cash price as a prudent measure when stress testing the financial model's ability to repay the loss if operating difficulties or engineering problems should occur. A greater part of this discount, however, is due to the historic volatility of zinc prices and the risk that the producer will not meet its obligations if zinc prices are depressed. Yet the producer could dramatically improve its creditworthiness if it purchased put options with a strike of $1,300. The zinc company has to pay a premium to purchase the options but, if the hedge is integrated into the financing agreement, it is then able to borrow an additional $200 per tonne on the discounted forward zinc price.

While it is true that in the public debt market the rating agencies may not give the zinc producer full credit for its hedge (unless they are specifically asked to rate a special purpose vehicle as we discuss below), banks and private placements/investors may recognise the value of the hedge if it is executed with a financially sound institution. Firms in developing markets have often used structures similar to these to gain access to Western credit markets. In Panel 6 we outline the Slovalco transaction involving the European Bank for Reconstruction and Development (EBRD) as an example of how integrated hedging can facilitate new investment.

Most lenders, and many non-equity investors, wish to protect themselves against metals price volatility. But sometimes finance can be raised from investors that are specifically searching for exposure to metals price rises without taking an equity stake in the company. For example, in the late 1980s the US mining house Magma Copper issued notes that were indexed against the price of copper. The value of the coupon the investor received increased as the price of copper rose, and decreased as the price of copper fell. Through this mechanism the company obtained a natural hedge at the same time as raising finance, while the investors gained a direct exposure to copper prices without the risk of an equity investment.

KEY FINANCING TECHNIQUES

The monetarisation of the forward price with a prepaid sales contract One common transaction that integrates finance with hedging is a prepaid sales contract. Typically, a bank will advance a loan to be repaid with the commodity production of the borrower. The lender subsequently converts this production into a stream of cash payments analogous to a loan's usual interest and principal repayments.

For example, a copper producer would receive a payment and agree to deliver an agreed

PANEL 6

SLOVALCO

In 1995, the European Bank for Reconstruction and Development (EBRD) made a $110 million loan to the Slovak aluminium smelter, Slovalco. (Significantly this is the largest investment the EBRD has made to an aluminium smelter to date, illustrating how integrated hedging and finance can facilitate investment in non-investment-grade countries.) This investment was on top of a $15 million equity participation in the plant (which was matched by Hydro Aluminium). The programme provided for a total of 172 new potlines with a primary smelting capacity of 108,500 tonnes, as well as secondary smelting facilities.

Before the decline in prices at the end of 1995, Slovalco converted its US dollar Libor-based EBRD loan to a loan in which the debt service cost became a function of the average monthly LME aluminium price for each quarter. Slovalco reviewed both its sensitivity to aluminium prices and also the instruments available to it to hedge this exposure. For its part, the EBRD was concerned that the company achieved core medium-term hedging, particularly over the period of greatest indebtedness and at levels above its break-even cost of production.

After reviewing its hedging alternatives, Slovalco decided that an EBRD aluminium-linked loan provided the most cost-effective and administratively effective method of hedging. It was helped to reach this conclusion by the EBRD's strong (AAA) credit rating and the bank's policy of passing on this benefit to its customers. Thus, Slovalco was able to obtain highly competitive pricing for its long-dated aluminium hedge because the loan's aluminium indexation was executed by the bank.

The loan's indexation was achieved through a financially settled fixed/floating aluminium price swap on a predetermined notional tonnage, under which the fixed payments made to Slovalco match its debt service cost and the floating payments paid by Slovalco match income received on metal sales. The transaction was documented under the bank's loan agreement and, as a result, Slovalco's cost of debt may be seen to fall as the price of aluminium falls, and rise as aluminium prices rise. On the proportion of the company's annual production represented by the notional tonnage amounts in the swap, the company is protected from aluminium price risk.

amount of copper cathodes, either directly to the lender or to an agreed third party - or it could repurchase the metal itself. The amount the lender will lend against the producer's copper assets is essentially a function of the net present value of the expected cashflow from those assets. The cashflow is secured by a hedging programme.

The US dollar sum paid up-front is determined by the following:

❑ the amount of copper sold in the sales agreement;

❑ the forward value of the copper (as defined by the LME, Comex copper markets, a third party or, where the company buys back its own material, the company itself);

❑ the US dollar market interest rates (or other, if non-US dollar borrowing);

❑ the company's cost of borrowing (determined by the lender's assessment of the production risk and/or any mitigating factors); and

❑ the contract's arrangement fees (if any).

This type of finance is very flexible. For instance, the producer may choose whether it wishes to repay the loan with a known tonnage of material at a fixed price, or whether it delivers an unknown tonnage at the price prevailing at maturity (ie, delivery date).

Inventory securitisation with a special purpose vehicle A weak or unrated company may be able to achieve a lower cost of funds by securitising its hedgeable inventories. In a methodology borrowed from the well-developed market in securitised payment receivables, a company removes inventory from its balance sheet by selling to a "bankruptcy remote" special purpose vehicle (SPV). The legal ownership of the inventory is transferred to the SPV and the firm receives a cash payment based on the discounted forward price of the commodity (Figure 1, overleaf). The SPV then funds itself in one of a number of ways: a private placement, commercial paper issuance, a bank syndication, or even through Islamic financing. In each case, the SPV will obtain a high credit rating due to its undisputed ownership of fully hedged assets.

In order to prove "ostensible ownership", the inventory must be clearly segregated and marked "held to the order" of the SPV. Nevertheless, the

1. Inventory securitisation with a special purpose vehicle

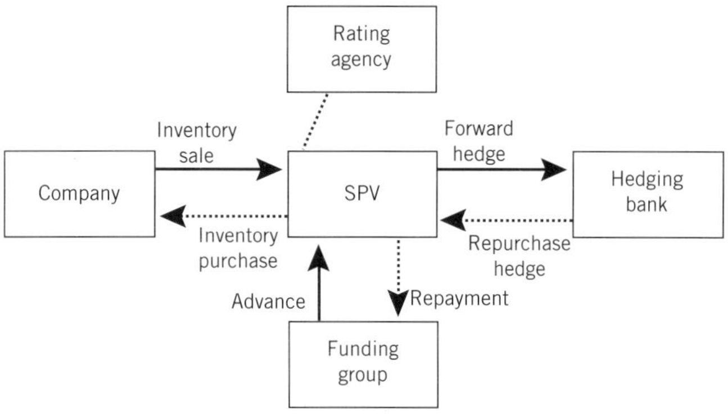

company is obliged to repurchase all the material on specific dates to coincide with the maturity of the hedges. In markets for which it is impossible to arrange forward sales, the SPV's creditors are exposed to the risk that the value of the assets could fall. The SPV would, therefore, only be able to borrow a proportion of the current value of its assets. In the case of a hedged transaction, however, an SPV may be able to receive 100% of the present value of the asset's forward price.

In order to maintain its credit integrity, the SPV is usually required to hedge with highly rated counterparties (ie, those with ratings of single A or above). This requirement is crucial because, if the hedge counterparty should fail, the SPV "shell" company would once again be reliant on the company to buy back the inventory at a fixed price. This would compromise its bankruptcy-remote status. In other words, the SPV's creditors once again become liable for any shortfall in the underlying assets.

Cross-subsidisation and integrated hedging: an extended example The incorporation of a commodity indexation into a finance package can offer an almost infinite number of hedging and cross-market subsidy combinations, depending on the company's desired risk profile. Let us look at an extended example of one such subsidy strategy.

Cu Smelt Co is a highly profitable integrated copper smelter/refiner. It has decided to expand its output following an increased demand for its LME deliverable copper cathode product. It has, furthermore, successfully signed a five-year fixed price contract with a high-cost copper mine to receive an annual quantity of copper concentrate. The copper mine is, in addition, happy to lock in fixed prices with the smelter because it is concerned that the predicted increase in copper concentrate production will depress the world price of copper concentrate, and that there will also be a shortage of copper smelting capacity. Because it has a high cost of production, the copper mine is unable to obtain credit for a strategic, five-year hedge at a reasonable cost, and is happy to accept the smelter's fixed price terms.

In contrast to the mine, Cu Smelt Co is highly creditworthy and confident that it can obtain US dollar financing to complete its planned $50 million expansion. Cu Smelt Co perceives three main threats to the profitability of its new productive capacity. Firstly, copper cathode prices could fall, reducing its sales revenue. Secondly, the cost of its energy could rise, increasing its cost of production. Finally, higher US dollar interest rates could also adversely effect its profitability by increasing the interest rate payable on the loan. In fact, higher interest rates would also have a detrimental effect on the project's financing: the cashflow generated by the increase in output would be discounted by a greater amount.

The company calculates that approximately 50% of the cost of a tonne of copper cathode would comprise copper concentrate purchases, with 30% comprising energy costs. Other operating costs (wages, maintenance costs, etc) are known. Owing to its strong bargaining position, because of the copper mine, Cu Smelt Co has successfully negotiated a low price for its copper concentrate. It is effectively "long" copper at this favourably negotiated rate.

Ordinarily, Cu Smelt Co's finance director would obtain US dollar financing at the most competitive rates available, while the sales manager would independently decide whether or not to hedge the copper output as part of a strategic hedge or separately against specific large customer contracts. This traditional approach, however, ignores several financing and hedging synergies. Cu Smelt Co decides to explore an integrated approach to hedging its exposures, while at the same time securing competitive financing.

The company can choose from a wide range of strategies. However, it decides to lock in the profit margin in the pre-negotiated concentrate purchase contract by hedging a proportion of its copper cathode sales. Cu Smelt Co is able to hedge its cathode production by selling forward over a five-year period. It agrees to sell forward at a price based on the average monthly settlement of the LME official second ring copper cash settlement price. The current forward copper price available is higher than the implicit copper price agreed in its concentrate purchase contract, enabling it to lock in a profit.

Because of its maturity, the copper sale is an off-exchange, OTC hedge. (The LME contract does not provide for copper price risk management beyond the 27 months quoted on the exchange.) Cu Smelt Co decides to enter into a copper sale at its favourably negotiated copper concentrate purchase rate (ie, lower than the market price), to create a financing subsidy, as well as to remove the risk that copper prices will fall below its agreed concentrate purchase rate. The financing subsidy is simply the difference between the copper price available as a hedge and the price it has negotiated in its concentrate purchase contract - in other words, the profit on the deal.

Rather than take this profit as an up-front payment, Cu Smelt Co is mindful of the possibility of higher US dollar interest rates, yet is reluctant to pay the high fixed rate for funds. It therefore chooses to purchase an interest rate cap with the profit from the concentrate purchase contract. Cu Smelt Co considers that its new plant's profitability is most vulnerable to a rise in interest rates over the three years of the loan. The interest rate cap's maturity is accordingly set at three years. The strike price is set at the lowest interest rate obtainable using the concentrate subsidy. To ensure consistency, the cap's notional volumes are matched to the outstanding balances of the loan over the first three years. The agreed loan is a straightforward amortising 10-year facility with interest paid semi-annually at a spread over six-month US dollar Libor. The interest rate cap amortises to match the value of the underlying debt, settling on the same matched, semi-annual basis.

Of course, should Cu Smelt Co successfully renegotiate the fixed price copper concentrate purchase at the end of the five-year period, it could once again lock in its copper price exposure with a forward sale. It may then be able to reapply a subsidy to its interest rate hedging. For example, it may decide to enter into another three-year cap, or a subsidised interest rate swap, or may even decide simply to reduce the interest rate margin payable.

The copper hedging programme improves the overall operating economics of the new plant by removing the risk that copper prices will fall below the smelter's fixed price concentrate purchase contract, while the interest rate cap sets a maximum interest cost over the initial three-year period.

From the lending and hedging institution's point of view, the strategy also makes sense. Volatilities are reduced, there are known parameters for copper prices and interest rates, and the loan repayment becomes more secure. The integrated transaction will also appear more attractive from the perspective of the bank group's earnings, because the hedging (both copper and interest rates) is a source of additional income, which would be taken into consideration when setting the borrower's margin.

Depending on the structure that is used, the documentation for the copper and interest rate hedging mechanisms can be incorporated into the financing itself, so that the package is fully integrated. This consideration is important when security has to be taken, and also helps remove definitional legal risks and hedging mismatches.

Future prospects

Increasingly, sophisticated cross-market hedging strategies, coupled with a more highly developed analysis of corporate commodity risk, are likely to be used to reduce costs in risk management and finance. An obvious growth sector is likely to be the hedging of commodity prices in conjunction with foreign exchange and interest rate risk. It is also probable that there will be more commodity-linked loans, particularly those that make use of asset securitisation, along with a greater use of cross-market hedging in the emerging markets, where credit risk is such a key obstacle to large project financings.

Conclusion

The last few years have witnessed an evolution in commodity price risk management as banks have moved from simply lending to their clients to offering a full range of integrated lending and hedging products. This change has been driven by the need to improve lending margins, increase the security of their loans and offer solutions to clients with complex risk requirements.

At the beginning of this chapter we showed how banks have refined their financial risk management products to incorporate commodity price exposures. Banks' familiarity with correlation trading has brought benefits, in the form of lower premiums, to clients with cross-market exposures. The primary aim of integrated financing and hedging packages is the facilitation of and reduction in the cost of finance. Banks are able to lower their lending margins by recognising that an integrated hedge reduces a transaction's inherent economic risk.

There is no reason why a cross-market hedge cannot be incorporated into a commodity-linked finance, to enable the client to fully maximise the synergies offered by cross-market hedging and integrated finance and hedging. Given the advantages outlined above, it is perhaps only a matter of time before a borrower decides to index its interest rate to a basket of metals/different markets and reduce the cost of finance still further.

We can only speculate when the first such deal might occur, but what is certain is that banks have become much more "solution driven" in their use of commodity hedging techniques. The hedging and financing transactions described in this chapter are, of course, only the bare bones of a successful integrated package. The real challenge ahead is for banks to innovate around a client's needs and overcome obstacles to this kind of sophisticated transaction by better understanding commodity business risks.

1 *Low gold lease rates are not very common, enabling the gold mining industry to access low and stable financing. Since 1982, lease rates have largely remained between 0.5% and 3%.*

RISK MANAGEMENT STRATEGIES FOR CORPORATIONS

5

Establishing Corporate Hedging Objectives and Strategies

Jud Roderick
FirstDerivatives
(A division of the First National Bank of Southern Africa)

The aim of this chapter is to consider risk management[1] from the perspective of a corporation exposed to metal price risk. Should such a corporation adopt a risk management strategy? If so, how can it structure the decision process involved in selecting specific hedges? The answers to these questions link in with the practical issues faced by corporate managers in implementing and monitoring a hedging programme.

Many of the examples used in this chapter describe mining companies or metal producers. This subset of corporations tends to be the most active in managing metal price exposure. However, the issues we discuss in this chapter apply equally across the broad cross-section of corporations that are exposed to metal price risk, including industrial end-users, metal traders, refiners and smelters. We will also touch on the subject of price risk management from the perspective of a bank, and briefly outline some of the issues involved in selling derivative-based risk management strategies.

To hedge or not to hedge?

The various reasons why a corporation might choose to hedge are summarised in Panel 1. However, the reasons given by corporations that are reluctant to hedge often also centre on the first point: hedging as a means of changing the risk profile of the company (expressed as an unwillingness to take a speculative position based on a view of future prices). This first point therefore forms the basis for our discussion below. The other points will be examined later in this chapter.

THE ARGUMENTS AGAINST HEDGING

The merits of implementing a hedging programme based on a view of future price moves have been strongly debated. A prominent view, espoused for example by Mercury Asset Management (MAM), one of the largest holders of South African mining equities, is that shareholders in mining companies *desire* exposure to the underlying commodity price risk and, therefore, mining houses should not sell forward their future production. Dr Graham Birch of MAM expanded on this view with the following points:

❑ while MAM acknowledges the use of derivatives for reducing credit risk on loan financing (thereby enhancing the ability of the company to raise capital), in the best interests of the fund investors they represent it is generally opposed to mining corporations instituting a metal hedging programme;

PANEL 1

POSSIBLE MOTIVATIONS FOR METALS PRICE HEDGING

❑ changing the risk profile of the company in response to a market view on future prices;
❑ dampening the volatility of company cashflows, irrespective of market view, often by managing timing mismatches between raw material costs and product sale prices;
❑ enhancing marketing flexibility by offering customers a choice of pricing terms without incurring price risk;
❑ creating a desirable financing structure;
❑ enhancing the creditworthiness of a "specific mining or production project to banks or other debt financers"; and
❑ altering the timing of revenue cashflows to optimise a company's tax position.

❑ shareholders will hold a mining share based on their assessment of management's effectiveness in geological exploration, bringing new reserves to production and mining these reserves with the greatest cost efficiencies. Should it wish, a shareholder such as MAM is capable of instituting metal price hedging programmes itself, as it does not need a mining company to do this on its behalf;

❑ the hedging forward of future production removes the very characteristic that many shareholders seek, ie, the possibility of unlimited "upside". A company that has hedged future production must, by its nature, be less attractive in the eyes of a potential shareholder; and

❑ the possibility of rogue traders or generally mismanaged hedge programmes is another negative aspect of the outcome of corporate hedging programmes. The recent Codelco and Sumitomo scandals, for instance, have highlighted the very real additional risk that a company undertaking hedging programmes can bring to its shareholders (see Panels 2 and 3, Chapter 3).

Geoff Campbell,[2] also of MAM, reinforced this anti-hedging view by stating that a gold producer that sells forward its gold production is sending three messages to its shareholders: it lacks confidence in the future price of gold; project economics are fragile; and management is inflexible in its approach to its mine plan.

These views carry significant influence, as investment funds such as MAM are large and often vocal shareholders of mining company equities. In South Africa, this approach to hedging is supported by companies such as Gold Fields SA and Palabora Mining Co (an RTZ-CRA subsidiary), both of which subscribe to a non-hedging policy.

The 1996 RTZ-CRA annual report states that: "RTZ-CRA's exposure to commodity prices is naturally diversified by virtue of its broad commodity spread and the group does not believe an active short-term commodity price hedging programme would provide long-term benefits to shareholders." Philip Crowson, head of the economics department at RTZ, expanded on this view in an article published in *Treasury Management International*,[3] in which he discussed the use of derivative instruments for price protection:

> This weakening of the nexus between present prices, underlying cost structure and the supply/demand balance carries some interesting implications for the longer term. An ever-widening use of price protection by producers raises the prospect of structural excess capacity re-emerging in the metals industry, with repercussions on prevailing prices. Also, the incentive for marginal producers to lower their costs through productivity improvements and other managerial actions is diminished, at least in the short term. These potential industry-wide effects are not, of course, of any immediate concern to individual companies. Not all have, however, taken advantage of the newer derivative products... RTZ's basic approach is that management's primary objective is to maximise the long-term rewards to the company's shareholders. They can invest in a portfolio of investments of different types and maturities in different industries and countries in order to satisfy their own unique risk profiles for a given expected reward. Shareholders invest in natural resource companies partly to gain exposure to fluctuating commodity prices and to overseas currencies. It directly follows that hedging of both currencies and price risk, no matter how it is done, partly usurps the shareholders own functions and prerogatives. If they are unhappy with a company's exposure, they can adjust their portfolios or even hedge directly.

A 1996 survey of copper producers, undertaken by E D & F Man International, indicated that 31% of these producers (of which RTZ is the largest) did not hedge.[4] The trend, however, appears to be towards an increasing use of derivatives to risk-manage production. The report informs us that 7 million tonnes of forward copper production had been hedged to date for 1996, compared with only 4.5m tonnes in 1994. Of the hedge positions in place for 1996, approximately 72% were in the form of bought put options.

While the statistics are not directly comparable, a survey of the main gold producing countries made in early 1996 revealed that Australian producers – the leaders in the use of forward markets – had hedged 630 tonnes of gold (equivalent to 28 months of future production) and that North Americans had hedged approximately 635 tonnes of gold, mostly through spot-deferred contracts. For the balance of 1996, the industry was approximately 43% hedged at an estimated price of $410/oz. A number of recent strategic hedging transactions undertaken by South

African producers has dramatically increased the hedged tonnage in this country (see Panel 6).

Companies often put forward other arguments against hedging:

❑ accurate price forecasting, either through technical or fundamental modelling cannot be empirically demonstrated to have been successful (suggesting that hedgers cannot systematically outperform the market);

❑ confidence in cost management rather than risk management as a means of protecting revenue; and

❑ diversification of exposures through vertical integration and business diversification is preferable to altering risk profiles through the use of derivative instruments.

THE ARGUMENTS FOR HEDGING

The counter-argument to these views is that shareholders actually desire the value that risk management expertise adds to a company over and above its natural exposure to the commodity cycle. Otherwise, it is maintained, they would simply hold the underlying commodity. Furthermore, it is suggested that most shareholders would be happy for companies to hedge, provided that such hedging and the resulting risk profile is transparent and public. While some shareholders may be risk takers and consequently desire the full exposure to price moves, it would seem likely that most shareholders are actually seeking an adequate risk-weighted return on capital, and are prepared to give up some potential gains in order to remove the risk of the company experiencing financial distress.

Empirical studies undertaken in a number of financial/commodity markets have indeed pointed to the *ineffectiveness of price forecasting*. While this suggests that corporations are unlikely to consistently outperform the market, many gold producers have been influenced by empirical evidence that longer-term forward selling (for example, five years or more) has consistently outperformed the average spot gold price achieved over the past 10 years. This has been a strong motivating factor behind recent gold hedging programmes.

The argument that a company that is actively hedging is *less likely to focus on production economics* appears tenuous at best, in that most hedging decisions are made at a higher operational level than the mine/smelter/factory, where production economics remain a critical performance variable.

Much of the academic literature on hedging effectiveness stems from a seminal work by Modigliani and Miller.[5] This paper, published in 1958, concluded that hedging does not add value in perfect markets. Subsequent analyses have stressed that, although Modigliani and Miller may be correct at a theoretical level, corporations could be justified in using risk management techniques in an imperfect world, ie, where artificial barriers to entry do exist, where shareholders are *not necessarily* risk averse and where market information is not equally available to all participants.[6]

One way of tackling the debate over the value of hedging is to communicate hedging policies clearly to investors, and allow them to decide whether this strategy is likely to add shareholder value. This open disclosure of hedge details is increasingly the approach that companies such as Barrick Gold Corporation have followed with their active gold hedging programmes (see Chapter 7). In South Africa this line has also been adopted by companies such as Gencor and JCI, with the publication of details of recent large gold hedging transactions (see Panels 2 and 7).

While many companies are voluntarily disclosing hedging information, regulators around the world are formalising this reporting requirement. Those responsible for these changes to accounting and reporting requirements in the US are the Securities and Exchange Commission (SEC) and the US Financial Accounting Standards Board (FASB). These reporting initiatives are being mirrored in other countries by bodies such as the International Accounting Standards Committee (IASC) and the Accounting Standards Board (ASB) in the UK (see Panel 4). This formalising process, however, has proved problematic, with draft documents being criticised by various industry groups. Common complaints were that:

❑ investors will be unable to determine the extent to which a derivative transaction will have a real risk reducing effect;

❑ the proposed disclosure rules put an unnecessary emphasis on derivatives (to the detriment of other financial information); and

❑ disclosure could put a company at a disadvantage by providing commercial information to its competitors.

Apart from the open disclosure of derivative positions, the accounting policy itself – and the way in which derivatives will be treated – can influence the nature of the hedging programme a company is prepared to undertake.

The arguments against hedging tend to oversimplify the debate, by implying that corpora-

PANEL 2

GENCOR LTD AND THE BEATRIX GOLD HEDGE

In a recent article, Mark Murning, the former treasury general manager of Gencor Ltd, discussed the company's approach to risk management. He pointed out that: "When entering into a risk management strategy, Gencor recognises that cognisance must be taken of shareholders' expectations. Given the cyclical nature of the commodity business, producers should aim to provide shareholders with as much upside as possible in a period of strong commodity prices, while providing some form of revenue protection during periods of weak prices."[1] He continued by arguing that shareholders' expectations can vary substantially. Shareholders of a marginal gold mine, for example, have an outlook that is quite different from shareholders of a mine with larger profit margins. "Thus, the risk management objective for each individual economic unit must be ascertained and a strategy put in place to achieve these objectives."

The Beatrix gold hedge

Michael Keeves (formerly Gencor Treasury)

Gengold, Gencor's gold division, evaluated the expansion of its Beatrix mine, particularly No. 3 shaft. This new shaft would increase the plant, reef mining and hoisting capacities of the Beatrix Mine, as well as extending the life of the mine by seven years, despite an estimated development cost of R575 million for the shaft. Gencor's treasury risk management team was requested to produce funding and/or hedging proposals for this new shaft. Working with a South African bank, they came up with a strategy to hedge the future gold production of Beatrix that would meet some specific objectives.

These structural objectives were twofold: firstly, the hedge had to secure the minimum required income streams and tax base to enable self-funding during the initial, developmental phase of the project; and, secondly, the hedge had to limit shareholder exposure to any funding shortfall during the second phase of the project – that is, the shareholders would not be required to contribute to funding as the hedge would ensure that the project was self-funded. Essentially, the hedging instruments provided protection against a fall in gold prices from the levels projected in the financial model that was being used to evaluate the project.

In July 1995, the Beatrix gold hedge was structured to fund the expansion of the No. 3 shaft.

The hedge structure The Beatrix hedge was constructed as a spot-deferred gold forward sale and gold call option structure, denominated in rand. The hedge was structured with a term of six years, maturing on a weekly basis and involving the forward sale of 2.9 million ounces of gold.

A spot-deferred sale was undertaken on these 90 tonnes (100% of Beatrix's total expected gold production) for the full six years and was sold forward at prices that were lower than the market forward curve at the time, but which were in line with Beatrix's minimum required revenue. Beatrix also purchased call options for 70% of the total production for the six years, with the strike prices set at the same levels as the forward sales. In addition to this gold hedging structure, Beatrix also purchased out-of-the-money rand/dollar call options for 30% of the value of total production, as an insurance policy against a severe weakening of the rand.

The purchase of the call options was funded by the present value of the difference between the market forward curve and the minimum required revenue line. In effect, Gencor forfeited this difference on the forward sales prices in return for a zero-cost (ie, self-funding) hedge.

The mechanics of the hedge The structure meant that, if rand gold spot prices were to fall below the hedge prices, Beatrix would be 100% hedged at the level of the forward selling prices on the spot-deferred forward sales. On the other hand, if rand gold hedge prices were to move above the hedge price, Beatrix would participate in 70% of any price moves above the hedge price by exercising the rand gold call options. The remaining 30% would, however, still be hedged at the price level fixed on the balance of the forward sales.

Beatrix does have flexibility on the spot-deferred forward sales, in that the remaining 30% of the forward sales could be rolled out to a future date. This means that Beatrix could obtain 100% participation in any upward movement in prices above the hedge level for a given sales period, although it would retain a hedge for future gold sales for the volume of production that was rolled out.

1 *Treasury Management International*, March 1995.

PANEL 3

THE IMPACT OF THE HEDGE FUNDS

There has been a lot written about the increasing profile of the hedge funds in the metals markets. In search of above average returns, these "speculative" investors have become dominant players in both the precious and base metal markets. Paradoxically, funds have occasionally been accused of both increasing volatility (see Chapter 8 on metals price volatility) and adding important liquidity to the metal markets.

The reasons behind investors' demand for gold are fairly clear, as bullion has long been a recognised investment medium. Base metals, however, have only recently become attractive to investors who are looking for a cyclical play on long-term economic growth. The negative correlation of returns with those of equity and fixed interest investments provides a strong argument for including commodities in a portfolio, in order to reduce risk through asset diversification. In addition, the strong negative correlation with inflation implies that commodity assets can be used as an effective inflation hedge for the financial assets in a portfolio. Risk-adjusted historical returns for commodities have been shown to be competitive with those achieved by equity and bond portfolios.

For a hedge fund trading directly on the metal exchanges, the use of metal derivatives in certain markets will be governed by liquidity constraints. Given the huge volume of funds under management, even a bullish view on, say, lead prices may not justify taking a position, due to the relative illiquidity of this metal. Liquidity constraints will also influence the nature of the position being taken: most base metals are traded in the short end of the price curve, where the volumes traded are largest. Likewise, because exotic instruments are in effect tailored to individual clients, they can be difficult to unwind.

The active marketing by banks of structured investment notes – where returns are linked to metal prices or an index of commodity prices – has also generated investment demand from a wider range of more "conservative" investment and mutual funds. This indirect investment in metals has increased the volumes traded on the terminal markets, such as the London Metals Exchange (LME). This type of trade tends to be of longer duration and is less influenced by short-term technical signals. The investment community, directly or indirectly, has consequently become an aggressive end-user of metal derivatives.

tions must either fix prices, or remain open to all price moves. The availability of *options*, however, means a company has the choice of unlimited risk profiles. In contrast to South Africa's Palabora Mining Company, a number of US copper producers (such as Phelps Dodge and Cyprus Amax Minerals) have actively used options to establish a floor price. The willingness of a company to pay for such price protection may be influenced by its cost of production. A company with a very low cost of production may consider that it has a natural buffer against a price fall and would only consider buying cheap insurance in the form of deep out-of-the-money puts. These strategies appear to be widely accepted by US equity analysts and are normally justified on the basis of providing price insurance, stabilising cashflow or enhancing credit risk for financiers.

The usual argument that options are expensive is synonymous with saying that insuring plant and equipment is expensive and therefore unjustified. In fact, given the easier access to historical price data, it could be argued that an options premium value (generated from an option pricing model) will better reflect the likelihood of an adverse event than traditional insurance premiums. The range of option hedging strategies are discussed in Chapter 2 of this book, but it is important to point out here that using options does not automatically entail an up-front premium – a cost that corporate boards or management often seem reluctant to incur. Panels 2 and 7, describing the Gencor and JCI gold hedges, illustrate the application of options in constructing zero-cost participating hedge structures.

The strongest justification for implementing a risk management programme has perhaps been that it *forces a company to identify and quantify its risks*. A hedging programme results in a conscious shaping of the company's risk profile. Too often the alternative is exposure to financial variables, resulting in volatile earnings flow, without a real understanding of the underlying exposure.

Is it hedging or speculation?

One motive for trading in metal derivative markets is the desire to generate profit directly from

PANEL 4

DISCLOSURE OF DERIVATIVE POSITIONS – REGULATORY CHANGES

Regulators in the UK, the US and other countries have been grappling with changes to disclosure requirements that are needed to adequately report the increasing use (and misuse) of derivative instruments. Both the Financial Accounting Standards Board (FASB) in the US and the International Accounting Standards Committee (IASC) have issued disclosure guidelines, although neither provides specific guidance on how these disclosures should be made. In December 1995, the Securities and Exchange Commission (SEC) released proposals that required US firms to provide quantitative information about the market risk of their financial instruments. The SEC proposals focus on the provision of "what-if" information, and would allow corporations to provide market risk information in three ways:

❑ tabular presentation of expected future cashflows;
❑ sensitivity analysis on each derivative position; and
❑ use of the value-at-risk (VAR) methodology.

In response to the SEC initiative, FASB released proposals for the accounting of financial instruments in June 1996, being an update to the nonmandatory FASB 119 proposals, which were published in 1994. FASB required companies to disclose the fair value of derivatives used for hedging. These changes in the value of derivatives would either be immediately recognised in earnings, or reported on the balance sheet in the equity accounts until realised.

For a derivative position to be designated as a hedge, the following criteria must be met:

❑ the designation is prospective and formally documented, the nature of the risk being hedged is identified, and the use of the derivatives is consistent with the entity's established risk management policies;
❑ the hedged instrument has a reliably measured fair value, which is expected to be offset by changes in the fair value of the derivative;
❑ if less than 100% of the exposure is hedged, the percentage hedged must be identified;
❑ the hedged item must be a single item, liability or firm commitment, or a portfolio of similar items; and
❑ the hedged item must expose the company to price changes that would affect reported earnings.

FASB would allow companies to report derivatives used to hedge forecast transactions outside of earnings only if certain conditions are satisfied. The companies must: define their hedging strategies in advance and allocate specific derivatives for that purpose; have a reasonable expectation that their hedging strategies will result in offsetting gains and losses; and ensure that the maturity of the derivatives used for hedging be similar to the forecast transaction.

In addition, the Accounting Standards Board (ASB) in the UK has issued a statement of principles for the reporting of financial instruments.[1]

1 A discussion paper, setting out the initial views of the ASB on accounting and disclosure for derivatives and other financial instruments, was published on July 18, 1996.

the trading activity. The hedge funds are one such group of speculators whose increased presence in base metal derivative markets over the past three years has had considerable impact on the risk management strategies of corporate hedgers (see Panel 3). The use of metal derivatives by corporations, however, can be motivated by two quite distinct aims:

❑ the mitigation of price risk; or
❑ the enhancement of profit through arbitrage or speculation.

For a corporate user of derivatives, the distinction between speculation and hedging is often not clear cut. Many corporations accept that their treasury departments are "actively" trading commodity price risk. In some cases this might be justified by the belief that the corporation has some degree of comparative advantage, perhaps by being a significant participant in the underlying physical market. Whatever the justification, the belief is that this activity will add value for shareholders. The problem arises, however, in differentiating and assessing the performance of such speculative trading from the simultaneous performance of hedging activities.

While the accounting guidelines define a hedge in respect of a specific transaction, in practice problems can arise when hedge programmes are managed dynamically, ie, when the percentage of a portfolio being hedged is continually being adjusted, or when a specific hedge transaction is lifted and repositioned. This

PANEL 7

WESTERN AREAS – SOUTH DEEP FINANCING TRANSACTION

Contributed by JCI Ltd

The merger of Western Areas Gold Mining Company Ltd (Western Areas) and South Deep Exploration Company in 1995 created one of the world's largest single exploitable gold ore bodies. At the time of the merger, it was announced that the cost of developing the South Deep section would amount to R2.7 billion (in July 1994 terms). This funding requirement would be met by internal funding of R1.6 billion, with the balance of R1.1 billion to be funded externally, based on a constant real gold price assumption of R44,000/kg.

These estimated funding requirements are dependent, not only on technical plans and cost estimates being achieved, but also on assumptions about the gold price, inflation and interest rates. As the South Deep section is vital to the earnings growth of Western Areas, and in view of the market conditions faced by producers, consideration was given to various funding alternatives, such as rights issues, gold loans, hedging and capitalisation awards.

Eventually, a funding programme was developed for the external funding requirement that encompassed equity and debt finance and the use of derivatives. It was implemented through:

❑ a rights offer of around R500 million, which took place in June 1995;

❑ capitalisation awards to shareholders, with options to elect shares instead of cash dividends; and

❑ a financial transaction that incorporates forward sales, rand/gold call options and rand/dollar call options.

The financial transaction

The quality and flexibility of the Western Areas ore body, in terms of size and gold content, enables the mine to plan for low working costs and consistent grades. Combined with recent developments in the South African financial and gold markets, this allowed Western Areas to avail itself of long-term gold derivatives to meet the objectives of the funding programme.

For the transaction, which commenced during the fourth quarter of 1995 and expires at the end of March 2004, Western Areas has sold forward its planned gold production of 7.3 million ounces of gold over 8½ years. Call options for 4 million ounces have already been purchased, which leaves an effective commitment to deliver 3.3 million ounces, representing 45% of Western Areas' planned production over this period.

The period of the transaction and the volume of the ounces of gold committed allow Western Areas to complete the funding requirements without shareholders being required to inject further capital into the South Deep project. They also eliminated the possiblility that Western Areas might have to raise external funds for South Deep at a time in the future when market conditions were unsuitable.

Raising of additional capital

In effect, the transaction restructured the market forward curve to give forward prices that would meet the projected working cost and capital expenditure requirements. As indicated in Table A and Figure A (overleaf), the forward sales were

Table A

Financial year ending 30 June	Average forward gold price (R/kg)	Average strike price of rand/gold call options (R/kg)	Average strike price of rand/dollar call options (R/$)
1996	47,000	47,000	–
1997	51,500	51,500	–
1998	59,000	59,000	5.66
1999	81,000	81,000	6.60
2000	94,000	94,000	7.42
2001	74,500	82,500	8.35
2002	75,500	85,500	9.39
2003	76,500	88,500	10.57
ending March 2004	79,000	91,000	11.71

A

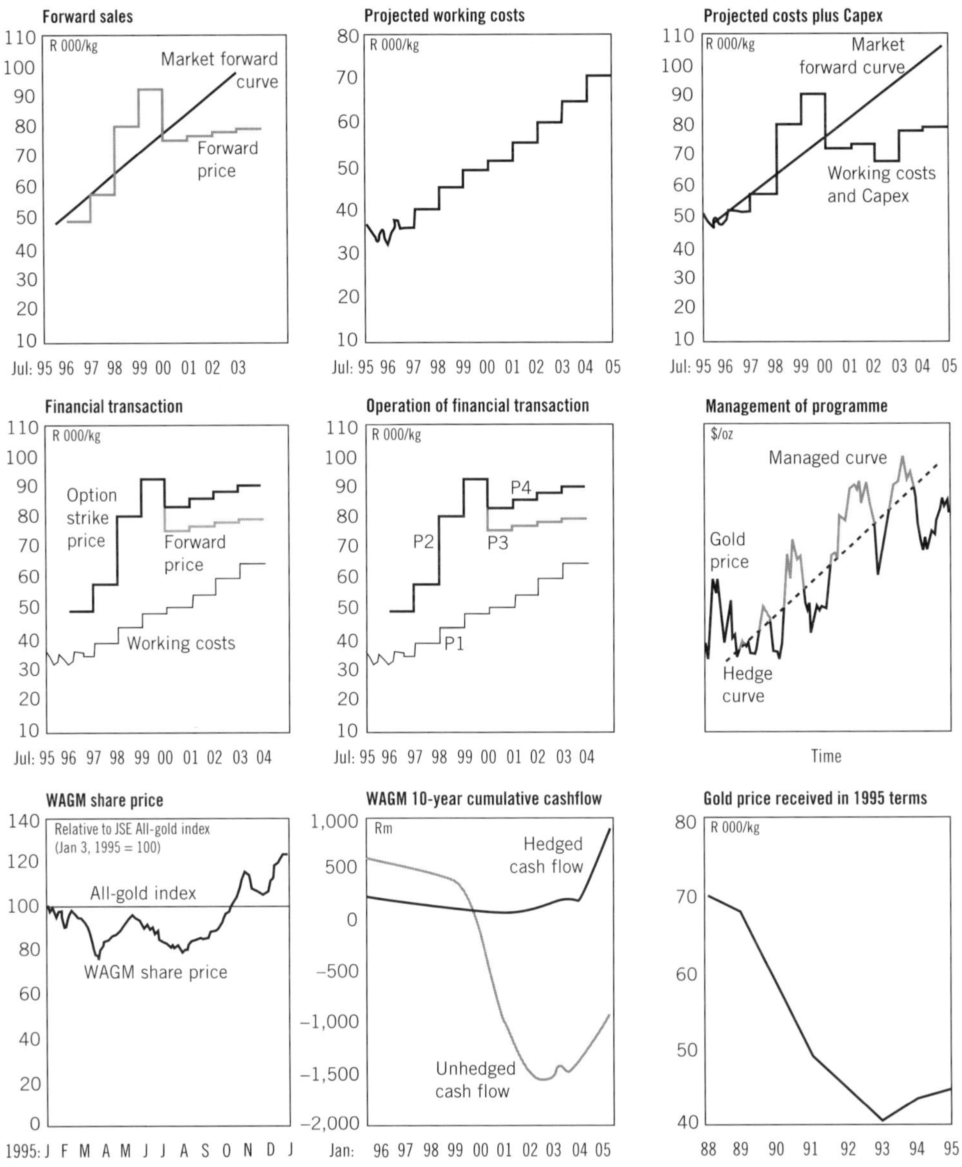

structured at prices higher than the market forward curve in the early part of the deal, and at prices lower than the market forward curve in the latter period of the deal. Although still at attractive forward prices, some potential revenue generated from the latter period was sacrificed to increase the revenue in the periods when capital expenditure would be at its highest.

Upside participation

Rand/gold call options were purchased for 55% of the volume sold forward, to allow participation in any upside movement in the gold price. Should gold enter into a new bull phase, Western Areas would be able to participate in at least 55% of such upside above the rand/gold call strike prices (see Figure A). This level of participation was developed consequent to significant modelling of the transaction under various adverse scenarios.

Another reason for the rand/gold call options is to protect the mine against gold price risk in the event of the production plan not being achieved, particularly in a high gold price scenario. Should production shortfalls occur, Western Areas is not at risk to deliver gold it is not able to produce.

Incorporating the rand/gold call options, therefore, results in an effective commitment of only 45% of Western Areas' production, but with 100% gold price protection on the downside.

Depreciation of the rand

A further component to the financial transaction involved the purchase of rand/dollar call options for 45% of the maturing gold forward sales value to protect the integrity of the programme over the duration of its life (see Table A).

A dramatic depreciation of the South African currency would inflate operating costs to untenable levels. Western Areas would then be caught in a cost squeeze, where 100% of the costs are inflated while the company benefits only from 55% participation of the increasing rand/gold call options referred to earlier. With these currency call options, Western Areas will participate by up to 100% in the upside rand price above the rand/dollar option strike price resulting from a currency depreciation. The first trigger level is if the rand is weaker than R4.80 to the dollar for the month of July 1997. Any levels of the rand stronger than these currency call option strike prices are not covered, although Western Areas will still enjoy the 55% participation in the rand price above the rand/gold call option strike price.

Transaction in perspective

Western Areas has an expected mine life in excess of 65 years, of which the production for 8½ years has been sold forward with a commitment to deliver only 45% of the planned production. The life-of-mine payable reserves are estimated to be 198 million tonnes, containing some 60 million ounces of gold. The forward sale commitment encompassed in the financial transaction represents only about 5% of this estimated gold reserve, which equates to only 56% of current production – rising to about 80% of Western Areas' planned production by the time the South Deep section reaches full production. Given this, the production from the Western Areas section alone will be sufficient to meet the future commitments required by the programme.

Therefore, for 100% protection over 8½ years against a downside movement in the gold price, in effect only 5% of the payable ore reserve will not participate in any rising gold price above the contract prices. The 45% of the production which does not participate in any rising gold price can be spread more evenly over the life of the mine, by virtue of the flexibility of the financial transaction.

Had the South Deep project been funded by a rights issue of R640 million (in 1994 terms) at the end of 1995, instead of the funding programme, the dilution in the shareholding of investors would have been approximately 11%, based on a price of R65 per share – with no gold price protection. A share price lower than this would imply an even higher potential dilution. A subsequent drop in the gold price would require additional funding, resulting in further potential dilution. Shareholders wishing to increase their absolute shareholding in Western Areas remain free to purchase additional shares with funds that would otherwise have had to be used to follow their rights issue.

Structure of the transaction

Five years into the transaction, the strike prices of the rand/gold call options are set higher than the forward prices. This is due to cost. Making the strike prices coincide with the forward prices over the final 3½ years, as they do over the first five years, would have meant increasing the term of the structure or paying an additional premium, neither of which were acceptable. Because the strike levels diverge, when the gold spot price rises above the contract prices, the mine will not participate in any upside until the rand/gold price exceeds the rand/gold call option strike. This does not affect the rand/dollar call options referred to earlier, which will trigger at predetermined rand/dollar exchange rates over the last six years of the programme (ie, from July 1997 to March 2004).

Flexibility of the transaction

An outstanding feature of the programme is its flexibility. Whenever the spot gold price is higher than the contract price, Western Areas may, provided the mine plan is achieved, choose not to deliver at this price for the 45% of the volume not covered by the rand/gold call options. Instead, this volume (or a portion thereof) may be rolled over at the prevailing contango to a future date, thereby receiving 100% of the contracted volume at the ruling spot price. Western Areas may therefore obtain the greater of the contract price or the spot price.

Market impact

The transaction was implemented professionally, and over a period of time, in order to limit the impact on both the South African domestic markets and the international gold market. Short-term gold lease rates rose significantly in the fourth quarter of 1995, but this was unrelated to the Western Areas gold sale and did not materially affect the pricing of the transaction.

PANEL 8

MANAGING RISK BY MANAGING QPS – AN EXAMPLE

Imagine that a "risk averse" South African metal refiner has negotiated its supply contract for metal concentrates such that the price it pays is based on the average London Metal Exchange (LME) cash price of the month after delivery (m + 1). The refining of the metal takes on average 30–45 days, with the metal being sold at the month of refined metal delivery –1. As both pricing periods coincide, a natural hedge is achieved and the refiner has eliminated price risk.

A more efficient and potentially more profitable way of managing this price exposure is to use base metal derivatives. This alternative strategy involves the company widening its quotation periods (QPs) gap by renegotiating its concentrate supply contracts – so that it buys at the LME average of the month of concentrate delivery, and sells the refined metal at month of delivery two months later. The refiner would then be exposed to a fall in the price of metal over this two-month gap.

To manage this risk, the company could hedge on the LME. As a paper trade with a bank or LME broker, the smelter would sell forward the first month – at a price to be determined by the (as yet unknown) average of that month – but roll this position forward so that it is settled promptly by the second working day of the month following the metal sale. At the same time, it would agree to buy forward to this same date at a price to be determined by the (as yet unknown) LME cash average of the selling month.

If the LME average cash price of the month of metal sale fell sharply, the refiner would receive a cash payment from its hedging counterparty equal to the price difference. The advantage of this approach is that:

- the refiner receives the additional benefit of the carry (ie, picks up the ruling contango when it rolls forward the hedge position); and
- the hedging flexibility removes the need to continually match QPs.

In practice, the refiner may experience difficulty in renegotiating its QPs, as the concentrate sellers will try to manipulate the QPs so that they also benefit from any contango.

needed to finance the project was heavily dependent on cashflow; and, of course, Dubal wanted to hedge against the possibility of a cyclical aluminium price fall. The solution adopted was a synthetic put embedded in a public syndicated loan. Following a two-year grace period, the loan was repayable in six instalments, with the instalment amount being dependent on the average aluminum price over the previous six months. This structure had three effects: it guaranteed a minimum price for the company's production, thereby fixing a minimum net margin and project return; it linked payment amount with ability to pay; and it reduced the credit risk exposure taken by the lenders (which improved the pricing on the syndicated loan).[12]

This credit enhancing role is particularly important for a company trying to obtain bank credit for resource projects in developing countries. Hedging can create debt capacity, as it increases the percentage of the value per tonne on proven reserves against which an investor is prepared to lend. While production uncertainty and political risk will remain, the uncertainty due to price volatility is removed.

In South Africa, derivatives have also been used to transfer profits between mines, in order to improve the net tax position of the mining company. The ability to do this is limited by the "ring fencing" legislation, which limits the transfer of profits to within defined lease areas. The tax effectiveness of a mining project might also be enhanced by changing the cashflow profile of future revenue streams, to ensure that capital expenditure can be deducted.

Elimination of the possibility of company failure Intuitively, it would appear that a company's share price would increase if the likelihood of financial distress is reduced in the eyes of risk-averse shareholders. This is particularly true in the current South African context, where the new government is sensitive to the impact of unemployment. For example, if the price of the metal falls below a threshold level, the political risk to a mining house of closing a marginal mining operation may be unacceptable in the current environment.

Protection of budget rates This, again, is a fairly commonly stated objective of corporate hedging programmes. Provided that forward pricing allows the budget rate to be achieved (and budget forecasts could be based on the pricing struc-

PANEL 9

ALUMINIUM PRICE MANAGEMENT – THE ALUSAF EXAMPLE

Alusaf is a South African-based aluminium smelter owned by Gencor. With the completion of its new Hillside smelter, its nameplate production capacity has been increased to 640,000 tonnes per year, while actual production levels have been running at 665,000 tonnes per year – making it one of the world's Top 10 producers. Around 230,000 tonnes of annual aluminium production are contractually committed as part of a toll smelting arrangement with its alumina suppliers Alcoa, Billiton and Alusuisse. In addition, there are medium-term contracts of three to five years with international consumers, and a number of short-term but effectively "evergreen" contracts with Far East and Japanese buyers. Approximately 80% of full capacity output is exported.

Alusaf's sales of aluminium are priced by reference to ruling London Metals Exchange (LME) month-average dollar prices, exposing the company to the influence of fluctuations in both metal prices and exchange rates. To reduce the effect on Alusaf's financial performance, long-term contracts have been put in place which link the costs of its two major inputs – electricity and alumina – to the LME aluminium price.

Alusaf has a break-even level of approximately $750 per tonne that reflects its open-ended power and alumina supply agreements. In contrast to many other producers, these tariff agreements have no floor or ceiling. While this leaves Alusaf exposed to upside moves, it also allows it to operate at the lower end of the cost curve.

Alusaf's electricity costs, expressed as a percentage of the LME floating price and therefore as a percentage of Alusaf's revenue, are around 16%. Similarly, the overall weighted average of Alusaf's alumina costs, as a percentage of the LME price, is 24%. The net effect of these contracts is that Alusaf's exposure to the aluminium price is reduced, from 100% of sales to approximately 60% of sales. This is considered Alusaf's natural exposure position.

Subsequently, Alusaf sells its aluminium on either a fixed or variable price basis, depending on the requirements of its customers. On a given tonnage, the effect of a fixed price sale is to reduce Alusaf's exposure on that tonnage from its natural exposure level of 60% to 40%. This is because revenue is no longer exposed to aluminium price movements; the two inputs of electricity and alumina remain exposed. Consistent with Gencor's global risk management philosophy, Alusaf then uses LME futures to realign its LME exposure closer to its natural risk position.

The Alusaf treasury department has actively worked with its marketing team to offer flexible pricing terms to customers. This has tended to reduce the demand for hedging products in "downstream" companies. An aluminium can manufacturer that requires fixed price aluminium, so that it can sell cans at a fixed price to a beverage company, is able to negotiate a fixed price supply agreement from Alusaf. As a result, LME hedge transactions have normally been executed by Alusaf, rather than by the downstream aluminium consumers.

First National Bank, as a seller of hedging products, would argue that each player in the production process should consider running its own hedging programme. The can manufacturer, for example, could have fixed its prices using a rand-denominated aluminium hedge. In contrast to a fixed price supply agreement, a hedging transaction can be easily unwound if the fundamental market view changes; more importantly, it can be structured to achieve a broader range of risk profiles (for example, by using option-based strategies).

ture offered by the forward curve), any manager whose performance is measured against the "naive" benchmark of hitting a budget target, has a strong incentive to hedge.

Creating profit through an active or speculative hedge programme For shareholders to be comfortable with this objective, they should be made aware of both target profit and the capital put at risk to achieve this profit. David Shimko[13] has outlined a framework for implementing such an approach, which emphasises that the appropriate capital cost includes interest foregone (relative to the benchmark) and an opportunity cost for capital implicitly allocated to the trading activity.

HEDGE EXECUTION – SOME CONSIDERATIONS
Following approval for the implementation of a hedge programme and the definition of objectives, the execution and subsequent monitoring

of the hedges brings with it a new set of responsibilities. Some of the issues that should be considered prior to executing a specific hedge structure include:

❑ *who is going to execute the hedge transactions?* The execution of the specific hedge programme may, in larger corporations, be handled by the treasury. In many smaller corporations, however, this execution role becomes the responsibility of either the purchasing manager or the financial manager, neither of whom may be accustomed to dealing in derivative markets. In some cases, separating the hedging from the physical purchasing department can create internal tensions, which can best be addressed by delineating performance benchmarks for each function;

❑ *obtaining market information or competitive quotes* Ultimately, the onus must be on the corporate hedger both to understand the structures it is executing and to establish that the pricing is fair. Access to financial data via Reuters/Telerate/Bloomberg is the first step in this exercise. Often, however, screen indications may be considerably different to the prices at which the market is trading. Many corporations rely on a process of obtaining competitive quotes to ensure fair pricing;

❑ *taxation and accounting implications* Organisations need to ensure that, before entering into derivative transactions, they fully understand both the accounting treatment that will be applied and the required accounting disclosures. In addition, they should fully evaluate the tax impact of receipts and payments of the instrument (including any VAT). In some instances, metal derivative transactions have been entirely tax driven, although the opportunity for such tax arbitrages is generally limited, as the tax authorities will normally focus on the intent of the underlying derivative transactions;

1. Alusaf MTP vs LME av three-month rand aluminium

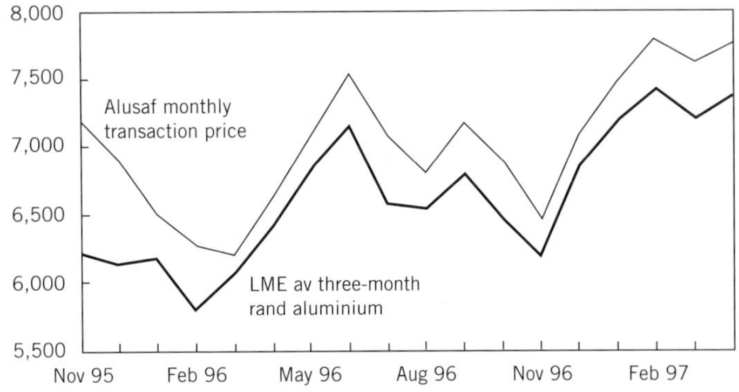

❑ *identification of expected cashflows and ensuring that the board and senior management view the hedge in combination with the value of its underlying physical position* A company reporting negative cashflows on a hedge position is too often forced to suspend its hedging programme, as the board has not considered the offsetting gain on its underlying physical position. While a fixed rate supply contract might also result in an "opportunity cost", the board is unlikely to view the negative cashflow on a hedge position in the same light;

❑ *implementation of adequate risk management systems* The difficulty of finding integrated risk management systems for a reasonable cost has meant that many corporations continue to rely on spreadsheets for position keeping and management reporting. Upgrading of technology is often driven by a desire for enhanced control or efficiency, but may require a threshold level of deal volume to justify the cost of buying off-the-shelf software; and

❑ *often hedging programmes will require prior board approval* It is important that such approvals are documented with an overview of current market parameters and of the basis on which the hedging decision is being made. Without documentation, board members may be tempted to back-track on their earlier decisions.

Hedging risks (the imperfect hedge)

Often, the hedging instruments available to the corporate hedger will not provide a perfect hedge for its physical position. In other words, the price moves of the hedging instrument will not be perfectly correlated with the price moves of the commodity that is being hedged. The resulting risk, known as basis risk, can be categorised into the following types:

❑ *location basis* is the price difference resulting from the separate geographical locations of the hedging instrument and the physical metal. In base metals this could, for example, reflect the pricing of the metal for delivery in Johannesburg versus LME pricing. In many cases, a corporation may choose to hedge only the LME component of its price risk, but in this instance there should be formal recognition and reporting of the basis risk. For many base metals sold in South Africa, the domestic pricing is founded on a fixed margin over the average LME cash settlement price. Provided this margin remains fixed – although it may change at discrete points in time if, for example, the import tariff changes – the basis risk is eliminated (see Figures 1 and 2, illustrating

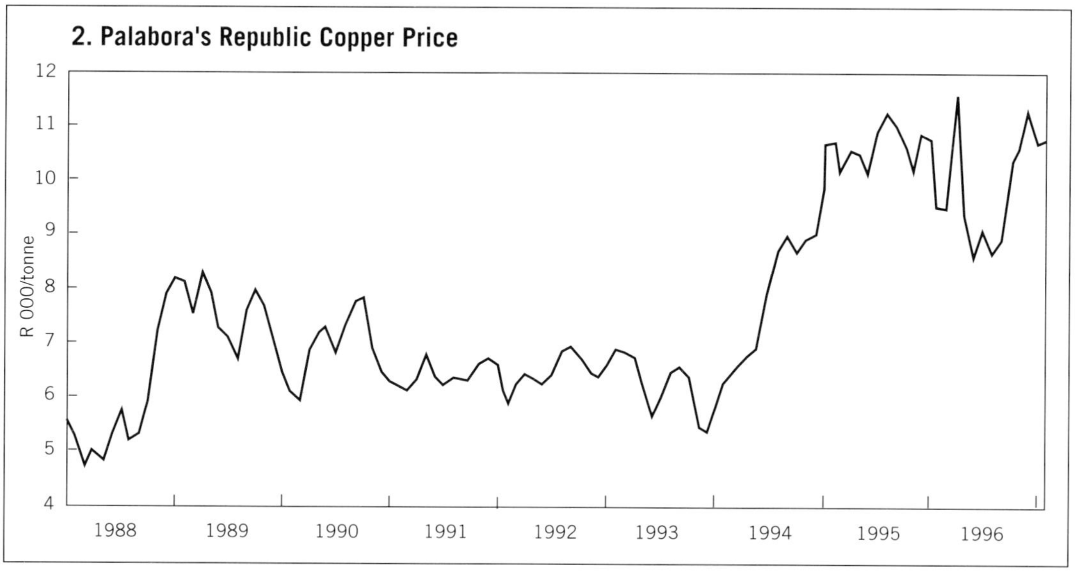

South African Alusaf's aluminium monthly transaction price versus the LME price and Palabora's RCP, respectively).

❑ *product basis* is the pricing differential resulting from a variance in the quality specifications of the hedging instrument and the physical metal. For LME base metals, the deliverable grades for which prices are quoted are carefully monitored to meet defined quality specifications. Metals that do not meet these quality specifications will trade at a discount to the LME grade. An illustration of this in the South African market is copper scrap which, depending on its quality, will trade at various discounts to the LME copper price. While the LME contract can be used as a hedge for scrap metal sales, a basis risk will exist that reflects the relative supply and demand for that particular grade;

❑ *time basis* arises when a hedge position is placed in a contract month which differs from the underlying exposure. This situation is most likely to occur when a longer-dated exposure is hedged using LME futures that only trade out to 27 months (the length of the LME strip may differ for other metals (ie, lead is 12 months). Placing hedge positions in the shorter dates, with the intention of rolling them out to match exposures, introduces considerable basis risk. The ability of a bank to offer such longer-dated structures will often depend on an ability to "warehouse" (ie, to take this risk on to its own trading position) such risk until a counterparty with an offsetting natural position can be found.

Another instance of a time basis risk that can arise in the base metal markets is the hedging of an average price exposure with a vanilla LME hedge contract settled against a cash price. Given the availability of average rate LME contracts, this is most likely to occur as part of a conscious hedging strategy for those metals where average rate pricing is less competitive.

With all of the above examples, the corporate hedger will have to decide whether the magnitude of the risk is acceptable; this can normally only be ascertained by undertaking a statistical analysis of the historical moves of the basis risk. In some cases, a bank or counterparty may be prepared to take on that risk and offer the corporation the desired hedge. This tailored hedge will, however, have an implicit cost attached to it and may also result in a less liquid position which is difficult to unwind.

This introduces the concept of *liquidity risk*, which can arise when a hedge is placed in a less liquid hedging contract. Unwinding such a contract can be costly, as the bid/offer spreads will naturally be wider in an illiquid market. An example of this could be faced by a company trying to hedge cobalt price risk. A few specialised minor metal trading houses are prepared to make forward prices (even option prices) on paper cobalt hedge structures. However, such structures may be expensive to unwind if the reversal has to be executed with one of the same few counterparties.

For South African companies, the underlying metal price exposure is usually rand denominated. From the corporation's perspective, then, the decision is whether to transact an integrated rand-denominated hedge or, alternatively, to hedge the metal and currency legs separately. Often, as companies become more sophisticated in their risk management, they feel that they should execute these legs individually. This often reflects a suspicion that banks will take a wider spread on an integrated hedging structure. The reality is that, while the company should have the ability to value the individual components of any transaction, there may still be merit in executing the integrated hedge. With option transactions, the volatility of the rand/metal will generally be less than the combined volatilities of the components – there is, therefore, an advantage in executing the integrated hedge (see Chapter 4 for further discussion).

Counterparty risk is a term normally used to describe the credit risk of a counterparty, which in itself can be significant for non-clearable contracts, given the small balance sheet of many LME brokers. In a wider sense, however, it also describes the risk of the counterparty to a corporate transaction misunderstanding the objective of the hedge transaction. The complex terminology of the base metal markets (such as the different types of average rate transaction) increases this risk. From a corporation's point of view, the benefit of having fewer counterparties that understand their business may outweigh the dubious benefit of playing the market for the best pricing.

Risk management controls

The recent Sumitomo copper trading scandal, following on the heels of the Codelco losses, highlights the critical need for comprehensive risk management controls and policies. In most of these recent cases of "unauthorised derivative trading", losses have resulted from trading over a sustained period of time in trading environments where the most basic control procedures were not being followed. In the Sumitomo example, the losses are estimated at over $2.5 billion from unauthorised copper trading, over a period of 10 years.

The subject of risk management controls is complex and will only be covered briefly in this chapter. A number of practitioners, including most of the major international accounting firms, have published recommendations designed for corporate users of derivatives. Many of these points have evolved from the wider study by the Group of Thirty (G30) Global Derivatives Study Group.[14] An overview of this subject is provided by the UK Futures and Options Association's *Managing Derivative Risk – Guidelines to Endusers of Derivatives*,[15] which summarises six core principles for managing derivative risk and includes suggestions on the practical steps for implementing them.

The following recommendations have been drafted from this report and various other documents (which are listed in the bibliography). They cover the key principles on which there has been general concurrence.

Recommendation 1 End-users should use derivatives in a manner consistent with the overall risk management policy approved by their board of directors. These policies should be regularly reviewed as business and market circumstances change. Policies governing derivative use should be clearly defined and should specify the purpose for which these instruments are to be used. Senior management at all levels should enforce them.

Procedures should be documented, and address:

- ❑ treasury objectives, which should be consistent with the strategic, commercial aspirations and risk appetite of the underlying business;
- ❑ acceptable hedging instruments, outlining the instrument and means by which they can change the risk profiles associated with each exposure;
- ❑ acceptable levels of risk, as the financial risks need to be identified and quantified. The use of derivatives to modify/decrease/increase risk also needs to be defined; and
- ❑ dealing limits, which need to be explicitly defined for all personnel, as well as emphasising the necessary implementation procedures.

Recommendation 2 A senior management level of understanding and education should be maintained, in line with the complexity of the risk management programme. The approval for the use of derivatives should be undertaken on the basis of a full analysis of the risks involved. A company should, of course, attempt to cover its risk by the use of instruments for which all risks are fully understood, as well as with instruments that can be managed and accounted for on internal systems.

Recommendation 3 As appropriate to the nature, size and complexity of their derivative activities, end-users should adopt the same valuation and market risk management practices that are recommended for financial institutions. Specifically, they should regularly mark to market their derivative transactions for risk management purposes.

This approach is, however, rather idealised – in practice, those corporate treasuries that hold all derivative positions to maturity (ie, they will not be trading out of positions) will feel this requirement might be replaced by an analysis of the payoff profile at different price levels on maturity. The changing values of the derivative position over its life may not be as important as its possible values at maturity. Board and manage-

PANEL 10

CORPORATE RISK MANAGEMENT RESPONSIBILITIES

Position	Risk management function	Reports to
The board	Defining risk appetite of company Formally approving risk policy Ratification of treasury benchmarks Monitoring performance and adherence to policy	Shareholders
The treasurer	Defining hedge objectives commensurate with risk appetite of company Creating hedge programmes that will meet hedge objectives Monitoring execution performance relative to benchmarks	The board
Treasury manager	Execution of hedge transactions Reporting hedge performance Reporting existing exposures and hedge positions	Treasurer
Back office	Confirmation of all trades Independent reporting of performance re benchmark System control Cashflows resulting from hedge transactions	Finance director

ment must, however, have a full understanding of the risk profile and the cashflows that can result at the maturity of the hedge.

Recommendation 4 End-users must ensure that derivative activities are properly supervised and are subject to an effective independent framework of internal controls and audits. Adequate systems must be available for data capture, processing, settlement and management reporting, to ensure that derivative transactions are conducted in an orderly and efficient manner, in compliance with management policies (see Panel 10). Systems for recording and valuing derivative transactions need to be adequate for the volume and complexity of derivative deals. The ability of trading staff to amend the records of deals already in the system should be carefully restricted.

Companies often overlook the need to ensure that support and reconciliation staff are adequately trained and have an adequate level of technical knowledge.

Recommendation 5 Procedures should be set down for the monitoring and management of legal risk. They should cover issues of legal capacity and authority, compliance with relevant statutory requirements, and appropriate documentation between counterparties.

Given the complexity of many counterparty dealing agreements (such as the standard documentation provided by the International Swap and Derivatives Association, ISDA), companies may want to seek independent legal advice. Creation of a master agreement will streamline future document negotiations.

Recommendation 6 Procedures should also be set down for the provision of full analysis for all counterparty credit risk and the practical management of such risks through the use of credit limits for each counterparty. These provisions should cover the organisation's aggregate exposure to that counterparty.

For OTC transactions, credit risk is normally split into market contingent risk - estimated by applying an appropriate factor to nominal deal principal, added to current market value - and settlement risk on the day of cashflows.

The FOA report, mentioned above, summarises the intention of these recommendations by emphasising the need for "tighter and more comprehensive internal operational controls, clearer segregation of functions, more and better training and education, higher standards in accounting and risk evaluation and better use of collateralisation and margining".

Selling risk management – a South African bank's perspective

In a "sophisticated" market, banks and brokers (the sellers of risk management) can fall into the trap of marketing risk management instruments without understanding and helping to develop the underlying risk management framework for their target clients. Recently, there have been a number of highly publicised examples of banks selling inappropriate strategies - such as using highly leveraged instruments, where the payoff profile bears no relationship to the underlying exposure - which do not fully take into account the risk profile of the end-user. The fault does not lie entirely with the banks - inadequate risk management frameworks have allowed corporate treasuries to enter into these inappropriate strategies with impunity, until the strategy fails.

In an "emerging market", such as South Africa, where commodity price hedging is relatively new, risk management providers may have to commit resources to build the foundations of a corporate risk management framework before transactions can be executed. Internationally, certain banks also appear to be pursuing this philosophy of enlightened self-interest (an example being the release, by JP Morgan, of the RiskMetrics package), with the expectation that increased deal flow will result from an informed client base. Without this corporate risk management framework, a bank marketing hedging services is often faced with inertia on the part of its corporate clients. This is not simply because the transactor has difficulty obtaining the necessary internal approvals (although a comprehensive risk framework will streamline this process); more often, it is because the transacting company cannot confidently identify a good price level at which to hedge. Concern that a poor hedging decision will be criticised by the board can often lead to the "safer" course of doing nothing.

In the past, derivative marketing has been driven by the need to demonstrate innovation. Problems have arisen where such innovation has outpaced the needs of the end-user. This situation has been exacerbated by the proliferation of derivative products offering a plethora of risk/reward profiles. Without a well-constructed and documented risk management framework, the average corporate manager faces an unenviable task in attempting to assess their suitability. Many give up in despair or are eventually seduced by the persistence of the salesmen, often to their peril. This has contributed to the slightly jaundiced view, expressed by corporates, of derivatives and derivative salesmen. This unfortunate situation has been largely self-inflicted, arising directly from the product-driven marketing strategies of the developers. The onerous demands of the major accounting standards bodies, with regard to financial instrument disclosure requirements, have certainly not enhanced this situation.

However, there is some light at the end of the tunnel, particularly for those risk management providers adopting a more solutions-driven approach. Where product development has been driven by end-user needs, it has led to a higher volume of OTC derivative deals and an enlarged role for banks (as opposed to traditional LME brokers). Asian option technology has in the past been an example where the OTC instrument was able to provide a better hedge for corporations exposed to average rate pricing on their physical base metals. This has driven the LME towards making its TAPOs a clearable instrument.

The effective marketing of derivatives involves an understanding, both of the corporate clients' risks, and of what motivates the transactor to execute a specific hedging transaction. This process can be time consuming, especially when the need for risk management has not been formally recognised. Applying a form of cashflow VAR analysis in a corporate context can demonstrate clearly the impact of unhedged exposures on a company's balance sheet and income statement. This modelling, sometimes called "cashflow at risk" (CFAR), defines risk in terms of earnings - or some other measure of a company's operating performance - rather than hedge profitability. By demonstrating the impact of changes in financial variables (such as commodity prices on key accounting ratios), risk management can be sold using a language that the financial director and key decision makers within a company are comfortable with.

1 *For our purposes, risk management can be defined as the active management of the financial exposures that will affect a corporation's cashflows and, ultimately, its share price.*

2 *In a paper presented at the 1996 FT World Gold Conference.*

3 *October 1994.*

4 *Quoted in* Metal Bulletin, *April 22, 1996.*

5 *F. Modigliani and M.H. Miller, 1958, "The Cost of Capital, Corporation Finance and the Theory of Investment",* The American Economic Review, *vol. 48 (June), pp. 261–97.*

6 *While these propositions will not be expanded upon in this chapter, it was argued by Smith and Stulz (1985) and Froot, Scharfstein and Stein (1993) that, under specific assumptions, risk management could add value by either reducing taxes, reducing the cost of financial distress or facilitating optimal investment. An up-to-date summary of the theoretical debate over corporate hedging can be found in G. Fenn et al, "Does Corporate Risk Management Create*

Shareholder Value?" in Financial Risk Management and the Corporate Treasury, *Risk Publications (1997), pp. 13–32.*

7 *See Mary Ellen Stocks, "Value-at-Risk: A Risk Management Tool for Corporate Treasurers",* Financial Risk Management for the Corporate Treasury, *Risk Publications (1997), pp. 77–92.*

8 *David Shimko, 1996,* Risk, *vol. 9, provides a simple example of how the VAR of a trading portfolio could be measured against the VAR of a defined benchmark.*

9 *Mary Ellen Stocks, "Value-at-Risk: A Risk Management Tool for Corporate Treasurers",* Financial Risk Management for the Corporate Treasury, *Risk Publications (1997), pp. 77–92.*

10 *A $5 bid/offer spread in the near dates for an aluminium quote can easily widen to over $50 beyond the 27-month LME clearing limit.*

11 *A QP is the specified time period over which the contract pricing is fixed.*

12 *This transaction won Merrill Lynch the* Corporate Finance *magazine structured deal of the year in 1995.*

13 *Shimko, David, 1996, "How to Speculate",* Risk, *vol. 9, no. 2.*

14 *Group of Thirty, Global Derivatives Study Group, 1993,* Derivatives: Practices and Principles.

15 *Published in 1995.*

BIBLIOGRAPHY

Crowson, P., 1994, *Metal Price Hedging*, pp. 17.

Davis, H., 1996, "Standard Fair", *Risk*, vol. 9, no. 6.

"Dubal Loan a Perfect Fit for the Project", *Corporate Finance*, December 1995, pp. 44.

Heston, C. and G. Greiff, 1990, "Defining the Risk Profile" *Corporate Finance*, August, pp. 10–14.

McNew, L., 1996, "Reducing Reynolds Risk", *Risk*, February, vol. 9, no. 2.

Maguire, F., 1994, "Base Instinct", *Futures and Options World*, October, pp. 43–47.

Metal Bulletin, 1996, April 22, pp. 7.

Mining Journal Gold Service, 1996, *International Gold Mining Newsletter*, vol. 23, no. 7.

Murning, M., 1995, "Managing Complex Risks", *Treasury Management International*, March.

Risk Publications, 1995, *Managing Energy Price Risk*, various chapters.

Shimko, D., 1996 "How to Speculate", *Risk*, vol. 9, no. 2.

Shimko, D., 1996, "VAR for Corporates", *Risk*, vol. 9, no. 6.

Smithson, C., 1996, "Value at Risk (2)", *Risk*, vol. 9, no. 2.

Turner, C., 1996, "VAR as an Industrial Tool", *Risk*, vol. 9, no. 3.

Yafie, R., 1995, "Protection Racket", *Futures and Options World*, July, pp. 54–55.

6

Linking Shareholder Utility, Corporate Goals and Risk Management

Chris Harris
BZW

Risk management means different things to different people. It can be *commission* to a hedge salesman, *livelihood* to a risk manager, *increased ability to plan* to a process manager, *profit* to a corporate treasury trader, *sleep at night* to a chief executive, or *altered financial performance* to an investor. Certainly there are many more dimensions than this, and yet within the area of markets there is only one kind of risk management tool: the exchange of one deliverable entity for another.[1] To hedge successfully, all of these dimensions of risk must be managed and reconciled with a simple two-dimensional exchange.

This chapter looks at how corporations in the metals markets can approach this problem. Unlike other chapters in this book, we make no attempt to analyse what the risk is, beyond its generic form in each sector, or the mechanics of *how* the instruments can refine or mitigate it. The purpose here is to provide a framework of communication so that all the stakeholders in metals industry corporations can transmit their needs efficiently through the "hedging infrastructure". This requires an interpretation, or at least a measure, of their respective needs in the rarefied language of market transactions (buy, sell, material, volume, price, date).

Underlying much of the debate about corporate hedging strategies is the question of whether hedging *can* specifically and independently add (or remove) value by itself, without invoking corporate risk arguments. While this subject is not extensively covered in this chapter,[2] some examples are provided in Panel 1 on pages 106–07.

The chapter is divided into four sections:

❑ *Shareholder utility* The role of the company is to deliver value to the shareholders. The simple maximisation of return is not a sufficient response to shareholder value, because different shareholders have different approaches to risk. This section defines the relationship between the subjective utility of the shareholders and market parameters.

❑ *Corporate identity and goals* Corporations must generate revenue above the risk-free rate of return. To do so they must constantly create and exploit competitive advantages. Paradoxically, to succeed in this may require a company focus that is not easily interpretable in terms of the risk and reward functions of a generic investor. As shareholder utility is maximised *only* if the financial performance profile of the company can be reconciled to the expectation of the investor, it is important to be able to characterise company goals and their outcome in investment language.

❑ *Corporate risk infrastructure* A risk infrastructure (procedures, information and communication systems, etc) must assist the management to assess potential costs, potential opportunities and the mechanisms by which the firm can reposition itself in the marketplace. This section discusses how this can be established, and how high-level corporate goals can be transmitted to the business through the risk infrastructure.

❑ *Control* Any activity that is significant enough to affect the financial performance of the firm needs managing carefully at all levels. Risk management is no exception. This section addresses the resolution and policing of conflicts of interest, as well as the general control system.

Shareholder utility

Shareholders come in all shapes and sizes, and companies are expected to provide "value" to them all. This value must be *measurable*, so that the company can be held accountable for its performance and so that different companies can be compared with each other. It must also approximate as efficiently as possible what the investors

1. The utility and marginal utility of wealth

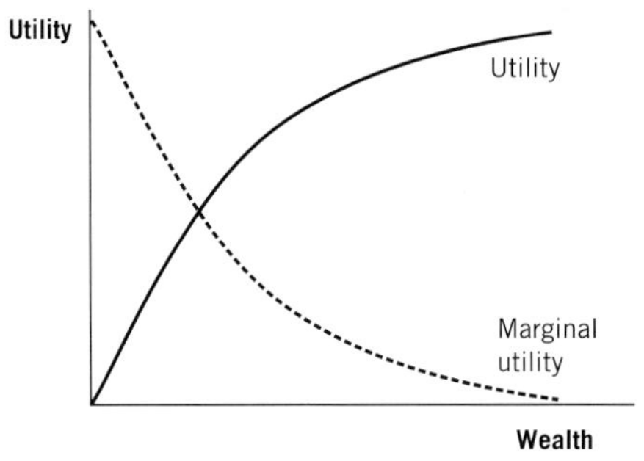

2. The utility cost of risk

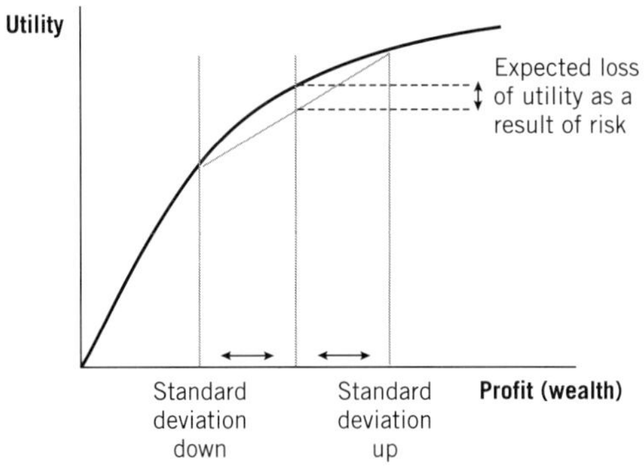

3a. The simple relationship between risk and utility

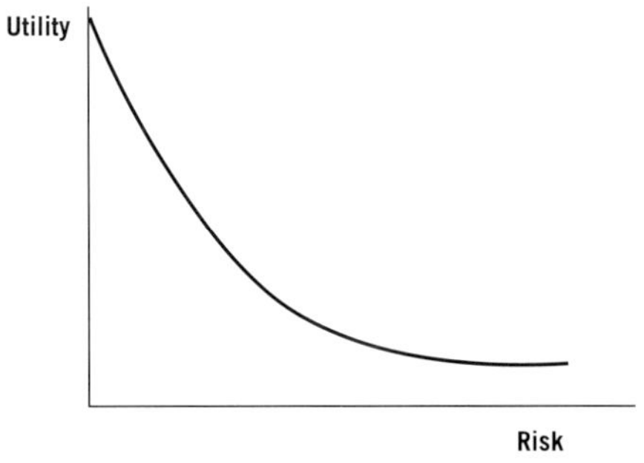

3b. Iso-utility, or indifference curves

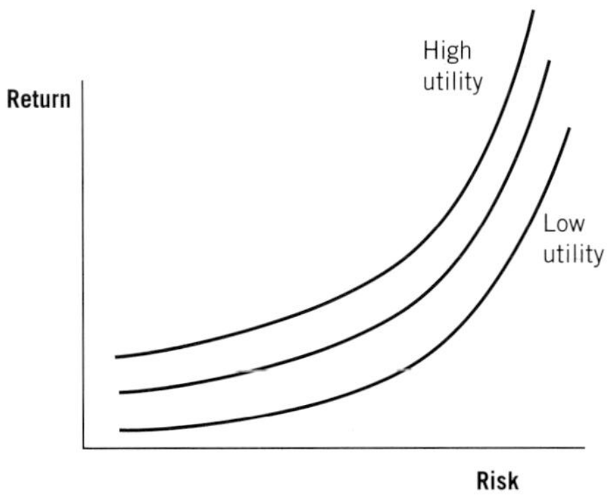

"want" or "need". Fortunately, we have two key benchmarks, both of which are measurable to a first approximation. These are:

- *return*, most conveniently measured as annual return on investment; and
- *risk*, most conveniently measured as the volatility of return.

Later on in this chapter, we will spend some time looking at more precise measures of risk.

There is also the question of who to please, and how to measure how pleased they are. For example, should performance be optimised for an "average" investor? Should the company consider the utility of company performance to non-voting investors? How much should time preference, domicile, average tax status and ethical considerations be taken into account? Can a company legitimately optimise its risk/reward with no consideration for investors, using the argument that a specialised investor base will migrate to the shares?

In theory, an affirmative answer to the final question answers all the others. Taking an evolutionary perspective, unsuitable marriages of investor and company will cause a long-term migration of the "right" kind of investor to the "right" kind of company. In practice, this process of learning by mistakes is enormously wasteful – far better to get it right first time. We will begin by looking at how risk valuation relates to investor needs.

All risk valuation rests on a central assumption – that the marginal utility of wealth decreases with the amount of wealth (Figure 1). In simple terms, this means that an extra penny to a poor man is "worth" more than an extra penny to a rich man. As the number of pennies owned by one person increases, his eagerness for the next one diminishes with his increasing pile. The converse is also true: that the rich man is less worried by a unit diminution than the man with a small pile of coins.

It follows that the effect of risk can be illustrated by using the utility curve (Figure 2). A starting point on the curve is taken, and it is assumed that market conditions will cause a movement on the wealth curve in one direction or the other, each with a probability of 50%. The average utility of the two points is then marked out. As is clear from the figure, the average utility is distinctly less than that of the starting point. This is the disutility, or cost, of risk.

From the curves in Figures 2 and 3, we can construct "indifference curves": the investor is indifferent to where exactly he is on each of the curves in Figure 3b – although if he could, he would shift himself onto a better (higher utility) line altogether. Note also that a particular form of utility curve is often assumed (a circular arc), and that a particular measure of risk is used (standard deviation of the normal distribution).

By and large, most observed factors in the real world,[3] from height of children in a class, to the change in inflation rate over time, show a very "well behaved" statistical variation called the *normal distribution*. The measure of variation of a factor is called the *standard deviation*, which is a good all-purpose risk measure. (As we mentioned above, on the reward axis the annual return on investment is the most useful measure.)

For a single investor, with a single investment, in a single stock which has a normally distributed return, this is as far as we need to go. In the real world, we need to consider some extra facets of risk. For the purposes of this chapter, they are *negative skew*, *positive skew*, *alpha* and *correlation*.

4. Negative skew of mining companies in relation to the normal distribution, and the effect of option insurance

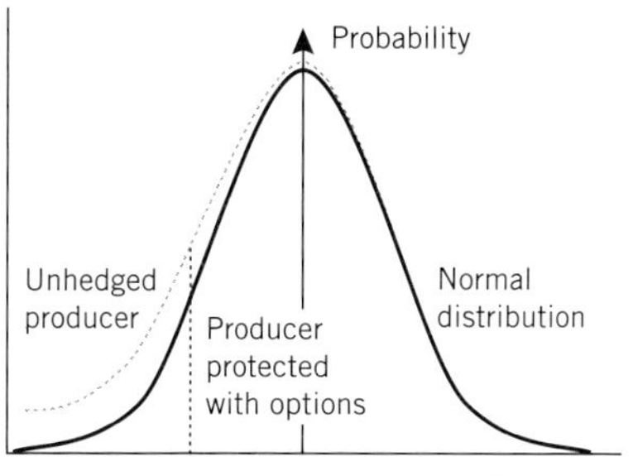

5. Risk profile of a company with a strong positive skew

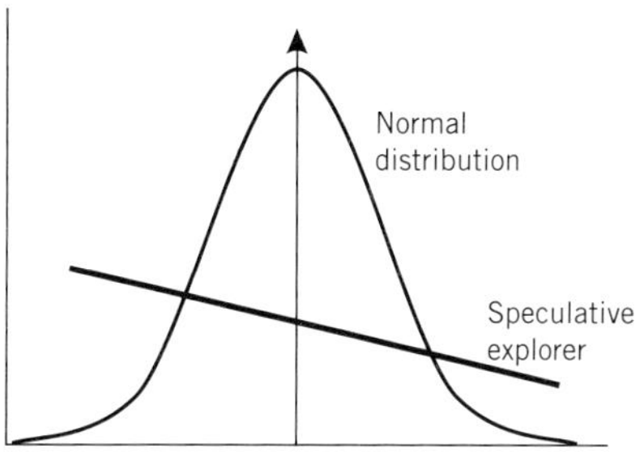

Negative skew describes the risk of an increased probability of negative events, when compared with their probability of occurrence in a diagram showing a normal distribution. Negative skew is shown in Figure 4 in relation to a typical unhedged metals producer. As we can see by looking at the left-hand of the diagram, the unhedged producer has more chance of suffering from a "worst case" reduction in return than if returns were normally distributed. This is particularly important in mining debt, because hedging has a very strong effect in this sector. "Worst case" analysis is particularly important for the mining debtholders[4] – because they will not share in any unusually high profits which, for the shareholder, may partly offset the disutility of worst-case scenarios.

Negative skew arises primarily for reasons of cashflow, and occurs in companies which are either highly leveraged or which incur high cash operating costs. Hedging can only alleviate *short-term* negative skew and can do little to affect long-term risk. The diagram shows the negative skew suffered by mining companies as their liquidity declines rapidly with profits, and also the strongly beneficial effect of option protection on the worst-case cashflow. Most investors are intolerant with respect to negative skew.

Positive skew is the possibility of extreme upside. Despite the high volatility of commodities, price movement rarely results in extreme upside share movement unless, for example, the mine is already near collapse and the share price is near zero. However, mining is one of the few industrial sectors that has *some* shares with stellar gains. Frequently, attempts by investors to gain positive skew are not justified by investment analysis in the cold light of day – but in the mining sector, speculative hope as a dimension of investor utility cannot be discounted. Positive skew can considerably distort the risk diagram, and standard deviation is an ineffective measure in these cases.

Alpha is the expected gain arising from an active picking of stocks. A high alpha stock is one that is expected by the investor to generate a higher rate of return than the return already discounted by the market price of the stock. Because investors also buy and sell to adjust the correlation of investment returns in their portfolios, alpha return is hard to separate from correlation (beta[5]), especially as an investment pattern created by the beta needs of one set of buyers influences the price and therefore the alpha of the stock.

In this context, alpha arises for two reasons: firstly, that the *sector* the company is operating in

PANEL 1

ADDING VALUE BY HEDGING

Hedging is essentially a value neutral activity, although not exactly so. There are a number of ways in which pure market activity can make money. These include beating the "zero sum game" market by exploiting better information, or making better use of information (subjective value gain); bid/offer, arbitrage or other direct profit extraction; and, lastly, exploiting the systematic structure of the market (objective value gain) in ways that can be identified and assessed by statistical and fundamental analysis.

The apparent dichotomy of hedging and speculation is more easily resolved if it is accepted that hedging can make a value gain. Consider the hedging of a producer in a market that is believed to be cyclical. The investor will, in general, wish to increase its exposure to the market when prices are low, and decrease it (to lock in gains) when prices are high. The extent of strategic hedging *should* therefore depend on the future outlook of the price. However, to make a value gain by hedging clearly invokes an element of "speculation".

Fair value gain/loss

All trading and risk management is underpinned by the Theory of Rational Expectations.[1] This theory implies that the mean expectation value of any forward price at any time in the future is equal to its current price. In other words, the expectation profit of any trade, regardless of when it is entered into, or for how long it is planned to hold the position, is zero. Although the theory forms a solid foundation for risk management, there are deviations from it in the real world – as outlined in Chapter 10 of this book.

For example, a consistent market structure for a particular metal can cause a consistent (systematic) deviation of the market price in a particular tenor from its expectation price (plus/minus random forces). Figure A shows the generalised curves for base and precious metals. Forward hedging creates an expectation[2] profit or loss. Note that, if this hedging is begun with the expectation of hedge gain, it should be continued over at least one economic cycle.

There are also a number of reasons commodity prices can be temporarily thrown off kilter. If there is a good likelihood of equilibrium returning before the contract expires, then this also creates an opportunity for hedge gain. This includes storage arbitrage (Figure B), economic cycling, hedge liquidation of large positions (Figure C), etc.

A. Market curves in relation to fair value curves for base and precious metals

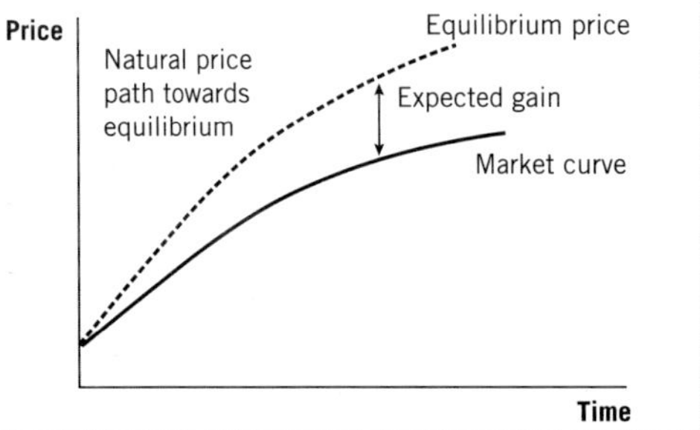

Industrial options

Producers and processors of metals often possess one or more of a wide array of "industrial options", ie, the option to adapt processes so that they depend upon or produce a different product or grade of product. Some of these options have a value that is easily definable in financial terms, and some do not. There are many instances in which the value of the industrial option cannot be realised unless it is actively managed using financial contracts. To take a hypothetical example,

B. Non-equilibrium forward price resulting from arbitrage

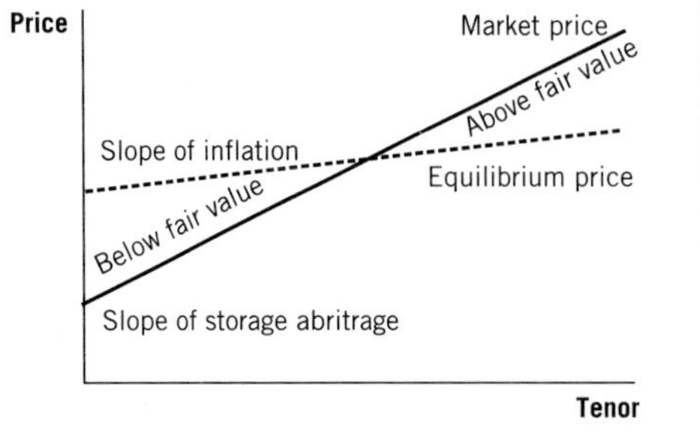

C. Non-equilibrium forward price effects arising from forced liquidation

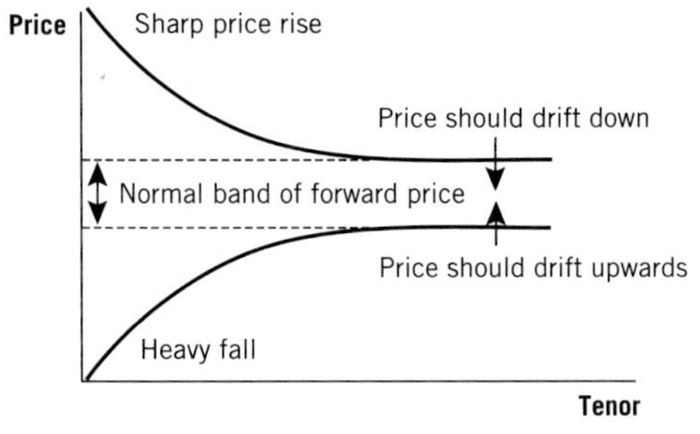

suppose that a small investment is required to change a process such that it can use either of two metals. By buying one metal forward and selling the ratio option on the two metals, it may be possible to raise enough premium to make the investment (Figure D).[3]

It should be noted that the active realisation of industrial options with market options tests corporate governance and risk infrastructure. Few corporations presently have a risk infrastructure that is sufficiently robust to allow them to sell (as opposed to buy) strategic options.

Managing processes more efficiently

As well as allowing firms to make use of their industrial options, hedging can also create efficiency, by allowing companies to use market-based transfer pricing. This practice links the management of processes much more closely to market prices. The best example is inventory management (see detailed example in main text), in which inventories are raised, lowered or altered (upstream or downstream) to make use of high or low prices or backwardation and contangos.

Financial gains

Hedging, off-balance sheet financing, securitisation and other market actions can have a direct effect on the financial analysis of a company, which should result in a lower debt service cost (see also discussion in Chapter 4 of this book).

Reduction of default risk

This is most easily demonstrable for producers, because the economic exposure of a producer to a terminal metals market is very apparent. An unhedged producer with fixed costs has a default risk that can be analysed with a fair degree of accuracy. The science of yield curves is very advanced, and it is an easy matter to evaluate the effect of reducing or increasing the amount that

D. Realisation of the industrial option value for a fabricator that can alter its process to use either of two metals

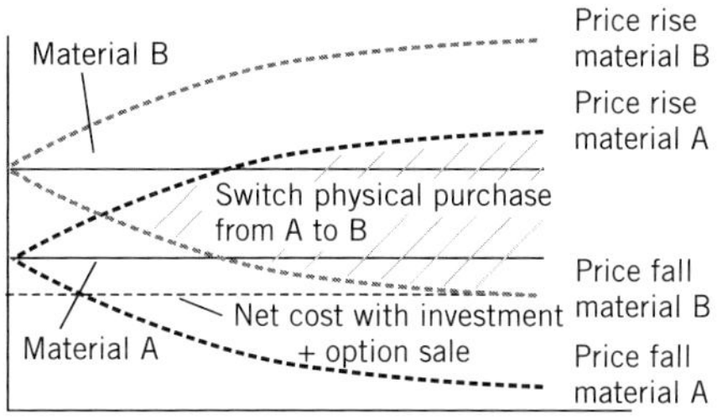

has to be set aside to cover the risk of default. This can be done in terms of basis points per year on borrowing costs, or in terms of a single present value. The default provision itself can be accurately estimated using the "delta"[4] of an option struck at the market price that precipitates default. It follows that hedging can create a definable saving in debt costs (Figure E).

The risk of a consumer/fabricator is considerably less apparent, and the existence of a hedging programme is unlikely to convince lenders to reduce the credit premium. The benefit from hedging arises from a consistent and long-term reduction of earnings volatility, proved in hindsight (Figure F).

Gearing

Hedging not only decreases the cost of debt, it also increases the amount that can be borrowed (by increasing earnings stability). Increasing the gearing of the company reduces the effective marginal cost of capital, because debt investors expect a lower rate of return than equity investors.

1 "No arbitrage" is the dominant theory in market trading, but rational expectations are still relied upon to connect "real world" prices to market prices.
2 This is the frequently termed "yield curve slippage".
3 This example would be a bold use of the industrial option, and is used for illustration purposes only.
4 The delta is the hedge ratio of the option and is easily caclulated using the Black–Scholes formula. See Chapters 2 and 9 of this book.

E. The relationship between break-even cost, market price, market volatility and default

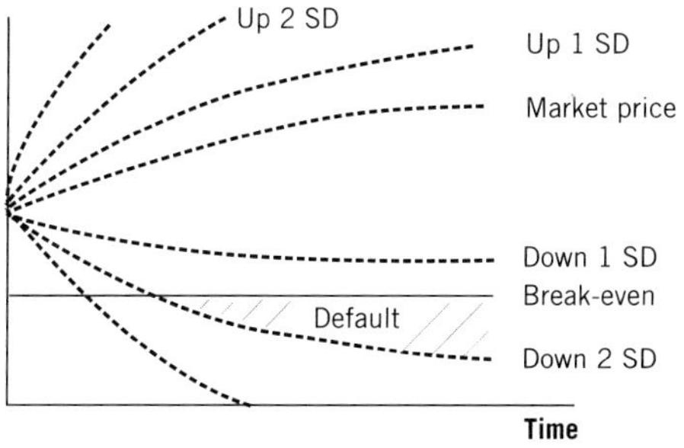

F. The relationship between default risk and borrowing cost (this evaluation is very precise in practice)

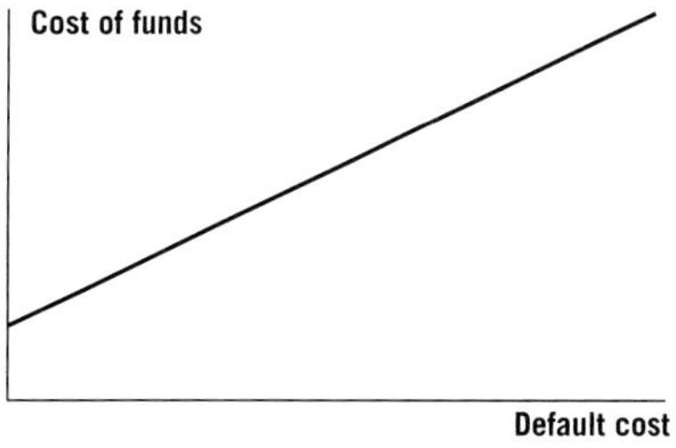

6. Alpha

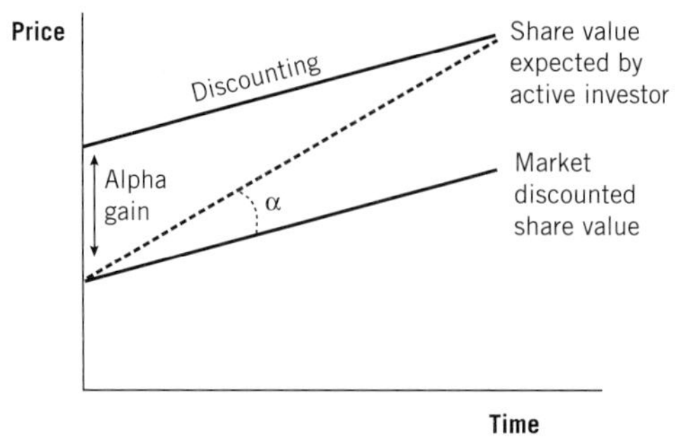

7. The risk/reward line that can be achieved from a basket of uncorrelated shares

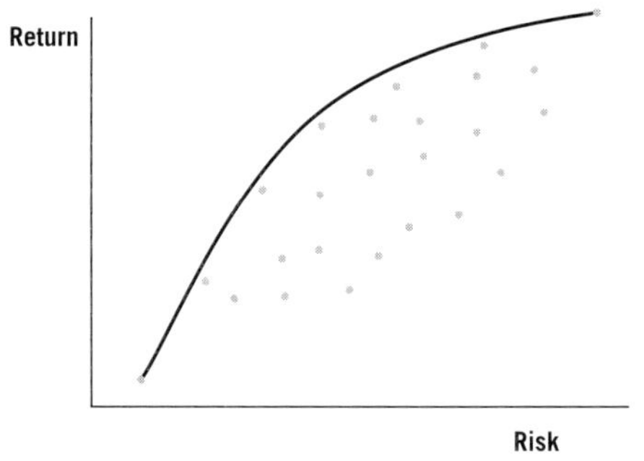

8. The potential movement of the efficient frontier, achieved by hedging

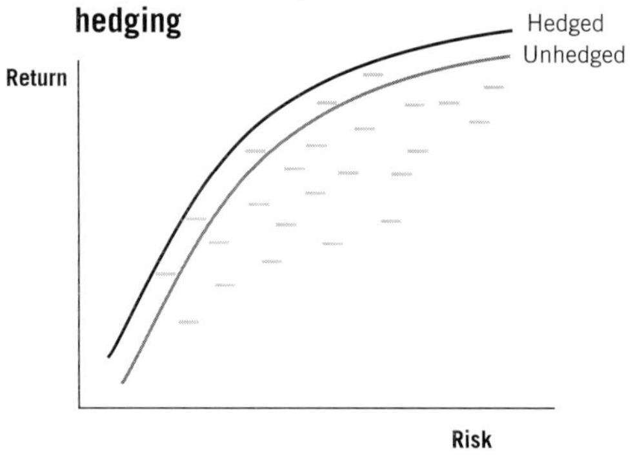

is expected to be more profitable than is discounted by the share prices in the sector and, secondly, that the *company* is expected to operate more profitably within the sector than is discounted by the individual share price (Figure 6). Metal price is frequently mixed up with alpha by investment analysts, and indeed metal prices *can* deliver an alpha gain. However, in almost all cases the rationale for seeking metal price risk is the correlation effect. And if the metal price is the source of alpha, then *direct* participation in the metals markets (eg, owning metal rather than owning metals companies) is the best form of exposure. (A complication here is that the covenants of equity funds often preclude activity outside of share price dealing.)

Correlation is the third most important variable after expected return and standard deviation of return. Correlation defines the extent to which changes in the value of risky assets are related to each other. In general, moves in share prices can be looked on as happening because of:

❑ *random risk,* ie, risk that has no identifiable relationship with other market factors; and

❑ *correlations* with the market portfolio of shares, and with other factors.

The volatility of a basket of truly randomly moving risky assets decreases as the portfolio size increases, and the risk is said to be diversified away. However, that portion of risk in each share that is correlated to the movement of the portfolio as a whole cannot be diversified away. For this reason, investors with large portfolios of shares are much more concerned with correlation than with random risk. (The most widely used share asset valuation theory, the capital asset pricing model, or CAPM,[6] uses correlation rather than standard deviation of return as its risk denominator.)

Just as positive correlation to the portfolio is undesirable, negative correlation is beneficial, and investors commonly search for shares and share sectors that are (at the time) negatively correlated to the stock index (Figure 7). This complicates the situation for metal shares (and therefore metal hedging) considerably, because there are times when investors will actively seek out metal price exposure.

The effects of positive correlation and negative correlation, and the fact that random risk is important to the smaller investor, make it dangerous to generalise about the optimum desired risk performance of the mining share. However, we can say that for each *investor criterion* – as opposed to each investor – there is an optimum portfolio.

The attainable portfolio performance for the standard share portfolio is called the efficient frontier, shown in Figure 8. Note that risk, in this case, is a measure specific to the investor, and depends on relative preference for lack of positive correlation, specific negative correlation, or random risk. It is not the generalised measure of risk generated by the CAPM model.

In the situation shown by the figure, provided that correlations remain unaltered, hedging can be used to move the points to the left and create a new (and better) efficient frontier.[7]

An important aspect of hedging in mining and, particularly, in the processing business is that hedging refines the ability to distinguish between company performances and make "alpha bets". It also changes the correlations. For example, a hedged company has a cost base and a net revenue that reflects *local* conditions; its general performance becomes more correlated with the local manufacturing sector, and less correlated with the international price of a commodity.

Negative correlations between share prices and market factors are surprisingly common, and are especially important in the manufacturing sector. For example, a processor will often experience reduced short-term profits when raw material prices rise. Correlations, in fact, tend to be *sporadic*. The phase difference between commodities, equities, bonds and cash is called the global liquidity cycle; and, just as prices are cyclic, so are correlations (Figure 9).

The effect of the correlation of a single stock to the market portfolio on the efficient frontier is shown in Figure 10.

It is clear from the above that investors must be able to picture the risks of a company in a way that is detailed enough to be useful, but also general enough to be applied to all potential investments. One way to do this is to chart company risks on a diagram. In Figure 11, the total importance of each factor is ranked at 100% and each is apportioned appropriately. The diagram is constructed so that the two major axes (return and general risk) are adjacent, and the main indifference curve can be constructed between them.

Figure 11 is one way of summarising the generic financial performance risk of the company. The purpose of the company is to deliver value (utility) to the shareholders. In theory, and given the choice, the shareholder base will reshuffle[8] to fit the profile of the company, ie, those with the best fit will outbid the others (Figure 13 overleaf).

By changing its hedge policy, the company changes all of the dimensions of risk and return on the diagram, and courts the appropriate investors. How can the company maximise shareholder utility by reference to this? Several things must happen. Firstly, there must be a direct transmission of strategy through to action across the whole company (this is discussed in detail later). Secondly, there must be a mutual communication of the needs of the shareholders, and the corporate strategy by which the company can deliver those needs. This communication is essential, because, if there is a systematic mismatch

9. Apparent correlation changes due to phase differences in economic cycles (very short-term measure used)

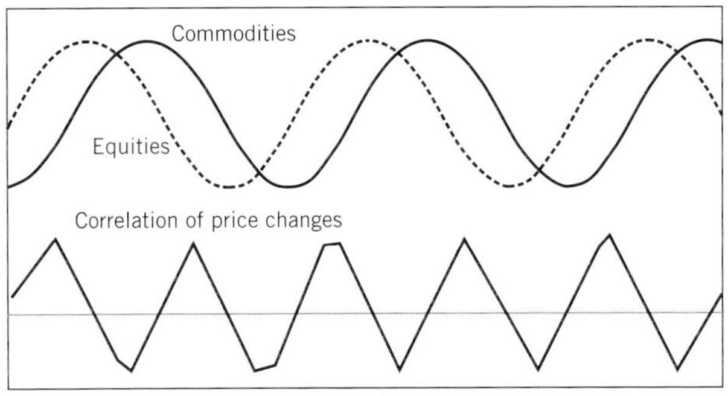

10. Addition of a single stock to the market portfolio, for the cases of positive, zero and negative correlation

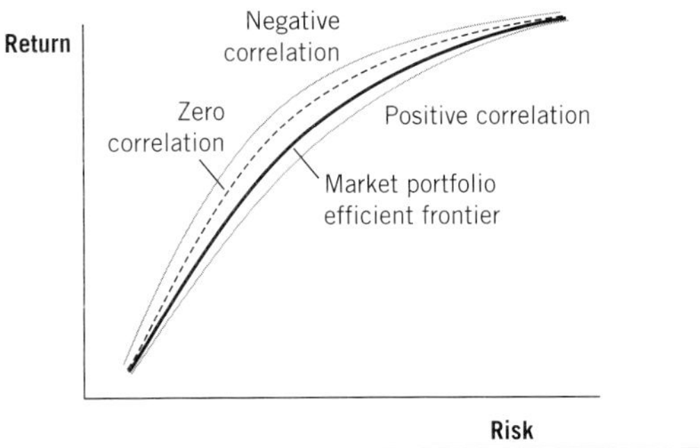

11. Risk map

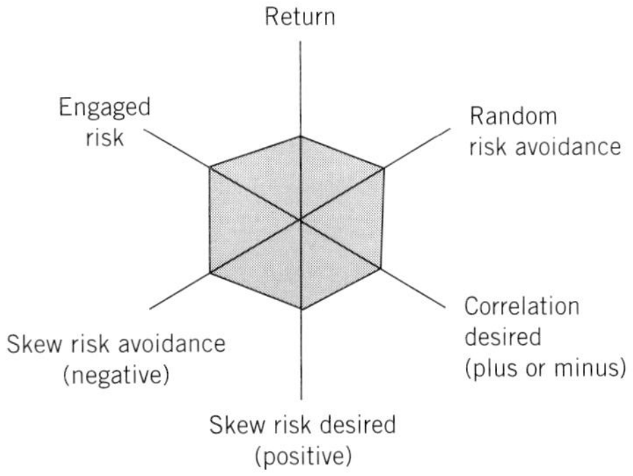

12. The risk/reward curves on the indifference map

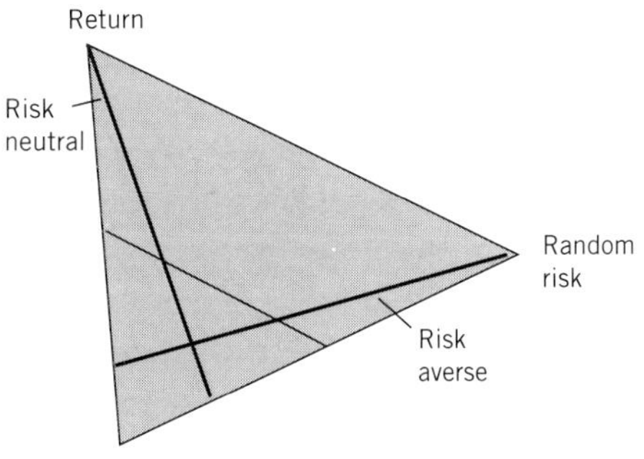

13. Investor migration

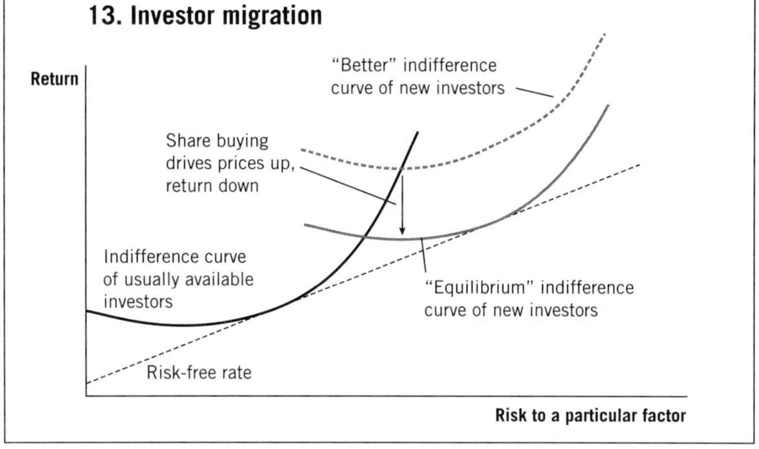

14. Front loading the revenue stream to gain cash from a new asset

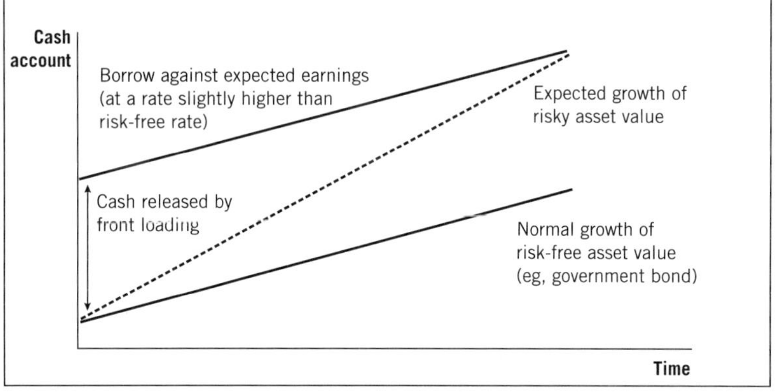

between the investor's interpretation of return/risk/correlation characteristics and the performance of the company, then the investor loses utility. This communication is increasingly common among mining companies (see Chapter 7 for a detailed example), some of which have indicated quite directly to investors that: "If you don't like our hedging, don't buy our shares!"

This section has looked at the company from the perspective of the needs of the investor. The next section links this to the search for, and communication of, corporate goals and corporate identity both within and outside of the company.

Corporate identity and goals

Whether companies decide to adapt their strategic policies to the perceived needs of investors, or whether they encourage the migration of investors that covet the company's existing risk profile, both they and the investor need to create an accurate map relating the business of the company to its risk profile. This can be done by identifying the driving force of the company – that is, the particular competitive advantage the company intends to exploit to deliver shareholder value.

In the mining and fabrication sector, the driving force of most companies can be characterised as one of the following:

- ❑ exploration;
- ❑ country expertise;
- ❑ extraction/processing technology;
- ❑ growth/financial engineering;
- ❑ size/long term; and
- ❑ production stability.

Below, we attempt to relate the risk management needs of each of these different types of company to its driving force and to the needs of investors.

EXPLORATION COMPANIES

Exploration companies create value by finding things. Their competitive advantage tends to be entrepreneurship, mobility, rapid response, very high average personal experience of employees and geological expertise (usually specific to a rock type). The role of exploration in mining has changed significantly over the last few years, and increasingly this sector is funded through a new investor base. So effective has this funding been that exploration no longer needs to be vertically integrated with a mining company to pay for the operations. In fact, exploration companies in recent years offer a good example of the effective and targeted delivery of a specific risk map to the appropriate investor base. The key to this has been the ability to realise value quickly once a find is made. This in turn has been made possible by "front loading"[9] the revenue stream through the hedging of price risk and the securitisation of the asset (Figure 14).

The share prices of exploration companies are capable of extraordinary rises (and falls). Subsequent events notwithstanding, an example might be Bre-X, which raised over \$2 billion before producing any revenue from the gold of deposits it claimed to have discovered in Indonesia.[10] Hedging is not the direct concern of an exploration company per se, but hedging becomes an issue if and when the company *changes* nature, as is common, by working the discovered body of ore.

Shareholder communication for this kind of company is quite simple, as the purpose of the company is obvious. A specific kind of investor is attracted – and is likely to exit once the company changes driving force, and look for new exploration companies to invest in. Timely communication of the strategy change is essential to maximise utility for the investor.

COUNTRY-EXPERTISE COMPANIES

Country-expertise companies are those which depend for their competitive advantage on a knowledge of the culture, working practices, risks, government, and financial system of a particular country. They develop contacts and influence to maintain smooth operations. This is a fascinating sector, because this company type has the most diverse roots and the most changeable nature. The companies in this sector present a wide array of types (size, other activities, country, etc), and hence this sector is well diversified except for one thing – metal price risk. Investors are bound to have different hedge requirements for these companies as they are often searching for "country alpha", ie, the assumption that it will be easier to operate in the country than is expected by the market. Some will wish to strip out the metal price risk and some will wish to keep it as a "leveraged metal play". The company response should be to hedge to optimise its performance according to internal targets (right growth rate, gearing, use of economic cycle, etc) and to communicate whatever overall risk strategy it uses to its investors. This is a wide enough asset class and investor class for there to be a smooth investor migration from share to share.

EXTRACTION/PROCESSING TECHNOLOGY COMPANIES

Technology companies create value by exploiting reserves or material that is inaccessible to competitors, and increasing the yield and quality of the product above that of competitors. In the metals sector, technology companies tend to evolve from size/production companies (see below) and tend to work within a small sector (a minor metal, or a small number of production sites). Investment in a technology company has an interesting effect in default, because the company asset becomes worthless (if they cannot exploit it, no-one can).

A technology company effectively has two divisions: a cash generator that relies on spent R&D money, and a research and investment function that relies on the cash stream. To continue to be successful as technology companies, these companies must continue to plough the profits from the cash generator into research. There are many instances where new technology cannot make any significant value gain and the technology company then becomes a production stability company (described later). Technology companies have a very specific position on the risk map. In particular, a good technology company will attract "alpha investors". The small size of technology risk companies exposes them to high negative skew and a high sensitivity to random risk. Therefore, aggressive hedging of metal price risk is *essential*. Investors requiring metal exposure can access it more efficiently by investing in other types of metal company.

GROWTH COMPANY

Growth companies create shareholder value by expanding the net asset base of the company. This is achieved by simultaneously acquiring and locking in a new revenue stream (by expansion, project acquisition and company acquisition) that is greater than its associated cost stream, and continuing this process as rapidly as possible. The need to borrow large amounts at cheap rates makes hedging *mandatory*. The expansion cycle is shown in Figure 15. In brief, money is borrowed and a producing activity is acquired/expanded. The net revenue stream is hedged and borrowed against (front loaded), releasing cash for a new acquisition. This is a highly effective strategy for a growth company, but it gives the company some quite specific attributes: very high exposure to liquidity crises (created by front-loading profit instead of leaving profit accrual as a cushion); the need to constantly grow; low exposure to metal price; and exposure to a high correlation between metal prices and operating costs.

No business can front-load profits better than one that creates a stable and monetised commodity. Hence, for the investor looking for growth companies in the general universe of shares, the metals mining sector is very significant. Of all the types of metals company, it is this sector in which the driving force (ie, being a *growth company*) is most likely to take precedence over the underlying activity (ie, being a *metals company*).

15. The expansion cycle

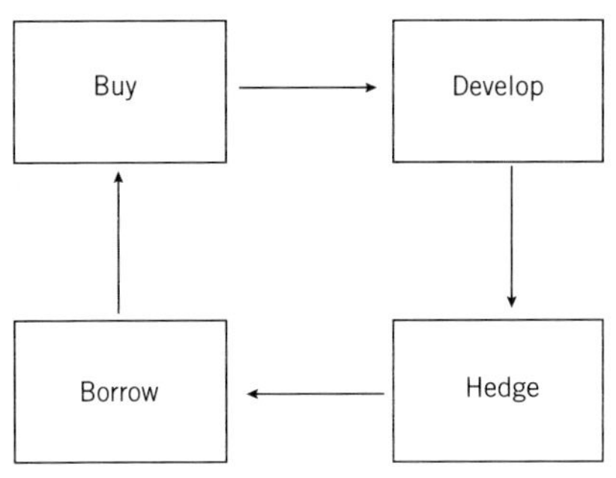

16. Potential mismatch between investor base and company performance in a growth company

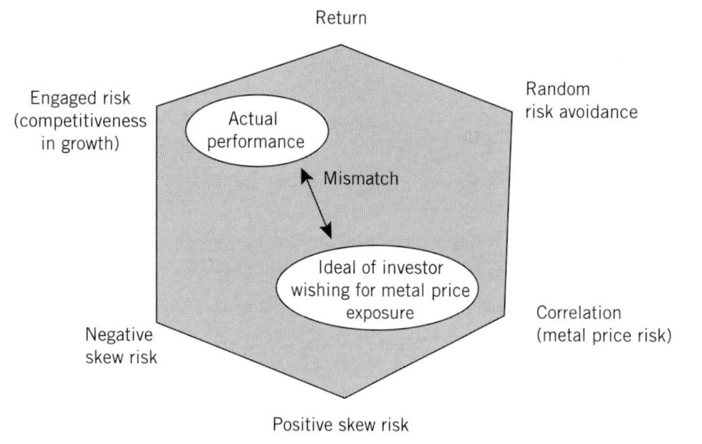

It follows that growth companies are those with the greatest need to educate and inform their shareholders about the nature of their metals price exposure (Figure 16).

SIZE/ LONG-TERM COMPANY

In these companies, size itself provides the competitive advantage. This is because the size of the company allows it to raise very large amounts of money at very cheap rates (equity money with a low risk premium, as well as debt money with a low credit premium). In the global investment markets, the investment timescale becomes ever shorter – yet the commitment required for very large metals projects remains very long term (10 years or more). This leaves a market niche for a company that is large enough to take on projects with a very long lead time to profitability, knowing that there are a stream of projects (invested in long ago) that can accrue the revenue to finance the debt stream. In the mining sector, this type of company relies on a relative scarcity of competition in purchasing very large deposits with low operating costs. (It follows that there are only a small number of companies in this class.)

The growth of the "growth companies", as described above, is a constant threat to size companies, because the growth companies can pay more for the asset if they can gain access to the expansion cycle shown in Figure 15. For this reason, the size companies often focus on buying assets that cannot easily be hedged and front loaded[11] (ie, projects that are very long term, have unstable costs, a high capital cost or unhedgeable types of metal, etc).

The prevailing strategy for the size/long-term companies is to maintain a stronghold in the lowest cash-cost quartile of metals production. Assuming that the net revenue stream available from an ore body has an effect on its purchase cost, then the assets purchased must have a high ratio of capital cost (purchase, royalties, development, sunk cost) to running cost. These are properties that the growth companies are less well placed to compete for, as the costs of debt service precede the revenues – whereas the running costs are simultaneous with the revenue stream.

The asset type has a strong effect on metal price exposure. The effect of metals price risk on the net asset value (present value of revenue stream minus cost stream) is considerably less than the high cash cost producer but, because this company type tends to hedge very little, the short-term revenue stream is highly exposed. Therefore, the share price is likely to vary lightly with metal price, while the annual profit is likely to be very strongly affected. This invokes the question of the relationship between dividend and profit – a relationship that is highly dependent on investor type.[12] While this type of company can in principle hold a single asset, in practice there is no mechanism for it to become a single-asset size/long-term company except by decline. Because this kind of company must, by definition, be able to raise very large amounts of funds at cheap rates, they tend to be blue-chip companies with a very strong historic heritage, growth companies that have run out of opportunities or investors, or country companies that have grown organically over a long period.

There is no glib answer to the hedging needs of this type of company. However, because so many of the other company types *need* to hedge, it could be argued that this company type is apposite for the investor that *wants* metal exposure (for either alpha or correlation reasons). The exposure of the company to metals price risk is already highly diluted by diversification and the low cash cost, and therefore this kind of company does not need to hedge to protect cash liquidity.

There is, however, a very important hedge item that is frequently overlooked by these companies. When metal prices are high, investors may wish to reduce metal price exposure (and correlation to other companies in this asset class), and they will certainly want to "make alpha" by being *short* instead of long on metal. Companies that do not hedge in the top quartile of the price cycle are not maximising shareholder utility. If the metal price is cyclical then

17. Changes in stock alpha in relation to market price of metal in cyclical market

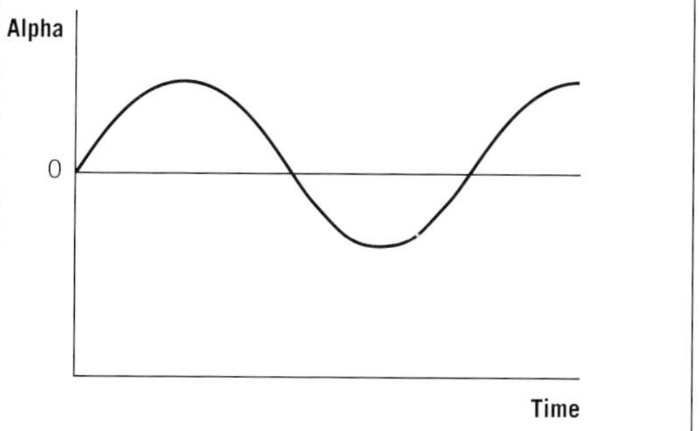

18. Evolution of production stability company

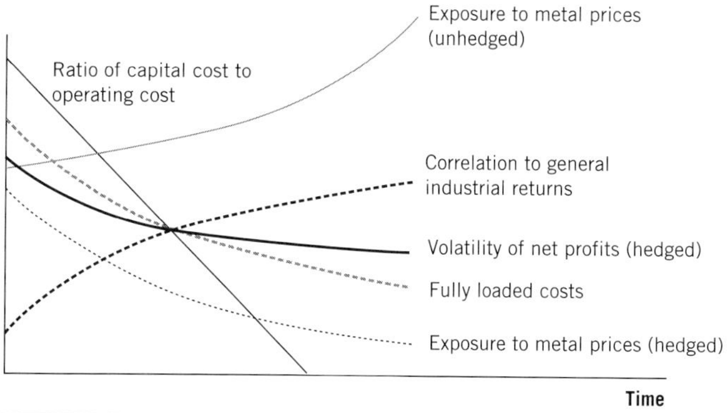

there is an alpha and correlation gain to be made by hedging, as the hedge makes money if the price falls (Figure 17). If the price is not cyclical (ie, it follows random walk with no autocorrelation, or reference to the historical average price), then the purchase of new productive assets can restore any desired upside price exposure.

Size companies have unassailable positions in the short term, and tolerant investors. However their position in the lowest cost quartile is constantly threatened by the exploration companies and the growth companies. To maintain their position it is important to partially hedge when forward commodity prices are in the highest historic quartile.

PRODUCTION STABILITY

The competitive advantage of production stability companies is *cost*. Production stability companies evolve out of country or technology companies, or (in manufacturing) from companies that have secured a strong wholesale or retail franchise. By and large, therefore, this type of company is a mature business, trading on a cost advantage. Low cost and stability are at a premium (Figure 18).

The nature of production stability companies is that they are low margin, high volume and undiversified. In addition, the debt costs and depreciation are low in relation to cash costs. They are highly vulnerable to downward price moves, as their margin is low already and there is no "war chest" to tide them through bad years, as there is for size companies. The vulnerability of cashflow means that negative skew must be protected against. Frequently, the financial exposures of production companies are hard to hedge, because the small net revenue stream means that the hedge must be fine-tuned. Here, it is important to take account of the positive correlation between production cost and output price. There is also a very high degree of optionality and price leverage in the risk exposure. Production companies can, in some instances hedge by selling call options and, in fact, this is the company class which is in the best position to actively use its industrial options to exploit market conditions. The industrial option in this case is essentially to produce more (or not) and faster (or not). The hedge infrastructure required to make use of industrial options is described later in this chapter.

Processing companies have a different risk profile to that of mining companies, because they do not have the underlying risk of the asset base. Therefore, the economic risk posed by metals prices is minimal (provided that their customers cannot easily substitute their product for one made from another material), while transaction and translation risks are high. Rolling mills are a good example of this company type; here, the *process* of producing standard products has become a commodity of sorts in its own right.

IMPLICATIONS: COMMUNICATING COMPANY TYPE

These examples of company types are intended to be descriptive rather than definitive. The important point is that there is so much diversity in the metals and mining manufacturing sector, that the investor *must* be able to identify where the company is on the risk map by identifying the driving force. Finding out in retrospect is not good enough. One method of communicating driving force is the expression of corporate goals, such as "we will grow", "we will invest in Ghana", "we will continue to maintain our position in the lowest cost quartile", etc. Together with the kind of analysis attempted above, these statements provide enough information for the interested investor to identify a company's position on the risk map.

Corporate risk infrastructure – where should risk be managed ?

Now we have a risk map of the investor, the risk map for the company, and a reconciliation of the company goal. How should hedges be implemented in practice so as to create maximum shareholder utility?

By far the most common and practical method is to run a hedge book within the treasury, and to overlay the treasury profit/loss with the departmental profit/loss. This is a reasonable approach - especially considering that many companies have not reached even this stage - but it is only a partial solution. To really drive the company forward requires a far greater commitment to a hedge infrastructure. An overlay hedge system creates a broad smoothing of the perceived aggregate risk of the company to market prices, but it is extremely difficult to feed *back* the hedge results into the business. (Indeed, the information on aggregate risk tends to deteriorate in quantity and quality as it flows up through the hierarchy.)

A good hedge infrastructure has a two-way information flow: information about the risks assumed travels up, market parameters travel down. With more information about risk and opportunity it is possible to *affect the physical movement of material* in a manner that uses market forces most effectively.

While there are certain common ground rules, hedge infrastructure is highly idiosyncratic in a metals business, particularly downstream businesses, and it is not possible to cover all the permutations here. There are also numerous factors in promoting an efficient infrastructure, including efficient data aggregation and reporting, automation, connectivity between divisions, unambiguous division of responsibility and non-reliance on individuals. But information flow is surely the single factor of greatest importance, and here we aim to demonstrate how information flow can be created and how it can be used most advantageously.

The idea behind the approach is extremely simple. It is to break down the business into very small cost accounting units, formalise the transfer pricing between the units with the greatest possible reference to external prices, and give the units flexibility on the risk management tactics they adopt. The business operates within the following framework:

❑ Every section or division of the business has a purchasing manager, a process/inventory manger, and a sales manager (one person can wear more than one hat, but the roles must be distinct).

❑ Material cost is transfer priced "at market" from one stage to the other.

❑ The value date for at market transfer should approximate to the time taken to convert the material into the commodity, or the last commodity-indexed value date against which it can be priced as product.

❑ Each stage bids and offers to the other on a committed forward premium, or value-added, basis. Interdepartmental contracts should be as long as possible.

❑ Each stage is allowed limited physical and hedge access to the external market.

❑ Hedge positions must be justifiable and of a size and tenor commensurate with the throughput.

❑ Hedges and exposures are passed up through the hierarchy, and any aggregate risk (split into transaction, translation and economic risks) is overlay hedged by the treasury.

Note that, provided the necessary information can be captured at each boundary or "node" of the business, it is not necessary to alter the internal divisions of responsibility. What is important is that risk is sufficiently localised for opportunity to be perceived on a transaction-by-transaction basis. This ideal structure is represented in Figure 19.

19. The modularisation of the financial functions of the processes

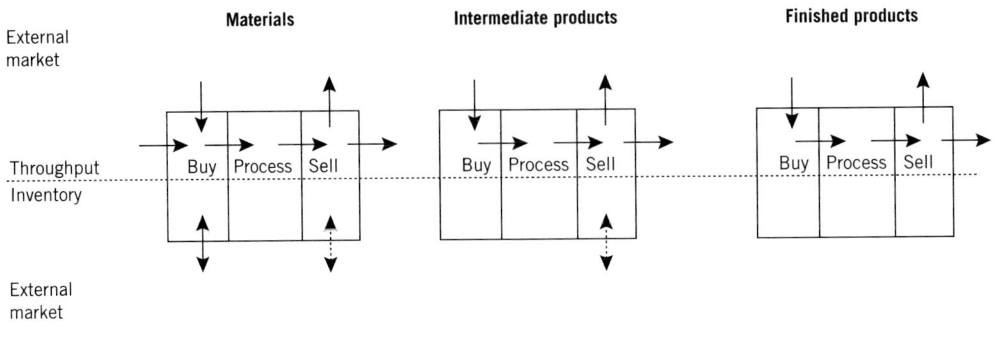

Let us consider a linear process in which a raw material is processed at one end of a business and a finished product is produced at the other. There are several internal stages, some of which purchase or produce an intermediate product that is also made externally by other companies and has the characteristics of a commodity (such as a transparent external price).

To make the example tangible, let us consider an integrated secondary smelter and foundry in aluminium. This business involves buying scrap aluminium, melting it, casting to ingots, transporting to the foundry at a separate site, melting and casting into artefacts.

How could this company gain the *automatic* ability to increase value in a way that does not involve a long communication process, and which could not be replicated by the standard treasury overlay hedge mechanism? Consider these situations:

1) *The purchase manager has identified a correlation with a six-week lag from the London Metals Exchange (LME) secondary aluminium price to the scrap price movement.* He therefore increases his scrap buying when LME prices rise, and hedge sells on the LME to protect his inventory value.
2) *The market has a pronounced backwardation for forward prices dated three months out.* The scrap inventory manager and inventory manager lend forward/forward. If the backwardation decreases, they borrow back. If the backwardation widens and prices feed through to casting prices, they borrow back and sell the casting based on the nearby price. If the casting cannot be sold, passing on the cost of a nearby quotation period, they stop making castings, make LME deliverable ingots and deliver into the short position.
3) *The market develops the maximum contango dictated by arbitrage.* The inventory manager (with treasury support) buys up a large supply of scrap and simultaneously hedges its value by a forward sale on the exchange. As his future intake will be priced "at market", and as his all-in costs are less than his hedge sale price, he makes a saving. (Here, we assume that his physical storage cost is low, whereas the market price discounts storage at commercial rates.) He must be sure to cover his backwardation risk by either ensuring that he can deliver out his material or by pricing out his finished product using the nearby LME price.
4) *Ingot composition specification premiums become variable.* The ingot inventory manger does not know which material he will need. He therefore shortens his bid period and committed volume and destocks. The scrap inventory manager increases his inventory to ensure that he can meet all ingot specifications. Both wait until they can sell the highest premium material and appropriate ingots are made. In effect, this process "upstreams" the stock.

The fundamental change here is a shift from "all-in" cost-based pricing, to "pass through" pricing of all factors for which there are external benchmarks (such as material price). This change in the internal transfer pricing method also creates some subtle changes in external pricing methods, and the relationship between the (external) buyer and the seller.

Let us examine this in relation to a second example, this time of a *buyer* of semi-fabricated product that wishes to secure a steady price. This buyer considers changing the way prices are agreed between himself and his external supplier:

1) *Old method* The buyer purchased from the seller on a long-term contractual fixed price basis but with varying volumes, on a price that was agreed to be "fair". However, when raw material prices fell, the buyer often either reduced buying volumes, cancelled his orders, or negotiated a discount.
2) *New method* The buyer purchases from the seller, on a long-term contractual basis, product that has only a small flexibility of volume. The price is equal to the market price *at the time of delivery*, plus a value-added premium that is agreed at the time the contract is signed. In addition to this, the seller engages in a market contract with the buyer. This is a separate contract. The buyer then has a fixed net price for all material that has an associated hedge.

The new system creates a material flow and cashflow that is the same as in the old system. However, the risk of abrogation on the physical contract is considerably less, because the physical transaction is at market and will not be significantly undercut (the volatility of value-added premium is a lot lower than the volatility of the raw materials). Although technically there is a risk of a default on the hedge, an abrogation of a hedge is treated as an actionable default rather than as an acceptable cancellation.

Clearly the seller makes a significant gain, because he has eliminated what was, in effect, a short option position. However, the buyer also gains because he receives quotes on a slowly changing value-added premium, rather than an "all in" price that is either very inefficient (because the possible market price changes are loaded in) or rapidly varying. The effect is much greater price transparency, allowing quotes to be compared much more efficiently.

Note also that both buyer and seller can make a credit and efficiency gain by executing the hedge with a bank, instead of arranging it between themselves. This is because banks have strong credit ratings, and regulation makes it impossible for them to renege on hedge contracts. In fact, this is usually what happens soon after contracts are deconstructed in this way.

Simply through changing the quotation mechanism, the short-term risk that the seller had hitherto absorbed is removed and the buyer's risks (always there, but spread out over time), have become immediately visible. Risk management has clearly been pushed downstream.

Now we can see more clearly how risk infrastructure can lead to changes in a business. Suppose that the purchased product could be made from another material. With the new purchasing method, the purchaser receives (stable) value-added bids from different sellers. He can attach these bids to the forward curves of the market prices to compute available total prices in the future (Figure 20). He then evaluates his process costs, and bids on to the next stage. As the competing product will have a different value to the current one (it may be lighter, for example), the buyer at the next processing stage within the same company evaluates the net of value minus cost and, if there is an available gain, he schedules and commits to switch material at some *determined* time in the future.

These examples are much simplified, but they show the effect that risk infrastructure can have on a business, and the key role of information flow. Treasury overlay hedges cannot achieve the same effect. However, they do have advantages with certain types of price risk, as we discuss in Panel 2.

20. Effect of forward price curves on material scheduling

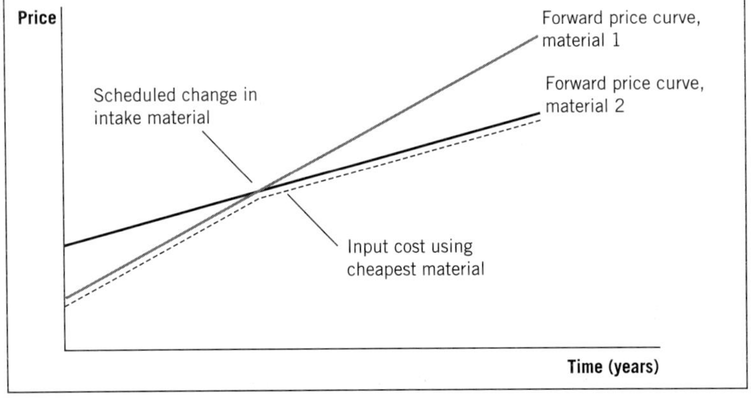

Control

Without a strong infrastructure, it is impossible to control hedging operations of any complexity. Almost all of the major control failures in banks and corporations involved in risk management have resulted from a breakdown in the transmission of information caused by weak infrastructure (see Panel 2, Chapter 3).

Furthermore, if *all* a control system does is control, then it will not be actively used for making business decisions. The control system should really be a refinement of the risk infrastructure.[13]

The purposes of control are threefold:

❑ protect against the implementation of actions that are knowingly suboptimal to the firm;
❑ protect against clerical mistakes; and
❑ protect against a misunderstanding of the possible outcomes of an action.

The first is the most important. Expressed in this way, it is far stronger than controlling fraud – it permits only those actions that have *beneficial* effects on the firm. The infrastructure described in the previous section creates a devolution of responsibility that enables the flux of small events to alter the course of the whole company, but it does so in a way that is visible at the operating levels of the business (the exclusion of invisible domains, such as new material, new countries and new products is of importance). In this way the firm "runs itself" in normal operation, and the job of senior management changes, from trying to make the small decisions more efficient, to the taking of (holistic, strategic) decisions that cannot be made using the particular information available at any of the series of small steps that the infrastructure engenders.

There is clearly a spectrum of suboptimal action, with fraud at one extreme. For virtually all companies, small-scale fraud is virtually impossible to prevent. At the same time, a sound risk infrastructure makes large-scale fraud by a *single* individual extremely difficult to enact. It also helps resolve conflicts of interest by enfranchising staff who, with the devolved power structure that infrastructure can create, add value in a visible manner. Imagine, for example, that a manager spots an opportunity that can be captured by hedging but which would otherwise be too risky for a small division of the company. Only if

PANEL 2

FOREIGN EXCHANGE RISK MANAGEMENT AS A TREASURY OVERLAY

In the main text we stated that the greatest transparency and stability of quote makes for the greatest efficiency in finding the best supplier. This has an important consequence for the currency of the quote. For maximum stability, the quote on the value added should be in the currency of cost, not in the natural currency of the buyer. This means that the relative attractiveness of different suppliers will vary with the strength of their local currency (a well-known effect in business!).

While changes in underlying commodity prices hit all users of the same commodity by the same amount, the effect of foreign exchange movement is specific to the country of origin. From the perspective of the buyer, random moves in foreign exchange rates cause random changes in the relative competitiveness of suppliers. This risk is hard to manage within business divisions, and the foreign exchange risk to a competitive position has to be overlay hedged by the treasury.

The overlay creates a cross-subsidy or cost to the various divisions of the business that is not fed back into their internal budgets. It is simply a smoothing function, and protracted rises in the value of a supplier's local currency will, rightly, cause budgetary pressure on the divisions. If this is extreme enough to cause losses in the division, then the decision of whether to close[1] the division will be taken at treasury/strategy level, taking into consideration the possibility that currency may revert to purchasing power parity levels.

It is the fact that foreign exchange risk does not affect all competing companies in the same way, but has a differential effect on different companies, that makes the process of risk managing it so different from the risk management of raw material prices.

1 In many cases the short-term view created by the hedge infrastructure cannot guide a long-term decision. It implicitly assumes that the marginal cost of production increases with volume. Where economy of scale or acceleration on the production experience curve can be altered, a strategic overview is required.

the hedge is precisely and simultaneously tied to the action can the strategy be entertained, but to do this the division must have access to a market hedging book. This hedge book need not be linked directly to the external market. If desired, it could be structured as an internal hedge account that flows through the treasury (which may, or may not, lay off the hedge in the external market).

One reason large-scale fraud has remained unprevented in companies is that those most likely to understand and have reservations about colleagues' activities also suffer from the strongest conflicts of interest. There is often no incentive, in fact a very strong disincentive, to be a "whistle blower", and this may be aggravated by a tendency for managers to turn a blind eye to the activities of profitable departments. This suggests the most important rule when designing a control system: irregularities must be reported through the infrastructure *automatically*, without any reliance on human communication or judgement at any one step of the information path. Irregularities would include large positions in relation to prescribed limits; large ledger movements in relation to reported profits; increases in the level of bank guarantees and credit exceptions. Many banks are now creating systems that operate according to this rule – even in simpler corporate trading systems, the rule holds true.

Banks also tend to build in several fail-safes to their risk infrastructure systems, so that if one information path fails, the correct operation of another path will report a mismatch. Although clerical errors are frequent, only a very small percentage of errors carry over to the next day, and the percentage lasting to the next day (after which time the likelihood of detection falls) is extremely small. Despite some recent heavily publicised disasters, the banking systems are generally very strong – and very costly. It makes sense for market users to leverage off the bank risk infrastructure. For example, if the original documentation is suitably specified,[14] then the corporate trading can be automatically restricted in the following ways:

- ❑ only authorised traders may trade;
- ❑ only authorised signatories can sign, and these may not include traders;
- ❑ credit limits may not be exceeded;
- ❑ trades at off-market prices are either disallowed or heavily restricted and generate exception reports that are delivered to the control department of the company; and
- ❑ telephone taping, trader recaps, trade confir-

mations and monthly statements deter wrongdoing.

In addition to this, traders in banks now have increased professional responsibility for estimating when personnel at companies do not trade *ultra vires*, or create risks for the company that are wholly inappropriate or excessive. While some responsibility exists through guidelines and precedents, actual malpractices are prevented by internal company rules (signed compliance manuals) or local regulation (eg, the Securities and Futures Association); supranational regulation is, and will remain, minimal.

Unfortunately, few corporations make use of their bank's investment in risk infrastructure. The exchange of documents between companies is at present an extremely inefficient process, with reams of largely irrelevant clauses that are never invoked, concerning market technicalities. Lawyers, who do not necessarily understand the core risks in the business, often concentrate on the details of credit default and market disruption conditions. So laborious is this process that neither party is keen to add the rules that really count, such as trader/limit authorisation.

This chapter has focused on the micro-management of risk. But the approach also helps firms measure risk at the highest level. The reporting of risk should be in the form of "weight-rate-date", ie, the amount of material or currency (possibly weighted by a probability of delivery), the price and the date of delivery. No matter what proprietary system is used to calculate and manage risk at local level, the upload must be in weight-rate-date form. The totals for the divisions are aggregated through the hierarchy until there is a single final figure for the company as a whole (Figure 21).

The company need not invest in writing a large static computer system. What is necessary is that the upload of data is straightforward. This necessitates a simple and common software, a common flat file or relational database, common network, hardware and protocols. A physical business will have to devise proprietary systems for their actual operations; however, the proprietary systems should be written with standard conventions (data dictionary, security access, good coding practice) so that they can be modified. (Given this, the systems will in fact gradually migrate from the business area managers into the hands of the Information Technology managers.)

The situation becomes more complicated when options and more complex derivatives are used to execute a strategic overlay hedge.[15] The weight-rate-date upload provides a good snapshot of risk, but gives no indication of the leverage that has been incurred - and which may cause sudden losses if there are large market movements (Figure 22).

Banks use a number of scenario-based analyses to cope with this problem, and the methodology they have developed to measure the daily value at risk (VAR) of contract portfolios is spreading to corporations.[16] Fraud apart, it is trading short positions in leveraged instruments *in the absence of an industrial option to back the position* that tends to cause the largest "derivative disasters". For obvious reasons, this is more common in financial institutions than in industrial corporations.

Of course, the risk infrastructure that we have described only represents the immediate risks to the firm. While it may be a pointer to the economic risk, it only measures the risks that are visible from current trade flow. The opportunities and threats from materials, products, locations and industries that have no current interface with the business are not included.

It is trying to cope with this level of risk that most often leads to the final factor in risk control

21. Hierarchic aggregation of risk

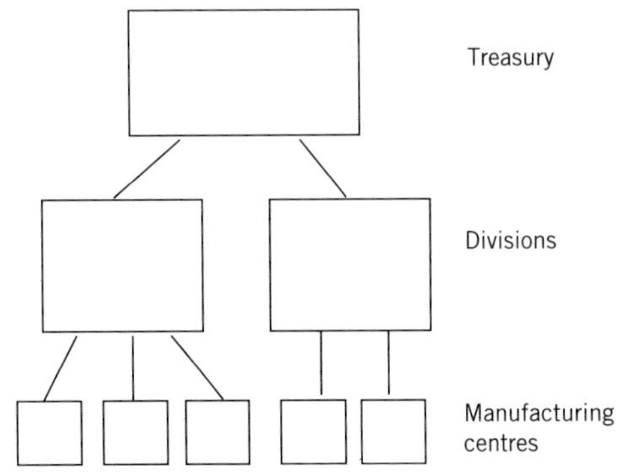

22. Example of a risk scenario with a snapshot at the current price and time

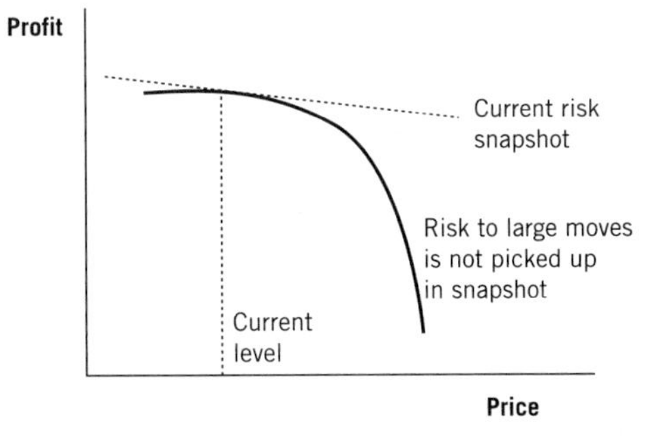

– *unintentional* effects of risk management. These are rarely a problem at operating level, because transaction-based risk management is directly connected to material flow and identifiable risks. Senior managers, however, have to take strategic decisions that are not intuitively obvious from the information flowing through the infrastructure; for example, to contract one business area in favour of another. Many of the economic (as opposed to transactional) market risks are similarly intangible, and can often only be understood by looking at the activity of the firm within a broader framework, rather than by analysing its cashflows.

Conclusion

In the case of dedicated trading companies, risk analysis is now a fine art, and financial risks are aggressively monitored and reduced. For many corporations, risk management remains quite primitive. This chapter discussed the two main reasons for this: firstly, because it is not certain what risk profile the shareholders actually want; and secondly, the risk faced is hard to analyse because risk information is not gathered at an operational level.

Gradually, but inevitably, the approaches to risk management developed in trading houses, investment institutions and major mining companies will influence the practice of risk management in smaller companies and major manufacturers. Risk management for the corporate treasurer will evolve, from a subjective evaluation of operating risks, to an automatic evaluation and hedging of operating risks plus an information-led strategic approach to economic risk.

1 *That is, the forward hedge, by far the most actively traded instrument. The other derivatives are refined versions of the forward hedge.*

2 *A recent review of the arguments as they apply to corporations (including, but not only, commodity corporations) is provided by George Fenn et al., "Does Corporate Risk Management Create Shareholder Value?: A Survey of Economic Theory and Evidence", in* Financial Risk and the Corporate Treasury: New Developments in Strategy and Control, *Risk Publications (1997), pp. 13–32.*

3 *This can be explained by a mathematical theory called "the central limit theory".*

4 *Strictly speaking, debtholders' interests are not important when considering investor utility. However, they are important in practice, particularly for metal companies.*

5 *Beta is the correlation of the stock to the relevant asset, usually the market portfolio.*

6 *When considering investment within a sector, correlation to the sector is of greatest importance and for this analysis a theory called Arbitrage Pricing Theory (APT) must be used.*

7 *Note that, if metal prices are negatively correlated to stock market prices, then hedging can reduce utility. By precisely specifying the risk axis, the effect on utility of hedging can be determined in all cases.*

8 *This can be viewed from the company perspective as a share price optimisation exercise. The most suitable investors will pay the highest price for the shares.*

9 *"Front loading" simply means bringing forward the net revenue stream and turning it into cash by borrowing against it.*

10 *At the time of going to press, Bre-X underwent a well-publicised collapse in share price.*

11 *Note that accounting for profits via accrual of revenue rather than present value of asset is an essential practice for the "size" companies. The increasing trend towards securitising and present valuing, and the potential practice of the valuation of the option value of uneconomic resources, is a direct threat to this type of company.*

12 *Institutional investors are generally indifferent to dividend (Fisher separation), but private investors are not.*

13 *Control generally applies purely to hedging. However, as many companies now actively use market factors in contract negotiations, those that do not may find themselves at a systematic disadvantage. When this happens, ignoring the terminal markets becomes a control issue.*

14 *In fact, this is rare. As we note in the main text, hedgers usually simply assume that their bank will follow "best practice", and banks are unwilling to add complications to trading arrangements unless they are specifically requested by the client.*

15 *The problem tends not to arise when the hedge is applied directly to an industrial option, as even if the extent of the industrial option is misjudged its general action is not often misunderstood.*

16 For example, see Mary Ellen Stocks, "VAR: A Risk Measurement Tool for Corporate Treasurers", in Financial Risk and the Corporate Treasury: New Developments in Strategy and Control, *Risk Publications (1997), pp. 13–32.*

BIBLIOGRAPHY

Brealey, R. and S. Myers, 1996, *Principles of Corporate Finance*, McGraw Hill.

Copeland, T., 1995, *Valuation: Measuring and Managing the Value of Companies*, J. Wiley.

Copeland, T. and F. Weston, 1988, *Financial Theory and Corporate Policy*, Addison Wesley.

Elton, E. and M. Gruber, 1991, *Modern Portfolio Theory and Investment Analysis*, J. Wiley.

Hayes, R. and S. Wheelwright, 1984, *Restoring Our Competitive Edge - Competing through Manufacturing*, J. Wiley.

Markovitz, H., 1959, *Portfolio Selection: Efficient Diversification of Investments*, J. Wiley.

Phillips, D., et al., 1987, *Operations Research - Principles and Practice*, J. Wiley.

7

American Barrick Resources Corporation

Managing Gold Price Risk

Peter Tufano and Jon Serbin
Harvard University

In this chapter we reproduce, with minor revisions, a detailed study of the gold hedging strategies of an individual corporation. The bulk of the study deals with risk management techniques used by American Barrick (now known as Barrick Gold Corporation) between 1983 and 1992, and compares the corporation's approach to the more general strategies on hedging with prices utilised by the industry. Panel 1 overleaf brings the story up to date, and describes some controversial hedging decisions (and reactions to them) which have kept the corporation in the news.

Background

During 1992, the financial team of Toronto-based American Barrick Resources Corporation, one of the world's fastest-growing and most financially successful gold mining concerns, met regularly to review strategic and tactical issues related to managing the firm's exposure to gold price risk. Many major gold mines prided themselves on hedging none of the price risk of their output. If unhedged, a gold mine's sole output (and hence its profits, cashflows and stock price) was tied to gyrations in the price of gold. However, American Barrick had in place a gold hedging programme that was an integral and much-publicised part of the firm's corporate strategy. In an environment of falling gold prices, the firm's hedge position had allowed it to profit handsomely and to sell its commodity output at prices well above market rates. For example, in 1992 American Barrick produced and sold over 1,280,000 ounces of gold at an average price of $422 per ounce, while the market price was about $345 per ounce.[1]

American Barrick's gold hedging programme, and indeed all the corporate finance and treasury functions of the $4 billion market capitalisation enterprise, were managed by a trio of relatively young but experienced financial executives: Gregory Wilkins (executive vice president and chief financial officer), Robert Wickham (vice president, finance) and Randall Oliphant (treasurer). Wickham and Oliphant were responsible for the day-to-day management of American Barrick's highly regarded hedging programme, and reported to and worked closely with Wilkins. Gregory Wilkins and Robert Wickham had been with the firm since its start-up, and Randall Oliphant had joined the firm in 1987.

The gold hedging programme was a distinguishing and permanent characteristic of the firm's strategy, and there was no discussion of abandoning the activity. Nevertheless, the implementation of the hedging programme raised a number of issues, and American Barrick's latest gold find, the Meikle Mine, naturally brought to the forefront questions of when, how much, and how to hedge its gold production. The recently announced Meikle Mine Development Project required capital investments exceeding $180 million and was projected to yield 400,000 ounces of gold annually for 11 years, beginning in 1996.

In addition, the processing of unexpectedly rich ore bodies would increase production to a level much higher than was anticipated. While this development was good news, the firm's output would then be hedged far less than planned. Putting on a new hedge position in an environment of low gold prices and low interest rates challenged the finance team's ingenuity, and its commitment to its hedging programme.

American Barrick Resources Corporation

Peter Munk, a successful Canadian entrepreneur and financier, was the chairman, chief executive officer and founder of American Barrick.

PANEL 1

UPDATE ON BARRICK GOLD CORPORATION

Peter Tufano

The American Barrick Resources Corporation of the 1992 case study has transformed itself into today's Barrick Gold Corporation. Beginning in 1993, the firm proclaimed itself a "growth company" in presentations to analysts and investors and, to date, its performance has lived up to this claim. From 1992 to 1995, the firm's reserves grew by 59%, production by 138% and operating cashflow by 42%. In the decade ending December 1995, Barrick's stock grew by 42% per annum, three times the rate of the S&P 500 Index and four times that of the Toronto Stock Exchange Gold and Precious Minerals Index.

To fuel its growth, Barrick continued its acquisition strategy, most prominently in its battle for control of LAC Minerals in 1994. Through this acquisition, Barrick added 13 million ounces of reserves, much of which was outside North America. In addition, the aggressive development programme also targeted Asia and West Africa as sites for future development. This broadened geographical strategy, dubbed "expanding our frontiers" in the 1995 annual report, was reflected in the firm dropping "American" from its name.

Barrick's ability to acquire new properties, and its success in taking over LAC, was due to financial strength. While much of this strength was a result of the firm's good fortune on the Goldstrike property (as described in the main text), part of its superior financial performance was attributable to its hedging programme. In the period 1993–95, Barrick realised an average price of $406 per ounce on its sales of gold, which was 8% above the market average of $376. This differential translated into additional pre-tax revenues of $191 million in these three years.

From the end of the period described in the case study until early 1996, Barrick maintained the hedging strategy described, relying on spot-deferred contracts to protect its output prices. At the end of the period of the case study, Barrick faced the "problem" of having richer ore than planned, and thus would have been underhedged if it had not adjusted its hedge positions. At that time, it did make the adjustment, and it subsequently maintained its policy of hedging 100% of the following three years of production. Its contracts of choice remained spot-deferred contracts, which gave Barrick the choice of delivering on the forward sale contract or rolling it over to another period.

Late 1995 and early 1996 was an extraordinary time for gold. Spot prices rose above $400 for the first time since 1990, but more importantly the premium that mines received for selling gold forward (contango) dropped, as the gold lease rate rose relative to the interest rate (see Chapter 1 of this book). The low forward-selling premium made the expected economic return of selling gold forward unattractive, compared with historical levels. In this environment, Barrick made a decision in late 1995 to scale back its hedging:

Although he had had no prior experience in the gold mining business, he had created and guided one of the world's premier and fastest-growing gold mining firms. From its entry into the business in 1983, American Barrick had grown from an equity market capitalisation of $46 million to one of about $5 billion by the end of 1992, ranking it as Canada's eighth-largest publicly traded company. From 1984 to 1992, its annual production grew from 34,000 ounces to 1.325 million ounces, and its proven and probable reserves increased from 322,000 ounces to nearly 26 million ounces.

American Barrick's growth came in part through almost annual acquisitions, coupled with good fortune in finding gold on its acquired properties. In 1983 the company purchased interests in small Canadian and Alaskan mines, and the next year it purchased an interest in the Pinson Mine in Nevada and acquired the Camflo Mine, which would produce more than 30,000 ounces annually. The Camflo acquisition provided American Barrick with skilled technical and engineering staff, including Robert Smith, American Barrick's president and chief operating officer since 1985. Camflo almost tripled American Barrick's reserve base. In 1985, American Barrick made an even larger acquisition, purchasing the Mercur Mine near Salt Lake City, Utah, from Texaco, Inc. In late 1986 and early 1987, it purchased the Goldstrike Mine and surrounding properties in Nevada. At the time it acquired Goldstrike, reserves on the property were estimated to be about 600,000 ounces. Over the following years, American Barrick discovered additional reserves on its Goldstrike

> Increased producer hedging ... raised gold lease rates which, together with low prevailing interest rates, made hedging less and less attractive. As a result of these considerations, we decided to adjust our hedge positions and are now maintaining a cover of about two years' production, against the former three years. Naturally, as a new market equilibrium is established, we may review and adjust our exposures again.[1]

On January 30, 1996 the firm announced that it had reduced its gold hedging from 9 million ounces to 6 million ounces at the end of 1995. Barrick's chief finance officer made it clear that: "Barrick continues to be committed to gold hedging, but we aren't stuck in the mud." Its change in policy merely signalled that the firm felt the cost of hedging had become prohibitively high.

Just as Barrick's hedging policies had been controversial, its announcement to scale back its hedging was equally contentious. One competitor criticised Barrick for changing its strategy "overnight" because of changes in the market, saying that a quick unwind "says that the strategy that they had in place before was wrong".[2] However, the broad market response to Barrick's announcement was very positive. The news was a surprise, even to gold experts, and it received wide coverage in the financial press on January 31 and for the next few days. In the five days following its announcement, Barrick stock rose 7.8% (or 5.4% after correcting for movements in the market and the price of gold).[3] In dollar terms, this translated into a $570 million–825 million increase in the market value of the firm in one week. One interpretation of this reaction was that investors agreed with Barrick's assessment that market conditions justified the change in hedging policy.

When Barrick started hedging, it was considered a relatively novel concept for a gold mining firm, but by 1996 hedging was a well-established tool for mining firms. Hedging activities of producers had become so important that some attributed the rise in gold prices (to over $410 an ounce in early February 1996) to Barrick's trend-setting announcement of its reduced hedging activity.[4] Whether or not this link exists, it is clear that gold price hedging has progressed, from being an oddity to being an important element of the gold mining business and the gold industry.

1 Barrick Gold Corporation, 1995 Annual Report.
2 "Amax Gold Dislikes Sudden Hedging Changes", Reuters Financial Service, March 12, 1996.
3 The correction for market and gold movements was carried out by estimating a two-factor market model (including both the return on gold and the S&P 500) on Barrick Gold returns over the 90 days prior to the announcement, and using the coefficients from this regression to calculate the expected return on Barrick stock for the five business days, January 30, 1996 through to February 5. On January 30, Barrick also announced its final quarter earnings. It is unlikely that the earnings announcement would have led to a large rise in the firm's stock price, as earnings came in slightly below analysts' expectations. According to Zacks Investment Research, the mean analyst estimate was $0.23 per share, versus the actual $0.22 per share. See "Consensus: US Corporate Earnings Surprise Data", Reuters Financial Service, January 30, 1996. By February 8, there were published rumours that Barrick might merge with Newmont Gold, and its stock fell in value by 5.2% on the day preceding the publication of the rumours.
4 For example, see Deborah Hargreaves, 1996, "Funds drive gold still higher", *Financial Times*, February 2, pp. 25.

property, and by 1992 reserves on the property were estimated to be 20.1 million ounces, and its annual production was approximately 1.1 million ounces. American Barrick's growth was expected to continue through the 1990s as the firm began to look overseas for additional mines. Table 1 (overleaf) gives information on the firm's operations since its inception.

American Barrick was not only rapidly growing but was also quite profitable. It generated large operating cashflows, which it continued to invest in its mines (see Table 2). Its rising profitability, despite the drop in gold prices, came from a variety of sources. American Barrick acquired its gold mines for relatively low amounts when gold prices were depressed in the mid-1980s, and it later found massive reserves in Goldstrike that enabled it to enjoy scale economies. In its Mercur Mine, the company was able to cut expenses and increase production to capacity, thus increasing profits. Finally, the firm's gold price management programme enabled it to sell its output at above-market prices and to profit while other firms could not. Table 3 provides comparative financial data on American Barrick and its major North American rivals for 1991.

From the outset, American Barrick's mission was determined by Munk's vision. In the early 1980s, he had sensed a demand by European and North American investors for holding gold stocks without the political risks of holding South African investments. In its first annual report as a publicly owned firm, American Barrick expressed its intention to meet this need: "The corporate strategy is to acquire or develop a

Table 1. American Barrick's operations, 1984–92

	1984	1985	1986	1987	1988	1989	1990	1991	1992
Gold production (oz)									
Renabie Mine, Ontario	8,098	14,858	17,504	19,307	19,408	20,051	21,751	15,187	–
Valdez Creek, Alaska	3,880	5,878	3,108	7,501	10,436	13,975	–	–	–
Camflo, Quebec	18,500	34,637	31,850	29,763	30,888	26,629	24,416	25,001	36,273
Pinson Mine, Nevada	3,600	8,289	22,603	20,116	21,612	19,028	15,966	15,504	13,376
Holt-McDermott Mine, Ontario	–	–	–	–	23,848	63,354	59,164	60,728	43,325
Mercur Mine, Utah	–	52,290	111,007	108,278	115,390	117,536	122,043	127,280	121,239
Goldstrike, Nevada	–	–	–	40,144	119,418	207,264	352,880	546,146	1,108,219
Total	**34,078**	**115,952**	**186,072**	**225,109**	**341,000**	**467,837**	**596,220**	**789,846**	**1,322,432**
Proven and probable gold reserves (oz)									
Renabie Mine, Ontario	100,000	85,000	159,100	123,200	98,200	112,000	27,700	–	–
Valdez Creek, Alaska	–	23,000	39,600	28,400	51,300	94,700	–	–	–
Camflo, Quebec	170,000	135,000	102,000	91,200	76,800	62,100	44,800	19,900	–
Pinson Mine, Nevada	52,000	123,000	123,800	115,500	129,500	130,000	105,700	100,500	83,700
Holt-McDermott Mine, Ontario	–	476,000	456,000	308,000	249,000	354,400	387,100	447,300	251,200
Mercur Mine, Utah	–	1,000,000	1,400,000	1,467,000	1,297,100	1,127,700	1,027,100	876,300	739,800
Goldstrike, Nevada	–	–	625,300	8,679,100	15,181,000	17,995,700	17,918,000	18,448,000	20,149,000
Meikle Mine, Nevada	–	–	–	–	–	–	–	4,485,000	4,485,000
Total	**322,000**	**1,842,000**	**2,905,800**	**10,812,400**	**17,082,900**	**19,876,600**	**19,510,400**	**24,377,000**	**25,708,700**
Cash cost/ounce ($/oz)[1]									
Renabie Mine, Ontario	376	253	239	283	353	360	373	301	–
Valdez Creek, Alaska	270	237	324	469	451	308	–	–	–
Camflo, Quebec	200	214	219	237	272	294	319	295	164
Pinson Mine, Nevada	175	169	133	169	157	178	215	238	260
Holt-McDermott Mine, Ontario	–	–	–	–	268	284	298	331	356
Mercur Mine, Utah	–	248	199	216	235	253	238	249	259
Goldstrike, Nevada	–	–	–	312	325	352	393	318	199
Weighted average cash cost/oz	**247**	**217**	**200**	**246**	**280**	**307**	**343**	**305**	**210**

Source: American Barrick Corporation, annual reports.

1 Cash costs include site costs for all mining (including deferred stripping costs), processing and administration, but do not include royalties, capital costs, exploration costs, resource taxes, depreciation and financing costs.

diversity of gold producing interests exclusively in North America."[2] It immediately listed its shares in Toronto, Montreal and the US, later adding listings in London, Paris, Zurich, Geneva and Basle.

A second tenet of the American Barrick strategy was to maintain conservative financial policies, by issuing little debt and by moderating the firm's gold price risk. The firm's insistence on bearing low financial risk was attributed to an earlier failed business experience of Peter Munk, and his subsequent distrust of high leverage. It also flowed from his stated belief in the benefits of flexibility: "Our financial strength not only ensures our existing development plans, it will allow us to take advantage of the decade's opportunities." American Barrick's subsequent growth necessitated greater amounts of leverage but, in his 1991 letter to shareholders, Munk continued to emphasise the importance of having a "strong, liquid balance sheet".

In his original conception, an integral element of financial conservatism was to moderate, although not completely eliminate, American Barrick's exposure to gold price risk. He felt that target investors would be interested in a gold mining firm that lowered the risk of movements in gold prices. American Barrick's appeal would be its positioning as a well-run, low-cost commodity producer, willing to sacrifice potential profits from gold price peaks in order to level out potential losses in the troughs. Investors might desire some exposure to gold prices, but they would want this exposure managed prudently.

In general terms, there are three ways to moderate risk: by diversifying it, selling (or hedging) it, or by insuring against it.[3] Given its clear focus on being a gold mining firm, American Barrick could not diversify away its gold price risk. It could, and did, sell (hedge) and insure against its risk. Its earliest efforts to manage price risk involved selling the risk to others; its later efforts used insurance strategies. While American Barrick had a conservative financial orientation with regard to the level of its indebtedness and the price risk it was willing to bear, it was adept at using innovative financing techniques and instruments to finance itself and manage the firm's financial risk.

By 1992, it appeared that Munk had communicated the unique features of American Barrick to shareholders. The firm's shares were held by

Table 2. American Barrick's financial performance, 1983–92 ($000s, except per share data)

	1983	1984[1]	1985[2]	1986	1987	1988	1989[3]	1990	1991	1992
BALANCE SHEET DATA										
Assets										
Cash and short-term investments	3,093	1,041	2,110	2,215	167,163	51,411	304,673	311,778	252,140	288,023
Note receivable	–	–	–	–	46,161	–	–	–	–	–
Marketable securities	–	1,460	455	99,478	312	–	–	–	–	–
Bullion settlements and other receivables	2,527	5,650	4,044	6,439	9,841	16,786	28,314	32,601	35,193	25,100
Inventories and prepaid expenses	437	1,961	7,547	9,596	15,946	18,760	35,067	46,852	41,114	40,248
Current assets	*6,057*	*10,112*	*14,155*	*117,727*	*239,423*	*86,957*	*368,054*	*391,231*	*328,447*	*353,371*
Investments	–	33,102	15,332	15,120	120,005	143,144	32,526	–	–	–
Property, plant and equipment	31,158	122,644	126,760	171,151	289,304	455,776	633,791	716,046	921,701	1,094,402
Other assets	3,207	2,630	9,082	14,885	27,050	14,958	15,698	39,606	56,189	56,520
Total assets	**40,422**	**168,489**	**165,329**	**318,884**	**675,785**	**700,825**	**1,050,069**	**1,146,883**	**1,306,337**	**1,504,293**
Liabilities and equity										
Accounts payable and accrued liabilities	4,165	6,950	11,627	16,793	24,811	26,209	42,019	28,528	54,532	58,804
Dividend payable	–	–	–	–	–	–	–	–	3,105	–
Notes and loans payable	1,365	26,323	4,102	53,658	–	–	–	–	–	–
Current part of long-term debt[4] & deferred revenues[5]	–	311	934	24,536	27,807	16,860	46,760	82,973	54,624	79,968
Current liabilities	*5,530*	*33,584*	*16,663*	*94,987*	*52,618*	*43,069*	*88,779*	*111,501*	*112,261*	*138,772*
Long-term debt[4]	2,783	41,490	9,619	61,942	137,010	91,834	61,271	331,401	262,996	260,098
Deferred revenues and other liabilities[5]	–	5,293	65,894	47,598	142,104	164,300	358,114	31,193	47,989	62,117
Deferred taxes	–	7,070	6,208	5,565	5,612	11,147	16,387	27,912	42,438	50,577
Total liabilities	*8,313*	*87,436*	*98,384*	*210,093*	*337,645*	*310,350*	*524,551*	*502,007*	*465,684*	*511,564*
Capital stock	37,845	100,175	103,389	98,315	315,850	325,562	427,509	534,707	653,102	664,410
Retained earnings	(5,736)	(19,121)	(36,444)	10,476	24,144	49,799	77,140	92,745	169,766	326,273
Foreign currency translation adjustment	–	–	–	–	(1,557)	15,124	20,869	17,424	17,785	2,046
Shareholders' equity	*32,109*	*81,053*	*66,945*	*108,791*	*338,437*	*390,485*	*525,518*	*644,876*	*840,653*	*992,729*
Total liabilities and shareholders' equity	**40,422**	**168,489**	**165,329**	**318,884**	**675,782**	**700,835**	**1,050,069**	**1,146,883**	**1,306,337**	**1,504,293**
INCOME STATEMENT DATA										
Revenues	1,286	4,407	37,327	69,106	92,127	147,509	206,069	251,624	344,725	540,437
Operating expenses	(1,180)	(7,635)	(23,315)	(39,482)	(48,090)	(79,545)	(111,010)	(132,356)	(175,357)	(234,205)
Administrative expenses	(1,197)	(2,312)	(2,607)	(4,036)	(5,547)	(6,756)	(8,728)	(10,570)	(11,951)	(14,241)
Income from operations	*(1,091)*	*(5,540)*	*11,406*	*25,588*	*38,490*	*61,208*	*86,331*	*108,698*	*157,417*	*291,991*
Depreciation, depletion and amortisation	(351)	(3,504)	(8,845)	(11,868)	(17,383)	(25,681)	(35,266)	(42,954)	(49,277)	(68,971)
Exploration and deferred mining costs written off	–	–	(345)	(135)	(3,010)	(501)	(8,299)	(6,925)	(3,465)	(4,310)
Interest and other income	215	3,509	5,315	4,547	10,658	15,369	21,945	31,487	23,961	13,330
Interest expense on long-term obligations	–	(4,343)	(2,935)	(3,844)	(9,985)	(10,671)	(12,770)	(12,787)	(9,427)	(9,296)
Other expenses	–	–	–	–	8,287	–	(9,487)	–	(4,243)	–
Income before taxes	*(1,226)*	*(9,878)*	*4,595*	*14,288*	*27,057*	*39,724*	*42,454*	*77,519*	*114,966*	*222,744*
Income taxes	–	822	1,500	2,700	6,487	9,229	8,719	19,314	22,526	47,804
Net Income	**(1,226)**	**(9,056)**	**3,095**	**11,588**	**20,570**	**30,495**	**33,735**	**58,205**	**92,440**	**174,940**
Net income per share	*(0.02)*	*(0.12)*	*0.08*	*0.28*	*0.18*	*0.26*	*0.28*	*0.45*	*0.68*	*1.22*
STATEMENTS OF CASHFLOW										
Cash from operations		71	12,646	24,466	37,276	61,693	76,801	94,040	160,233	282,782
Cash from investment activities		(99,015)	(20,682)	(95,679)	(192,871)	(195,175)	(114,569)	(160,263)	(303,346)	(272,209)
Cash from financing										
Capital stock		63,392	3,250	31,389	213,190	7,316	102,252	107,198	118,395	11,308
Renabie Gold Trust[6]		5,762	–	–	–	–	–	–	–	–
Long-term liabilities		5,505	2,471	–	–	–	–	–	–	–
Gold-linked 5.25% notes[7]		–	–	52,903	–	–	–	–	–	–
Gold Company of America		–	40,778	–	–	–	–	–	–	–
Gold loans and long-term liabilities: proceeds		–	26,826	–	171,004	50,166	218,818	–	–	77,000
Gold loans and long-term liabilities: repayments		–	(40,563)	(13,178)	(13,427)	(74,357)	(22,024)	(21,940)	(76,806)	(40,172)
Gold purchase warrants[8]		–	–	4,248	–	–	–	–	–	–
Note receivable[9]		–	–	–	(46,161)	46,161	–	–	–	–
Dividends		–	–	–	(2,220)	(4,840)	(7,896)	(11,263)	(15,000)	(18,433)
Other[10]		(2,716)	(959)	(1,914)	(1,441)	(2,466)	(796)	(1,019)	1,826	(3,105)
		71,944	**31,803**	**73,446**	**320,945**	**21,980**	**290,354**	**72,976**	**28,415**	**26,598**

Source: American Barrick Resources Corporation, annual reports.

Note: Financial data for 1983–87 were originally reported in Canadian dollars. Subsequent American Barrick financial reports translate these into US dollars at a fixed rate of 0.77 US$/C$. This convention is used here.

1 Does not include 1984 extraordinary loss of $9,523,000 attributable to divestment of non-mining properties (oil and gas). 2 Does not include 1985 extraordinary loss of $20,305,000 attributable to divestment of non-mining properties (oil and gas). 3 In 1989, Barrick changed the way it accounted for exploration and deferred stripping costs. Financials for previous years have not been restated to reflect this change. Accordingly, there is a mismatch in some accounts when comparing pre-1989 data. 4 Long-term debt includes gold loan obligations at original value. 5 Deferred revenues include gains arising from early repayment of gold loans and adjustments made to value the loan at market prices prevailing at the balance sheet date. In earlier years, deferred revenues included all gold loan obligations as well as long-term obligations to financing trusts and purchase contracts. Other liabilities include reserves for future environmental and land reclamation costs. 6 The Renabie Gold Trust receives a variable percentage of Renabie production, which varies from 3-10%, based on the price of gold. 7 The Gold Company of America entered into gold purchase agreements to purchase gold from the Camflo mine. The percentage of the contract delivered each year varies with the price of gold. The rate is 8% at $365 gold and increases or decreases by 1% for each $35 change in the price of gold. 8 In September 1986 the company issued 2 million units at $21.5/unit, consisting of one common share and two gold purchase warrants. Each warrant entitled the holder to purchase 0.02oz gold at $9.50 until September 1990. At issue, the warrants were valued at $1.50 each. 9 A portion ($46.1 million) of the proceeds from the October 1987 equity issue was used to purchase a note receivable, which was repaid in 1988. 10 Also includes costs incurred in raising capital.

Table 3. Operating and financial performance of major gold mining firms in 1991 ($ million, except per share and per ounce data)

	American Barrick	Amax Gold	Battle Mtn[6]	Echo Bay	FMC Gold[6]	Homestake Mining	LAC Minerals	Newmont Gold[7]	Newmont Mining[7]	Pegasus Gold	Placer Dome
Operating information											
Production (000oz)	789.8	300.2	408.0	733.9	357.0	1,045.2	1,040.0	1,576.9	1,420.9	315.3	1,684.0
Average realised price/oz[1]	438	427	368	392	361	361	413	363	391	389	399
Cash costs/oz[2]	205	195	178	249	210	307	245	203	203	226	223
Total costs/oz[3]	274	346	376	390	343	448	390	288	288	351	415
Total reserves (million oz)	25.3	6.2	7.1	1.3	2.6	13.2	10.6	20.1	18.1	4.0	16.8
Reserve replacement costs/oz[4]	13	17	19	23	66	29	33	9	9	54	104
Risk management activities											
% of 1992 production "hedged"[5]	94	50	0	15	0	0	80	0	29	68	24
Average price/oz of "hedged" production[5]	424	497	–	417	–	–	396	–	431	380	421
% of debt gold-linked	100	6	0	100	0	0	26	–	100	25	4
% of revenue from gold sales	100	100	95	91	92	94	85	100	89	79	70
Financial information											
Cashflow from operations	160.23	50.90	53.84	97.57	48.91	23.80	122.95	181.77	98.33	32.56	276.60
Cashflow from investment	(303.35)	(53.70)	(125.92)	(56.34)	(21.19)	(45.23)	(184.48)	(176.46)	(83.68)	(38.33)	(354.00)
Cashflow from financing	28.42	12.10	8.16	(52.32)	(3.67)	(50.16)	126.42	(5.24)	(126.13)	60.14	(26.90)
Capital expenditures	245.50	60.00	147.00	60.00	19.40	138.42	95.15	97.27	95.50	38.70	226.00
Total assets	1,306	198	525	875	275	927	1,346	817	818	351	2,291
Total debt	336	26	128	234	127	52	348	0	224	71	310
Stock price information											
Shareholders' equity (book) value	841	198	315	492	244	669	778	735	201	246	1,481
No. of shares in millions (Dec 31, 1991)	140.9	60.6	79.8	105.1	73.5	99.5	146.9	104.9	67.8	27.9	236.7
Closing price per share (Dec 31, 1991)	27.88	11.63	7.88	7.50	5.00	16.00	8.13	39.75	40.38	12.37	11.00
Standard deviation of returns (1988–92)	0.020	0.024	0.027	0.025	0.028	0.024	0.024	0.021	0.020	0.025	0.021
% of firms owned by officers and directors	25	0.60	1.03	1.14	0.01	9.08	2.46	0	0.56	1.22	0.52
Total common stock return (1988–92)	218.7	–46.9	–70.0	–77.0	–60.0	–35.3	–41.0	–9.6	–38.1	37.1	–12.2

Source: Company annual reports, 10Ks and proxy statements, S&P stock reports, First Boston analysts' reports, JP Morgan analysts' reports.

1 Average Comex price of gold in 1991 was $362. 2 Cash costs include site costs for all mining (including deferred stripping costs), processing and administration, but do not include royalties, capital costs, exploration costs, resource taxes, depreciation and financing costs. Data courtesy of Paul Zink, JP Morgan. American Barrick's definition of cash costs in Table 1 includes its deferred stripping costs, by which the expenses of removing waste rock that lies above ore bodies is amortised over the life of the mine. American Barrick's treatment of deferred stripping costs differs from that of other firms. The costs in this table have been adjusted so that American Barrick's costs can be directly compared with other mining firms' costs. 3 Total costs add depreciation, royalties, capital costs, exploration costs, resource taxes and financing costs to cash costs. Data courtesy of Paul Zink, JP Morgan. 4 Reserve replacement costs are the sum of capitalised additions to exploration/development expenditures and exploration expenses divided by the net new ounces added to reserves for 1987–91. Data courtesy of Paul Zink, JP Morgan. 5 At December 31, 1991. Data from Ted Reeve, 1992, *North American Hedging Report*, First Boston Corporation. (See Table 6 for details.) 6 FMC Corp owns 79% of FMC Gold and hedged 88.7% of its share of 1992 production. FMC Gold officers and directors own 943,032 shares of FMC Corp. 7 Newmont Mining owned 90.1% of Newmont Gold and hedged 29% of its share of production as indicated.

1. Return to American Barrick common stock and common stocks of other major gold mining firms, 1987–92

Source: Data from the Center for Research in Security Prices.
Note: This chart shows the value of $1 invested in American Barrick on the date of its listing on the New York Stock Exchange (Feb 25, 1987) and reinvested in the shares of American Barrick as dividends were paid. The line labelled "other majors" shows the value of $1 invested equally in the other major gold mines on the same date, with dividends reinvested in an equal-weighted portfolio of these firms. The "other majors" include Amax, Battle Mountain, Echo Bay, FMC Gold, Homestake, International Corona, LAC Minerals, Newmont Gold, Newmont Mining, Pegasus and Placer Dome.

European, Canadian and US investors.[4] Shareholders included many investors which shied away from traditional gold mining investments:

> Barrick's investor base has now broadened to include institutions that traditionally avoid gold investments. They invest in Barrick because it has an excellent track record, an expectation for future growth, a recognised, proven management team and a strong balance sheet.[5]

Finally, the market seemed to respond positively to American Barrick; its stock out-performed the market and other major gold mining firms (Figure 1).

Gold

While the current primary "uses" of gold are for jewellery (80% of current use) and for industrial and commercial applications such as dentistry and electronics, to understand gold one must appreciate its unique historical role in the international economy as a currency and as a purported hedge against political instability and inflation. Archaeologists have found evidence that gold served as money as early as 2000 BC, although the use of gold as metallic money is generally traced back to Greece in the seventh century BC. Over the next 3,000 years, gold served as a currency and as backing for paper money. In the late nineteenth century, the relationship between money and gold was one of great political importance. William McKinley, US presidential candidate and supporter of a gold standard, defeated his opponent, William Jennings Bryan, who insisted that defining currency in terms of gold content would "crucify mankind upon a cross of gold". Debates over the proper role of gold in a macroeconomy, and its impact on real growth, inflation and deflation have preoccupied politicians, bankers and economists for centuries.

In 1992, gold no longer played the central role it once did in the world economy, and central banks no longer needed to back up their currency with gold reserves. Free of the requirement to hold gold, and aware of the profitability of selling or lending gold, central banks had begun to sell gold. From 1968 to 1991, central bank holdings of gold fell from 886 million ounces to 726 million ounces, a drop of nearly 20%.[6] Canada, Belgium and the Netherlands announced outright sales of their gold, and other governments saw opportunities to earn profits on their gold reserves through gold lending and participating in the swaps and options markets. Many metals analysts predicted that sales by the official sector would depress the real price of gold, even though industrial demand for gold was projected to outstrip the new supply created by mines.

Some analysts and investors viewed gold as an inflation hedge and a store of value. It was argued that, in times of economic and political instability, investors demand gold, driving up its price. It was also commonly held that, in times of inflation, the purchasing power of gold increases, while that of money decreases. Unfortunately, academic research failed to bear out this conventional wisdom. Gold appeared to be an ineffective hedge against inflation and political uncertainty in short and medium horizons, although it may have been effective over long horizons and against cataclysmic events.[7]

Figure 2 plots the price of gold in nominal and real terms, along with the inflation rate, from 1980 to 1992. In the two decades prior to 1992, the price of gold fluctuated from a low of $24 per ounce in 1971 to above $850 per ounce in the early 1980s. Prices slid through much of the

2. Price of gold and the relationship between inflation rates and changes in gold prices, 1980–92

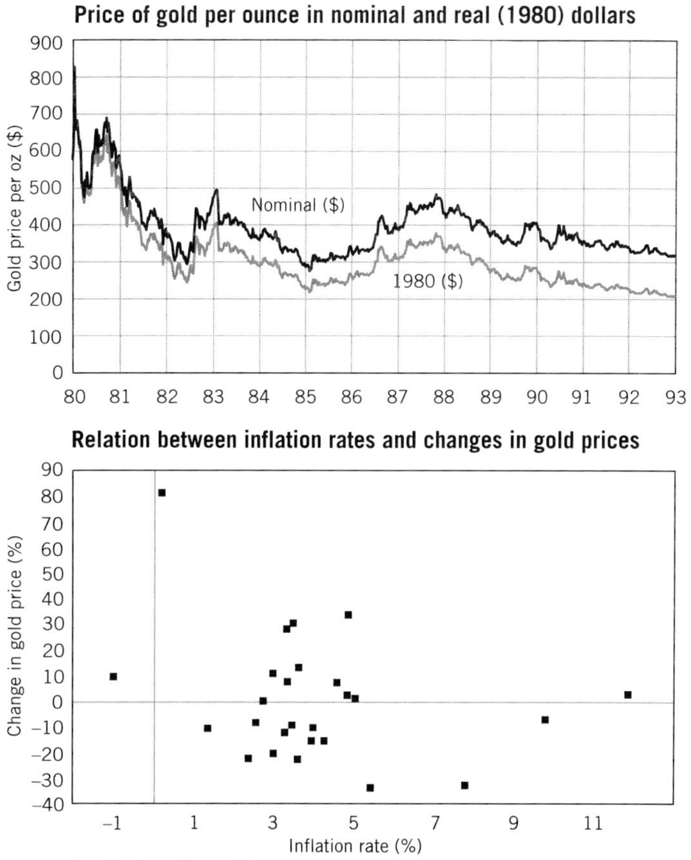

Source: Data from IDC Datasheet.
Note: Annualised inflation rates calculated for each non-overlapping six-month period from January 1980 to December 1992. Annualised changes in nominal gold prices are calculated for same periods.

1980s, with an upturn around the stock market correction of 1987. Since then, gold prices have declined steadily, although daily prices remained quite volatile. Research has shown that gold prices are likely to experience more extreme movements, both up and down, than other assets, and that positive returns are likely to be followed by subsequent positive returns.[8]

Some analysts predicted that gold would become increasingly commodity-like, enjoying only modest nominal price increases and real price declines. However, large global government deficits might lead countries to monetise their deficits and incite inflationary fears, driving up the demand for gold. Political instability in both South Africa and the former Soviet Union, whose mines produced 35% of world output, could disrupt supplies of gold. Some commentators voiced fears that the massive sales of gold for future delivery by bullion dealers and mines, taken in aggregate, would continue to depress current prices.[9] Finally, it was always possible that a major new gold field would be found, as in the gold rushes of California (1848), Australia (1851) and South Africa (1886).

Gold producers and production

As producers of commodity products, gold mining firms had virtually no marketing or distribution costs. There was always a ready market for their product, at market prices, once extracted from the earth and refined. Therefore, a gold mine's profits were a function of the quantity of its production and the difference between the prices at which it sold its output and its costs.

Over the long term, one gold producer can have a competitive advantage over others, based on its costs of gold production, driven by the physical features of its gold deposit and the efficiency of the firm's operations. Mines with gold closer to the surface, with ores richer in gold and with ore in physical forms more amenable to recovery, have natural cost advantages over others. Large amounts of ore must be mined, whether in open pits or underground shafts, and then processed to extract small quantities of gold. For example, the ore in American Barrick's Goldstrike Mine contained an estimated 0.127 ounces of gold for each ton of ore, meaning that, to produce a single ounce of gold that might sell for $300–400, American Barrick would need to mine and process almost 16,000 pounds of rock. Once mined, the ore was treated by a combination of processes that included crushing the ore, heating it, sorting by density, chemically treating it and, finally, refining it to remove impurities. Both mining and processing were costly activities. For example, at Goldstrike, mining and processing costs were roughly equal in magnitude, varying directly with the amount of ore mined and processed.

In the short term, mining firms have a limited ability to adjust production to changes in the price of gold. They can slightly adjust their rate of mining, or they may be able to choose which ore grade to mine and process. For instance, an open-pit mine may be able to stockpile ores, allowing the producer to adjust the grade of ore processed depending on market conditions; underground mines typically have greater flexibility to select the grade of ore they will mine and process. At the extreme, a mining firm can choose to shut down a mine, although practical concerns (eg, mine floodings) can make this decision nearly irreversible. American Barrick's policy was to mine and produce as much gold as quickly as possible; thus its production decisions were not affected by the market price of gold.

The differences among the major producers, in the natural endowments of their mines and the economic efficiency of their operations, caused marginal costs of production to vary widely in the industry (see Table 3). Gold mines also needed to make large fixed or sunk costs. The geology and economics of gold mining required firms to invest large sums of money, to create the infrastructure necessary to dig and process the ore. For example, the Meikle Mine, American Barrick's newest ore deposit, was projected to demand a capital investment of $180 million (in 1992 terms) spread out over four years. The incremental capital investments of this particular project were relatively low, for the new mine lay only one mile north of the firm's Goldstrike properties and could use the same processing and maintenance facilities, and access roads.

Once at full production, the Meikle Mine was expected to produce 400,000 ounces of gold per year for 11 years. If there were no financial contracts by which American Barrick could lock in, or at least set bounds on, the prices at which it could sell the output of the Meikle Mine, the expected value of the project could fluctuate widely. Fortunately, the gold industry had at its disposal a wide range of contracts to manage risk, ranging from indexed borrowings to esoteric options. According to analysts of gold mining firms, American Barrick was not only one of the most active users of these opportunities, but also one of the most adept.

The diversity of risk management practices in the gold industry

The level, type and horizon of risk management activities varied considerably among gold mining firms. Australian producers were early and heavy users of risk management vehicles, while North American firms tended to use fewer risk management contracts, and South African producers managed little of their price risk. For example, according to estimates by one leading gold analyst, by the end of 1991 Australian producers had hedged 17 months of production, North Americans 9.6 months and South Africans under four months.[10]

Among North American producers, there was a wide range of risk management policies and practices. Table 4 gives aggregated information about the risk management activities of the North American producers over time, while Table 5 provides survey results showing the risk management activities, as at the end of 1991, of North American producers by level of production. Table 6 (overleaf) gives details of the risk management activities of the top 11 North American firms.

The degree to which firms managed their output price exposure was well tracked, with firms differentiating themselves on the basis of these policies. At one extreme stood large producers like Homestake, which engaged in no risk management activities whatsoever and justified this policy in public statements:

> So that its shareholders might capture the full benefit of increases in the price of gold, Homestake does not hedge its gold production. As a result of this policy, Homestake's earnings are more volatile than those of many other gold producers. The company believes that its shareholders will achieve maximum benefit from such a policy over the long term.[11]

At the other end of the spectrum stood American Barrick, for which managing gold price risk was an integral part of business and one of the firm's four stated business objectives. The value of managing price risk to shareholders was made clear in Peter Munk's letter to shareholders:

> Our unique gold hedging programme gives American Barrick extraordinary financial stability. It protects us from the impact of dips in the gold price, allows us to plan our cashflows with confidence and, in combination with our rising production, offers investors a predictable, rising earnings profile in the future.[12]

Table 4. Percentage of production covered by price risk management activities by major North American gold producers, 1990–92

	Percentage of production hedged					Spot price at	Number of
Survey date	1991[1]	1992[1]	1993	1994	1995	time of survey ($)	firms surveyed
Jun 1990	22.7	–	–	–	–	352	35
Sep 1990	32.8	–	–	–	–	408	38
Dec 1990	41.8	24.3	16.1	–	–	386	40
Mar 1991	49.0	25.3	16.4	–	–	356	47
Jun 1991	57.0	30.1	17.4	8.3	–	368	53
Sep 1991	53.1	31.1	18.7	14.0	–	349	53
Dec 1991	–	37.4	21.5	15.3	–	353	52
Mar 1992	–	42.4	24.3	18.0	7.3	341	52

Sources: Data from Ted Reeve, *North American Gold Monitor and Global Gold Hedge Survey*, First Boston Equity Research. Gold prices from IDC Datasheet.

1 Shows percentage covered by price risk management activities as of date shown for the remainder of the year.

Table 5. Percentage of production covered by price risk management activities by major North American gold mines at December 31, 1991

	1992	1993	1994	1995
Seniors	41	21	17	7
Intermediates	48	16	9	5
Juniors	15	7	4	7
Total	**39**	**18**	**13**	**6**

Sources: Data from Egizio Bianchini, *Gold Producers Based in North America, Hedging Survey*, vol II, Nesbitt Research, Spring 1992.

Note: Senior producers are those with estimated 1992 production of more than 400,000oz. Intermediate producers have estimated 1992 production of 100,000–400,000oz. Junior producers have estimated 1992 production of under 100,000oz.

Between these two extremes lie a wide variety of firms whose policies evolved over time. For example, in 1990, the management of Battle Mountain Gold announced a major change in policy:

> The company expects to hedge up to 25% ... of its first six months' gold production in 1991. This change in strategy was not taken lightly. We have long held the belief that investors appreciate a gold equity which does not cap upside potential in gold price rallies. However, a recent study of the market indicates that there may now be a share price premium, rather than penalty, for hedging.[13]

Finally, there were hybrid arrangements, where investors could choose to buy shares in identical mines, differing mainly in the degree to which they were protected against gold price movement. For instance, investors could buy the stock of Newmont Gold, which engaged in no gold

Table 6. Price risk management activities of 11 leading North American gold mining firms at December 31, 1991

	1992 Ounces	1992 Price/oz ($)	1992 % of production	1993 Ounces	1993 Price/oz ($)	1993 % of production	1994 Ounces	1994 Price/oz ($)	1994 % of production
American Barrick									
Forward sales	289,273	415		–	–		–	–	
Spot deferred	424,997	439		681,250	450		1,025,937	411	
Gold loans	100,886	455		168,750	419		164,063	402	
Puts	309,844	400		350,000	429		60,000	450	
Total	1,125,000	424	94	1,200,000	440	96	1,250,000	412	96
Calls sold	–	–		140,000	449		18,000	450	
Amax Gold									
Spot deferred	139,880	507		–	–		–	–	
Puts	12,000	410		42,000	425		42,000	440	
Gold loans	4,000	400		–	–		–	–	
Total	155,880	497	50	42,000	425	12	42,000	440	12
Battle Mountain Gold			0			0			0
Echo Bay									
Forward sales	81,000	412		–	–		–	–	
Gold loans	27,670	432		27,670	432		89,670	388	
Total	108,670	417	15	27,670	432	4	89,670	388	12
FMC Gold[1]			0			0			0
Homestake			0			0			0
LAC Minerals									
Forward sales	840,000	395		488,000	399		–	–	
Gold loans	52,500	414		70,000	414		70,000	414	
Total	892,500	396	80	558,000	401	49	70,000	414	6
Newmont Gold[2]			0			0			0
Newmont Mining[2]									
Forward sales	8,700	434		–	–				
Gold loans	250,000	449		250,000	449				
Puts	158,500	403		–	–				
Total	417,200	431	29	250,000	449	16	0		0
Calls sold	166,500	455		–	–				
Pegasus Gold									
Forward sales	114,065	420		44,565	494		50,565	492	
Puts	150,000	350		–	–		–	–	
Total	264,065	380	68	44,565	494	10	50,565	492	10
Placer Dome									
Forward sales	372,000	425		231,000	427		231,000	427	
Gold loans	7,000	431		10,000	431		10,000	431	
Puts	34,000	378		–	–		–	–	
Total	413,000	421	24	241,000	427	14	241,000	427	14
Calls sold	31,000	425		–	–		–	–	
Calls purchased	7,000	435		–	–		–	–	

Source: Data from Ted Reeve, 1992, *North American Hedging Report*, First Boston Corporation.

1 The FMC Corporation owned 78.9% of FMC Gold and hedged its pro rata share of production. As of December 31, 1992, it had hedged 88.7% of its 1992, 79.6% of its 1993 and 0% of its 1994 share of production. 2 Newmont Mining owned 90.1% of Newmont Gold.

price risk management. Yet Newmont Gold was 90% owned by Newmont Mining, whose shares were also traded publicly and which managed part of its gold price risk.

Vehicles for managing gold price risk

American Barrick's hedging programme evolved over the corporation's 10-year history and used a wide range of tools to manage gold price risk. With gold financings, forward sales, options strategies and spot-deferred contracts, American Barrick shed some of its gold price risk, while maintaining flexibility to profit from rising gold prices.

GOLD FINANCINGS

Before 1986, most of American Barrick's gold price management activities were incorporated in financings for its mines. In 1983, it funded its purchase of the Renabie Gold Mine in northern Ontario by issuing common shares, but then needed an additional $18 million for capital expenditures to develop the mine. To fund this expansion, in February 1984 it raised $17 million through an innovative vehicle, the Barrick-Cullaton Gold Trust. Marketed in Canada and Europe, this trust was the first publicly traded gold royalty trust in Canada. The gold trust paid investors 3% of the mine's output when the price of gold was at or below $399 per ounce, rising to 10% of production when gold was at $1,000 per ounce. In its first annual report, American Barrick explained what it believed to be the win-win nature of this financing:

The investor benefits, not only from increased volumes of gold to the trust, but also from increased gold price. Barrick shareholders benefit from the low-cost development funds for mine expansion today, and only pay increased royalties in future if there are future gold price increases.

The firm used a related structure to raise $40 million for its Camflo Mine in 1984.[14]

American Barrick's next two large acquisitions used bullion loans and gold-indexed Eurobond offerings to raise capital. To fund the acquisition of the Mercur Mine, in 1985, the firm entered into a bullion loan with Toronto Dominion Bank, in which it received 77,000 ounces of gold, which it immediately sold on the market for net proceeds of $25 million. Over the next four-and-a-half years, American Barrick was to repay the loan in monthly instalments in ounces of gold at an interest rate of about 2% per year.[15] The bullion loan was collateralised by the assets of the mine (valued at $54.3 million) and a guarantee by American Barrick. In addition, American Barrick was required to make accelerated deliveries to the lender equal to 50% of the cashflow from the mine after deducting approved capital expenditures and mandatory deliveries for the preceding year.[16] As part of its massive capital needs to fund Goldstrike and its other properties' capital needs, American Barrick raised funds through additional bullion loans collateralised by its mines. Its 1,050,000 ounce bullion loan used to finance Goldstrike Mine was the largest gold loan in the world at the time. As at the end of 1992, gold loans in place required the firm to deliver the following ounces of gold: 33,750 ounces in 1993; 224,063 ounces in 1994; 213,125 ounces in 1995; and 315,000 ounces in 1996–97.

American Barrick also raised funds through gold-indexed underwritten offerings. In February 1987, when gold was about $400 per ounce, the firm offered $50 million in 2% gold-indexed notes to Euromarket investors, which were typically European fund managers which purchased the issue either for their own accounts or for their clients. Investors paid $1,308 per note and received annual interest payments of $26.16. In addition, the investors were entitled to redeem the notes at any time between February 26, 1988, and February 26, 1992. If redeemed at the first possible opportunity, the holder could choose to receive an amount of cash or gold bullion whose value equalled 3.2150 ounces of gold. This redemption amount increased over time, so that, if it were held to maturity, the investor would receive 3.3804 ounces of gold. Unlike bullion loans, this offering was not collateralised by the firm's mines, whose production had been pledged as collateral for its bullion loans.

FORWARD SALES

In a forward sale of gold, a party commits to deliver a specified quantity of gold, at a specific date, for a price set at the beginning of a contract. Before the termination of the contract, no money changes hands. Forward contracts are private over-the-counter (OTC) transactions between principals, typically for 10,000 ounces or more, and their terms (such as the maturity of the contract and the size of the transaction) can be tailored by the contracting parties. Most forward contracts do not trade before delivery, although the parties are free to close out their positions through a negotiated settlement. As a practical matter, forward sales are usually for relatively short delivery periods of under a few years.[17]

In most markets, forward sellers receive a premium (commonly called contango) above the current gold price. For example, when gold prices are $350 per ounce, one ounce sold for delivery in one year might be priced at $367.50, a premium or contango of 5%. In effect, by contracting today to deliver gold in one year, the forward seller earns a guaranteed 5% rate of return.

Contango is equal to the difference between the interest rate for lending dollars and the interest rate for lending gold, called the gold lease rate. If the gold lease rate is 2% per year and the current price of gold is $350, someone who lends one ounce of gold today will be paid back that ounce plus $7 in cash ($350 × 2%) at the end of the year. If the one-year dollar lending rate is 7% and the one-year gold leasing rate is 2%, then the contango for selling gold forward is defined to be 5% per year. In this example, if spot gold prices (for immediate delivery) are $350, and a forward contract is struck for delivery in one year, then the price for forward delivery at the end of one year would be $350 × (1 + 0.05) = $367.50. If the forward price differed from $367.50, bullion dealers and others could earn arbitrage profits. Table 7 (overleaf) shows the gold lease rate, the dollar interest rate and contango over time.

A sharp drop in gold prices in 1984 and 1985 led to the first explicit forward sales of gold at American Barrick. As prices fell to levels equal to

Table 7. Gold lease rate, Libor (London interbank offered rate), contango, spot and forward gold prices, 1982–92

	Gold lease rate (%)	Libor (%)	Contango (%)	Gold price ($ per oz)	Forward price ($ per oz)
Jan 1982	1.35	16.83	15.48	384.11	443.56
June 1982	1.45	15.63	14.18	314.93	359.59
Jan 1983	0.65	9.45	8.80	479.88	522.11
June 1983	0.85	10.28	9.43	412.82	451.75
Jan 1984	1.05	10.45	9.40	370.86	405.72
June 1984	1.25	13.40	12.15	377.64	423.53
Jan 1985	1.35	9.60	8.25	302.77	327.75
June 1985	1.20	8.33	7.13	316.39	338.95
Jan 1986	1.50	8.31	6.81	344.58	368.06
June 1986	1.50	7.60	6.10	342.77	363.68
Jan 1987	1.20	6.19	4.99	408.31	428.69
June 1987	0.70	7.86	7.16	449.57	481.76
Jan 1988	1.30	7.75	6.45	476.57	507.29
June 1988	1.45	8.24	6.79	451.34	481.96
Jan 1989	1.70	9.77	8.07	403.99	436.60
June 1989	2.25	9.19	6.94	367.59	393.11
Jan 1990	1.40	8.48	7.08	410.12	439.17
June 1990	1.45	8.54	7.09	352.31	377.28
Jan 1991	2.40	7.40	5.00	384.47	403.70
June 1991	1.30	6.94	5.64	366.70	387.37
Jan 1992	1.15	4.52	3.37	354.43	366.38
June 1992	1.10	4.54	3.44	340.80	352.52
Dec 31, 1992	1.80	4.06	2.26	333.33	340.86

Sources: IDC Datasheet, Reuters, Chase Manhattan Bank.

Note: Gold lease rates, Libor, contango and forward prices are quoted for periods of one year. Data are averages for each month, except for December 31, 1992.

Table 8. American Barrick's forward sales of gold (excluding gold financings and spot-deferred contracts), 1984–92

	Ounces sold forward (000s)	Date of longest forward sale	Average price at delivery ($)
1984	0	–	–
1985	79.4	12/86	336
1986	92.6	12/87	364
1987	37.9	1/89	497
1988	56.6	12/92	486
1989	117.4	12/91	427
1990	0	–	–
1991	0	–	–
1992	0	–	–

Source: American Barrick Resources Corporation, annual reports.

the firm's estimated break-even (and threatened to fall even further), the company's profitability was jeopardised. American Barrick reacted by selling forward about 20,000 ounces in 1984 to protect itself against possible continued declines in gold prices. The gold market soon recovered and prices rose. The forward sales proved costly in hindsight, for the firm lost the opportunity to sell at the higher market prices. Nevertheless, this experience sparked new interest in using the financial markets to manage gold price risk, and Robert Wickham (treasurer at that time) began to study ways to protect the firm against adverse price movements using forward sales and option strategies. Table 8 shows the firm's forward sales of gold from 1984 to 1992.

OPTIONS AND WARRANTS

As its forward selling in 1984 and 1985 demonstrated, hedging not only eliminated American Barrick's downside exposure, but also its ability to benefit if prices rose. From 1987, it began to experiment with option-based insurance strategies that could mitigate the risk of price declines while allowing the firm to retain some of the benefits of rising prices.

In executing a "collar" strategy (also known as a participating min/max programme or a bull spread), the firm simultaneously bought put options and sold call options on gold.[18] The calls and puts had the same maturity, but the exercise price of the puts was below that of the calls. The options were purchased in the OTC market from one of American Barrick's 15 trading partners.[19] By using the premiums received from the sale of calls to purchase puts, a collar strategy required no initial cash outlay, which made it more acceptable to the firm's board of directors.

By adjusting the exercise prices and ratios of puts and calls, American Barrick could determine the degree to which it chose to participate in gold price rises. For example, market prices might allow it to buy one put with an exercise price of $420 per ounce and sell one call at $550 per ounce, financing the purchase of the put exactly by the sale of the call, because the two options had the same premium. This pair of market prices contracts would effectively set a minimum price of $420 from American Barrick's perspective. Between $420 and $550, it would capture all the upside of increases in the price of gold, and above $550 it would enjoy none of the increases in gold prices. Instead of selling one call with an exercise price of $550, the prevailing market prices for gold options might permit it to sell 0.5 calls with an exercise price of $485 and receive the same premium. Then, it would benefit fully from all price increases between $420 and $485, and would enjoy half of all increases above $485.

Table 9 shows American Barrick's option portfolio over time. As the firm became more comfortable with options, its positions grew. But as spot prices declined, it lowered the call strike price and the put/call ratio of its collar positions so as not to allow its floor level to drop. This meant that the firm had to surrender more of the upside potential to protect against drops in gold price. Furthermore, the OTC market in which it transacted with other principals rarely wrote options contracts longer than five years, and the market was liquid only for contracts with maturities under two years. This horizon was far shorter than the 20 years of expected production currently in reserve. In 1990, the firm stopped adding new options positions and began to use spot-deferred contracts extensively.

Table 9. American Barrick's year-end gold option positions, 1983–92

	Put positions			Call positions		
	Ounces (000s)	Avg exercise price/oz ($)	Longest maturity (yrs)	Ounces (000s)	Avg exercise price/oz ($)	Longest maturity
(yrs)						
1983	–	–	–	–	–	–
1984	–	–	–	–	–	–
1985	–	–	–	–	–	–
1986[1]	–	–	–	–[2]	–[2]	–[2]
1987[3]	549.3	426	3	215.4	578	3
1988[3]	1,084.7	430	4	556.4	533	4
1989[3]	1,700.0	417	4	886.9	461	4
1990[3]	1,471.4	418	4	723.5	445	4
1991[3]	1,009.1	417	3	447.3	427	3
1992[4]	410.0	432	2	–	–	–

Source: American Barrick Resources Corporation, annual reports.

1 In 1986, American Barrick entered into an agreement with a third party to carry out trading in gold options, with profits split equally and losses borne completely by the other party. 2 On September 25, 1986, American Barrick issued 2 million units at $21.50 each, consisting of one share of common stock and two gold purchase warrants. Each warrant allowed the holder to buy 0.02 ounces of gold at $9.20 (or $460 per ounce) at any time over the following four years. 3 In all years the net premium paid for all new option positions was zero. 4 In this year, American Barrick added no new options contracts to its position.

SPOT-DEFERRED CONTRACTS

A spot-deferred contract (SDC) is a type of forward sale of gold. In a standard forward sale, a delivery date is set, and on that date the forward seller delivers gold to the buyer at the pre-arranged forward price. In an SDC, there are multiple delivery dates, with the final one being five or 10 years after the initiation of the contract. The SDC seller chooses on which of these rollover dates it will deliver the gold and has the right to defer the delivery until the end of the contract. Ultimately, the SDC seller must deliver the quantity of gold called for in the contract, but it has a choice when to deliver it.

At the initiation of an SDC with one-year delivery or rollover dates, the prices paid for delivery were set only for the first rollover date. Gold that American Barrick delivered at the end of the first year would be paid the one-year forward price. At that rollover date, American Barrick could deliver on the contract (if the contract price was higher than spot), or it could roll the contract forward to the next period and sell the gold in the spot market. If it chose the latter, no money or gold would change hands between the SDC trading partners at this time, and the price would be set for delivery of gold on the next rollover date. The price set for delivery in the next period would be based on the prior contract price plus the prevailing contango premium on the rollover date. From both American Barrick and its trading partner's perspective, the price for the next rollover would be set such that both parties would have an indifferent attitude towards rolling over the contract for another year and closing out the contract and initiating a new one-year forward contract.[20]

American Barrick's initial SDC trading agreements called for ultimate delivery within three or four years but, as a result of its large reserve base and strong financial position, it was able to negotiate subsequent agreements that gave the firm 10 years within which to make delivery. SDC contracts were typically written by large producers with bullion dealers, covering not less than 100,000 ounces of gold. An integral feature of spot-deferred trading agreements was the covenants that the company's 15 trading partners required it to meet. If American Barrick's finances weakened considerably, or if its reserves deteriorated, its ability to continue to roll over its positions could be suspended. Weaker mining firms (with low reserves, high costs and high leverage) were unable to enter into long-term SDCs, or may have been required to deposit funds with their trading partners (or post margins) at each date when the contracts were rolled over.

American Barrick saw SDCs as a way to profit from increases in the price of gold and yet set a minimum price on its sales of gold. From 1990, American Barrick's use of SDCs grew rapidly, supplanting its other hedging vehicles, with 1,035,000 ounces pledged to contracts in place at the end of 1990, 2,248,202 ounces at the end of 1991 and 4,341,827 ounces at year-end 1992. As it became more comfortable with SDCs, American Barrick began to experiment with vehicles to manage the inherent contango risk of these contracts by using interest rate forwards and options.

Summary: hedging at American Barrick

Throughout the 1980s and early 1990s, as American Barrick's reserves and financial strength improved and the market for gold hedging vehicles matured, the company's risk management activities grew in size and complexity. Moving from gold financings to forwards to options to SDCs, the firm used virtually every instrument available to manage its gold price risk.

Gold price risk management at American Barrick evolved out of the conservative financing orientation of the firm. However, specific events in the corporation, like the 1984 experience with selling gold forward, or the discovery of nearly 18 million unexpected ounces of gold reserves at Goldstrike, accelerated the pace at which hedging activity took place. With Goldstrike, American Barrick's board set a guideline for risk management: the firm would be fully protected against price declines for all production out three years, and 20–25% protected for the following decade. Specific details of the methods and implementation were left to the financial team, which reported the firm's position to the board of directors on a regular basis.

While the programme was dedicated to ensuring that American Barrick was protected against falls in the price of gold over the long term, in the short term the financial team strategically managed its positions to capitalise on its expectations of movements in the price of gold. For example, in early January 1991 gold prices were about $386 per ounce. Later that month, as military forces massed near the border of Kuwait, the price of gold began to rise. On the evening of January 17, 1991, while President George Bush made a television address telling of the initiation of Operation Desert Storm, gold prices surged to almost $410. In roughly an hour the company's finance team sold approximately one year of production in the spot market, to capitalise on what it perceived was a short-term uptick in prices. The bet proved correct, for gold prices later in the year never approached this level.

Because it lacked the technical training and in-house models to price the various gold derivatives, the financial team made a point of obtaining competitive quotes for its derivative transactions. Given American Barrick's financial strength and reserve base, the finance team felt that it could enter into contracts that many other mines and most gold stock investors could not. Furthermore, the terms of these contracts were more favourable than those other mining firms and investors would receive. Over time, as the finance team became more proficient at using the derivatives, it began to develop customised contracts, using financial instruments available from major dealers.

American Barrick's largest positions were established in conjunction with Goldstrike when gold prices were much higher than in late 1992. As a result, as gold prices declined, American Barrick was able to deliver its production against contracts for prices far above market prices, and would continue to be able to sell above market prices. Table 10 shows the spot prices of gold and the average price that American Barrick realised on its sales throughout the firm's history.

American Barrick made a point of communicating its risk management programme to the investing public. Table 11 is an excerpt of information about the programme presented to analysts, including published details of the firm's hedge position. The firm's hedging was prominently mentioned in public reports (including on the cover of the 1990 annual report), and executives gave speeches and wrote articles about the firm's hedging activities. Using publicly available information, analysts attempted to value its futures, options and SDC positions and, while these estimates differed, there was a broad consensus that these financial transaction activities had proven to be wise choices in hindsight.

Table 10. American Barrick's realised price for delivered gold versus Comex spot price, 1984–92

	Average price for gold delivered during year ($)	Average ounces delivered	Comex price ($)
1984	311	34,078	360
1985	333	115,952	317
1986	348	185,359	368
1987	410	219,776	447
1988	446	330,479	437
1989	436	472,452	393
1990	437	575,656	384
1991	438	787,735	362
1992	422	1,280,320	345

Source: American Barrick Resources Corporation, annual reports.

Table 11. Public disclosure of American Barrick's consolidated gold price risk management position at December 31, 1992

	1993		1994		1995	
	Ounces	Avg price ($)	Ounces	Avg price ($)	Ounces	Avg price ($)
Gold loans[1]	33,750	515	224,063	402	213,125	400
Put options	350,000	429	60,000	450	–	–
Scheduled deliveries	383,750	437	284,063	412	213,125	400
Spot-deferred contracts[2]	4,341,827	–	–	–	–	–

Source: American Barrick Resources Corporation.

1 Beyond 1995, the company had delivery obligations under its gold loans of 315,000oz at an average price of $400 per ounce through to 1997. 2 Spot-deferred contracts have no fixed delivery date and may be rolled forward for up to 10 years under the terms of American Barrick's trading agreements. On each rollover date, the value of the contracts increases with the accumulation of the contango. Uncommitted gold available from production will be delivered against these contracts when the spot price of gold is less than the price of the contracts. If the spot gold price exceeds the contract price, uncommitted gold available from production will be sold on the spot market and the contracts will be rolled forward for future delivery at a higher price through the accumulation of additional contango. Assuming the spot price of gold remains below the contract prices, the company will realise a minimum average price of over $400 per ounce for all its production through to the end of 1994. If the spot price exceeds the contract price, the company's average realised price will be higher, as the contracts will be deferred for future delivery and production will be delivered into the higher spot market. From 1995, the minimum average price for the unutilised portion of the existing spot-deferred contracts will be in excess of $400 per ounce. Ultimately, Barrick's realised price could be significantly higher, depending on the timing of deliveries and the forward premiums achieved.

Pleasant surprises challenge the hedging programme

In 1991 and 1992, American Barrick's good luck in the minefields put new demands on the firm's hedging programme. In September 1989, the firm's geologists began exploring the "Purple Vein", located one mile north of its Goldstrike property. While these early explorations turned up gold in 10 of the 17 holes drilled, the amount, the technical feasibility and the economic attractiveness of the find could not be determined by the end of 1989. The gold lay under the water table, at depths where the ground water temperature was over 140°F. In 1990, exploration continued, with an additional 31 holes drilled, which indicated that perhaps over 5 million ounces of gold lay in the deposit. But the technical details of mining the gold were daunting, and over the coming year technicians would need to visit deep-shaft South African mines and consult with ventilation and cooling engineers to ensure that the gold could be extracted. During this time, there was substantial technical uncertainty.

Finally, in February 1992, the firm felt confident that the ore could be extracted, and publicly announced the proven and probable reserves of 4.5 million ounces, renaming the mine the Meikle Mine in honour of the American Barrick executive who was instrumental in acquiring and exploring the Goldstrike property. In announcing the mine, analysts were told that "given full consideration of the risks inherent in mine development, it has been determined that the economics of the deposit are very attractive, even at $350 per ounce gold", although the break-even level of the mine was far lower than $350 per ounce (see Table 12 for details of the Meikle Mine project). Construction would not be completed until 1995, with full production commencing in 1996. The finance team had to determine when, during the period in which Meikle was being explored and then constructed, it would begin to manage the price risk of the mine's production and which mix of instruments it would use.

While Meikle promised to boost the firm's production in the long term, good fortune unexpectedly produced a new challenge for the hedging programme in the short term. In the fourth quarter of 1992, engineers determined that American Barrick's mined ore was richer in gold than originally anticipated. The firm had planned to produce roughly 1.2 million ounces annually of gold by 1995 and had hedged itself fully at this level for the period 1993-95. The newer estimates suggested that production would be closer to 2 million ounces annually by 1995; thus the firm suddenly became substantially more exposed to gold price swings, as measured against its policy guidelines.

With the price of gold and interest rates at historically low levels, the sudden need to enter into options, forwards or SDCs became more complicated for American Barrick. While industrial demand for gold was projected to outstrip newly mined supply, and the large bullion sales by the central banks had been absorbed, gold prices were not projected to increase. While some analysts projected a rebound in gold prices, with

Table 12. Projected data on Meikle Mine project

(Dollar figures in millions, except per ounce statistics)

	Amount[1] ($)	Timing of expenditure
Capital costs prior to production[2]		
Surface facilities and mine shafts	55	mid-1993–94
Underground development	31	1994–95
Refrigeration and ventilation	12	1994–95
Dewatering	23	1994–95
Mine equipment	12	1995
Capitalised preproduction	48	mid-1993–95
Total capital costs	180	
Operating costs per ounce of gold[3]	125	
Royalties[4] (% of sales)	4	
Estimated land reclamation costs at termination of project[5]	2.5	
Effective tax rate[5] (%)	20	

Source: American Barrick Resources Corporation.

1 In 1992 dollars. 2 Includes contingency of approximately 10%. 3 Planned reserves of 4.5 million ounces were projected to be produced over an 11-year period beginning in full production in 1996. Approximately 400,000 ounces of gold would be produced each year from 1996 to 2006. 4 Royalties paid by American Barrick to the firm that had a royalty interest on the property on which the Meikle Mine was located. 5 The taxation of gold mining firms is quite complex: mines can enjoy both depreciation and depletion tax benefits. The effect of these tax shields was to reduce American Barrick's effective tax rate on its operating profits on the Meikle Mine to approximately 20%.

Table 13. Gold prices and other capital markets data, 1990–92

	Jan 1990	Jun 1990	Jan 1991	Jun 1991	Jan 1992	Jun 1992	Dec 1992
Gold price ($/oz)	410	352	385	367	354	341	333
$ interest rates (%)							
Libor: one year	8.48	8.54	7.40	6.94	4.52	4.54	4.06
One-year Treasuries	7.92	8.10	6.65	6.36	4.15	4.17	3.61
Three years	8.13	8.40	7.38	7.39	5.40	5.60	4.93
Five years	8.12	8.43	7.70	7.94	6.24	6.48	5.83
Gold lease rates (%)							
One year	1.40	1.45	2.40	1.30	1.15	1.10	1.80
Three years	2.90	2.80	3.50	2.60	2.10	1.80	2.25
Five years	4.00	3.75	4.75	3.50	2.90	2.25	2.70
Implied volatility of gold[1] (%)	18		12		9		7

Sources: American Barrick Resources Corporation, IDC Datasheet, Chase Manhattan Bank and Paul H. Zink, *The North American Gold Industry: A Market in Transition*, JP Morgan Report, July 1, 1992.

Note: All data except for implied volatilities are averages for each month, except for December 31, 1992. Implied volatility figures are annual estimates, except for December 1992, which is a monthly estimate.

1 Approximate implied volatilities on European options on gold with maturities of five years or less. Implied volatilities for gold options had been over 50% in 1980, about 18% in 1987 and 12% in 1988 and 1989. In late January 1991, implied volatilities reached over 20%.

higher US inflation because of President Clinton's economic proposals, others discounted the possibility of inflation. Furthermore, the proliferation in interest rate, currency and commodity derivatives gave investors alternatives to manage inflation risk more directly and efficiently than gold. Many held that, despite upheavals around the world, the fear of global war had declined and gold would not be bid up in these relatively peaceful times. With the fall in the price of gold, mining firms were reported to be cutting back exploration and development efforts, and analysts estimated that perhaps one in three mines was unprofitable at current prices.

Table 13 shows the price of gold, along with capital market rates, with the representative quotes on various gold derivatives available to the American Barrick financial team at the end of 1992. The team needed to decide what to do: whether to stand committed to the guideline of managing all of the price risk of the next three years of production and, if so, how to deal with the unexpected 1.7 million ounces of additional production for that period.

1 *All figures in this case are expressed in US dollars unless otherwise noted.*

2 *As of 1992, all properties of American Barrick were in North America, although it contemplated looking abroad.*

3 *See Merton, R.C., 1993,* Operation and Regulation in Financial Intermediaries: A Functional Perspective, *Stockholm, Economic Council, for additional insights into the general treatment of managing risk. To define these three terms, Merton gives the example of the owner of a ship. To manage the risk of loss, a ship owner can: diversify by buying a portfolio of ships to avoid a complete loss if one ship sinks; sell (or hedge) the ship and have no economic exposure to its subsequent outcome; or buy an insurance policy that pays off if the ship sinks, but allows the ship owner to profit if it does not. Merton uses the term "hedging" to mean entering into a position such that the payoff is the same regardless of the outcome, which could be accomplished through selling the ship today or entering into a binding forward contract to sell it at some point in the future.*

4 *An important group of American Barrick shareholders comprised its managers and directors. At the end of 1991, the officers and directors as a group owned directly or indirectly 31.2 million shares, with options to purchase an additional 4.1 million shares. At December 31, 1991, there were 140.9 million shares outstanding. The closing price per share on December 31, 1991 was $27.875. In 1992, there were 141.9 million shares, of which officers and directors owned 29.6 million. The closing price per share on December 31, 1992 was $31.00.*

5 *American Barrick Resources Corporation, "Letter to Shareholders",* 1991 Annual Report, *p. 5.*

6 *See Zink, P.H., 1992, "The North American Gold Industry: A Market in Transition", JP Morgan Securities Inc,* Equity Research.

7 *See Sherman, E.J., 1986,* Gold Investment: Theory and Application, *New York, Prentice-Hall, and Jastram, R.W., 1977,* The Golden Constant: The English and American Experience, 1560–1976, *New York, Wiley.*

8 *See Aggarwal, R., and L. Soenen, 1988, "The Nature and Efficiency of Gold Markets",* Journal of Portfolio Management *vol. 14(3), pp. 18–21, and Aggarwal R. and P.S. Sundararaghavan, 1987, "The Efficiency of the Silver Futures Market",* Journal of Banking and Finance, *vol. 11, pp. 1–16.*

9 *See Gooding, K., 1991, "Financial Engineering Tames the Gold Market",* Financial Times, *July 26, p. 24.*

10 *Ted Reeve, 1992,* Global Gold Hedge Survey, *First Boston Equity Research.*

11 *Homestake,* 1990 Annual Report.

12 *American Barrick Resources Corporation,* 1991 Annual Report.

13 *Battle Mountain,* 1990 Annual Report.

14 *In the Camflo transaction, investors got a return of 8% when the gold price was $365 per ounce, and this rate increased or decreased by 1% for each $35 change in the price of gold, to a maximum of $1,500 per ounce.*

15 *In 1988, the company retired this gold loan when it entered into a 125,000 ounce revolving gold loan with a term of seven years. This loan, collateralised by the assets of the Mercur Mine, required payment of interest at 0.75% over the gold lease rate, and was amortised over seven years with quarterly payments.*

16 *In 1986, the mandatory payments on this loan were 9,282 ounces and the accelerated payments were 7,937 ounces.*

17 *Futures contracts on gold also exist, although American Barrick and other mining firms did not use them in their hedging programmes. These futures contracts trade on exchanges such as Comex. Unlike forward contracts, futures contracts are "marked to market" on a daily basis, requiring daily transfers of funds among the parties. The longest traded futures contract has a maturity of approximately four years, although contracts with delivery dates of more than two years trade infrequently.*

18 *A put option gives the holder the right to sell an asset on a certain date for a pre-specified exercise price. A call option gives its holder the right to buy an asset on a certain date for a pre-specified exercise price.*

19 *Alternatively, it could have bought and sold gold options (and options on gold futures) on a number of organised exchanges, including Comex (New York), the European*

Options Exchange (Amsterdam) and Liffe (the London International Financial Futures & Options Exchange). Exchange-traded gold options have maturities under one year.

20 *If American Barrick were to roll one-year forward contracts, it would be required to recognise its gains or losses on these contracts at the end of each year for both taxes and financial reporting. The tax and financial reporting treatment of the newer SDCs was unclear, as they had not been tested in the courts. American Barrick's legal counsel believed that, because SDCs were long-term contracts for which delivery was not required in the short term, no gains or losses would be recognised on these trading agreements before the company delivered gold against its SDC commitments.*

RISK ANALYSIS: VOLATILITY, VALUATION AND FORWARD CURVES

8

Non-Ferrous Metals Price Volatility

A Fractionally Integrated Process?

Gilles P. Teyssiere, Christopher L. Gilbert and Celso Brunetti
Queen Mary and Westfield College

Metals are both industrially produced and consumed goods, subject to the standard "laws" of supply and demand, and financial assets. The same is true of other primary commodities, particularly petroleum. When one takes a medium- to long-term view of the evolution of a metal market, it is important to consider trends in production and consumption levels, as well as production costs. However, when one takes a short-term perspective, these factors become less significant and metals prices behave very similarly to the prices of other financial assets. It is this latter perspective that we adopt in this chapter.

Introduction

To begin with, it is important to distinguish between the first-order (mean) process and the second-order (variance or scedastic) process for any asset price. If one transforms the price into a holding return, market efficiency implies that there should be little or no systematic predictability in the first-order process. Models which claim to forecast short-term changes in metals prices rightly command very little respect. This is not to say that an astute individual cannot out-guess the market, but rather that it is not possible for a college graduate with no industry knowledge to systematically outperform the consensus reflected in futures market prices. First-order processes for financial asset prices are therefore uninteresting, and best modelled either as random or mildly autoregressive.

By contrast, second-order asset price processes are rich and complicated. These processes describe the evolution of asset price *variability* over time. One can, therefore, hope to predict whether or not a price will be variable without having any knowledge about which way it will vary. If a company announcement is anticipated, one may reasonably expect the share price to move significantly up or down, even though no information is available that would help one to predict the direction of movement. The impact of announcements is less important in metals markets, although markets do range from being very quiet at certain times to being highly volatile at others. It is, therefore, reasonable to expect to be able to predict metals price variability (or volatility). Furthermore, because price volatility increases the riskiness of any unhedged position, it may also be important to predict volatility.

Of course, many metals market participants hedge and, to that extent, are unaffected by volatility. Increasingly, however, hedging is undertaken through the purchase of options – put options to shield against downside price risk, or call options to shield against upside risk. The writer of the option carries that risk, the extent of which is reflected in the option's price. Writers of options must, therefore, be very conscious of likely price volatility over the term of any options contracts they write. Access to a methodology that assists in the prediction of volatility will provide the writer of an option with a competitive advantage, in terms of accurate pricing; it will also help them decide when to write, and when to avoid writing, a particular contract.

Two features of the scedastic processes associated with asset prices have been emphasised by academic economists. These are:

- ❑ periods of high volatility tend to bunch together, as if markets were either in "active" or "passive" mode (volatilities exhibit positive *short-term* autocorrelation); and
- ❑ changes in volatility, although not permanent, are highly persistent (these positive short-term associations persist into the *medium term*).

We can add a third conjecture:

❑ over long periods of time, volatility is trendless (volatilities are trendless in the *long term*).

All three of these features may be observed in non-ferrous metals.

The bunching of price variability in financial markets is often attributed to the uneven way in which market news arrives. In an efficient financial market, all currently available information is discounted into market prices. It follows that price changes (strictly, excess holding returns)[1] can only be due to the arrival of new information. However, information arrives unevenly over time. In part, this reflects the fact that some periods (hours, days, weeks) are typically more active than others (for example, low activity occurs on Mondays or in December). More importantly, markets occasionally take time to reach a consensus on issues that affect prices. In the metals context, such issues may relate to the strength of metals demand, or to Russian or Chinese intentions in delivering to the London Metals Exchange (LME). In periods such as these, prices tend to bounce around over a period of days, or even weeks, as traders take positions on their information and/or with respect to these issues. This produces a clustering of volatility. Contrastingly, in other periods markets may appear to be asleep, with prices listlessly "moving sideways".

The bunching of volatility has been modelled by the Arch (AutoRegressive Conditional Heteroscedasticity) and Garch (Generalised AutoRegressive Conditional Heteroscedasticity) classes of model. In essence, Arch/Garch models relate current levels of volatility to volatility levels in previous periods, so that high volatility today predicts high volatility tomorrow, and vice versa. We discuss these models in a later section of this chapter.

Autoregressive models are useful because they allow models shocks to persist. That is, an event which raises volatility today, will also raise volatility in the future, albeit to a lesser extent. However, in standard autoregressive models such as Arch/Garch this persistence decays relatively quickly (technically, the persistence decays at an exponential rate). Processes in which shocks decay rapidly are said to exhibit short memory. By contrast, financial market volatility appears to persist for longer than these models can easily accommodate. In other words, volatility appears to be a *long-memory* process. Frequently, in order to make the model predictions fit the observed degree of persistence at *medium-term* horizons, one would need substantially higher estimates of the autoregressive parameters than is suggested by the autocorrelations at *short-term* lags. What is required is a model which allows relatively modest degrees of autocorrelation to persist for a long period of time. A further extension of the Arch/Garch class to Figarch (Fractionally Integrated Generalised Auto-Regressive Conditional Heteroscedasticity) models does just this.

Standard Arch/Garch models impose stationarity on the data. In general terms, stationarity implies that time-series plots of the series will look very similar at different dates. In particular, the series will have the same (unconditional) mean and variance at different dates. Stationarity therefore implies mean reversion. To say that a scedastic series is mean reverting is to say that the (unconditional) variance of the original series is constant over long periods of time. In contrast, a non-stationary series may be described as integrated, implying that differencing (ie, replacing x_t by $Dx_t = x_t - x_{t-1}$) will reduce it to stationarity – ie, if x_t is an integrated series, $D^r x_t$ will be stationary for a suitably high value of r (generally one or two in financial and economic applications). Whereas a shock to a stationary series will have only short-run effects, a shock to an integrated series will persist indefinitely.

Series with a fractional degree of integration are intermediate between these two cases. Fractionally integrated series may be either stationary or non-stationary, depending on the fractional integration parameter. This means that their shocks are more persistent than shocks applied to stationary series, but less persistent than those applied to integrated series. Figarch models and their application for LME metals will be analysed later in this chapter.

There is an unresolved question as to why the variances of financial time series do generally appear to be fractionally integrated. One conjecture is that this is a consequence of speculation. When speculators establish a position they do so with the intention, subsequently, of unwinding it. A purchase of a metals futures contract today will inevitably be followed by a sale at some future date, so that transactions become paired. A burst of volatility today will, therefore, imply high trading volumes over the coming weeks, which will maintain volatility at relatively high levels – even after the market has achieved an element of consensus on the informational content of the events which triggered today's activity. This account tallies well with the observed persistence of financial market volatility for around 50 trading days.

While short- and medium-term volatilities tend to be positively associated, long-term volatilities, at least in metals, appear trendless (stationary).[2] However, this conclusion conflicts with the widespread industry view that metals volatility has tended to rise over recent years, particularly as a consequence of activity by speculative funds.

Long-term trends in metals volatility

We start by looking at recent trends in volatility in non-ferrous metals. Our data set consists of a complete record of daily data on LME settlement prices from January 1972 to December 1995 for the six LME metals: aluminium (Al), copper (Cu), nickel (Ni), lead (Pb), tin (Sn) and zinc (Zn). Data on aluminium and nickel, however, are available only from October 1982.[3] The volatility for metal j in month m is calculated as the intra-month standard deviation of daily log dollar price changes (ie, daily holding returns), as shown in Box 1.

In the metals industries, it is more usual to calculate volatilities using monthly average or end-month figures. The advantage of using daily figures is that one obtains a higher frequency series than when one calculates the volatility using monthly returns. In the case study presented here, the use of daily data generates a sample of 288 monthly observations over the 24-year period 1972-95. If we had confined ourselves to using the annual standard deviations of monthly prices, there would only have been 24 observations. Daily data, therefore, generate potentially much more informative volatility measures.

Table 1 summarises the data by averaging over three-year periods, while Figures 1 and 2 depict the aluminium and copper volatility series, respectively. Four conclusions stand out and are explained below.

CONSISTENCY OVER TIME

It is apparent both from Table 1 and Figures 1 and 2 that there has been no observable trend in non-ferrous metals volatility over the past 25 years. This conclusion is confirmed by rigorous statistical analysis.[4] Anyone who asserts that metals are more volatile now than in the past is simply demonstrating poor memory or lack of knowledge.

CONSISTENCY OVER METALS

The temporal pattern of volatility movements is similar across all six metals. Volatility was high in

Box 1: Volatility measurement

This is a standard historic volatility measure. We measure the volatility of metal j as:

$$\mathrm{Vol}_{jm} = \sqrt{\frac{1}{n_m - 1}\sum_{i=1}^{n_m}\left(\Delta \ln p_{jmi} - \frac{1}{n_m}\sum_{i=1}^{n_m}\Delta \ln p_{jmi}\right)^2}$$

where p_{jmi} is the dollar value of the LME settlement price of metal j on day I of month m, and where the LME traded on n_m days in month m.

Table 1. Average monthly volatilities (%)

	Aluminium	Copper	Nickel	Lead	Tin	Zinc	Average
1972–74	-	2.01	-	1.86	1.40	2.46	1.93
1975–77	-	1.20	-	1.72	1.16	1.35	1.36
1978–80	-	1.66	-	2.42	1.32	1.81	1.80
1981–83	-	1.26	-	1.90	0.98	1.53	1.42
1984–86	1.45	1.12	1.29	2.06	-	1.77	1.54
1987–89	2.59	2.30	2.84	2.22	-	2.11	2.41
1990–92	1.25	1.38	1.62	1.84	0.92	1.54	1.43
1993–95	1.15	1.37	1.72	1.63	1.31	1.18	1.39
Entire period[1]	**1.58**	**1.54**	**1.84**	**1.96**	**1.15**	**1.72**	

1 This period is October 1992–December 1995 for aluminium and nickel, and January 1972–October 1985 plus August 1989–December 1995 for tin.

1. Aluminium volatility, 1983–95

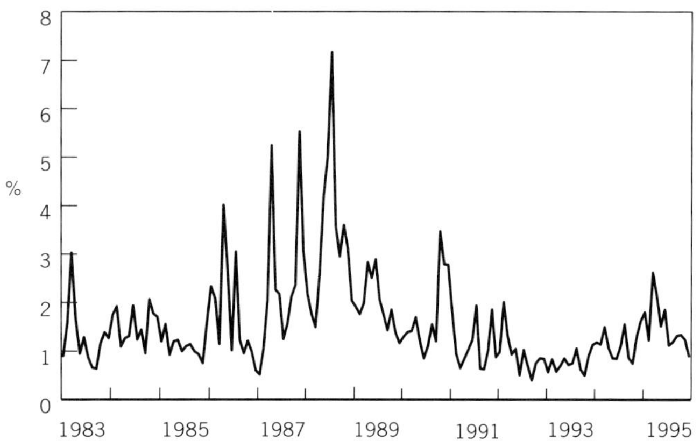

2. Copper volatility, 1972–95

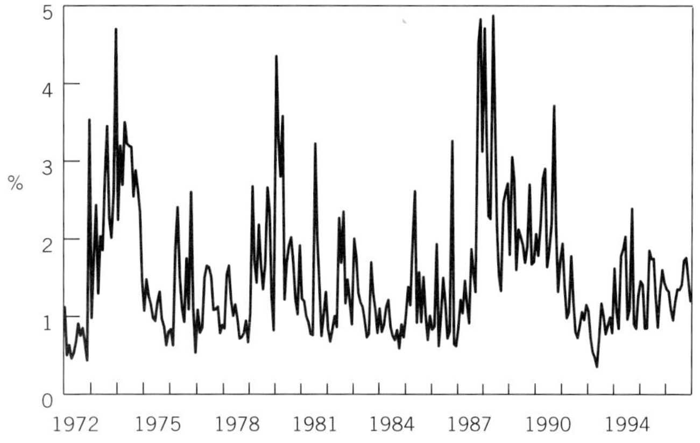

the period 1972–74, and again in 1987–89, but was low in the early 1980s and early 1990s. Detailed statistical analysis indicates that volatilities in aluminium, copper and nickel move particularly closely together, with lead and zinc volatility sharing a common idiosyncratic component.[5]

HIGH VOLATILITY IS ASSOCIATED WITH TIGHT DEMAND

Two periods stand out as exhibiting high volatility: 1973–74 and 1987–90. The common feature was a low level of LME warehouse stocks, resulting from sharp and unanticipated upsurges in metals demand (in 1973 and 1988, respectively). In a slack market (ie, when warehouse stocks are high), a small increase in metals requirements is easily met from stock, and hence gives rise only to a small price increase. In a tight market, on the other hand, stocks are held by potential metal users, which will require a large price incentive to release them on to the market. Hence, under these conditions, the same small change in metals requirements will result in a significantly larger price rise.

VOLATILITY WAS NOT EXCEPTIONALLY HIGH IN 1993–95

A sharp rise in demand was also a feature of 1994, but this came against the backdrop of high LME warehouse stocks (particularly in aluminium), so that the effects on volatility were more muted. Except for tin, volatility over the three-year period 1993–95 was lower than its historic average level. There was a significant increase in copper volatility in the latter part of 1995 and the first months of 1996, but it transpires that the trading strategy of a major Japanese corporation was responsible for artificial tightness in the copper market (see Chapter 3, Panel 2).

As noted in the introduction, this conclusion conflicts with the view that the activities of speculative funds have tended to increase metals markets volatility since 1993. To be sure, it appears[6] that a number of bursts of high volatility may be attributed to large movements on the part of speculative funds; and it must be acknowledged that volatility in 1994 was higher than in the early 1990s. Nevertheless, volatility levels over this recent period remain largely in line with historical experience, and are nowhere near as high as in the mid-1970s and late 1980s. Instead, these year-to-year changes in volatility appear largely to be due to changes in the overall tightness of metals markets. Volatility is typically high in periods during which stocks are low and supply is tight, whereas when stocks are plentiful shocks are easily absorbed by the market and have little impact on price. The modest increase in metals volatility experienced over recent years is primarily due to the tightening of the balance between supply and demand, rather than fund activity. Fund activity may even have reduced volatility by increasing market liquidity.

The Garch class of models

Over the last few years, there have been many types of volatility model advanced. Observing the frequent clustering of time-series variability, Engle proposed the autoregressive conditional *heteroscedasticity* (Arch) class, which models the *conditional second moments* of the time series (see Panel 1 for an explanation of italicised technical terms, and Panel 2 for references to key theoretical contributions). An Arch(p) model may be defined by:

$$\begin{aligned} y_t &= \mu_t + h_t^{1/2}\varepsilon_t \\ h_t &= \omega\left[1 + \alpha(L)\varepsilon_t^2\right] \\ \varepsilon_t &\sim N(0,1) \end{aligned} \qquad (1)$$

where $\alpha(L)$ is a *lag polynomial* of order p, L is the *lag operator* such that $Lx_t = x_{t-1}$ and $\alpha_0=1$. This model represents the local variations at time t around the conditional mean μ_t by a varying variance function h_t which depends on the *information set* W_{t-1} available on day $t-1$. In other words, equations (1) describe a regression function in which the regression variance varies over time in an *autoregressive* manner.

By analogy with standard conditional mean representations (standard regressions), one may refer to h_t as a *scedastic* or conditional variance function. In a financial context, it is natural to think of y_t as the asset return, which is well approximated by $y_t = 100(\ln P_t - \ln P_{t-1})$, where P_t is the asset price.[7] The conditional mean, μ_t, may be any regression function, although in principle an *unconditional mean* μ should be sufficient in applications to informationally efficient financial markets. In the results which are discussed later in this chapter, the conditional mean is allowed to be autoregressive:

$$\mu_t = \mu + \xi y_{t-1} \qquad (2)$$

This model represents the regression variance h_t as a *moving average* of the variance shocks ε_t^2 but, because one can generally represent a high-order moving average process by a low-order

European options, as it is simple to augment the volatility simulation with simulated metals prices. This will often be acceptable for the valuation of standard American calls on metals futures, but for puts (and also for calls in backwardation periods) it will be necessary to account for early exercise. This makes the valuation procedure significantly more complicated.

As an illustration, consider LME copper options on December 1, 1995. LME cash copper traded at $2,915.50 per tonne, while three-month copper was $2,708 per tonne. Trades were reported in December puts and calls with $2,900 strikes, February calls with a $3,000 strike and February puts with a $2,800 strike. In Table 2 we have priced these options using the Black formula, with three alternative estimates of the variance over the option term:

- ❑ the average volatility over the previous week;
- ❑ the average volatility over the previous three months; and
- ❑ the forecast volatility from the Figarch(1,d,0) model reported in the next section of this chapter.

We also give the reported trade prices for comparison.

The correspondence of the actual and calculated prices is poor, but this probably reflects the fact that we have estimated the required three-week (December) and 11-week (February) futures prices by linear interpolation - market participants would have had access to the actual price at which this intermediate date was trading. Also, we have failed to take into account the possibility of early exercise, which may have been important with the December call in view of the sharp backwardation (premium of the spot price over three months). More importantly, however, there are considerable differences in the implied premiums depending on the volatility estimate employed, with the Figarch forecast lying outside the range of the two historical volatilities.

Option trading on the LME takes the form of buying and selling volatility (implied volatilities rather than premiums are quoted), and these numbers suggest that standard estimates of future volatility may seriously misrepresent likely behaviour. In particular, it seems possible that market participants may over-discount recent periods of high volatility (which are likely to persist more than conventional estimates suggest).

Two other considerations may be relevant. Non-normality, which is highly evident in metals price data (see the next section), suggests that there may indeed be merit in simulating the options price directly, rather than in adopting the plug-in method, as the Black options formula relies on normality as well as constant variance. This does, however, imply that the non-normality should be taken into account in simulating the options price. A straightforward way of doing this is to "bootstrap" the innovation distribution, by sampling from the empirical distribution of the estimated residuals from the volatility model employed. Secondly, although standard plain vanilla puts and calls are generally fairly insensitive to alternative volatility estimates, this is not necessarily true of all exotic options (such as "down-and-out" options). This suggests that, even if plug-in estimates work well for the plain vanilla options, more caution should be employed in pricing exotics.

Box 5: The Ljung–Box statistic

The Ljung–Box statistic of order k is defined as:

$$Q(k) = n(n+2)\sum_{j=1}^{k}\frac{\rho_j}{n-j}$$

where ρ_j is the jth order autocorrelation of the standardised residuals and the sample size is n. Under the null hypothesis of no residual serial correlation, it is distributed as $\chi^2(n-p)$, where p is the number of parameters in the regression function. It provides a "portmanteau" test for serial correlation of order up to k but is sensitive to choice of k. The second-order Ljung–Box statistic $Q^2(k)$ provides a portmanteau test for residual heteroscedasticity. One uses the same statistic, but in this case based on the autocorrelations of the squared residuals. The statistic now has degrees of freedom n−q where q is the number of parameters in the (Garch) conditional variance function. See Ljung G. and G.E.P. Box, 1978, "On a Measure of Lack of Fit in Time Series Models", *Biometrika*, 65, pp. 297–303.

Table 2. LME copper options, December 1, 1995

Date	Strike ($)	Put/call	One-week historical volatility ($)	Three-month historical volatility ($)	Figarch (1,d,0) ($)	Actual price ($)
Dec	2,900	Call	7	15	17	30
Dec	2,900	Put	43	51	53	16
Feb	3,000	Call	2	11	28	57
Feb	2,800	Put	102	125	153	120

Estimated Figarch models for non-ferrous metals

There is by now a growing experience in applying fractionally integrated volatility models to stock market and bond returns, but relatively little awareness of how these models can be applied in metals and other physical commodity markets. However, the issues are broadly similar, and it is therefore useful to examine the applicability of these models in this context. In what follows, we report ML estimates of the AR(1)-Figarch(1,d,0) model:

$$\begin{aligned} y_t &= \mu + \xi y_{t-1} + h_t^{½}\varepsilon_t \\ h_t &= \omega + \beta h_{t-1} + \left[1 - \beta L - (1-L)^d\right]\varepsilon_t^2 \end{aligned} \quad (9)$$

on daily data for each of the six LME non-ferrous metals: aluminium, copper, nickel, lead, tin and zinc. Estimates are over the period January 1972 to December 1995 for copper, lead and zinc; October 1982 to December 1995 for aluminium and nickel; and January 1972 to October 1985 plus August 1989 to December 1995 for tin.[12] The first five rows of Table 3 list the sample statistics for the daily returns over this period. It is apparent that there are substantial departures from normality, due almost entirely to excess kurtosis (see definition in Panel 1). This is normal in financial data, but it does caution against putting too much faith in estimated parameter standard errors, as discussed below.[13]

The final four rows of Table 3 report Box-Pierce portmanteau statistics for the squared returns over ranges of 10, 20, 50 and 100 lags (see Box 5). These all exhibit very high degrees of dependence. This may be seen visually in Figure 6, which shows the correlogram (sample autocorrelation function) of the squared daily aluminium returns. This should be contrasted with the theoretical autocorrelation functions illustrated in Figures 3 and 4 – the sample function corresponds closely to the theoretical function from the fractionally integrated process (Figure 4), and looks quite different from that of the short-memory process with the same autoregressive and moving average parameters (Figure 3). This is a clear visual demonstration of the presence of long memory.

Parameter estimates for the AR(1)-Figarch (1,d,0) model (9) are given in Table 4 (approximate standard errors in parentheses). It is important to note that:

- the autoregressive parameter ξ of the AR(1) first-order process is estimated as negative for all metals except tin, but it is only significantly different from zero in the case of copper. A negative coefficient may be rationalised in terms of trading processes in which prices bounce between bid to offer levels;
- the autoregressive coefficient β of the Figarch process, by contrast, is estimated as positive for all six metals and lies in the range 0.25–0.38;
- the fractional differencing parameter d is estimated as significantly greater than zero but significantly less than unity for all six metals, confirming both fractional integration and stationarity. The parameters all lie within the range 0.42–0.52, and this suggests possible extension to a multivariate model with a common fractional integration parameter; and
- the conditions for the variances to remain positive ($\omega > 0$, $0 \le \beta < d \le 1$) are satisfied for all six metals.

Table 5 provides diagnostics to assess the adequacy of the estimated models. The first two rows show the skewness and excess kurtosis of the standardised residuals, while the subsequent rows give Box-Pierce portmanteau statistics for the squared residuals over ranges of 10, 20, 50 and 100 lags. The standardised residuals exhibit substantially less kurtosis than the returns (see Table 3) for all the metals except copper. Perhaps of greater importance, the Box-Pierce portmanteau statistics in general fail to reject the null hypothesis of no serial correlation in the squared

Table 3. Sample statistics

	Al	Cu	Ni	Pb	Sn	Zn
Mean	0.018	0.016	0.020	0.018	0.016	0.017
Standard deviation	1.783	1.762	2.181	2.127	1.343	1.965
Skewness	−0.669	−0.122	−0.533	−0.198	−0.043	−0.394
Excess kurtosis	11.32	6.68	13.78	7.09	7.56	11.84
Normality $c^2(2)$	3,271	3,614	4,536	3,850	3,612	7,073
# Observations	3,343	6,056	3,343	6,056	5,104	6,056
$Q^2(10)$	1,377	1,094	1,113	1,997	1,824	2,800
$Q^2(20)$	1,992	1,907	2,212	2,262	2,352	3,645
$Q^2(50)$	3,012	2,980	3,319	2,370	2,691	5,338
$Q^2(100)$	3,564	4,531	4,137	2,738	3,309	7,421

6. Simulated autocorrelation function, aluminium squared returns, October 1982–December 1995

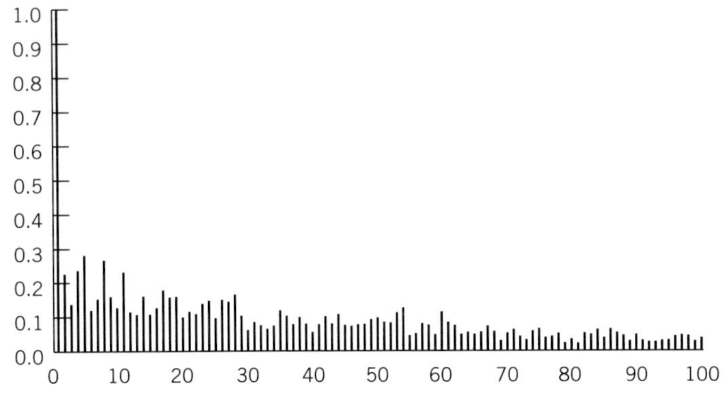

residuals, indicating that we have adequately accounted for the sample autocorrelations. Furthermore, these statistics are, without exception, an order lower than the corresponding statistics for the squared returns reported in Table 3. These statistics suggest that, despite their apparent simplicity, the estimated Figarch models adequately account for the long-range dependence in the volatility series.

Conclusions

Volatilities in financial markets present interesting and novel problems which are only beginning to be understood. Standard time-series models do not appear adequate to capture the variability of volatility at a daily level, and metals are no exception in this regard. What is required are models which:

- allow for the possibility of short bursts of activity;
- allow the volatility effects of these bursts to persist into the medium term; but
- impose reversion to a stationary long-run level in the long term.

These features of metals volatility have implications for the pricing of options on LME contracts.

We have suggested that the Figarch class of models satisfies these requirements. Estimates for the LME metals over the period 1972–95 confirm that simple models of this class account for observed volatility persistence, and show that the volatility processes of all six metals examined are very similar. Models of this sort allow an extension of standard options pricing procedures, to take into account temporary bursts of volatility – either through the plug-in approach, or by more extended numerical simulation.

Table 4. QML parameter estimates

	Al	Cu	Ni	Pb	Sn	Zn
μ	0.477	−2.90	−2.93	4.138	0.736	3.975
(x100)	(2.121)	(1.629)	(2.284)	(1.997)	(1.247)	(1.815)
ξ	−0.083	−6.907	0.055	−4.121	0.755	- 0.912
(x100)	(1.903)	(1.393)	(1.974)	(1.439)	(1.602)	(1.410)
ω	0.1295	0.1637	0.1525	0.2174	0.0682	0.1923
	(0.0246)	(0.0236)	(0.0336)	(0.0303)	(0.0126)	(0.0251)
β	0.3278	0.2831	0.2543	0.3734	0.2552	0.3436
	(0.0490)	(0.0449)	(0.0456)	(0.0499)	(0.0408)	(0.0529)
d	0.4483	0.4243	0.4579	0.5171	0.4589	0.4745
	(0.0432)	(0.0365)	(0.0375)	(0.0452)	(0.0334)	(0.0463)

Table 5. Model diagnostics

	Al	Cu	Ni	Pb	Sn	Zn
Skewness	0.155	−0.346	0.230	0.012	−0.005	0.080
Excess kurtosis	6.46	10.64	5.38	6.11	5.25	5.50
$Q^2(10)$	6.64	5.41	4.57	7.40	21.32	27.22
$Q^2(20)$	9.55	9.95	12.77	14.29	31.40	31.58
$Q^2(50)$	38.33	22.22	47.35	37.98	69.73	59.06
$Q^2(100)$	85.51	72.35	108.16	105.19	117.91	99.41

1 *A share price will fall as the share goes ex-dividend; this fall will be correctly anticipated by the market. However, it is not possible to use this information to generate an excess holding return. For a theoretical account of volatility clustering see Gallant, A.R., D.A. Hsieh and G. Tauchen, "On Fitting a Recalcitrant Series: The Pound-Dollar Exchange Rate, 1974–83", in Barnett W.A., Powell J. and G. Tauchen (eds.), 1991,* Nonparametric and Semiparametric Methods in Economics and Statistics, *Cambridge University Press.*

2 *This has been documented in Brunetti C. and C.L. Gilbert, 1995, "Metals Price Volatility, 1972–95",* Resources Policy, *21, pp. 237–54.*

3 *Tin was not traded on the LME from November 1985 to July 1989. At the start of the sample, the LME traded entirely in sterling, but by the later years of the sample all contracts had become dollar denominated. All prices have been converted to a dollar basis at the current day's dollar/sterling exchange rate. Daily price data are available from the LME from January 1989. Data prior to this are taken from World Bureau of Metal Statistics,* World Metal Statistics *(various issues). The dollar/sterling exchange rate is the official LME dollar/sterling exchange rate from 1989, although it is taken from Datastream for dates prior to 1989. These exchange rates will not be synchronous with the metals prices. The data is available in spreadsheet form (also including three-month prices) from the authors on request. A small charge will be requested from non-academic users.*

4 *See Brunetti C. and C.L. Gilbert, 1995, op. cit.*

5 *See Gilbert, C.L. and C. Brunetti, 1996, "Harmless Speculation",* Risk, *vol. 9, No. 5, pp. 56–60.*

6 *See Brunetti C. and C.L. Gilbert, 1995, op. cit.*

7 *Alternatively, the excess return obtained by subtracting the interest rate. On daily data, this correction makes little difference.*

8 *Beran J.,* Statistics for Long-Memory Processes, *Chapman and Hall, 1994, is the best general introduction to the statistical theory relating to long-memory processes.*

9 *An Arfima process is a fractionally integrated Arma process. Arma and Arima processes are special cases of the Arfima class in the same way that Garch and Igarch processes are special cases of the Figarch class.*

10 *Hurst C.E., 1951, "Long-term Storage Capacity of Reservoirs",* Transactions of the American Society of Civil Engineers, *116, pp. 770–799. Hurst analysed annual flow rates in the River Nile.*

11 *Gemmill G.,* Option Pricing: An International Perspective, *McGraw-Hill, 1993, recommends use of the Cox and Ross CEV model for pricing commodity options. See Black F., 1976, "The Pricing of Commodity Contracts",* Journal of

Financial Economics, *3, pp. 167–179; and Cox, J. and S. Ross, 1976, "The Valuation of Options for Alternative Stochastic Processes",* Journal of Financial Economics, *3, pp. 145–166.*

12 *The copper, lead and zinc models were also estimated over the shorter sample used for aluminium and nickel. The results were very similar to those reported for the full sample.*

13 *It also implies that, strictly, one should interpret the estimates as quasi-maximum likelihood (QML) rather than ML.*

9

Special Issues in Valuing Metals Derivatives

Oliver Frankel
Goldman Sachs

To any professional engaged in the fabrication or valuation of derivatives, the metals markets present their own distinctive character.[1] And just as the metals markets are distinct from those in stocks and equities, so the risks that need to be evaluated in the base metals markets differ from those encountered in precious metals. The purpose of this chapter is to illustrate how the general Black–Scholes framework for option valuation[2] – and the extensions of it that are necessary to cope with exotic options – can be applied to base and precious metals.

As is well known, the Black-Scholes theory relies on certain fundamental assumptions: normally distributed returns,[3] frictionless markets, zero taxes and the ability to trade continuously. Without challenging these assumptions – except the first, as applied to the metals markets, which we discuss at the end of this chapter – we still need to make explicit a series of related tenets that are implicit in applications of the Black-Scholes theory (and its extensions) in the equity and currency markets, and re-examine them in the context of metals.

The first tenet is that forward prices in a market are consistent with spot prices carried forward – accomplished by financing the cost at the spot price, and lending the asset out to term. Where this tenet holds true, it is possible to hedge long forward positions with short-term or spot positions while assuming only "carry rate" risk. (Carry rate risk is the risk that either the financing or lending rates may change over the course of the life of the forward – in foreign exchange, both rates can be hedged in any case, while with equities only the financing rate can be hedged). Thus daily returns from spot positions are the same as those obtained from long-term forward positions, at least. While such carry arguments are approximately true in the case of precious metals, they cannot be assumed when trading in base metals. Not only do base metal returns differ across maturity, but it also appears that they are often far from 100% correlated; on some days, forward prices move in the opposite direction to the cash price!

Precious metals, however, do appear to be similar to currencies – at least in the short term. As with foreign exchange, the banking reserve system maintains large gold reserves, the short-term lending of which provides stability in the gold lease rate market, and liquidity for dealers to carry forward short spot positions as hedges against long forward positions (Chapter 1 of this book discusses the mechanics of this in some detail). Thus many points presented here as adaptations for valuing precious metals derivatives also apply to longer-term currency and equity hedging. That they are seldom relevant is, I believe, because the terms of most currency and equity derivatives are quite short – under two years – while gold derivatives can span five or even 10 years of risk.

Pricing base metals derivatives requires modifications to the Black-Scholes theory for reasons that have nothing to do with long tenors. While users and traders in base metals maintain substantial inventory stocks as protection against vagaries in supply, transport costs prohibit their lending for short periods (outside of the exchange). This is in complete contrast to precious metals, the lending of which can be effected via reallocation among accounts held in the same bank vault. Without the stabilising effect of a lease rate market, there arises a separate and volatile effect in the dynamics of near-term prices – an effect also evident in the energy markets. In consequence, not only are base metal forward prices more volatile as they become

PANEL 1

FISCHER BLACK'S COMMODITY OPTION PRICING MODEL

At first sight, to apply the original Black-Scholes option pricing model to commodities it would appear necessary to develop an imaginary dividend yield that would accrue to holders of the commodity, even when they bought the commodity on a forward basis. What is more, since the forward price curve – in the case of base metals, at least – can change considerably over a day of trading, it would appear necessary to provide a stochastic model to describe the dynamic behaviour of this imaginary dividend yield.

In his seminal paper of 1976, Fischer Black showed that all this was unnecessary. According to the framework of derivatives pricing – using risk-neutral arguments – each dated forward price must follow a geometric random walk. In consequence, given an annual percent volatility of V, the distribution of possible forward prices for any later date – eg, at option expiration – is simply a lognormal distribution. That is, the log of the future forward price centres around $\log(F) - V^2T/2$ with standard deviation $V\sqrt{T}$, where F is the current forward price and T is the future time in years.

Given this insight, it is possible to price a call option directly as the present value of the expected payout:

$$C[F,K;V,T,r] = e^{-rT}\{FN(d_1) - KN(d_2)\}$$

where,
F is the current forward price,
K is the option strike,
V is the volatility,
T is the time to expiration (in years),
r is the discount rate,
and, similar to the original Black-Scholes model,

$$d_2 = \frac{\log(F/K) - V^2T/2}{V\sqrt{T}}$$

$$d_1 = d_2 + V\sqrt{T}$$

Probability distribution for a one-year forward price of 1,600 and 20% volatility

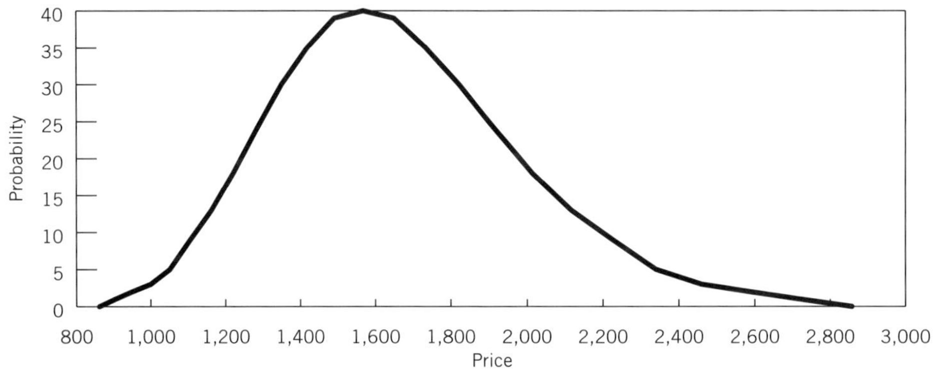

prompt, but also the correlation between short- and long-term prices breaks down.

As an example, the correlation between the spot price for aluminium and the price of contracts for aluminium 15 months forward ("15-month aluminium") has averaged a mere 65% over the years 1995 and 1996. For copper priced on the London Metals Exchange (LME), the story is even more dramatic. In 1996, the correlation of the cash (spot price) and prices for 15-month aluminium averaged only 47%, and the correlation of the cash price and three-month prices averaged little more at 56%. We must infer that no single factor prescribes how aluminium and copper forward prices move! (This is in contrast to, say, gold or silver, where the spot price dictates the dynamics for its entire forward price curve.)

Note, however, that this is not always the case. In the past there have been periods - 1993, for example, when LME inventories were at historical highs - in which aluminium forward prices became temporarily consistent with financing from spot prices, and when the correlation of the cash and 15-month prices hit very high averages (97% for a time in 1993). During these times, percentage changes in the 15-month price mirror those seen in the cash price. Thus, we note that base metals can behave like currencies in certain market environments, when inventories are high. At such times, forward prices - obtained by financing and carrying metal inventories - may be lower than any expected future cash price that takes into account future projected supply and demand levels: instead, the forward price is driven by the marginal desire for shorter-term metal.

So when, under what circumstances, do we need to adapt the single-factor Black-Scholes theory? Regular European-style options can be effectively priced and managed against forward prices by using the option-pricing formula specially adapted for commodities that was published by Fischer Black in 1976 (the "Black '76 model" described in Panel 1).[4] In essence, the option premium to be paid today is the discounted expected value of the option payout, under the assumption that the current future price is a fair reflection of its future value (and that the forward price probability distribution is lognormal). The volatility parameter to the model describes the "width" of this distribution, once we have de-annualised it by multiplying by the square root[5] of the time to expiration.

Figure 1 charts the price history of gold from March 1, 1992, and the forward curve on that date. In addition, two curves describing the plus one and minus one standard deviations around the forward curve are superimposed, assuming a constant volatility of 12%. Note how the spread between the plus and minus one standard deviation curves increases with the square root of time. This illustrates how a constant volatility assumption corresponds to the width of terminal distribution of progressively longer-maturity forwards.

1. Spot gold price distribution:
12% volatility, 3.5% contango, Mar 22, 1992–Mar 14, 1997

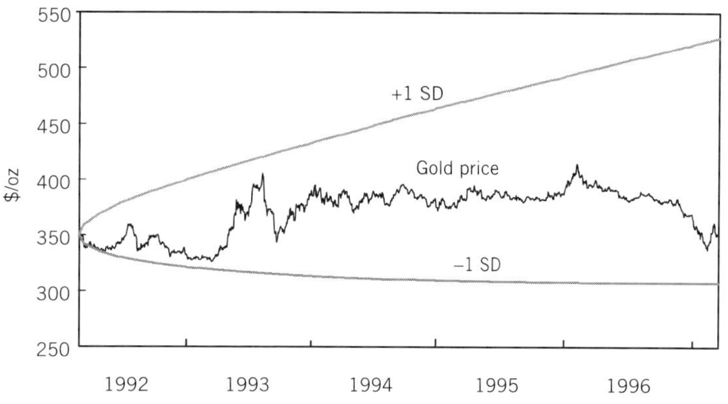

Table 1. COMEX gold volatilities as of last week of August 1996

Spot price was 381.5

Strike	1m	2m	3m	4m	6m	8m	10m	12m
340	29.0	18.3	14.3	10.9	11.0	10.0	9.3	9.5
350	23.5	15.0	11.8	9.0	9.7	9.0	8.7	9.0
360	18.0	11.8	9.2	8.0	8.3	8.0	8.0	8.2
370	12.5	8.5	7.5	6.4	7.1	7.3	7.3	7.6
380	6.7	6.4	6.3	6.0	7.0	7.2	6.9	7.0
390	4.9	5.8	6.0	6.2	6.5	7.1	7.0	7.1
400	8.7	6.4	6.6	6.7	6.7	6.7	6.7	7.1
410	12.7	7.6	7.6	7.5	7.4	7.0	7.3	7.1
420	17.5	9.6	9.1	8.2	7.8	7.7	8.0	7.7
430	22.0	12.4	10.8	9.5	8.8	8.7	8.4	7.9
440	26.2	15.0	11.7	10.6	9.9	9.2	9.0	8.4
450	30.3	17.4	13.6	11.3	10.7	10.2	9.5	9.0
460	34.2	20.6	15.5	12.0	11.9	11.1	9.8	9.5

In the metals markets, forward prices are readily available in the form of prices for the relevant exchange-traded futures contracts. The exchanges also list call and put options with a variety of expiration dates and strike prices.[6] Using the Black '76 commodity option model we can "back out" the volatility parameter that the market is using to price options, and obtain a table of volatilities organised by expiration and strike.

Note that the volatilities vary not only by term but also by strike. While the variation by term can be worked into the Black-Scholes theory – by allowing the volatility of the metal spot price to vary over time – the variation by strike is distinctly at odds with the theory's assumption of lognormal prices (or normally distributed instantaneous returns). We will postpone our discussion of this until the last part of this chapter, partly because it is a difficult problem, and partly because it is not peculiar to the metals markets. Until then, we shall note the variation by term to expiration, and make this the subject of our main analysis.

Under what circumstances, then, do we need further theory to take into account the special features of metals, when both forward and option prices are readily available from exchange markets?

The standard European option payout depends on the realisation of a single forward price on a particular day. While we are treating returns as normally distributed, the Black '76 formulation holds as long as the volatility parameter is appropriate for the option expiration and forward value date. When the optionality of a derivative on a forward price ends earlier than the regular option (as in the case of an "early expiration" option), or when it starts later (as in the case of a "delayed start" option,[7] where the option strike is set some time after the date of trade), versions of the Black '76 formula can be applied: discounting is applied from the option settlement date, while the option time term depends on when the optionality starts and ends. However, the setting of the volatility parameter demands some thought.

Take, as an example, an early expiration option which grants the holder a three-month call on a five-year forward price. Should one use a volatility implied from three-month exchange options, or from regular European five-year options? Or do we need a volatility derived from a more complete theory which projects, in a manner consistent with market option prices, how the expected daily volatility of a given forward price will change over time? A volatility profile, if you will. With such a profile, one would be equipped to evaluate, not only short-term options on longer forwards, but also delayed start options, compound options and certain varieties of American options and knock-out options. The common feature of all these instruments is that the contingent payoff depends on realisations of the same dated[8] forward price over a number (or continuum) of times up to expiration.

Apart from the market-implied volatilities, we have one other source of information to help us derive plausible volatility profiles: recent or typical historical volatility relationships. We may note, for example, that forwards with a certain maturity tend to possess a volatility that is 10% higher (or lower) than the spot price volatility. Equipped with similar observations, and the requirement that the volatility over the life of the option must be that implied from the market, we can pursue one key objective of this chapter: to provide a means to derive a period volatility for a given dated forward, for any pair of start and end dates within the life of the regular European option associated with the forward.

In other instances we have to evaluate an option on a payout that is described by more than one dated forward price. Average price options (Asian options) and forward spread[9] options are obvious examples, but regular American, lookback and knockout-style options are also in this category. An American option can be exercised against a given term forward price (eg, spot price or three-month price) at any time. The payout of a lookback option depends on the maximum or minimum spot price obtained. Similarly, a regular knockout option is knocked out against a given term price, the spot price for precious metals and the three-month price for base metals. Each of these familiar option styles depends on the whole curve of forward prices and their projected evolution over time, and thus their combined statistics. In these cases, when the derivative payout depends on the realisation of more than one forward price, valuation models must incorporate the relative movement between forward prices as a correlation, a covariance or, more explicitly, as the conditional distribution of one forward price given the price of another.

In general, the problem boils down to deriving a period covariance between a given pair of dated forward prices. If we can derive this, then the period correlation – the usual parameter required in option pricing formulas – can be easily calculated by dividing the covariance by the period volatilities of the two forwards (and the length of the period).

There are a good many books that describe these and similar options, and show how to evaluate them.[10] However, as yet no text explains how to think about the volatility (and correlation) parameters that should be used with the given formulas within the context of the metals markets. The over-arching objective of this chapter is, therefore, to show how we can derive appropriate and consistent volatility and correlation estimates by examining metal price behaviour – estimates which can then be confidently applied to the textbook option pricing formulas.

Metal forward prices and their statistics

To focus the investigation, and as a first step, let us consider how we can think about the evolution of volatility of a dated forward, as it matures over time – the "volatility profile" we mentioned above. Furthermore, how can we use this to price early expiration options?

The first requirement of any approach is that it is consistent with market prices. If volatility for a given forward price is going to evolve over time, then the total volatility up to the market option expiration date must be the same as the volatility implied by market option prices. It is also a basic tenet that markets are efficient: changes in dated forward prices on one day are independent from changes that have occurred earlier. In other words, all market forward prices follow random walks.[11] And, as with all random walks – indeed, as with our method for estimating volatility, the standard deviation being the square root of variance – it is variance that accrues with the progression of time. When we speak of total volatility we mean the square root of the total variance, so that our consistency condition is that, given a volatility profile, when squared (to give a "variance profile") and summed, our method has to lead to the same total variance that we back out from market option prices. (The latter is simply the market-implied volatility parameter squared, times the time in years of the life of the option, and can be referred to as the market-implied variance.)

Another consideration is that the volatility profiles associated with each dated forward should be consistent with one another. This consistency condition will vary from metal to metal, as we shall see below. For now, note that strict Black-Scholes theory requires that, at every instant, each forward price should undergo the same percentage change. That is, at every instant, they must experience the same volatility; and further, their moment-to-moment returns must be completely correlated (in fact, identical). Under these strict conditions, a two-year forward price must experience the same volatility as that of a three-month price, over the same period. The answer to our question as to what volatility to use for an early expiration option is straightforward: use the volatility implied by a three-month option. Similarly, the volatility to use when pricing a delayed start option - consistent with market-implied volatilities - must be that found by subtracting the three-month market-implied variance (MIV) from the five-year MIV; after annualising it (dividing by the active term of the option, 5−0.25 = 4.75), the square root gives the necessary volatility.

This precept, and the consequent calculus, is used in the pricing of equity and foreign exchange derivatives. Before we apply it in the metal derivative context, we should first check to see whether actual statistics of metal forward prices exhibit these properties. We shall start our investigation with gold, as the precious metal par excellence.

Precious metals

A first experiment is to measure the average volatilities of various term forward prices, over a given period. Under Black-Scholes, the volatilities should all be equal. Figure 2 shows the 1996 historical average volatility of forward prices, with maturities from spot to seven years, plotted against the volatilities predicted by the Black–Scholes model.

We note that the actual volatility of forwards appears to have been larger than the corresponding spot volatility, and that it was increasingly larger with increasing term to maturity. The average three-month volatility appears to have been approximately 6%, while the five-year forward price experienced an average volatility of 8% over the same period - 33% larger! We draw the conclusion that not all the Black–Scholes precepts hold precisely for precious metals.

The second prediction that Black–Scholes supports is that the forward prices will be fully correlated. Table 2 shows how well spot prices correlated with the various forward prices during 1996.

2. Forward price volatility by maturity, historic average in 1996

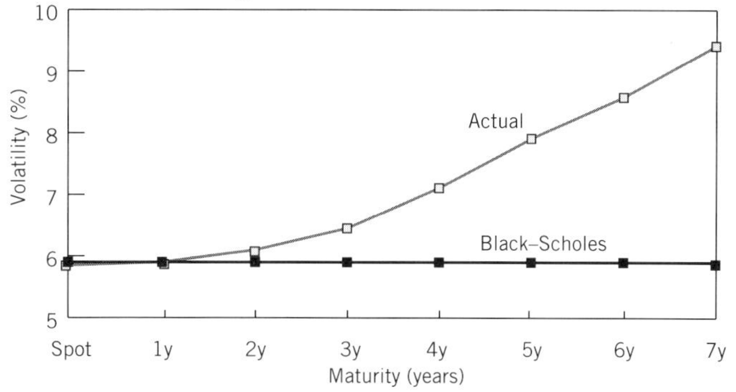

Table 2. Correlation of spot and forward prices in 1996

Term	1y	2y	3y	4y	5y	6y	7y
Correlation	0.998	0.995	0.992	0.990	0.987	0.985	0.982

Table 3. Average historical volatility by term in 1996

Teim	1y	2y	3y	4y	5y	Cy	7y
Correlation	1.000	1.050	1.120	1.205	1.341	1.454	1.595

As can be seen from the table, gold forward prices are indeed very highly correlated. It is consistent with these statistics to suggest that forward prices undergo a change in the same direction in each instant; even if, on average, forward prices with longer terms respond more (on a percentage basis). If this is the case, then market-implied term volatilities should also reflect this in some way. We have been looking at average daily volatilities. What is the relationship of these to term volatilities, ie, to the projected average volatility of a forward as it matures towards the spot price?

If we make the following two assumptions, we can reconcile the theory and the data, and thereby derive period volatility parameters that are consistent, both with forward price volatility characteristics and with market option prices:

1. The spot price is projected so that it is subject to a time-dependent volatility in the future.
2. Forward prices experience a volatility that is a factor larger than the future spot price volatility, the factor depending upon their remaining maturity at that time.

A table of factors can be extracted from the chart (Table 3) to illustrate the average historical volatility by term in 1996; for each term we have divided the volatility seen in that term by the average spot volatility.

With these factors in hand we can now itera-

PANEL 2

GOLD VOLATILITY TERM STRUCTURE AND RELATIONSHIP TO INTEREST RATE AND LEASE RATE VOLATILITY

We can relate the dynamics of the gold forward curve to interest and lease rates using a simple model. The model exploits the fact that the returns of a given dated forward of price F with maturity T, under arbitrage-free pricing, must, at all times t, follow a random walk:

$$\frac{dF_t^T}{F_t^T} = \sigma dW + \eta(T-t)dZ;\ dW.d_t = \rho dz$$

where σ is the gold price volatility and η the volatility, expressed in per cent per annum, of the gold contango rate. The variance to maturity is then expressed as:

$$\sigma_0^T = \sqrt{\frac{1}{T-t}\int_t^T E\left\{\frac{dF_s^T}{F_s^T}\right\} ds} =$$

$$\sqrt{\frac{1}{T-t}\int_t^T \left(\sigma^2 + 2\rho\sigma\eta(T-s) + \eta^2(T-s)^2\right) ds}$$

which, at t = 0, evaluates to:

$$\sigma_0^T = \sqrt{\sigma^2 + \rho\sigma\eta T + \frac{\eta^2 T^2}{3}}$$

The relationship between contango rate volatility and interest and lease rate volatility can be expressed via:

$$\eta^2 = \chi^2 R^2 + \lambda^2 L^2 - 2\nu\chi\lambda RL$$

where:

χ is the interest rate volatility and R the forward interest rate;

λ is the lease rate volatility and L the forward lease rate; and

ν is the correlation between interest and lease rates.

tively calculate the market projection of the future spot price volatility.

Starting with one-year options, as the one-year factor is one, we set the one-year spot price volatility to that of the term volatility implied by the price of one-year options in the market. Let us say that this volatility is 6%, and that two-year options are quoted at 6.5%. While the spot price was moving at 6% volatility, our theory (and Table 3) suggest, that the two-year forward price was moving at 6% × 1.05 = 6.3%. If the market projects a total two-year variance of:

$$6.5\% \times 6.5\% \times 2 = 0.00845$$

and the forward experiences a variance for the first year of:

$$6.3\% \times 6.3\% \times 1 = 0.003969$$

then the forward variance for the spot price will be the difference, or 0.004481. We then take the square root to calculate a projected volatility for the spot price in one year for one year as 6.69%. We can continue this calculation to project the future volatility of the spot price for as far into the future as we have market option prices. Once we have the future volatility of spot we have, from the same factors, the future volatility of forward prices of all terms at any future time.

Let us apply this to the pricing problem we posed earlier: how to find suitable volatility parameters for pricing early expiration and delayed start options. For a one-year option on a five-year dated forward, we should use the market one-year term volatility of 6% and then multiply by the five-year factor:

$$6\% \times 1.341 = 8.046\ \%$$

Note that this will, in all likelihood, be far greater than the five-year term volatility. If the future volatility of spot were 6% throughout, this would predict a five-year term volatility of 6.9%, which we can see as follows. Take the product of each factor with 6% to calculate the forward volatility of the dated forward as it matures over time; sum the squares of these products to get the total variance; and divide by five to annualise. The square root of this is our projected term volatility of 6.9%.

To find a volatility parameter for a delayed start option, we proceed along similar lines. For an option on the dated five-year forward with a strike price that is set at the market price of that forward in one year, one must project the variance that the forward will experience, starting not today but once the strike has been set. In one year's time, the exercised contract would start to behave like a four-year forward which, in a further four years, will mature into the region of the spot price. Consequently, we must apply the factors that correspond to the one-year to four-year terms to the forward volatility of the spot price for years two to five (as backed out from the volatilities implied by the market for those terms).

The use of a table of empirically derived factors is not completely satisfying. Where is the structure that dictates that the longer-term forwards are subject to larger volatilities? How do the factors that we have derived statistically relate to spot price volatility and to other market rates and prices?

To develop the theory further, remember that forward prices in precious metals markets are derived from spot prices via financing and lending. Indeed, forward prices are quoted in terms of the carry (or forward) rate. This forward rate is, loosely, the difference between the interest rate and lease rate as they apply to the term of the dated forward. Thus, even without a change in the spot price, a forward price will respond to changes in carry rates – in particular, to changes in interest rates. This observation can be developed into a complete model that links forward price volatility to that of interest rates and lease rates, taking into account correlations between them and spot price returns. Indeed, if we assume a low correlation between carry rates and spot prices,[12] the daily forward price variance is approximately the sum of the spot price variance and the effective variance due to carry rate moves. The latter variance is proportional to the term of the dated forward – explaining why longer-term forwards are more volatile. With long-term carry rates of around 4% experiencing an average volatility of around 25%, we can estimate the price volatility of a five-year forward as:

$$\sqrt{6\%^2 + (25\% + 4\% + 5)^2}$$

where 6% is taken as the average spot price volatility.

This calculates to roughly 7.81%, a result that is not inconsistent with the historically measured volatility of forwards of this tenor (7.91%).

We can now test the approach by deriving forward volatilities for 1996, using the lease rate volatilities and correlations among the spot price and rates. Figure 3 compares these volatilities

3. Forward price volatility by maturity, historic average in 1996

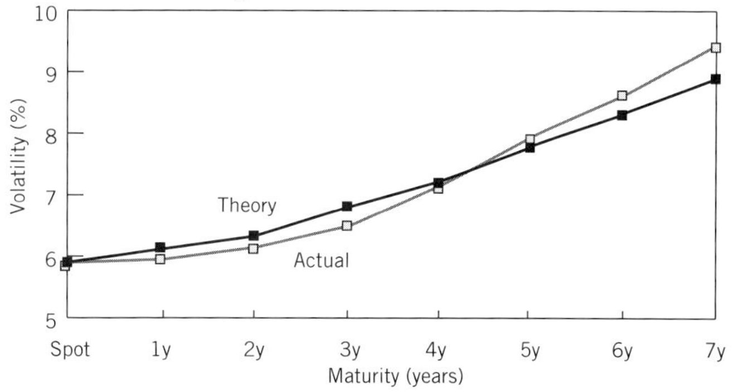

derived from theory with the volatilities seen in the market. While the calculations do not match the actual rates perfectly, the chart suggests that the approach is worth exploring further.

Base metals

The behaviour of forward curves in the base metals markets is very distinctive – both in contrast to the precious metals and among the different base metals. As with all commodities, the organisation of storage and transport governs the relationship between the spot price and the forward price. In the case of base metals, storage practice varies from metal to metal, as the structure of the producing industry varies (see also Chapter 10).

Consider the copper and aluminium industries. Consumers of these metals rarely use the metals in the form in which they are "deliverable" according to the exchange contract (see Chapter 3) ie, copper cathode or aluminium ingot (sows or T-bars). Instead, to suit the user, the metal is reformed – copper into rod, aluminium typically into sheet. This service is usually performed by the producer or, in some cases, by an independent manufacturer (only occasionally by the end-users themselves). While converting copper cathode to rod is a relatively simple process, aluminium sheet rolling is highly capital intensive and very expensive to interrupt and restart.

In consequence, the aluminium sheet manufacturer is motivated to maintain sufficient inventories of exchange-quality material to buffer supply uncertainties and demand fluctuations. A rolling operation must both perform a metal inventory and plan purchases and operations against a forward price. In contrast, the copper rod producer may run its operation to process whatever material is available: the rod producer buys copper at the spot price.

The effect on the two exchange markets is profound. There is little demand for aluminium in the

4. Aluminium and copper 1996 volatility

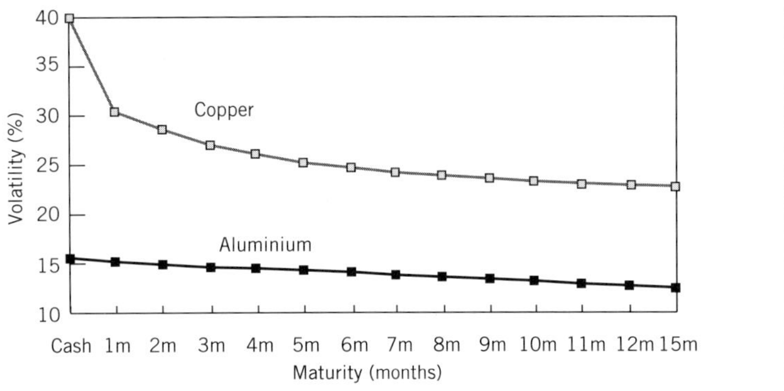

5. Precious metals, aluminium and copper correlation, spot prices to forward prices, 1996

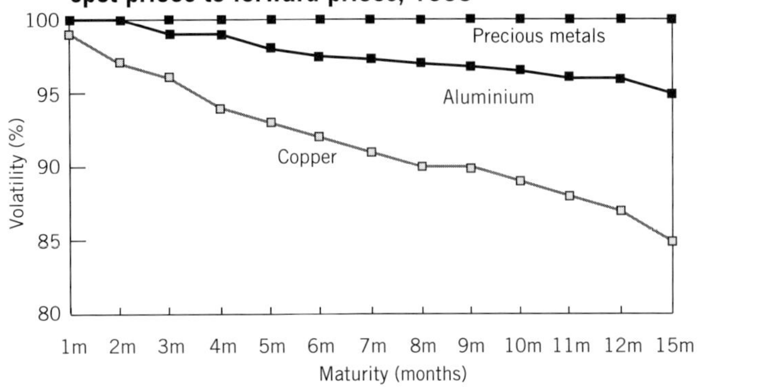

cash market, either from the producer or consumer. Typically, the cash price is only a little over the price necessary to fund carrying the metal from the cash market to the more liquid three-month forward price (ie, the price necessary to take into account financing and LME warehouse storage). Indeed, the "cash-to-threes" (ie, the spot price minus the three-month price) segment of the curve has been in backwardation for only 29% and 1% of the time over the last 10 and five years respectively. Looking at the price relationship from another angle, we can say that the spot price volatility is typically very close to that of the three-month price, 15.6% to compare with 14.6% in 1996. Furthermore, the price of 15-month aluminium has in periods (1992–93, for example) risen as high as the cash-and-carry price (ie, the price calculated by adding the appropriate cost of carry to the prevailing cash price).

In contrast, the copper industry has no such systemic need to maintain inventories, which means that there are usually no copper reserves to buffer the temporary supply-demand imbalances that affect the copper cash price. In consequence, the spot price undergoes a very high volatility – much higher than the forward prices of one-, three- and 15-month copper contracts.[14] In addition, the relationship of cash to threes is usually backwardated (positive). It has been in backwardation for over 60% of the time in the last 10 years, for example.

These examples suggest that modelling the forward price behaviour of base metals will be quite complex! As with the precious metals, we start our investigation by examining recent statistics for forward prices. Figure 4 illustrates the average forward price volatility for both aluminium and copper during 1996. (The traded forward market for base metals is much shorter than for precious metals, so we examine tenors of from cash to 15 months).

In contrast to the precious metals market, base metal forward prices are less volatile the further forward they are. Most commodities exhibit this behaviour: precious metals are the exception. Indeed, copper shows the more typical behaviour, with very pronounced spot volatility.

The correlations between spot prices and forward prices also reveal a different pattern to the correlations seen in precious metals. As can be clearly seen in Figure 5, the correlations of these prices in the cases of aluminium and copper are significantly lower than the 100% correlations shown by precious metals. Furthermore, the strength of the correlation declines as the tenor of the forward contracts increases. In the case of the precious metals, with all correlations close to unity, we were able to use a model of forward prices driven by a single random factor: a model in which each forward price, each day, underwent a percentage change driven by the same "force", even if it responded differently. In the case of base metals, a model driven by a single random factor could not possibly generate the kind of empirical data we see illustrated in Figure 5.

However, before we discard Black-Scholes (and all exotic extensions) and start experimenting with much more complex multi-factor models, we should remind ourselves what we are trying to achieve. We want to be able to price varieties of European options, such as early expiration and delayed start options: that is, we want to derive the volatility of a forward over any period of its life – any period volatility of a given forward, let us say. We would also like to obtain the correlation or covariance between two forwards over any given period. And finally, we must maintain consistency with volatilities inferred from market prices.

If not for the last constraint, we might be tempted simply to apply recent measurements of daily volatilities to projected period volatilities for a given forward: for example, as the period return

PANEL 3

HEDGING BASE METAL FORWARDS

The problems of pricing and hedging derivatives are closely linked: solutions to the former suggest ways to effect the latter. As a general formulation, the hedger has as an original exposure a certain amount of a forward-dated material, and must cover this position using some amount of either one or two other-dated forwards. The trick is to select positions and amounts that minimise the daily variation in value of the resulting combined position. (By value we mean present value, and by variation we mean the expected variance.)

If F1 and F2 are the forward prices relating to dates D1 and D2, and df1 and df2 are the discount factors associated with those dates, then given one unit of the second forward, we need to derive the amount of the first forward, X say, that minimises:

$$Q = E[df1\ dF1\ X + df2\ dF2]^2$$

where dF1 and dF2 are random variables representing daily changes in F1 and F2. Assuming that the distribution of prices is lognormal, if F1 and F2 are assumed to experience daily volatilities of s1 and s2, with correlation r12, then:

$$Q = df1^2 F1^2 s1^2 X^2 + 2\ df1\ df2\ F1\ F2\ X\ s1\ s2\ r12 + df2^2 F2^2 s2^2$$

The best hedge ratio X is obtained at a minimum of Q, at which the derivative of Q with respect to X, DQ/DX, is zero. We use this to obtain the equation for X:

$$DQ/DX = 2\ df1^2 F1^2 s1^2 X + 2\ df1\ df2\ F1\ F2\ s1\ s2\ r12 = 0$$

$$2\ df1^2 F1^2 s1^2 X = -2\ df1\ df2\ F1\ F2\ s1\ s2\ r12$$

$$X = -df1\ df2\ F1\ F2\ s1\ s2\ r12 / df1^2 F1^2 s1^2 = -df2\ F2\ s2\ r12 / df1\ F1\ s1$$

Note that daily volatilities and correlations are used, corresponding to the maturities of the respective forwards, and are those we collect in our statistics (ie, daily expected movements).

Similarly, if the problem is to find the best hedge using two forwards, a pair of equations is obtained. In general, the problem reduces to solving a linear system of equations.

of a given forward price must itself follow a random walk, we can project the period volatility using the trick we described above. As an example, suppose we want to discover the volatility for the period starting in one month and ending three months from now (1m to 3m), on a forward contract that is maturing in six months. Suppose also that we have extracted the volatility measurements in Table 4 for one-month to six-month volatilities from daily forward price returns.

Now, assuming this recent volatility for forwards were to persist, we could simply sum the squares of the volatilities in Table 4, divide by six, and calculate the square root - presenting us with a term volatility of 24.94%. In this calculation we are assuming that, for the first month the price of the forward contract will behave in the same way as a six-month forward (ie, exhibit a volatility of 21%); the calculation for the second month assumes the forward price will behave like the current five-month forward (as it will have one less month then to maturity); and so on. By summing the variances, annualising and taking the square root, we arrive at a projection for market term volatilities.

Similarly, looking again at Table 4, we can obtain a 1m to 3m volatility by applying the same calculation to the 5m, 4m and 3m table entries, which correspond to the maturity of the forward over the 1m to 3m period. We obtain 23.53%.

Now, assume that we know that the current implied volatility for the six-month term is, in fact, 27% not 24.94%. One is tempted to re-scale Table 4 so that it meets the level of volatility implied by the market. By multiplying the table's historical volatility by the ratio of 27%/24.94%, we would meet the market constraint. But would the resulting 25.48% volatility for the shorter 1m to 3m period (23.53% multiplied by this ratio) be sensible?

Figure 6 (overleaf) illustrates the results of the method we have just described (the "summation of forward variances" technique) when the author used it to project term volatilities for LME copper prices at the start of 1997, using as a basis for the calculation the actual daily forward price volatilities from late-1996.

Table 4. Volatility measurements for one-month to six-month volatilities

Term	1m	2m	3m	4m	5m	6m
Volatility (%)	30	27	25	23.5	22	21

6. Projected and market volatility curves, LME copper, January 2, 1997

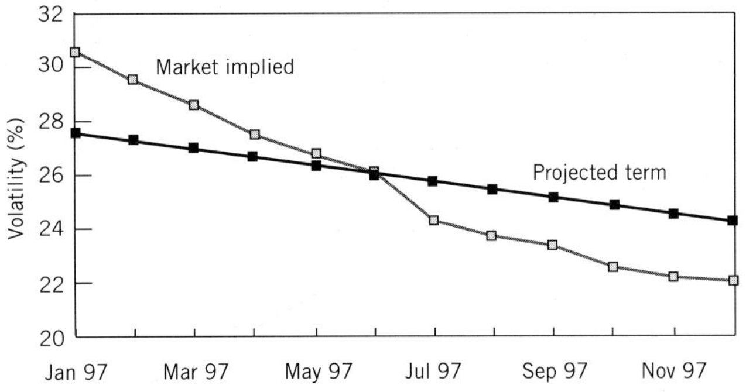

The figure shows that, while the projected term volatilities are close to the market-implied volatilities, the latter are higher than the former for short terms, and lower for longer-term maturities. To apply the scaling technique, we would need the projected term volatilities and the market-implied volatility curves to be in the same ratio to each other at every maturity. As an alternative, which does seem to work for the period volatility problem, one can calculate a scaling factor for each month going forward by iteratively satisfying the market constraint term-by-increasing-term, applying the prior scaling factors as one proceeds.

The factor scaling technique leaves one less than satisfied. When we used a factor scaling technique for precious metals we were, at least, able to identify exogenous variables (financing and leasing rates) and fold them into the calculations. For base metals, the effects are endogenous, and we cannot learn from other markets how to apply the scaling statistics. For option payouts based on a single forward price the statistical scaling approach is fully justified and quite sufficient. But the approach does not address the relationship, or period correlation, between pairs of forwards.

Table 5. LME copper daily correlations between pairs of forwards: average over 1996

	Cash	1m	2m	3m	4m	5m	6m	7m	8m	9m	10m	11m	12m
Cash	100.0												
1m	99.0	100.0											
2m	96.7	98.8	100.0										
3m	95.7	98.0	99.6	100.0									
4m	94.5	97.2	99.2	99.8	100.0								
5m	93.4	96.4	98.7	99.5	99.9	100.0							
6m	92.3	95.6	98.0	99.0	99.5	99.8	100.0						
7m	91.2	94.7	97.3	98.5	99.2	99.6	99.9	100.0					
8m	90.5	94.1	96.8	98.0	98.8	99.3	99.7	99.9	100.0				
9m	89.8	93.5	96.2	97.6	98.5	99.0	99.5	99.8	99.9	100.0			
10m	88.9	92.7	95.6	97.1	98.0	98.7	99.2	99.6	99.8	99.9	100.0		
11m	88.0	92.0	94.9	96.4	97.5	98.2	98.9	99.3	99.6	99.8	99.9	100.0	
12m	87.4	91.4	94.3	96.0	97.1	97.8	98.5	99.0	99.4	99.6	99.8	100.0	100.0

How can we tackle this problem of period correlations? Note that the correlation itself does not form the basis of the computation, but rather the period covariance, which in turn is just the sum of daily covariance terms appropriate for the forward maturities of the forward prices. Each daily covariance term is the product of the appropriate volatilities with the appropriate correlation.

As an example, in pricing a two-month option on the spread between the three-month and six-month copper prices, a two-factor approach is clearly necessary, and one needs the following period parameters to apply any of a range of spread option formulas:[15]

- ❑ two-month period volatilities for both the three-month and six-month forward prices; and
- ❑ two-month period correlation between the three-month and six-month forwards.

This last parameter is simply the period covariance divided by the two volatilities and by the period time, so our efforts are concentrated in calculating a period covariance. We follow the same approach that we took earlier in calculating period variances for the volatility parameters. To do so we need a more complete set of daily average correlations, as shown in Table 5.

Initially, the correlation between our forwards is that of the three- and six-month forwards prices, which we find from our table to be 99%. One month later they will be two- and five-month forward prices, at which time their correlation will be 98.7%. And towards expiration of the option, their correlation will drop further to 97.2%: that of a one-month and four-month pair of forwards. Using the volatility table presented earlier (Table 4), we would take the six-month forward volatility to progress from 21% to 22% and end at 23.5%. Similarly, we would project the three-month forward volatility to be 25% initially, 27% in one month, to end up at 30%. The required variances and covariance are shown in Table 6.

The required correlation figure is simply 0.1791 divided by the square root of the product of 0.2254 and 0.1477, which is 98.17%. Were it not for the cash-and-carry constraint that limits the range of the spread of prices between a pair of forwards, we could claim to be ready to price spread options. At least, this technique can be used in conjunction with widely available formulas to provide an upper bound to the value of the option, and as a valuation technique it will be roughly correct when the forward curve is backwardated.

We have gained a lot of ground and are now well placed to price American and Asian options, swaptions (options on swaps), compound options and knockout options. Importantly, we have not had to introduce a complicated term structure, multi-factor model with parameters that are not easy to identify, measure or understand. To do so would have made the material considerably harder, without adding much usefulness. In the end, every two-factor model that is linear in returns is equivalent. The real value of any particular formulation is to make the model satisfy the constraint of generating option volatilities that match market-implied volatilities, while simultaneously reflecting the pattern of daily forward price volatilities and correlations. The rest – the calculation of period return volatilities and the correlations that we must use in many pricing formulas for exotic options – must follow the logic that we have adopted here, whether or not the approach makes use of a particular term-structure model of forward price dynamics.

Full carry constraint

The logic and simplicity of the approach described above is only possible because we restricted our models to those which provide returns with linear dynamics. However, it is always possible to undertake a metals inventory – unlike some commodities – the cash-and-carry price for a forward date places an upper limit on the corresponding forward price. This constraint affects the dynamics of forward prices and how they move with respect to each other and, properly modelled, it introduces a non-linear term into the dynamics.

As the market in LME copper is seldom in "full carry" (ie, forward prices consistent with cash-and-carry finance and storage costs), we shall focus on the market in LME aluminium. Figure 7 shows the behaviour of three- and 15-month aluminium from 1990 to 1997. The line labelled "carry price" shows the extent to which the 15-month price, expressed as a percentage of the cash-and-carry price, was taken out of the three-month price. (The cash-to-threes market itself is so frequently in, or close to, full carry that it is not particularly instructive to examine their relationship.)

Figure 8 displays how LME aluminium characteristics change as the forward curve moves into and out of full carry. Against the carry ratio (the ratio of the 15-month forward price to its carry price) are plotted the 60-day correlation between the three- and 15-month prices, and their volatility ratio (the ratio of the 60-day volatility of the 15-month price to the 60-day volatility of the the three-month price). Note that all three lines collapse to 100% in the same periods so that, as forward prices approach full carry, the two-factor model effect vanishes, and the metal starts to behave like a precious metal in its dynamics. Let us refer to the ratio of the 15-month price to its cash-and-carry price from three months as the degree of full carry.

The figure shows that both the correlation effects, and the characteristic decrease in volatility as term increases, tend to disappear as the market approaches full carry. Thus, when we are calculating period volatilities and the like, we must ensure that the period in which data is gathered exhibits a similar degree of full carry to that in effect at the time of pricing.

Volatility variation by strike

At the start of this chapter we noted that, in the metals markets, market-implied volatilities vary

Table 6

Pair of forwards	Variance and covariance expressions	Value
3m with 3m	$25\% \times 25\% + 27\% \times 27\% + 30\% \times 30\%$	0.2254
3m with 6m	$99\% \times 21\% \times 25\% + 98.7\% \times 22\% \times 27\% + 97.2\% \times 23.5\% \times 30\%$	0.1791
6m with 6m	$21\% \times 21\% + 22\% \times 22\% + 23.5\% \times 23.5\%$	0.1477

7. LME aluminum 3m carried to 15m

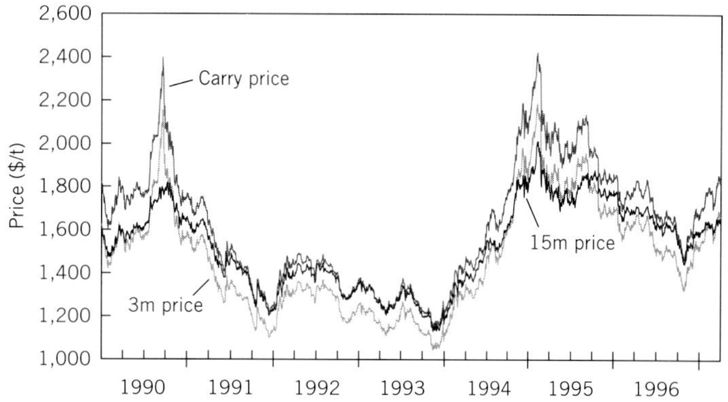

8. LME aluminium carry statistics

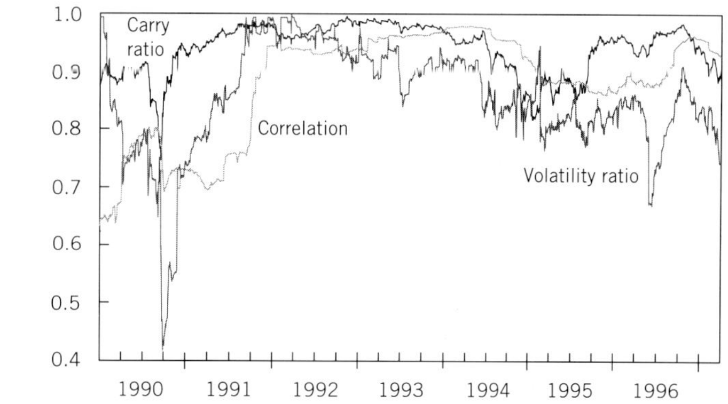

by term and by strike. For an options trader, the most obvious effect is that put strike volatilities are higher than those at the money. For base metals, the full carry effect described above partly explains this market characteristic. However, two other factors play a much larger part.

The first is the effect of supply and demand. For base metals in particular, the options markets are relatively shallow and dealers charge a premium for strikes that are in demand, as they are unable, generally, to find a source for options with a similar or more out-of-the-money strike. Alternatively, a large supplier of volatility to the market (eg, a fund embarking on a major programme of options selling) can cause a lowering of market prices for at-the-money strikes. Again, this is partly a simple effect of supply and demand. But, if the option seller does not hedge its position dynamically in the market, then the dealer's dynamic hedging can absorb the momentum of prices, and lead to a lower market-implied volatility.

The second factor – sudden jumps in market prices – explains a larger part of the picture.

A number of classic theories help us to understand this feature. The first theory is that the volatility depends, not only on term, but also on the level of prices. Take gold as an example. The theory, in line with popular belief, suggests that gold trades more actively, and that its price moves faster, when the price of gold is above $400 per ounce.

This appears to be quite reasonable – and immediately implies a non-linear model of prices. If we combine this model with the need to explain less than full correlation between pairs of forwards, we find we are faced with a formidable task, and a model that may not be tractable in terms of its calibration. However, for precious metals at least, this approach is feasible.[16]

Table 7 is a development of Table 1 from the beginning of this chapter. The spot price was around 380 at the time the data in the table was compiled. Note that, while the prices of options with higher strikes exhibit increased volatility, the volatility of options with strikes that are lower by about the same amount is just as high. This seems counter to the theory outlined above. Note also that the volatility variation is significantly higher for shorter expirations.

There are two theories that remain. Theory one can be disposed of immediately in that it predicts less variation at first, increasing variation later, followed by variation decreasing to almost zero with longer terms. This is the stochastic volatility theory, a good introduction to which is Hull and White (1987). The table shows, and this is typical, that the shorter the term the higher the variation by strike. Another point against the stochastic volatility theory – and it is not that the theory is not correct, volatility is volatile, it is that it cannot provide for the character of the data – is that if one estimates the "volatility of volatility" and the other parameters of the model, and prices options, one does not get such a pronounced picture as the data provides.

We are left with Merton's (1976) approach, which describes a process called "jump-diffusion". In Merton's model, the underlying price process usually follows a continuous random walk but, occasionally – the occasions (jumps) being driven by a Poisson process – the price jumps, producing a discontinuity in the price path. The jumps themselves are of random size: the model generates them using a lognormal distribution, and affecting the immediate returns.[17]

The calibration of the Merton jump-diffusion model to the table above yields quite stable parameters, varying only slightly by term to expiration; the model can therefore be said to explain

9. Gold price and volatility

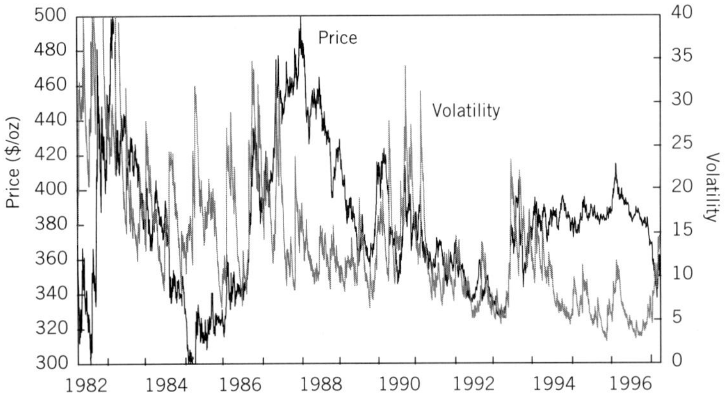

Table 7. Comex gold volatilities in the last week of August 1996

Strike	1m	2m	3m	4m	6m	8m	10m	12m
340	29.0	18.3	14.3	10.9	11.0	10.0	9.3	9.5
350	23.5	15.0	11.8	9.0	9.7	9.0	8.7	9.0
360	18.0	11.8	9.2	8.0	8.3	8.0	8.0	8.2
370	12.5	8.5	7.5	6.4	7.1	7.3	7.3	7.6
380	6.7	6.4	6.3	6.0	7.0	7.2	6.9	7.0
390	4.9	5.8	6.0	6.2	6.5	7.1	7.0	7.1
400	8.7	6.4	6.6	6.7	6.7	6.7	6.7	7.1
410	12.7	7.6	7.6	7.5	7.4	7.0	7.3	7.1
420	17.5	9.6	9.1	8.2	7.8	7.7	8.0	7.7
430	22.0	12.4	10.8	9.5	8.8	8.7	8.4	7.9
440	26.2	15.0	11.7	10.6	9.9	9.2	9.0	8.4
450	30.3	17.4	13.6	11.3	10.7	10.2	9.5	9.0
460	34.2	20.6	15.5	12.0	11.9	11.1	9.8	9.5
470	38.0	24.2	17.3	12.2	12.8	11.9	10.3	9.8
480	41.6	29.1	19.0	13.5	13.7	12.8	10.9	10.0

PANEL 4

PRICING BINARY OPTIONS UNDER THE VOLATILITY SMILE

Binary options – also known as digital options – provide an example of a terminal payout option with pricing that is independent of the type of model used to explain the volatility variation by strike. Terminal payout options can be expressed in terms of the discounted expected payout, and all that is missing is the terminal probability price distribution. However, given a complete volatility-by-strike description, one can back out the implied probability distribution, although in practice there are some numerical problems.

In the case of binary options the problem is especially simple – and interesting. The binary option payoff can be approximated as a call spread struck symmetrically about the binary strike, on an amount of metal such that the call spread strike differential times the amount of metal gives a value of one (ie, the binary payout if realised). So formulated, the binary option is, in the limit, the total differential of a call option (struck at the same level as the binary) with respect to strike. Bearing in mind that the volatility is now assumed to vary by strike, after applying the chain rule for total differentials, we find that the binary option (before discounting) is worth the textbook answer N(d2) – the partial differential of the call with respect to the strike – plus an additional term that reflects the differential of volatility with respect to strike. The result can thus be obtained without needing to model the cause of the volatility variation by strike.

the market data well. Applying the jump-diffusion model can be fairly straightforward, although it really depends on the type of derivative to be priced. Its usefulness stems from the fact that, apart from the number of jumps in a given term, the model follows a random walk - so regular option theory applies. In effect, the jump-diffusion option pricing formulas are infinite sums of regular option prices, conditional upon a number of jumps weighted by the (Poisson) probability of that number of jumps in the period. Only a few terms are taken, of course, as the probability of a large number of jumps is usually very small.

Conclusion

In this chapter, we have recognised the specific character that the metals markets possess in regard to their forward price dynamics. Rather than present a panoply of models that explicate anecdotal descriptions of metals price behaviour, the approach has been to collect the statistics necessary to price derivatives using available models, which any model of the price dynamics needs to match in any case to be a faithful model.

The statistical data necessarily relate to daily price moves,[18] collected by maturity. Although they are historical, the statistics provide us with the "character" of the evolution of forward price volatilities. Appropriate scaling, by forward period if necessary, allows us to incorporate this information into the implied volatilities by term collected from the market. The result is reasonable and consistent volatility profiles.

In contrast, the advantage of a dynamics model approach is that, properly designed, it can provide statistics similar to those obtained from historical data with just a handful of parameters. Such a model can also allow us to extend our reach to maturities not available for statistical analysis (four- and five-year forwards in the context of base metals, for example). The model parameters, not often directly observable, need to be estimated via a best-fit technique, to the collected statistics, a task which if not carefully done can lead to parameter estimates that vary wildly from day to day. When the objective is to derive period volatilities and correlations for forward prices that themselves follow random walks - a necessity following from an efficient markets hypothesis - our simple technique derived from summing daily variances suffices, and allows the use of readily available option-pricing formulas.

1 *Unlike the foreign exchange and interest rate markets, the use of second-generation derivatives for metals risk management has not been taken up and the market dynamics have been far from studied. The objective of this chapter is to open up the area a little more, to encourage a sensitivity to pricing practice, and thus allow for the design and acceptance of more appropriate hedging strategies.*

2 *The model was originally described in Black and Scholes (1973). Recent discussions of the underlying assumptions as they affect modelling outside the commodity markets can be found in Jarrow (1996).*

3 *That is, moment-to-moment returns are assumed to be normally distributed. This leads to prices being distributed*

lognormally and period returns distributed accordingly.

4 *For those unfamiliar with this formulation, with respect to the standard Black-Scholes formula, the forward price is substituted for the spot price and the dividend rate is set to the financing rate.*

5 *Volatilities are quoted on a percentage per annum basis. Annualisation (and de-annualisation) involves time scaling. The square root of time is used as, on average, the distance a random walk has travelled from its start in a certain time is proportional to the square root of that time. This result, due both to Bachelier and Einstein independently, can be easily derived from first principles, if we understand that what is meant by random is that the direction of each step is independent of the previous step, and any taken before it.*

6 *While the Comex options are American-style options (ie, exercisable at any time into the underlying contract), unless the options are deeply in the money, there is very little extra value to them over standard European-style options (exercisable solely at maturity); here, we shall consider them as European, and subject them to the same theory and model.*

7 *Options the strike of which is not set at the time of trade, but with reference to the forward price at a later date, before expiration of the option. Also known as "forward options", and "delayed start options".*

8 *The term dated forward price is used here to emphasise that we are interested in the price for delivery of metal at a given future date. This contrasts with a term forward price, such as the LME three-month price, which refers to a different date (three months in the future) on each (or most) of the dates the contract is traded.*

9 *Options expiring before a pair of forward dates that allow the purchase or sale of the second at the price of the first (at expiration) plus a specified spread.*

10 *Hull and White (1990), Nelken (1996), and Wilmott, Dewynne and Howison (1993) are some good example texts.*

11 *While this may not be the case in fact, it provides an arbitrage-free basis for pricing and hedging derivative instruments.*

12 *This is not completely wrong. The correlation was 4% over 1995 and –11% in 1996.*

13 *39.9% compared with 30.4%, 26.1% and 22.8% respectively, in 1996.*

14 *As discussed, this is not structurally correct, but good enough, given the statistics, for most purposes. An example of where the model would fail is in pricing an option on the gold forward contango.*

15 *As an example, see K. Ravindran (1993).*

16 *See Derman and Kani (1995) or Dupire (1995).*

17 *See Jarrow and Rudd (1987), Chapter 11, for a good treatment.*

18 *Rather than to market option term volatilities.*

BIBLIOGRAPHY

Black, F., 1976, "The Pricing of Commodity Contracts", *Journal of Financial Economics*, 3, pp. 167–79.

Black, F. and M. Scholes, 1973, "The Pricing of Option Contracts and Corporate Liabilities", *Journal of Political Economy*, 81, pp. 637–54; reprinted in *Vasicek and Beyond*, ed. Lane Hughston, Risk Publications (1996), pp. 3–17.

Derman, E. and Iraj Kani, 1995, "Riding on a Smile", *Over the Rainbow: Developments in Exotic Options and Complex Swaps*, ed. R. Jarrow, Risk Publications, pp. 277–84.

Dupire, B., 1995, "Pricing with a Smile", *Over the Rainbow: Developments in Exotic Options and Complex Swaps*, ed. Robert Jarrow, Risk Publications, pp. 271–76.

Hull, J., 1993, *Options, Futures, and Other Derivative Securities*, second edition, Englewood Cliffs, NJ: Prentice Hall.

Hull, J. and A. White, 1987, "The Pricing of Options on Assets with Stochastic Volatility", *Journal of Finance* 3, pp. 281–300; recently reprinted in *Hull-White on Derivatives*, Risk Publications (1995), pp. 19–40.

Hull, J. and A. White, 1990, "Pricing Interest Rate Derivative Securities", *The Review of Financial Studies*, vol. 3, pp. 573–92; recently reprinted in *Hull-White on Derivatives*, Risk Publications (1995), pp. 225–46.

Jarrow, R. and A. Rudd, 1983, *Option Pricing*, Irwin Publishing.

Merton, R., "Option Pricing When Underlying Stock Returns are Discontinuous," *Journal of Financial Economics*, May 1976, pp. 125–44.

Nelken, I., 1996, *The Handbook of Exotic Options*, Irwin Professional Publishing.

Ravindran, K., 1993, "Low-fat Spreads", *Risk* (October); reprinted in R. Jarrow, ed., *Over the Rainbow*, Risk Publications (1996), pp. 141–43.

Wilmott, P., J. Dewynne and S. Howison, 1993, *Option Pricing*, Oxford Financial Press.

10

Long-Term Metal Price Development

Chris Harris
BZW

This chapter attempts to characterise how metals prices develop through time, from the long-term market through to the spot market. It is not about predicting the level of future spot prices – a quite different exercise!

Where market prices are directly observable, characterising how they behave reveals methods of reducing risk and evaluating market anomalies. Outside the observable market – in the long-term or over-the-counter (OTC) markets where many bilateral agreements are struck – price characterisation can help create a sensible price measure, or help market participants to "synthesise" a price using readily available instruments or observable benchmarks.

Derivatives traders sometimes maintain that the pricing algorithms used in derivative markets are portable from one commodity market to another. This is incorrect. As this chapter reveals, the economics underlying each metal must be identified.

The chapter opens with a brief discussion of the theory of price. However, long-term price development is a large and difficult subject. Like the apocryphal blind man trying to understand an elephant, a picture of the whole is best gained by feeling around the different parts. For this reason, we move on quite quickly to develop some important themes of price and volatility characterisation, using a series of examples drawn from individual metals markets. The aim is to show that practical models of price characterisation can be developed without using complex mathematics.

Metals, money and currency

Metals are classed as commodities, and in general they behave as commodities "should". Production costs are easily characterised and are vulnerable to few risks that cannot be controlled (such as the weather, or disease). Consumption remains steady, or trends steadily from business cycle to business cycle. As tradable goods, they have a high value per unit, tend not to degrade, and are of high and testable purity.

Less obviously, *money* is also a commodity – which for the last two millennia has often taken the form of metal. (The direct equivalence, called metallism, creates some particular quirks when considering price theory in different metals.) How does the concept of money as a commodity relate to the problem of characterising prices – and especially long-term prices – for metals?

In a "perfect" world, price would be the same as value, and value could measured in relative utility. For example, we might compare one hour of pleasure with one hour of labour, or one acre of land with a tonne of potatoes. In the real world, utility is hard to measure directly, so a proxy is used to compare *relative* utilities: money. In this sense, money is simply the lingua franca of conversion between relative utilities.

Unfortunately, this lingua franca takes more than one form! In the case of metal, there are three important denominations:

- ❑ budgeting currency;
- ❑ trading currency (see Panel 2, overleaf); and
- ❑ true economic currency.

The true economic currency is the currency that determines the long-term shift in the supply/demand balance. Every commodity has an idiosyncratic "true currency", in which its long-term price remains relatively stable.

Since demand is only manifest in the short-term and is uncontrolled, while supply is automatically regulated by supply profit – the true currency is defined in terms of supply economics.

The true economic denomination is represented by the weighting of the cost mix. Although the *ultimate* denomination of the cost

PANEL 1

MODELLING

The use of models is ubiquitous in commercial and economic fields, as well as in science. Models offer an intuitive understanding of complex processes, provide a common ground on which to communicate with peers, and create a framework on which to "hang" the latest generation of theories. Models do not have to be "right", but they do have to approximate market behaviour well enough to be *useful*. There is a bewildering array of economic models from which we can "mix and match".

When analysing prices, we constantly – albeit often unconsciously – use models, or the theories from which models are constructed. One of the most fundamental of these is Lucas' Theory of Rational Expectations (RE).[1] In its strongest form, this states that information (and the ability to use it) is so readily available that only an infinitesimal speculative advantage over other market participants can be gained by the acquisition of extra "private" information.

Lucas recognised the apparently oxymoronic nature of this statement – ie, there is so much speculation that it is hardly worth speculating. The secret of RE is that "hardly" is enough to keep traders profitable for markets in which the model does apply, and that the model is not intended to be applied in *all* market situations.

The most important outcome of the model with regard to price is that it suggests that the price of a forward contract *now* is equal to the mean expectation price of the contract when it becomes *prompt*. To operate perfectly, it requires that the overwhelming majority of traders are risk neutral, and have full knowledge *and* understanding of all market forces in the tenor in which they are trading. Such people would certainly not need my advice! In fact, within the active market, and for active market practitioners, an entirely different theoretical basis, called "no-arbitrage", always dominates the RE determined prices. Indeed, "If there is an arbitrage price, any other price is too dangerous to quote".[2]

For our purposes – the examination of very poorly defined prices outside the no-arbitrage zone – we shall assume that RE is a useful framework on which to hang some models, and at the same time highlight the areas in which it does not operate very well. In effect, this chapter addresses the transition of prices between the RE model and the no-arbitrage model. Ideally, the model adaptations would smoothly overlap in the intermediate regions and therefore create consistent pricing from the very short to the very long tenors. (RE can also be a useful foundation for modelling prices in markets where there are arbitrage opportunities, for market users that do not run active hedge portfolios and which cannot or do not fully access the arbitrage market.)

The other ubiquitous model that we will use is the Black–Scholes model (a no-arbitrage model), which even in the commodity markets is the tool most traders use to price options. Given the very rigid set of conditions under which the Black–Scholes model is designed to work, its success in practical applications is extraordinary.[3] The great majority of option traders are not trying to find a better model, but are modelling how their market behaves in relation to Black-Scholes. We too will be using the model in this way.

We shall also be using a number of other models, and adapting existing ones (as economists will note). The essential difference between using models and making statistical analyses is that modelling takes a mechanistic view of the driving forces of a market. Statistical methods have the benefit of being relatively objective – but they can only view the future as a mirror of the past. Even clear signals from current events are ignored. For example, the recent copper market price fall that was *anticipated* by mineral economists was measured as *freak* by statistics.

1 The origins of this were extensively used by Keynes.
2 From *Financial Calculus*, M. Baxter and A. Rennie, Cambridge University Press: Cambridge (1996).
3 A recent discussion of the assumptions behind the Black–Scholes model can be found in the introduction to R. Jarrow, ed: *Over the Rainbow*, Risk Publications (1995).

mix is in labour cost, it is usual for the *intermediate* denomination of a commodity to be fairly discrete. For example, plastics have a high oil content, diamonds are predominantly mined in South Africa and Russia, and gold has a high finance cost that is linked to the dollar.

As the argument used in this paper is that long-term prices migrate towards the level of long-term costs, the true currency (or currency basket) must be identified if random effects (such as fluctuation in the trading currency) are to be separated from systematic effects.

PANEL 2

DOLLARISATION

The dominant trading currency for all commodities is the US dollar. Not only is the dollar the currency for trading physical commodities, but it is also the currency of denomination of any factor that requires accurate comparisons in the short term (seconds through to days).

For example, the price of *processes* (eg, rolling, smelting) and *services* (eg, commissions) are commonly quoted in dollars, even between two counterparties in the same country. Increasingly, the culture of dollar *usage* has created the dollarisation of decisions. The dollar does more than express value; it defines a method of finding value.

The dollar is used because of the great convenience of *instant* international comparability. As the time frame over which decisions are made lengthens, the need for dollarisation decreases. However, as decision times for major investments become shorter and shorter, the contracts prone to dollarisation extend further into the future.

Provided that dollars are used only as a lingua franca, dollarisation does not give rise to any major problems. This is particularly true in the short tenors – the dollars earned are spent before they have time to change in value.

However as the tenor extends, the dollar receipt/debt is likely to be held for long enough prior to exchange for its purchasing value to change. Unlike commodities, the value of dollars is not intrinsic and can instantly be altered by a change in US fiscal or monetary policy. This financial exposure must be taken into consideration if dollars are used as a long-term contracting currency.

In theory, the true economic currency can be found by identifying the currency basket in which the long-term metal price has the lowest volatility. However, as long-term prices are not visible, this is usually not possible. Instead, the currency has to be assessed by examining the cost base of metal production.

The true currency - and by implication the commodity nature of money - is especially important when we are looking at very long-term volatilities. In the very long term, the volatility of "metal" value is outweighed by that of the individual national currency in which the money value is measured. In effect, all metal volatilities tend towards the volatility of their true currency value in the very long term.

Price dynamics

The title of this chapter is worded quite carefully. In fact, it has three meanings, each of which is of profound importance to the understanding of the dynamics of metal prices. These are:

- the development of the economic forces that "make" prices;
- the development of the spot price as time moves forward; and
- the development of forward prices as time brings them closer to their prompt dates.

THE DEVELOPMENT OF THE ECONOMIC FORCES THAT DETERMINE PRICES

To model long-term prices, we need to find the true economic determination of value. For this, the work of the early political economists is of great use. In fact, much of political economies revolves around the real denomination of value.

Adam Smith provides the best starting point for our analysis. Writing after the end of the mercantile era of heavy state involvement in commerce, Smith asserted the aggregate importance of individual actions in the shaping of society. The search for personal fulfilment created an "invisible hand" that guided society - to the benefit of everyone. His ideas were developed by David Ricardo and formed two branches: Cost of Production Theory and Subjective Preference Theory.

According to the Cost of Production Theory, goods are produced if it is profitable to do so. Production increases significantly until it dampens the rise in price. The emphasis is on production, and production requires capital, land, labour and planning. This locates the production decision in the long term. A hundred years ago, under the Cost of Production Theory, prices were exposed to what Marshall, an important economist in this area, called the "hazards of mining". Nowadays, the uncertainty of mining costs is considerably less, and the Cost of Production Theory usually yields stable prices.

According to Subjective Preference Theory, the value, and therefore price, of a product is derived from its marginal utility. (In the spot forum, the market for goods is highly transparent, and the value of a good is measured in its exchange value as well as its utility value.) This

PANEL 3

COMPARATIVE COST STRUCTURE OF MAJOR METALS

The table below summarises the industry structure that underlies the major metals markets. The shading of horizontal columns illustrates the vertical integration of production in each metal. The sectors shown in bold type in the table tend to dominate by (generally) owning the other tiers, controlling the level and mechanism of transfer price, and by adjusting the extent of vertical integration of production of the commodity.

Vertical integration of metals markets

Metal	Dig	Concentrate	Purify/reduce	Fabricate/alloy
Aluminium	Bauxite	Precipitate pure oxide	**Smelt**	Extrude, roll, cast, etc
Copper	**Oxide, sulphide mixed**	Concentrate	Smelt/refine	Draw, etc
Iron	Iron ore	Agglomerate/ pelletise	Furnace	**Forge, roll, etc Alloy**
Lead/zinc	Oxide, sulphide ores	Concentrate	Smelt/refine	Cast, roll (lead) Cast, coat (zinc)
Gold	**Gold-bearing rock**	**Leach/bio leach**		Cast in bars. fabricate
Nickel	Nickel ore	Concentrate, smelt to matte	Smelt/refine	Castings Alloy in steel

places a clear emphasis on consumption - and brings the key decisions affecting price into the very short term. By the time a consumer decides whether or not to buy particular goods, the production decision has long been made.

Surprisingly perhaps, the third branch of economic thought that we will find useful is Marxian Abstract Labour Theory. Abstract Labour Theory, which underpinned the concept of a planned economy, states that everything can be valued in terms of hours of labour (in fact, Adam Smith also believed "sweat of the brow" to be the only true measure of value). While the political philosophy with which it was associated has never enjoyed much favour in the global markets, the underlying economic theory still offers a framework in which the Cost of Production Theory can be applied to the economics of mineral production. This is because job creation/protection remains a core function of modern government. For example, tariffs, subsidies, quotas, special economic zones, taxes and regulations are all examples of labour-driven market intervention. Abstract Labour Theory is, in fact, very amenable to a classical economic analysis of price. In addition, it is extremely useful for the very long dates in which no parameters can be quantified in currency (ie, relative) terms, and for which a more absolute value measure is required. Note that, while money currency may be used as the lingua franca, the true currency of denomination here is labour.

The three-way branching of price theory provides a neat division of tenor (economic zone) and "real" economic currency. This is summarised, crudely, in Table 1.

Table 1. Simplification of economic zones and related price theory

Economic zone	Short term	Long term	Very long term
	0 to two years	Two to seven years	Seven to 25 years
Useful theory	Subjective Preference	Cost of Production	Abstract Labour
Relevant authors	Friedman, Brittan	Keynes, Galbraith, Sraffa	(Ricardo), Marx
Denomination	Currency of trading	Currency of capital	Labour, utility
Activity	Speculation; short-term tendering	Strategic equity investment decisions; speculation on cycles; speculation on fundamentals	Government investment; investment in supply channels; long-term projects
Example	Buying commodity during price rise, etc	Smelter expansion; buying commodity during recession; vertical de-integration	Exploration; long-term power contracts; vertical integration; relocation

THE DEVELOPMENT OF THE SPOT PRICE AS TIME MOVES FORWARD

The term "spot price" means different things in different markets. For precious metals it denotes the price two business days ahead; for base metals it is either the price two business days ahead or the three-month forward price; and for futures it is the nearest contract (which itself has an implied date structure *within* the month[1]). In all markets, it is the most active contract for investors.

The most important aspect of the spot price is that, while *prompt date* is not constant (it moves forward every day), the *economic zone* that the spot price lies within is constant.

The Theory of Rational Expectations predicts that the most likely path for the spot price is along the forward curve. However, we have seen that each region of the forward curve is subject to very different economic forces. The agents trading the forward price are not those who trade the cash price, and their expectations are measured in different denominations. This is a blow for simple price modelling, as a single application of Rational Expectations (or no arbitrage) across all tenors cannot be made. This is of special importance when forward prices are driven off course by a *shift* in the tenor of the boundary between economic regimes, in ways that we shall examine later. However, in the absence of modelling, the forward price remains the *best guess* for the direction of the spot price.

The concentration of investor activity into spot trading has two important effects. Firstly, it compresses the short-term economic time zone into an extremely short time frame. Secondly, the extreme shortness effectively precludes any industrial response (ie, a strategic decision to produce/consume more or less) to price movements. A qualification here is that, to a limited extent, the time frame of the industrial response can be shortened by means of interim measures such as:

- stocking/destocking;
- price fixing;
- order-book changes; and
- other decisions made in one time frame that can have knock-on supply/demand effect in another.

The rapidity of changes in utility in the short-term market, allied with the relative constancy of underlying production/consumption, means that the spot price is effectively a *random variable*. There is no economic denomination in which the price can be stable.

There is one aspect of spot price development that is affected by economics, and which is not described properly by a simple random distribution. It is not the mean *price*, but the spot price *distribution*. If a pre-determined action is triggered by a cash price event, then medium-term decision making is drawn into the short-term economic zone. Many market participants set price triggers above and below the existing market price, and if an accumulation of triggers is set off then the normal distribution arising from the Theory of Rational Expectations is thrown off-kilter. Important trigger events may be caused by large open option positions in the market.

THE DEVELOPMENT OF FORWARD PRICES AS TIME BRINGS THEM CLOSER TO THEIR PROMPT DATES

The Theory of Rational Expectations tells us that all the information that is needed to estimate the future price of a particular dated contract is already discounted in the current forward price of that contract. The expectation price does not change as the tenor of the contract shrinks (excepting the price drift that arises from volatility effects).

However, the economic agents acting in the long term are not the same as those acting in the short term. In the long term, the price "tries" to reach equilibrium, by affecting supply and demand. Provided that rational agents can perceive the long-term price, they can endeavour to produce more, or consume less, metal. For equilibrium to prevail, these agents must have the *ability* to perceive opportunity, the *mechanism* with which to exploit it, and enough *time* to act. These three essentials keep equilibrium in the long tenors.

The short-term economic agents adjust price by buying and selling, not by making and consuming. The high velocity of paper exchange compared with physical flow, and the diversity of individual needs and preferences, prevents us from making useful observations about collective action. The unpredictability of actions effectively *randomises* the spot price of metal, from the perspective of both observers and participants.

Therefore, three important things happen to long-term prices as their tenors shrink. They:

- lose their identifiable connections with fundamentals;
- move faster; and
- randomise.

Prices drift (see Panel 4, overleaf) from a relatively unknown region, through a well-characterised equilibrium region, and into a random region. Note that *random* and *unknown* forces

PANEL 4

RANDOM PROCESSES AND DRIFT

Drift can be defined as the consistent movement of a forward price over time, in response to an economic force. As a factor in market pricing, drift is used in very different ways by traders, project financiers and academics.[1] Mathematically, it is expressed by a form of random walk called the Wiener (strictly, Gauss–Wiener) process.

The Wiener equation (adapted to include mean reversion) is:

$$dS / S = \mu dt + \sigma dz - k(S - Sm)$$

where
S = price (traditionally spot price)
μ = drift term
dt = time interval
σ = volatility of S with respect to t
dz is a Brownian motion term creating a price move
k = empirical mean reverting force
Sm = economic equilibrium price

The three currencies we discuss in the main text (budget, traded and economic) are reflected in the first (μdt), second (σdz) and third (k(S–Sm)) terms, respectively, and the drift is represented by the first term. Users of the Wiener process invariably assume that all three currencies are the same.

The Black–Scholes formula makes use of the Wiener process, but has the important ability to "retrofit" the key market parameter (volatility) to the observed market. The great success of the Black–Scholes model as a practical tool in the markets stems from its capability to normalise to the observed market, and to communicate with a single and simple parameter. The raw Wiener process cannot be married to the observed market in this way, and hence the parameters (starting price, volatility, drift, mean reversion force) remain subjective.

If we apply the Wiener process using the spot price as the starting price, and the long-tenor market implied volatility or long-term average cash historic volatility as the *volatility*, the result is of little practical use. However, if the long-term price is used as the start *price*, and the long-tenor forward/forward volatility is used as the *volatility*, then it is considerably more effective. In this way, the observed market can be used to model market prices in the short tenors, and the Wiener process can be used to model prices in the long tenors – with a good match between the two curves. Ideally, the long-term price used as the start price in the Wiener process would be in the *true economic currency* of the metal (see main text discussion).

1 Drift is the non-random component of the change in commodity price over time. For the purposes of this chapter, an intuitive understanding of drift in commodity price is promoted over its more rigorous analytical form.

are both manifest in market prices as volatility, but are the result of very different effects.

Equilibrium price is taken from analysts and, in many metals, the average error of analysts in predicting the average price of a year ahead is about equal to the average annual volatility of the metal. This is the same as saying that the spot price will be equal to the analyst (equilibrium) price (not forward price) plus/minus annual volatility. This implies that analysts only get predictions exactly right by being lucky!

True denomination currency equal to trading currency – copper

Copper is a good metal to start with, as it is very "well behaved" in terms of the mechanics of its dollar price movement. We can illustrate how it moves, why it moves and, most important of all, the very restricted environment that allows it to follow the rules.

What are the cost determinants of copper? Like all other metals, these are labour, debt, materials, energy and equity capital. Copper is particular in having a high ratio of capital cost to running cost for both mining *and* smelting. The opposite is true for copper fabrication (relative to other metals), but this does not provide a balancing effect because copper is a vertically deintegrated industry. The deintegration disconnects consumer (short-term) price behaviour from long-term price behaviour. The copper industry is also a highly dollar-denominated industry (see Figure 1). As a generalisation, copper miners are not historic copper specialists, but are capital-rich global miners, with debt costs denominated in dollars. Copper is also used as an investment vehicle in the capital markets. This, and the dollarised nature, has the effect of contracting its economic tenor from very long term, to long term, and suggests that the Cost of Production Theory may be useful when searching for the long-term dollar price.

The broad stability of the long-term price of copper is illustrated in Figure 2.

The fact that long-tenor prices tend to be relatively constant over short periods has in the past created a kind of pivot point. As cash prices rise, and long-tenor prices remain stable, *very long-term* prices may fall. This is in part due to overreaction by the market, and in part due to the effect that high cash prices have on investment in production.

So, in copper we have a long-term dollar price that is determinist, and a cash price that is effectively random. How can we connect them? There are number of different axioms that we could borrow from the foreign exchange or interest rate markets. I have opted for a very simple rule that makes intuitive sense and - very conveniently - retains its form when applied to volatility. (It is also intuitively similar to Newton's law relating force to power.)

I assume that the nearby price of copper is not at (cost of production) equilibrium, and that, over time, it will migrate towards equilibrium. As a starting point, let us state that the equilibrium price in the near term is equal to the equilibrium for the long term (neglecting inflation for the moment). If the intensity of use of copper[2] is relatively constant, then this is a reasonable assumption, good enough for the moment, and which can be unravelled later. Then we can say that the rate of change of the market price towards its equilibrium price is directly proportional to the difference from the equilibrium price ($S - Sm$ in Panel 4). There are other forces (manifest in its non-equilibrium nature), but they are random to the viewer, and therefore do not cause a systematic drift. Note that this model does not have to be "right". It is intended to be (and is!) useful.

This modelling approach, described in more detail in Panel 5 (overleaf), has the great advantage of allowing us to switch between tenor and time, and of having the same forms for price and volatility. The exponential method is *one* way of drawing the forward curve between the spot and forward price. Each metal has a "better" line of its own, but this is a very useful general purpose method to start with.

This method of using an exponential beta to model price and volatility employs a mean reversion of sorts, but it does not require a breakdown of the Theory of Rational Expectations or of the Black–Scholes model. Depending on the desired approach, an historic average price can be used to represent the equilibrium price (an autocorrelation analysis), or an analyst can provide the equilibrium price. We can, if we wish, build on top of this a mean reversion to a price that *does not equal* the forward price. This can be very useful for copper, but is beyond the scope of this chapter.[3]

1. Main copper production areas and the dollar zones

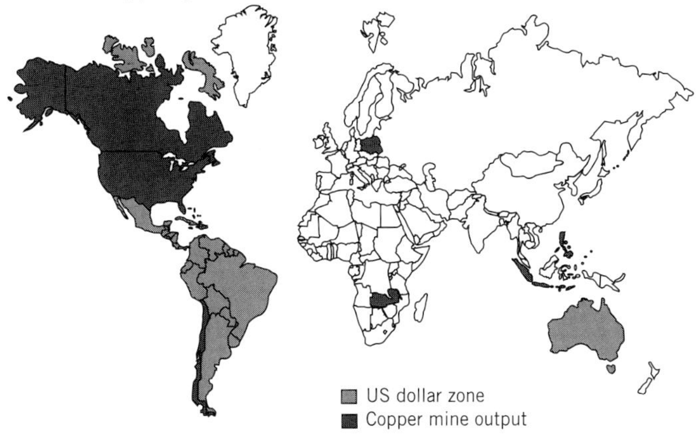

2. Copper price curve in successive years
(July 1992, May 1993, Feb, Dec 1994, July 1995, June, July 1996)

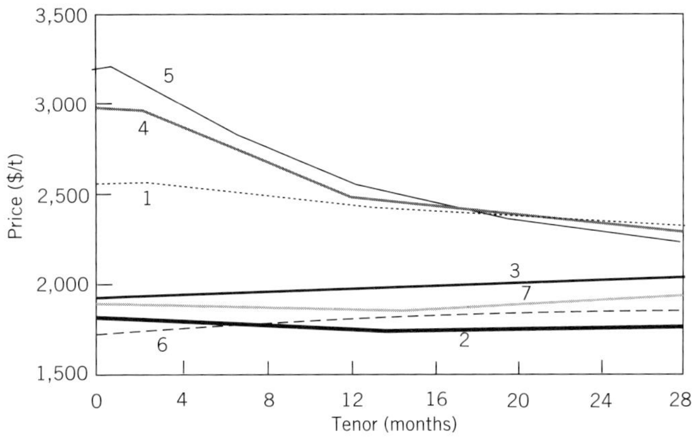

Because our exponential method assumes that there are strong systematic forces acting upon the market, it is most effective in market environments where there is a strong medium-term backwardation. The effects of arbitrage make the exponential method intractable in a contango market.

How does the model set out in Panel 5 relate to market realities? Let us look first at volatility. Figure 3 (overleaf) charts the decline of instantaneous historical volatility in relation to contract term for the copper market. Our long-term model suggests that the volatility of the price of copper, denominated in dollars, should fall to near zero in long tenors; the model for *very* long prices suggests that the volatility of the copper price should then rise to the volatility of the dollar itself.

Note that a straight line or simple polynomial could also be fitted to this. Our use of the expo-

PANEL 5

BETA MODELLING FOR COPPER

This panel introduces a way of characterising both price and volatility using a simple model. The model offers a rough and reliable method with an intuitive rationale – it is not intended to be rigorous. Here the relationship between the spot price and volatility, and forward price and volatility, is represented by a simple multiple, called the beta. The beta is very similar to the beta of the Capital Asset Pricing Model, and the methodology used in the decorrelation of interest rates. However, rather than merely using the beta as a correlation index, we make the stronger assumption that, once the initial conditions are characterised, the subsequent forward price movements are determinable from spot price movements. (It should be stressed that this is a first-order approximation and that forward price drift and other effects must be corrected for after the model is implemented.)

Copper is relatively easy to model in this way, because the same currency (US dollars) applies to its trading, budget and true economic value. The modelling approach described in this panel can be reconciled to the mean-reverting Wiener process described in Panel 4.

Let us assume that cash prices are non-equilibrium in their response to known forces, and that they are driven off course by unknown forces (such as investor demand). We will also assume that the cash price has a tendency to revert to the known equilibrium but that this process is slowed by inertia. Finally, let us also assume that the restoring force is directly proportional to the distance that the price is from its equilibrium value. In other words, the energy invested in production doubles when the difference of the market price from the equilibrium price doubles.

The modelling is as follows:

$$F = C_1(P_{\tau=0,t} - P_e)$$

Where F = restoring force, $P_{\tau,t}$ = price at tenor τ and time t, and C_n is a general constant, P_e is the equilibrium price.

Continuing our analogy with the physical world, we will assume that the speed at which the price moves towards its equilibrium is directly proportional to the energy acting to restore this price:

$$\partial P_{\tau=0,t} / \partial t = C_2 F$$

Combining the equations, and eliminating F, we have

$$\partial P_{\tau=0,t} / \partial t = C_3(P_{\tau=0,t} - P_e)$$

which can be integrated with respect to time so as to yield the exponential form:

$$P_{\tau=0,t} = P_e + C_4 e^{-kt}$$

where k is a constant and C_4 is dependent on the spot price and equilibrium price.

By applying the Theory of Rational Expectations (and assuming zero drift), we can make time and tenor equivalent:

$$P_{\tau=0,t} = P_{\tau=t}$$

Fitting the observed market to these equations means that we can characterise the parameters of the equilibrium price. We define beta by:

$$V_{\tau,t=0} = \beta V_{\tau=0,t=0}$$

where V = volatility, then

$$\beta = C_s e^{-k\tau}$$

It should be noted that, as the restoring force does not operate well in the short-term markets, beta does not characterise prices in those markets very well.

Strictly speaking, in order to apply the Theory of Rational Expectations it is necessary to make the equilibrium price equal to the price at the infinite tenor. However, the analysis can be used without this assumption.

Apart from making intuitive sense, the great advantage of this method is the reconciliation of both the forward price curve and the forward instantaneous volatility curve to the same form: the exponential. The exponential has long-term boundary conditions that are tractable. The inconvenient short-term boundary conditions are not important because they fall within a regime that is not bound by long-term economics – a regime in which we do not expect the model to be either observable or applicable.

nential is a subjective decision, based on perceived market mechanics.

In fact, from Figure 4 we can see that the long-term historical volatility tends to dip under the exponential curve in the longer dates. This effect is created by corporate governance. Producers tend to trade only as far into the future as the quoted market extends. This confines hedges to the last period of the quoted market. As they sell into price rises and curtail sales in price dips, the historical volatility seen in the prices of long-term contracts is, in general, *reduced* by their hedging activities.

However, we see just the opposite effect when we look at *implied* volatility. Nowadays, copper producers rarely sell options, and when they enter into long-term contracts they prefer to buy options rather than commit to forward sales. There is a supply/demand imbalance for long-dated options, thereby creating a rise in implied volatility that is above the expected historical volatility.

Because implied and historical volatilities (weighted over contract life) should in theory be identical, it is clear that producers and market traders are overriding both the Theory of Rational Expectations and the Black–Scholes model – leaving an arbitrage in their wake. Although there are structural reasons for the maintenance of this arbitrage (mainly capital adequacy rules), it is likely to reduce over time as traders seek new profit avenues.

An important additional complication arises when we try to convert the instantaneous historical volatility model into a curve representing implied volatility. The implied volatility is equal to the *average* volatility over the whole period, weighted by the time decay for the particular option – and to convert the instantaneous volatility to the weighted average volatility is rather awkward. This problem is not covered in detail in this chapter, although we do revisit it briefly in the section on gold prices, in the particular circumstance of a flat beta environment. Elsewhere in this chapter, we assume that the cash price volatility remains constant.

What about price? First we must find the equilibrium price. There is a standard mechanism for doing this: the cumulative supply curve is compiled from all the available data on production costs, and this is plotted against the expected demand curve for the year in question. The marginal (ie, equilibrium) cost can be read where the curves intercept (see Figure 5).

The three regions of the cumulative supply curve are usually quite well defined, and the lower-bound copper price can be read off from the intersection of the long flat line and steep line on the right. The curve is calculated for each year that is known, and the prices are corrected for inflation. The equilibrium price for each year in the long term is married to the known market curve, as shown in Figure 6 (overleaf).

Other measures of lower-bound price are also useful, such as historical troughs in cash prices corrected for inflation, and calculations based on minimum consumption estimates.

How can we adjust the theoretical long-term copper price to fit the market curve as it develops in the real world? One simple but relatively effective way to do this is to change all the parameters (equilibrium price, beta) each day by about 1% of their value. Long-term price should always move up when the cash price moves up.

The difference between the "settled down"

3. Actual beta curve (July 1996) normalised to the three-month tenor

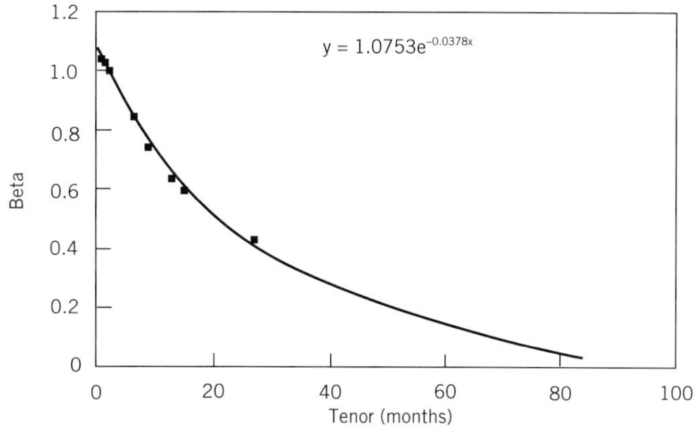

4. Copper volatility model

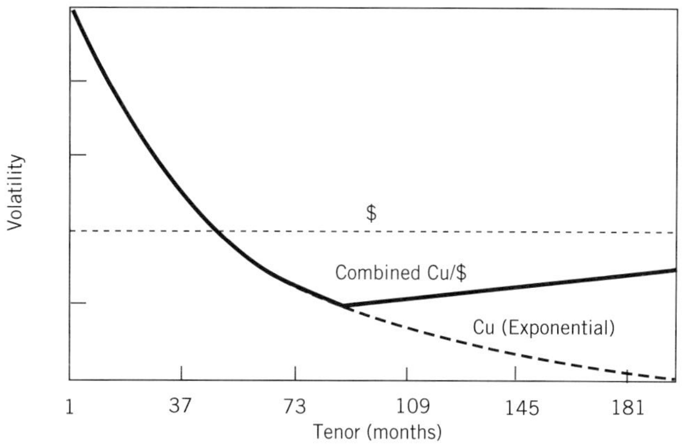

5. The standard price equilibrium curve

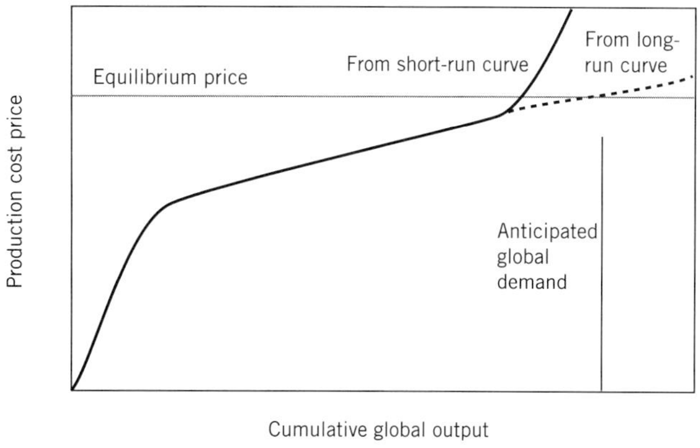

6. Construction of long-term copper price

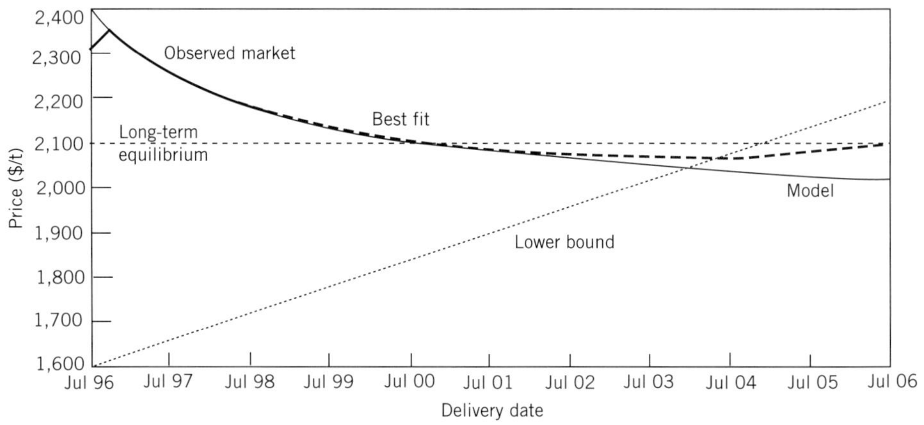

fitted price and the equilibrium price gives an indication of the drift term described in Panel 4.

How useful is the model we have described in this section? The answer is that it works reasonably well in a backwardation market with tenors that are longer than those affected by storage arbitrage (as described in our discussion of gold, below). Certainly, it is not a perfect fit. A perfect fit would imply that the model is fully understood and agreed, and that all traders calculated the exponentials each day. If this were the case there would be no need to write about it, and no trading opportunity to gain by exploiting the difference between the model curve and market reality. Figure 7 shows the modelled price curve against actual market prices – on a traded date that was chosen specifically for goodness of fit.

The exponential method is particularly useful for modelling *volatility*, but it is also sometimes useful for modelling *price*. The "goodness of fit" to the price curve can give an indication of aberrations in the volatility curve.

Note that the good fit illustrated in Figure 7 represents a disappointment to a trader, as it means that someone else got there first in terms of making useful analysis – and smoothed out the bumps.

Copper offers an excellent test bed for developing models for markets unaffected by arbitrage. In fact, price behaviour in most metals markets is best analysed in terms of how it differs from copper. When we want to understand price movements in a market strongly affected by arbitrage, the best example is gold.

7. Copper price in December 1995 with exponential fit

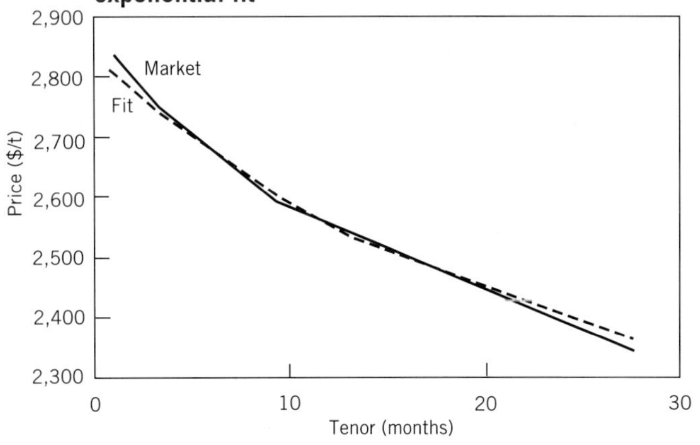

Contango arbitrage – gold

Gold is unique among metals in that its industrial utility is fairly insignificant, while its "psychological" value is paramount. Here, we assume that the psychological value of gold can be expressed in terms of utility, and that the utility of gold to the central banks and to investors is reasonably constant.

Because gold is not consumed to the extent that other metals are, and is extensively stored, the arbitrage opportunities of holders of gold are important in influencing medium-term gold lease rates, and therefore medium-term gold prices. This is as important as the effect described by the Theory of Rational Expectations.

The drivers of the gold market are the central banks (which drive the forward curve), the mass of investors (who slowly move the spot price), the mines (which produce a long-term effect on price and forward curve), and capital market investors (who produce short-term effects on the spot price).

It is safe to assume that central bank gold holding will continue for the next few decades at least, and that they will continue to attempt to reduce the lost opportunity cost in holding gold (see also Chapter 1). In the attempt, the central banks create the principal arbitrage of the gold market.

PANEL 6

GOLD ARBITRAGE FORMULA

How do the actions of participants in the gold markets give rise to a formula for gold arbitrage? Let:

S = spot price of gold in $
s = simple gold swap rate
F = forward price of gold in $
i = short-term simple $ interest rates
I = short-term gold interest rate

Now consider the actions in the gold market described in the table below.

Action	now Au	forward Au	now $	forward $
buy gold	1		–S	
lend gold	–1	1(1+It/360)		
borrow dollars			S	–S(1+it/360)
sell forward gold		–1(1+It/360)		F(1+It/360)

If we characterise the simple interest gold swap rates by:

$$F = S\left(I + \frac{st}{360}\right)$$

then we can see from balancing the forward cash-flow in the box above that:

$$S\left(I + \frac{it}{360}\right) = S\left(I + \frac{It}{360}\right)\left(I + \frac{st}{360}\right)$$

which gives:

$$i = I + s + \frac{Ist}{360}$$

In the short term, we can usually ignore the last term of this equation.

The relationship between simple, simple compounding and continuous rates is:

$$I + \frac{ist}{360} = \left(I + i_{comp}\right)^{t/360} = \exp\left(t_{cont}\frac{t}{360}\right)$$

The exponential form is useful, particularly as the beta has an exponential form.

There are two ways of holding a long position in forward gold:

- simply buying a forward contract; and
- borrowing money, buying gold and holding it.

Panel 6 illustrates how these actions give rise to a way of calculating the long-term price of gold.

In a perfect credit environment (in which gold would not be needed!), the long-term lease rate would trend towards zero. The buy/lend/store/sell arbitrage formula is used for the limiting contango in all metals. Obviously, the storage costs for base metals per dollar of value are much higher. The aluminium market of 1993 is a very good example of a market in contango with high implied storage costs.

Gold exhibits a highly complex relationship across economic zones. Because of the very strong relationship between the cash price and the forward price, the long-term metal price becomes very responsive to cash prices and – compared with other metals – the short-term economic zone extends forward a few years.

This has a peculiar effect on the cash price. Assuming that the utility/exchange value of gold, denominated in currency, remains constant in real terms, then the gold forward price should rise up the inflation curve. This implies that gold lease rates should roughly equal real interest rates. If gold lease rates are actually low, and utility/exchange value is normalised to the medium rather than the short term, then the implication is that cash gold trades at a discount to its "real" value.

How can we model the forward price? A simple starting model can be constructed using the following basic premises:

- there is a ceiling on the long-term lease rate for gold;
- the forward curve discounts the risk costs of gold lenders;
- a short forward/forward lending position has a positive return; and
- when the lease curve is in equilibrium, a short forward/forward lease position yields the same return on capital in all tenors.

The last point is an important equilibrium condition that is partly dependent on the regulatory capital measure for holding short lease positions, and partly dependent on the creditworthiness of the gold borrowers.

Figure 8 (overleaf) shows a simple construction of the gold forward rate using the assumption that the capital cost is proportional to the position tenor, and that the lease rate is capped by opportunist lenders. The peak lease rate is

8. Gold lease rate model

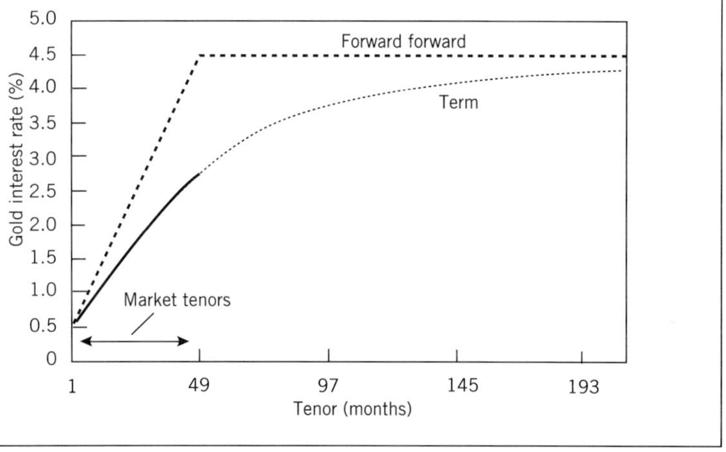

9. Gold volatility model

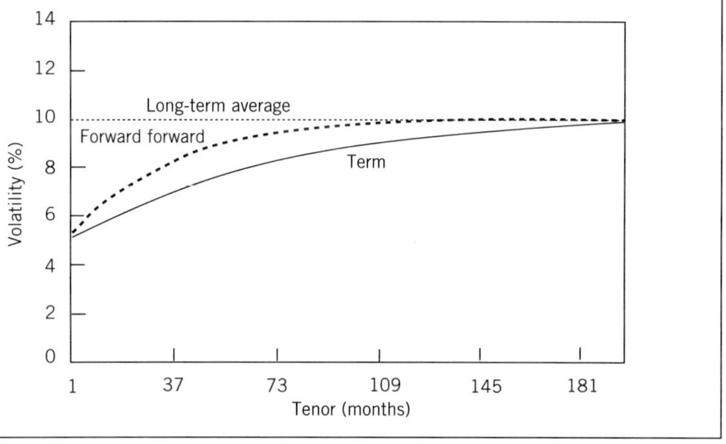

arbitrary and in reality appears gradually rather than sharply. The arguments for a peak rate are that, at a certain rate, central banks will lease long-term gold, or bullion banks will take more on to their "gap" books, and that, by borrowing gold instead of dollars at rates above international real interest rates, mines erode their profits and see a reduction in their equity value.

This model is about as far away as we can get from the Theory of Rational Expectations while still keeping things relatively simple and coherent. Naturally, there is much scope to build on it.

What about gold volatility? The close connection between cash and forward prices allows us to build a simple volatility curve that is not seriously complicated by tenor-dependent volatility (of the kind discussed in the previous section on copper). The tenor in which the utility of gold is measured should, theoretically, match the tenor in which the gold is expected to be mobilised (ie, sold or used as collateral). As gold is primarily a non-consumed asset, the utility should be normalised to a tenor measured in months or years.

The exponential method provides an effective and simple starting point. Let us make some simple assumptions:

- ❑ lease rate volatility is low;
- ❑ gold price volatility is independent of the measurement period (ie, it is "self similar");
- ❑ there is a long-term natural volatility for gold; and
- ❑ short-term economics prevail in all tenors.

The forward/forward one-day volatility in all times (not tenors) is modelled using an exponential. From this curve, a term volatility is constructed. This process is similar to the calculation of term interest rates from forward/forward rates, but is rather more complicated. This yields a volatility curve similar to the one shown in Figure 9.

The construction of the term curve is rather complicated. As it must be used in a real situation in which volatility is dependent on strike price as well as on tenor, an iterative numerical method offers the most flexible approach. Panel 7 presents the absolute bare bones of the method. (It is not for the faint hearted!)

Once this term curve has been constructed, the constricting assumptions can be unravelled. The most important change is to the assumption that the whole curve resides in the short-term economic zone: in practice, the summation of two exponentials with different exponents is required to correct for the zone transition.

True economic price denominated in utility – aluminium

Aluminium has a number of unique characteristics, all of which are of great importance in its price development. They cannot all be covered here, but the principal factors are:

- ❑ vertical integration;
- ❑ non-dollar based costs;
- ❑ dominance of smelting in the production process;
- ❑ smelter input indexation; and
- ❑ strong governmental interest/protection.

Vertical integration is important at the downstream end, because integrated metals companies are less sensitive to commodity price movements. Retail product prices are slower moving than market commodity prices. If aluminium prices rise, an aluminium company may gain on smelting and lose on extrusion.

Let us look first at the currency base of aluminium. There are three stages in the creation of an ingot: bauxite mining, refining to alumina and smelting to aluminium. The cost structure of each is quite separate.

PANEL 7

CONSTRUCTING A GOLD VOLATILITY CURVE

1) Construct a trial term volatility curve using an exponential forward/forward curve. Because this is a trial curve, exactly how it is formed is not really critical.
2) Value an at-the-money option on the 120th month's tenor using the trial term volatility curve.
3) Advance time by one month. Add together all the profits and losses (P&Ls) arising from the factors listed below (4–7)
4) Gamma – (diagram B) based on forward/forward expected historical volatility. This is equal to the forward/forward trial modelled volatility. This volatility is found by valuing a volatility timespread (short one option, and long the same option with one more month of duration) using the term volatilities of adjacent months, and then finding the volatility that gives the same timespread value using the same volatility for both options.
5) Theta – (diagram C) based on trial term volatility.
6) Vega – (diagram D) pick up/drop on the term volatility curve as the tenor shortens by a month.
7) Jump – (diagram E, expanded in F) volatility pick-up based on strike-dependent volatility. Jump gain is always positive and therefore must be included.
8) Weight over all strike prices. The number of strikes can be relatively few. This is because price change reduces the vega of near-the-money options and increases the vega of out-of-the-money options. This reduces the accumulation of strike-dependent volatility pick-up.
9) The P&L is converted via the option vega back to volatility change from the 120th month to the 119th month.
10) This is repeated for all months. The results are fed back into the trial curve for the second trial. Several iterations are required.

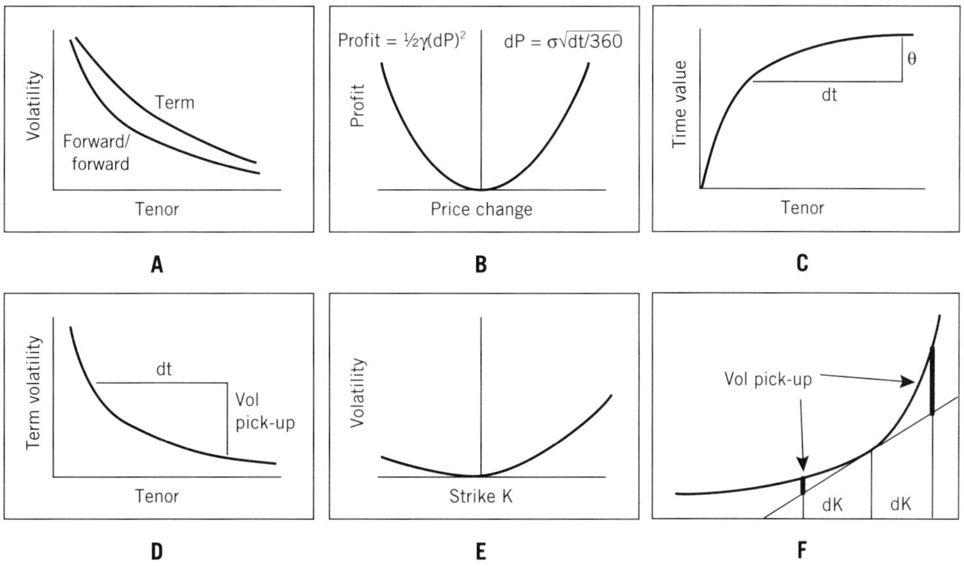

Bauxite mines are predominantly located in developing countries (Figure 10, overleaf) and, while the Western majors have an equity interest, there is usually strong state involvement. Bauxite mining is not capital intensive, and hence the cost is highly dependent on the local environment. Refining has no particular geographical location, apart from being near a port, for convenience of input and output of the bulk commodity. At present, aluminium smelting is frequently located near areas of high demand – although this is certainly changing. Smelting does incur a high capital cost, but not so high in terms of percentage of output price. In any case, the asset value of smelter plant is frequently "written off" after a few years, as is common practice with industrial plant.

Upstream costs (the alumina) have very little relationship to the US dollar. Power costs and alumina costs are very frequently indexed directly to

10. Main bauxite production areas and the dollar zone

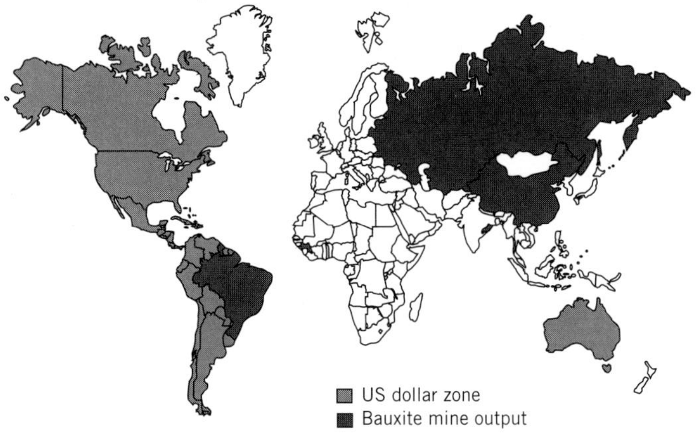

11. Aluminium volatility, denominated in dollars

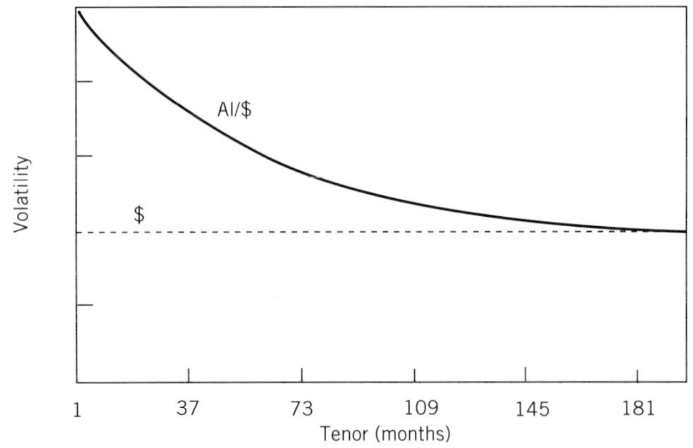

the aluminium price – in effect, they are denominated in aluminium.

The cost currency in which aluminium itself is denominated is hard to define. Labour cost is probably the best measure, particularly as power costs are based on local hydro or nuclear energy rather than being based on the international petrodollar. The best way to glimpse aluminium prices in their true currency would be to strip away the dollar dependence and see how the medium-term price has behaved over the last few years in other currencies. Unfortunately, the effect of the collapse of the Soviet Union and the associated collapse of the rouble, together with the effect of the Memorandum of Understanding of 1993, in which the producers, with government backing, multilaterally agreed to curtail output, have created too much distortion to allow a sensible statistical analysis.

12. Aluminium volatility in different denominations

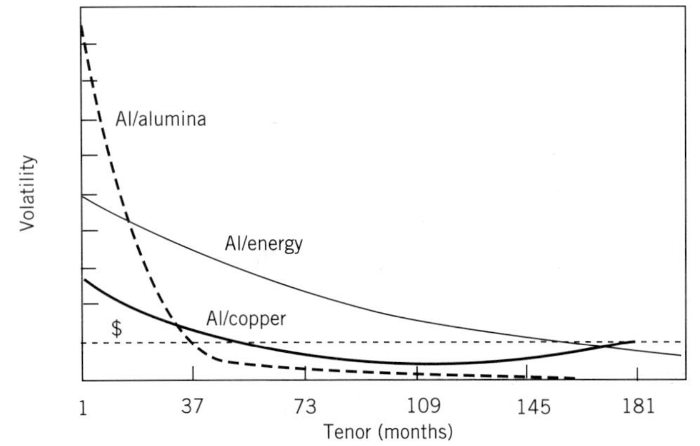

The denomination of the cost of production in a currency other than the investment currency makes it hard for economic agents to act. This is one reason there has been insufficient investment in aluminium production over the last three years. Figure 11 shows the effect on volatility of denominating the aluminium price in a currency other than its true economic currency (it can be compared with the volatility chart for copper in Figure 4).

Figure 12 shows the theoretical volatility of aluminium when it is denominated in other "currencies". Given this complex picture, what is the best model to use for aluminium prices? In practice, it may be best to use the same model as for copper. The rationale behind this is that, in the short term, the long-term dollar price is stable – because the value of the long-term dollar itself is stable. However, the parameters used to model the aluminium curve need to be adjusted far more frequently than they do for copper, and the parameters are inclined to trend in response to external factors.

The sell/wait/buy cycle and pricing culture – zinc

The Cost of Production Theory proved useful when we were analysing the long-term copper price. Abstract Labour Theory can be applied to long-term aluminium prices. The usefulness of the third theory we described in the first part of this chapter – Subjective Preference Theory – becomes apparent when we compare the zinc market with the others.

Let us first look at the industrial consumption of the three major metals over the last few years (Figure 13).

Investment funds were very quick to respond to the change in consumption we can see in the graph from early 1994, and shifted their funds from bonds to commodities. The key point here, however, is that zinc quite clearly performs "late". By the time the increase in demand for zinc had outstripped that of the two major metals, the investment money had moved on to equities.

This shows the great importance of trading for exchange, rather than trading for use. Zinc and aluminium started at similar values, and finished up with similar stock levels – but they ended up with very different stable values. Figure 14 demonstrates this and indicates that cash prices can be "non-equilibrium" for long periods.

Compared with aluminium, the demand for zinc is very inelastic. Of all the uses of zinc, the market in which we can most easily examine the relative value of zinc to the end-user is the galvanising market – which accounts for about 50% of zinc consumption. But even in this market, only about 50% of consumption goes towards custom or job galvanising in which the galvaniser's cost is mainly zinc, and not steel. For this reason, an investment-related price hike is unlikely to be dampened by substitution – as the price hike eventually was in the case of aluminium.

The short-term price has, therefore, been sluggish. What of the evolution of long-term prices? The first thing to look at is the currency basis of mine output. The geographical basis is shown in Figure 15, in comparison with copper.

Despite a fairly strong dollar content, the forward volatility curve for zinc is relatively flat. This is principally due to the slowness of movements in the cash price and the flatness of the forward curve.

The relative lack of speculative interference in the zinc price makes it possible to observe the transition of economic zones. Consider a tonne of zinc that is produced and then consumed. The zinc producer is likely to hedge his output into tenors extending beyond one year. However, the same tonne of zinc is not hedged by the consumer until its arrival is fairly imminent. (This is partly due to differences in corporate culture, but also because their zinc price risk profiles are quite different.) For our present purpose, the important point is that the zinc is "sold" by means of the hedge, and then there is a wait before it is bought again at a fixed price. This is known as the sell/wait/buy cycle (Figure 17 overleaf).

To see the effect of the cycle, we can use historical data to compare the forward price against the final cash price of the contract. Figure 18 (overleaf) illustrates this in the case of the 15-month forward contract. The analysis suggests that, by buying during the "sell" part of the cycle, a saving of $40, or nearly 4% of the price, could have been made. (While this statistical result is significant, it should not be construed as *proof* of the argument.)

13. Changes in world consumption of major metals

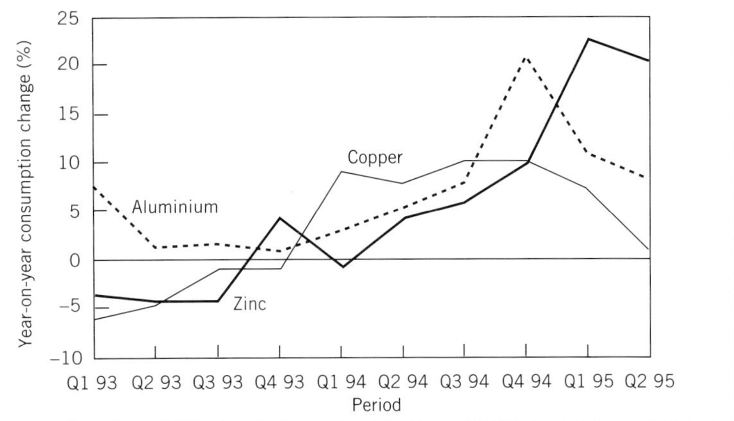

14. Changes in LME prices for major metals

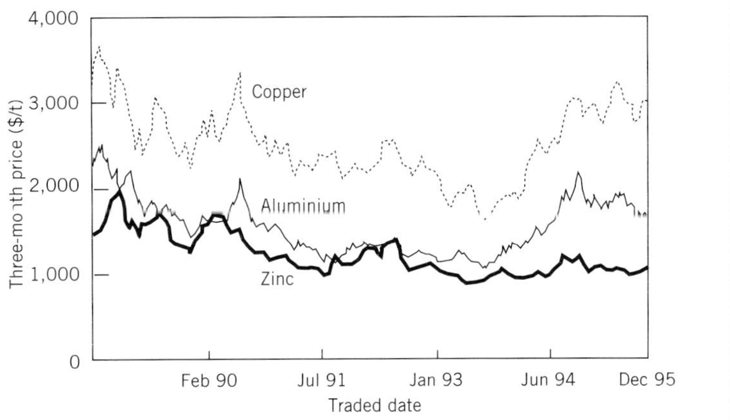

15. Production location of zinc and copper

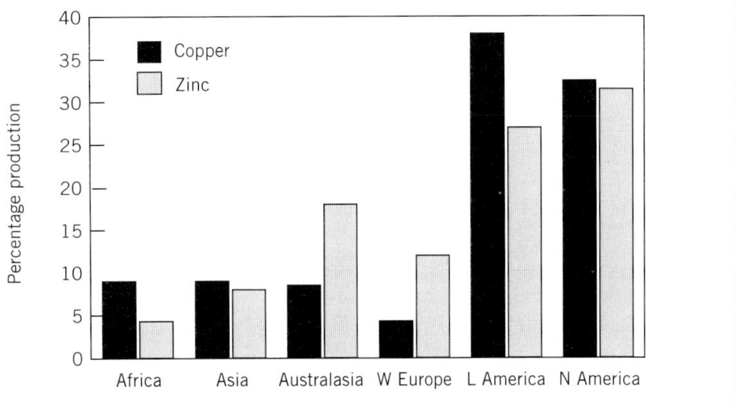

The sum of $40 represents the magnitude of the drift term described earlier in this chapter.

Finally, zinc is a good example of how "pricing culture", often rooted in the history of an industry, affects market dynamics. In the past, due to the inefficiency of the traditional smelting process, the zinc smelter would budget for a 15% loss of zinc through the smelting process itself. Nowadays, smelters are much more efficient and most of this zinc is recovered. However, the pricing formula for

16. Beta curves for copper and zinc, denominated in dollars

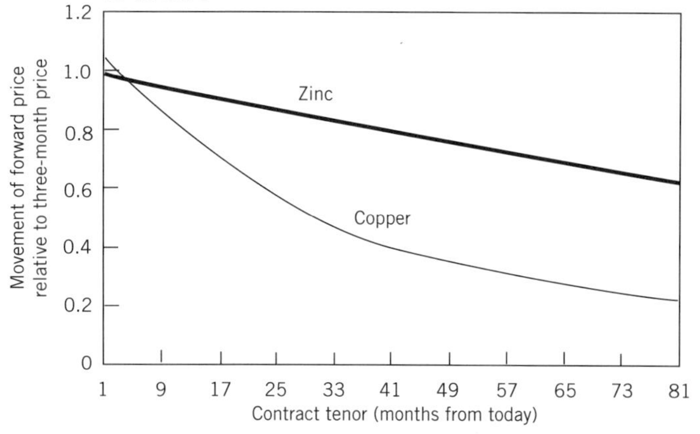

17. The sell/wait/buy cycle

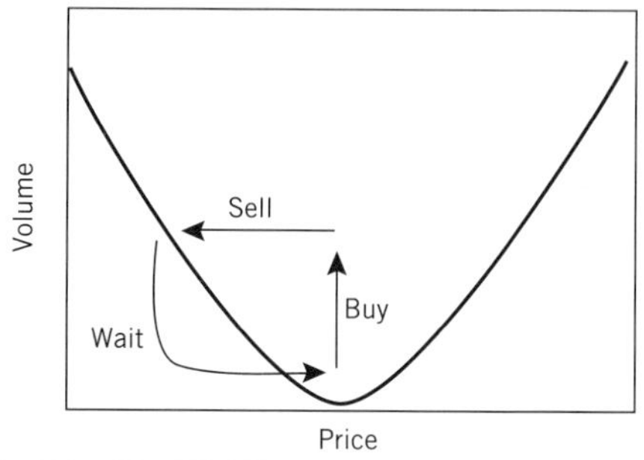

18. Historical benefits from selling late or buying early (15 months)

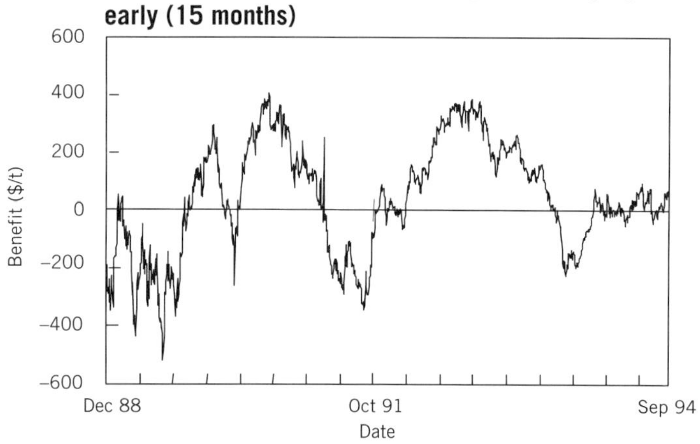

zinc concentrate maintained the 15% "free" zinc. Competition between smelters means that, in effect, smelters now "pay" producers for this free zinc by offering cheaper treatment. However, as a result they bear some of the market price risk for zinc and this creates an integration of sorts between smelter and mine. The risk sharing reduces the pressure on the weaker producers and delays closures when prices are low.

Short-term changes to long-term prices caused by process – nickel

Are there circumstances in which the long-term value of a commodity can suddenly change? The answer is yes, indeed. The price of oil is a very good example. Prices are not closely tied to production costs, but to the supply/demand balance. If an OPEC country announces that it will double production – and break its quota – in a year's time, then the cash price will hardly change, but the forward price will change significantly.

This is an example of how an *instant* decision can have an instant effect on the long-term market price. Breakthroughs in industrial *process* are somewhat more involuntary, but may have an equivalent effect on the long-term price.

What kinds of event in the base metals markets cause shocks to the long-term price? Firstly, there are the kinds of change that are the result of global dynamics rather than unilateral decisions. For example, changes in country risk, long-term real interest rates, tariffs, etc.

Secondly, there are changes in technology, such as:

- the use of bio leach in the gold industry;
- solvent extraction or plating on to stainless steel blanks in the copper industry;
- laterite extraction in nickel; and
- the "solvex" process for alumina.

This type of change could create step changes in price. In fact, this has not really happened very much, because the time taken from the initial development of a process to its use in a high percentage of global production is usually much greater than the tenor of the forward market discussed in this chapter.

Nickel probably provides the best example of a fast-moving production price (in effect, a modern example of the "hazards of mining" we mentioned earlier). Some key factors affecting the cost of producing nickel are:

Laterite extraction Laterite ores appear as a result of the deposition of the heavy metal over long periods. Falling reserves of non-laterite ores have put a premium on laterite extraction technology, and it develops by fits and starts. Both the total available volume of laterite ores, and the marginal cost of production, are very variable.

Polymetal production This is a common feature in metals mining: one metal is produced as a by-product of another. Nickel often appears with platinum and with cobalt. As the cost is shared between metals, the nickel cost is dependent on the market price of the co-metals.

Company nature Nickel is a re-melted commodity, rather than a fabricated commodity. This prevents much forward integration from production into the destination market. Nickel producers are also very weakly diversified into other metals, and are few in number. These factors mean that the producers cannot easily absorb changes in market price. Paradoxically, the fight to achieve economies of scale at economic troughs, and the need to gain the last pennies from an economic boom, make the nickel price more, rather than less, volatile (compared with a market that has many integrated and diversified producers).

On the consumption side, nickel price and nickel demand have little connection. Nickel is predominantly used in stainless steel, the demand for which is dependent on macroeconomic conditions. The nickel content of stainless steel (the austenitic ratio) is also relatively stable. The lack of elasticity of consumption means that there is little check on medium-term price movements.

The short-term market is a slightly different matter. The stainless steel market adopts the pricing culture of the steel market, which is inflation based rather than market based, and which has much in common with producer pricing. It is therefore very hard to pass on nickel costs, when they are not defined by a price surcharge formula. While the external market price (material not covered by longer contracts) remains volatile, the transaction price for long-term physical contracts is less volatile.

In summary, nickel is volatile in all tenors. This is includes the long term, because the hazards of mining make the cost of production very variable.

Short-term changes to long-term prices caused by decisions – lead

Environmental legislation is likely to have a profound effect on the metals markets in certain countries. Two laws have a particular impact. Firstly, the "superfund listing" in America, which makes a metal user or producer responsible for metal pollution created by other companies that are in some way connected to it. For example, the producer may have bought the site of an old mine, or supplied a company that dumps heavy metal waste. Secondly, in Europe, the Basel regulations currently restrict the recycling of waste (the rationale being that this forces the initial waste producer to redesign its process and so avoid producing it).

In copper, it is an unwanted by-product that is the environmental rogue. In lead, it is the lead itself. Self-regulation in the lead industry was developed well before the recent legislative stringency. Exposure has in the past arisen mainly from lead pipes, lead paints and contaminated soils. Even so, the lead industry has been extremely responsive to public concerns, and has developed secondary smelters with zero emissions. Public opinion is so important that, in at least one smelter, all rain water falling into the complex is collected and sold to the local water authority, with a lower lead content than the general water supply. The smelters are also responsible through superfund legislation for the eventual return of the batteries they sell.

The impact of legislation is unlike most other business risks in that it sometimes arrives in one fell swoop: unpredictable, sudden, arbitrary, far reaching, and sometimes even irrational. These are all ingredients for a volatile price.

Lead smelters must make a bet. Do they spend

PANEL 8

ENVIRONMENTAL ISSUES AND THE LOCATION OF PRODUCTION

A local environmental ruling in one part of the world can have a knock-on effect in another. For example, Dutch law requires zinc smelters to reduce their production of jarosite – a waste product that can be avoided by inputting concentrate that is low in iron. Meanwhile, the Century zinc mine in Australia (which produces zinc ore that has a low iron content) is subject to land rights claims. Hence, the economics of a smelter in Holland is in part dependent on the political and legal process in Australia.

By switching environmental effects between countries, an effective eco-export market is created by the local legal structures. This is extremely important in the very long-term price region.

Another example of this is provided by aluminium, which can be purified by using chlorine. When producing aluminium of a high purity, there is a trade off between the level of purity and the output of chlorine. The balance is dependent on local environmental laws.

a lot of money designing new plants to reduce toxic emissions to minuscule amounts - and incur the risk that legislation does not occur, or is relaxed, leaving the smelters which have not innovated with a cost advantage? In fact, over the last 20 years, the environmental laws have not just become more stringent, but they have been more stringent than expected. This has resulted in the closure of 22 of the 40 secondary smelters that existed 20 years ago in the US.

It is not the direction of change that is hard for industry to deal with, it is the unpredictability. Currently, the future direction of the law is unpredictable, and therefore the cost to the industry is unpredictable. It follows that the long-term price remains volatile.

In passing, it is worth mentioning that there is quite a difference between airborne pollution direct from the mine/smelter complex, mine waste and run-off, and all other forms of pollution. Airborne pollution can be very easily seen, measured and targeted. As a result, airborne pollution is a determinant in the choice of copper-smelter technology. However, as only 70% of copper output is smelted, and smelting currently only represents about 20% of cathode cost, this does not create high volatility in the copper price.

The price of lead, like the nickel price, is very volatile. Whereas nickel has a stable consumption trend, the search for lead substitutes makes the demand market as variable as the supply. So much so that the long-term market is very poorly defined.

Shift in the tenor of economic zones – silver

There are many ways in which the market paradigm of a metal can shift that are not dependent on technological processes. For example, there might be a temporary or permanent shift in the active economic zone (see Table 2), or a permanent change in the way the metal is used. The change in the role of silver in the investment markets provides a good example of the latter.

Historically, silver was used as a reserve currency for international trade - in fact, it was more prevalent than gold. This was largely because silver possessed a key quality of physical money - it is divisible (gold is too valuable to be used for common coinage of a practical size). However, divisibility is no longer so important and physical money forms a very minor proportion of money assets. While silver fell from grace as a money metal some time ago, it maintained some speculative exchange value - partly upheld by the Bunker Hunt incident. This has now eroded, and silver has effectively become an industrial metal. The particular importance for our purpose is that, while gold need only gravitate slowly to the marginal cost of mining (as one month's output represents only a small fraction of the total investment reserve), silver now gravitates towards the marginal cost at the same speed as a base metal. This has been disastrous for the price of silver. It is very unlikely that silver will re-emerge as a money metal, although it still has considerable short-term potential as a speculative metal.

What does this mean in practice? The contango arbitrage for gold and silver are virtually identical in nature - although silver tends to trade closer to the money curve due to the higher cost of physical storage. This gives the silver market a similar forward curve structure to that of the gold market.

In gold, the traded volume is dominated by the activities of investment and central banks, which perceive the asset value in the short-term tenor. The forward price is therefore a construct of the *spot* price. In silver, the volume of trade is dominated by the production sector, which allocates investment based on long-term prices. The spot price is therefore a construct of the *forward* price. We saw in gold how the contango can drive the spot price below the "fair price". In the silver market, steep contangos can depress spot prices below the levels that would be seen if trading for investment purposes was dominant.

What about volatility? The fact that much less silver than gold is traded for investment purposes means that it is much easier to drive up the silver market. Historically, this has meant that the natural volatility of silver has been higher than that

Table 2. Examples of shifts in economic zones and their effects

Example	Effect	Implication
Very long-term trading	Long tenors move into short-term economic zone	Increase in price volatility
Stock increase or decrease	Short-term market affects long-term market	Activation of production rate option
Psychological connection between zones	Long-term prices driven away from equilibrium	Increase in long-term price volatility
Capital market investment	Long-term tenors move into very long-term economic zone	Reduction of long-term price volatility
Tolling (for currency)	Less risk-capital market investment attracted	Long-term tenors, etc
Tolling (for metal)	All tenors move to very long-term economics	Lower volatility in "true currency", changed volatility in other currency

of gold. However, now that silver has made its paradigm shift to become a metal driven by the economics of production, it has assumed a long-term volatility that is characteristic of an industrial metal. The long-term natural forward/forward volatility of silver has always been high - market participants believe that every few years silver shows a very strong movement - but its volatility will move closer and closer to that of gold. In fact, because long-term silver prices should be dominated by Cost of Production Theory, and because gold will always be strongly influenced by Subjective Preference Theory, the volatility of the *long-term* silver price "should" fall below that of gold.

Cycles – copper revisited

As a general rule, economic cycles are not factored into forward prices in financial markets, even when the liquid forward price curve includes more than one cycle (eg, the long bond).

However, economic cycles are very important in metals markets because the markets are relatively inflexible in the adjustments they can make to production and consumption between tenors.

Consider the recent copper market, which exhibited high cash prices but relatively low producer costs. The high cash prices led (in part) to an increase in planned production that looks likely to generate a copper surplus in the year 1998.

The application of the Theory of Rational Expectations to this market environment dictates two outcomes: a low price in mid-1998, and a contango throughout 1998. This scenario can only come to pass if we steepen the backwardation from cash through to the end of 1997. The effect is shown in Figure 19.

The significance of this is that a subjective preference curve is forced onto a cost of production curve by the action of neutral investors. The copper price does not follow a supply/demand equilibrium, but the price response actually leads

19. Long-term copper price and the effect of rational expectations in a cyclical economy

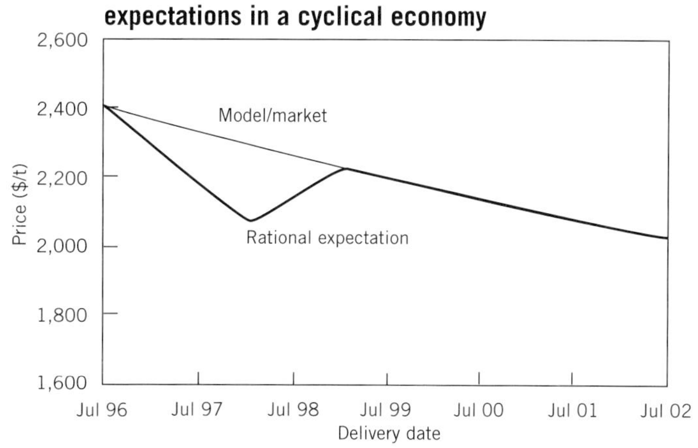

the physical factors that are the real drivers.

The action of investors in major metals markets nearly always causes the cash price response to precede the response of more fundamental market factors. Whether this lead is factored into the forward curve depends entirely on whether the investors extend the tenor of their economic activity into the long term. As market liquidity increases in the long term, and investors try to identify and take advantage of the systematic drift (the alpha of investment language), we may expect market cycles to become more evident in forward price curves.

Conclusion

Long-term pricing is a vast subject, and to date there has been little effort made to marry theory and practice. The first attempts to do so are bound to take a somewhat "homespun" approach to the idiosyncratic economics of the metals markets. Hopefully, however, this chapter has shown that both prices and volatilities can be modelled into the very long term. The characterisation of price can assist in evaluating financial decisions, and even in striking long-term "bargains". It is particularly important when market participants try to synthesise prices so that the short-term (and liquid) markets can be used to hedge long-term risks.

1 *In the futures market, contracts are quoted with one price per monthly contract. However, the seller can choose when to deliver the metal within that month. Whether the seller exercises its intramonth delivery option early or late depends in part on supply and demand in the physical market. The intramonth price structure in the physical market must therefore be taken into account when pricing futures.*

2 *Intensity of use is a term used to describe the amount of copper used by a country relative to its GDP.*

3 *Harris, C., 1994, "What Drives Long-term Metals Prices?",* Metal Bulletin Research Conference paper, *and Harris, C., 1995, "Copper Prices and Premiums",* Metal Bulletin Copper Conference paper.

BIBLIOGRAPHY

Dodd, N., 1974, *The Sociology of Money*, Polity Press: Cambridge.

Galbraith, J.K., 1975, *Money*, Penguin: London.

Keynes, J.M., 1936, *The General Theory of Employment, Interest and Money*, Macmillan: London.

Knox, P. and J. Agnew, 1994, *The Geography of the World Economy*, Edward Arnold: London.

Marx, K., 1891, *Wage, Labour and Capital.*

Ricardo, D., 1817, *Principles of Political Economy and Taxation*, London.

Smith, A., 1776, *The Wealth of Nations.*

Sheppard, E. and T. Barnes, 1990, *The Capitalist Space Economy*, Unwin Hyman: London.

Sraffa, P., 1960, *The Production of Commodities by means of Commodities*, Cambridge University Press: Cambridge.

GLOSSARY

This glossary provides short definitions of terms and abbreviations relevant to risk management in the metals markets. The glossary has been designed for general reference, so not all of the terms defined below are used elsewhere in this book. Longer definitions of terms used in financial risk management are available in an industry-standard glossary called The Chase/Risk Magazine Guide to Risk Management, *also available from Risk Publications.*

accelerated supply Sale of metals or other commodities in the market before the commodity has been mined or produced, by means of mine hedging contracts (eg forwards) and other financial transactions

accreting swap Swap contract with a notional amount that increases during the life of the swap (opposite of amortising swap, qv)

allocated accounts Accounts of secured creditors, offering precise description of metal assays and quantities, and with the customer's metals stocks kept physically segregated. *See also* unallocated accounts

all-or-nothing Digital option (qv). This option's put (call) pays out a pre-determined amount (the "all") if the reference price or index is below (above) the strike price at the option's expiration. The amount by which the reference price or index is below (above) the strike is irrelevant; the pay-out will be "all" or nothing

American option Option exercisable at any time up to expiration. *See also* European option

amortising option Option contract with a notional amount that decreases during the life of the option, such as an amortising cap, collar or swaption

amortising swap Swap contract with a notional amount that decreases during the life of the swap (opposite of accreting swap)

annuity swap Swap where, on the fixed payment side, the principal amount is amortised over the life of the swap

arbitrage Riskless profit gained from simultaneously buying and selling the same asset in different markets, or by means of different instruments, in order to exploit price differences (ie an inefficiency in the market overall). Arbitrage is often contrasted with speculation, which involves risk-taking

Arch AutoRegressive Conditional Heteroscedasticity, a technique used in the measurement of volatility

ASB Accounting Standards Board

Asian option *see* average price (rate) option

assay Test of purity or fineness of gold or silver

assay mark Mark stamped into a bar of gold or other precious metal to indicate its purity or fineness

asset-risk benchmark Benchmark (qv) against which the riskiness of a corporate's assets may be measured. In sophisticated corporate risk management strategies, the dollar risk of the liability portfolio may be managed against an asset-risk benchmark

asset-sensitivity estimates Estimates of the effect of risk factors on the value of assets

at the money An at-the-money option is an option with a strike price that is equal to the prevailing market price of the underlying asset. *See also* in-the-money and out-of-the-money

average cap Also known as an average rate cap, a cap on an averaged price or index rate over a given period, rather than on the rate prevailing at the end of the period (*see also* average price (rate) option)

average price (rate) option Option on the average spot or index price of a commodity (or other underlying) over a specified period. Four variables have to be agreed between buyer and seller: the premium, the strike price, the source of the commodity price data and the sampling interval (eg each day, or week). At the end of the life of the option, the average rate is calculated and compared with the strike price. A cash payment is then made to the buyer of the option equal to the face amount of the option times the difference between the two rates (assuming the option is in the money; otherwise it expires worthless)

backwardation Description of a market in which commodity forward prices are lower than the spot price

barrier option Option where the ability of the holder to exercise is activated or, alternatively, extinguished if the value of the underlying reaches a specified level. Also known as a limit option or trigger option

basis risk In a futures market, the risk that the value of a futures contract does not move in line with the underlying exposure. More generally, and in the over-the-counter market, the risk that the reference price or price index specified in the hedge contract does not move in line with the financial exposure that the hedger is attempting to risk manage

basket option Option based on the combined price of an underlying basket of metals (or currencies, equities, etc). The basket might be weighted to reflect the hedger's financial exposure to each type of metal

bear market Market in which prices are expected to fall. Derivative strategies using spread options (combinations of options with different exercise prices) can be devised to take advantage of this market view

bear spread *see* bear market

benchmark Criterion against which to measure the performance (or riskiness) of any of a variety of variables, including portfolios of metals-linked contracts. They also can be used to judge the performance of risk managers or fund managers

bid Price at which a buyer is willing to purchase an asset

bid/ask (offer) spread Difference between the buying price and the selling price of an asset at a particular moment in time

binomial tree Commonly used numerical solution, which traces various paths the underlying price can take and then calculates option values corresponding to the different price outcomes

break forward Forward contract which the customer can break at a pre-determined rate, allowing him or her to take advantage of any favourable market movements

bull market Market in which prices are expected to rise. Derivative strategies using spread options (combinations of options with different exercise prices) can be devised to take advantage of this market view

bull spreads *see* bull market

bullion Generic term for gold and silver, particularly when in bar, ingot or plate form

butterfly spread The simultaneous sale of an at-the-money straddle (qv) and purchase of an out-of-the-money strangle (qv). The structure profits if the underlying metal (or other) price remains stable and has limited risk in the event of a large move in either direction

calendar spread Strategy involving buying and selling options or futures with the same (strike) price but different maturities. Such a strategy is used in futures when one contract month is theoretically cheap and another is expensive. With options, the strategy is often used to exploit expected changes in the shape of the volatility term structure

call option Contract which gives the purchaser the right to buy an underlying at a certain price on or before a certain date (*see also* put option)

cancellable swap Swap in which the payer of the fixed rate has the option, usually exercisable on a specified date, of cancelling the deal (*see also* swaption)

cap Ceiling on the price level of an underlying (eg, commodity or interest rate), constructed from a strip of European options (qv). For example, if on prescribed reference dates a price reference or index is above a rate agreed between the seller of the cap and the buyer, the seller pays the buyer the difference until the next reference date. The opposite of a floor (qv)

CAPM Capital asset pricing model

capped option Option where the holder's ability to profit from a change in value of the underlying is subject to a specified limit

caption Option on a cap

carat Unit used to describe the proportion of precious metals in an alloy, 24 carat being pure gold. Also a measure of the weight of diamonds and other precious stones

carry rate risk Risk that either the financing or lending rates may change over the course of the life of a forward

cash & carry arbitrage Strategy in which a trader sells a commodity (or other) futures contract and purchases the underlying commodity to deliver into the futures contract when it matures, thus generating a riskless profit. For the strategy to work, the futures contract must be theoretically expensive relative to purchasing the commodity in the cash market, and (in the case of commodities) the trader must be able to secure storage at a rate that ensures a profit margin

cashflow at risk (CFAR) Expression of corporate financial risk where risk is defined in terms of earnings - or some other measure of a company's performance - rather than hedged profitability

CFTC *see* Commodity Futures Trading Commission

CIF *see* cost, insurance and freight (CIF)

collar Combination of the purchase of a cap (qv) and the sale of a floor (qv), or vice versa, to create the desired band within which the buyer of the collar wants the price of the underlying (eg, price of copper) to be held

Comex The Commodity Exchange in New York, now a division of Nymex (qv)

Commodity Futures Trading Commission (CFTC) Government agency that regulates the futures markets in the US

commodity-linked finance Debt where the principal and/or interest repayments are in some way linked to commodity prices

commodity swap Swap where one of the cashflows is based on a fixed value for the underlying commodity and the other is based on a floating index value. The commodity may be copper, gold or other metals (or energy or agricultural products). The end-users are consumers, who pay a fixed rate, and producers

compound option Option on an option, the first giving the buyer the right, but not the obligation, to buy the second on a specific date at a pre-determined price. Compound options are particularly common in the electricity market, rather less so in the metals market

consignment stocks Precious metal bars (gold or silver) that are consigned to a client, who guarantees payment to the owner at the prevailing price as the stocks are depleted

contango Description of a market in which the forward price of a commodity is higher than the spot price

contingent option Option where the premium is higher than usual but is only payable if the value of the underlying reaches a specified level. Also known as a contingent premium option

contingent premium option *see* contingent option

correlation matrices Statistical constructs used in the value-at-risk (qv) methodology to measure the degree of relatedness of various market factors

corridor Collar (qv) on a swap using two swaptions (qv)

cost, insurance and freight (CIF) The CIF designation indicates that the price/contract includes freight and insurance to the named destination (but may not include customs duties)

cost of carry Cost of owning and holding a physical commodity over a particular period, largely a factor of physical storage, insurance and funding costs. Funding costs represent the cost of financing the transaction, and are thus dependent upon interest rates

country risk The risks, when conducting business in a particular country, of negative economic or political conditions arising in that country. More specifically, the credit risk of a financial transaction or instrument arising out of those conditions

covered option Option for which the seller holds an offsetting position in the underlying asset (so that both positions cancel out the financial risk that each would incur if held on its own)

credit derivatives Financial contract that involves a potential exchange of payments in which at least one of the cashflows is linked to the performance of a specified underlying credit-sensitive asset or liability. *See also* credit swaps

credit risk Degree of uncertainty of the ability of a counterparty to fulfil its financial and legal obligations

credit swaps Agreement between two counterparties to exchange disparate cashflows, at least one of which must be tied to the performance of a credit-sensitive asset or to a portfolio or index of such assets. The other cashflow is usually tied to a floating-rate index, or a fixed rate, or linked to another credit-sensitive asset

cross In the foreign exchange markets, two non-dollar currencies in relation to each other, eg, Deutschmark/yen

cross-market risk Simultaneous price exposure to two or more markets

deferred pay-out option American option (qv) where settlement is at expiry

deferred start options Options purchased before their "lives" actually commence. A corporation might, for example, decide to buy a deferred start option to lock in what it perceives as current advantageous pricing for an option that it knows that it will need in the future

deferred strike option Option where the strike price is established at a future date based on the spot price prevailing at that future date

delivery date Date on which metal (or other) must be delivered in order to meet the terms of a contract

delta Measure used in the financial risk management industry to describe a change in the value of an option in response to a change in the underlying price (positive for calls, negative for puts)

digital option Unlike simple European and American options, a digital option has fixed pay-outs and, rather like binary digital circuits, which are either on or off, either pays out this amount or nothing at all. Digital options can be added together to create assets that exactly mirror investors' anticipated index price movements (see also one touch all-or-nothing)

discount swap Swap in which the fixed rate payments are below the internal rate of return on the swap, the difference being made up at maturity by a balloon payment

down-and-in option Barrier option (qv) where the holder's ability to exercise is activated if the value of the underlying drops below a specified level (*see also* up-and-in option)

down-and-out option Barrier option (qv) where the holder's ability to exercise expires if the value of the underlying drops below a specified level (*see also* up-and-out option)

drift Constant movement of a forward price over time, in response to an economic force

dynamic hedging Hedging technique whereby the percentage of a portfolio being hedged is continually adjusted, or when a specific hedge transaction is lifted and repositioned. By contrast, hedges that are not adjusted after being put in place are known as "static" hedges

efficient frontier method Technique used by fund managers to allocate assets

EFP Exchange of Futures for Physical

European option Option that can only be exercised at expiry (*see also* American option)

exercise The act of a call (put) option holder buying (selling) the underlying product (*see also* American option and European option)

expiry date Final day on which an option may be exercised

extinguishable option Option in which the holder's right to exercise disappears if the value of the underlying passes a specified level (*see also* barrier option)

FASB Financial Accounting Standards Board

Figarch *see* Fractionally Integrated

Generalised AutoRegressive Heteroscedasticity

floor Series of European call options protecting the buyer from a fall in the price of the underlying (eg price of copper) below a specified level; the opposite of a cap (qv)

floortion Option on a floor (qv)

forward Agreement to exchange a pre-determined amount of currency, commodity or other financial instrument at a specified future date and at a pre-determined rate

forward band Zero-cost collar (qv), that is, one in which the premium payable as a result of buying the cap (qv) is offset exactly by that obtained from selling the floor (qv)

forward break *see* break forward

forward/forward deposit Agreement by one party to make a deposit with another at a specified future date and pre-determined rate

forward swap Swap arranged at current prices but entered into at some time in the future

Fractionally Integrated Generalised AutoRegressive Heteroscedasticity (Figarch) Mathematical technique used in the calculation of price volatilities

Free on Board (FOB) indicates that the price/contract includes delivery of a commodity on board a transporting vessel. The cost of further transport or insurance will reside with the purchaser

front loading Bringing forward a net revenue stream (eg from a mine that is being developed) and turning it into cash by borrowing against it

fundamental analysis The study of "fundamentals" is the analysis of underlying economic and political factors likely to affect the supply and demand of a commodity. It is often contrasted with technical analysis (qv), the study of market price behaviour

futures contract Obligation to buy or sell a standard amount of commodity, currency, financial instrument or service at a pre-determined price and at a specified date. Futures are normally traded on exchanges and may incur margin payments (daily payments to or from the holder of the position that vary according to the profit or loss of the position)

Futures Commission Merchant (FCM) US commodity brokerage house focused on exchange-traded futures

gamma Measure used in the financial risk management industry to describe the change in the delta (qv) of an option in response to a change in the underlying price

gapping Feature of commodity markets whereby there are large and very rapid price movements to new levels, followed by relatively stable prices

Garch *see* Generalised AutoRegressive Conditional Heteroscedasticity

gearing (or leverage) In markets, the ability to gain financial exposure to large profits or large losses by using only a small initial investment

Generalised AutoRegressive Conditional Heteroscedasticity (Garch) Mathematical technique used to analyse price volatilities

gold loan Arrangement of funding in gold for a major project (eg mine development) or inventory. The gold exposure is thus hedged and a relatively cheap source of funding is tapped

gold warrant Naked or attached warrant exercisable into gold at a pre-determined price

"the Greeks" In the risk management industry, certain risk measures applied to options are described using Greek symbols (the Greeks). *See* individual entries for delta, gamma, kappa (listed under its more common name, vega), rho and theta

hedge Contract or market position entered into in order to reduce or negate an existing exposure to a market price

historical simulation methodology Method of calculating value-at-risk (VAR) (qv), using historical data to assess the likely impact of market moves on a portfolio

IASC International Accounting Standards Committee

IMRO The Investment Management Regulatory Organisation (an SRO (qv))

in the money An in-the-money option is an option with a strike price that is advantageous compared with the current market price of the underlying. The more an option is in-the-money, higher its intrinsic value and the more expensive it becomes. *See also* at-the-money and out-of-the-money

indexed notes Contract whereby the issuer usually assumes the risk of unfavourable price movements in the instrument, commodity or index to which the contract is linked, in exchange for which the issuer can reduce the cost of borrowing (compared with traditional instruments without the risk exposure)

ISDA The International Swaps and Derivatives Association

kappa *see* vega

knock-in option Option where the holder's ability to exercise is activated if the value of the underlying reaches a specified level (*see also* barrier option)

knock-out option Option where the holder's ability to exercise is extinguished if the value of the underlying reaches a specified level (*see also* barrier option)

legal risk Uncertainty arising from the possibility that a contract might not be enforceable

level payment swap Evens out those fixed rate payments that would otherwise vary, for example, because of the amortisation of the principal

leverage *see* gearing

limit option *see* barrier option

liquidity risk Risk associated with transactions made in illiquid markets ie those markets that lack substantial and regular trading, or in which trading may dry up in particular market circumstances

location basis The price difference resulting from the separate geographical locations of the hedging instrument and the physical metal

loco Location at which the physical inventory of the metal being traded is held (eg gold might be traded "loco London"), and for which a particular price premium or price differential is likely to apply

London Bullion Market Association (LBMA) Association incorporated in 1987 to express the interests of players in the wholesale bullion market, and to encourage the development of the London bullion market

London Good Delivery List This list names the smelters and assayers whose gold/silver bars meet the standards of fineness, weight, marks and appearance set by the London Bullion Market Association (qv)

London interbank offered rate (Libor) In the money markets, the rate of interest at which funds are offered in the London interbank market, for maturities ranging from overnight to five years. Three- and six-month Libor are widely used as reference rates for payments on floating-rate loans

lookback option Option that allows the purchaser, at the end of a given period of time, to choose as the rate for exercise any rate that has existed during the option's life

mapping The process whereby an institution or corporation's derivative positions are related to a set of risk "buckets" so as to facilitate calculations at the portfolio level eg value-at-risk calculations

margin Deposits of cash or collateral that may be demanded as security against open positions in the futures, forwards or options markets

margin call Request for additional cash or collateral to offset losses on forward or futures contracts (*see also* margin)

mark to market Contracts and positions are said to be "marked to market" when they are revalued according to prices in the prevailing market, as opposed to the value they may have had when the position was initiated or the value they may have at some point in the future

market comparables technique Technique for estimating the fair value of an instrument for which no price is quoted by comparing it with the quoted prices of similar instruments

market maker Market participant who is committed, explicitly or otherwise, to quoting bid and offer prices in a particular market

market risk Risks related to changes in prices of tradable variables, such as commodity prices (eg price of copper), exchange rate risks or interest rate risks

min-max option The purchase of one option and the sale of another option of the same specifications, so that the client effectively sets minimum and maximum price levels for its metal intake or sales. The sold option, in effect, subsidises the cost of the purchased option (to a degree, depending on the prices set)

Monte Carlo simulation Technique used to determine the likely value of a derivative or other contract by simulating the evolution of the underlying variables many times over. The discounted average outcome of the simulation gives an approximation of the derivative's value. Monte Carlo simulation can be used to estimate the value-at-risk (VAR) (qv) of a portfolio. Here, it generates a simulation of many correlated market movements for the markets to which the portfolio is exposed, and the positions in the portfolio are revalued repeatedly in accordance with the simulated scenarios. This results in a probability distribution of portfolio gains and losses, from which the VAR can be determined

naked option The opposite of a covered option (qv), this is the sale of a put option or call option that is not related to a holding in the underlying asset. In contrast to covered positions, naked positions tend to increase the financial exposure of the holder

negative skew Describes the risk of an increased probability of negative events, when compared with their probability of occurrence in a diagram showing a normal distribution

net present value (NPV) Technique used to assess the worth of future payments by looking at the present value of those future cashflows discounted at today's cost of capital

novation Replacement of a contract or, more usually, a series of contracts with one, new contract

Nymex The New York Mercantile Exchange

off-market swap Tax-driven swap strategy, in which the fixed rate payments differ significantly from current market rates

one touch all-or-nothing Digital option (qv). This option's put (call) pays out a pre-determined amount (the "all") if the index goes below (above) the strike price at any time during the option's life. How far below (above) the strike price the index moves is irrelevant; the pay-out will be the "all" or nothing

open interest This statistic describes, on a given day, the number of contracts of a particular type on an exchange that are still "open" (ie which are still active and have not been closed out)

open outcry On some exchanges the style of trading involves dealers facing each other in a pit or ring, crying out (open outcry) the contract specifications, quantity and price that they are willing to trade on

open position Market position that the holder has not closed out (ie to which they are still financially exposed)

open repo Open-ended repurchase, or repurchase closed at the discretion of either party

operational risk Term used to describe the risk of losses resulting from inadequate systems or controls, human error, or management failure (in contrast to pure market or credit risk, qv)

opportunity cost Value of an action that could have been taken if the current action had not been chosen

option The right, but not the obligation, to buy or sell a given commodity, stock, interest rate instrument or currency in the future at a mutually agreed price, known as the strike price (qv). The right is given in exchange for a premium

Ornstein–Uhlenbeck equation Standard equation that describes mean reversion. It can be used to characterise and measure commodity price behaviour

OTC *see* over-the-counter

out of the money An out-of-the-money option is an option with a strike price that is disadvantageous compared with the current market price of the underlying. The more an option is out-of-the-money, the less it is worth, since the chance of the holder being able to exercise it is reduced. *See also* at-the-money and in-the-money

over-the-counter (OTC) Customised derivative contracts usually arranged with an intermediary such as a major bank, as opposed to the standardised derivative contracts available on an exchange. OTC contracts are also sometimes described as "bilateral" (ie they are agreements between two parties) and "privately negotiated" (ie they are not available on an exchange)

over-the-top warrant Warrant with the same characteristics as an up-and-out option (qv)

participating forward Also known as a profit-sharing forward, an adaptation of the range forward (qv), in which only a floor (qv) is fixed. Instead of paying a premium, the owner/client undertakes to pass a percentage of any gain to the seller. The percentage (known as the seller's participation rate) varies in direct proportion to the level of the floor. For a low participation rate, the buyer must accept a low floor. The buyer is allowed to choose the level of either the participation rate or the floor. Based on that choice, the seller fixes the other variable

participating option Option where the holder forgoes a pre-determined percentage of any profits in return for paying a reduced premium

participating swap Swap where a counterparty incurs lower costs in return for giving up a percentage of any gain on the swap

path-dependent option Generic term for options where the pay-off, or sometimes the exercise style, depends, not just on the current price of the underlying asset or commodity, but also on the path it follows

periodic resetting swap Swap where the floating-rate payment is an average of floating rates that have prevailed since the last payment, rather than the interest rate prevailing at the end of the period

polymetal production Common feature of mining where one metal (eg silver) is produced in tandem with, or as a by-product of, mining for another metal. The nature of the supply curve, and thus price volatility, can be substantially affected by this economic fundamental

portfolio theory Theory which states that the variance of the return on a collection of assets will nearly always be less than the variance of the return on any subset of the portfolio

positive cashflow collar Collar (qv) other than a zero-cost collar (qv)

positive skew A greater likelihood of extreme "upside" movements in a share or market price than is described by a normal (ie bell-shaped) probability distribution

precious metals Metals of the highest value, usually held to include gold, silver, platinum and other platinum-group metals

product basis The pricing differential that results from any difference between the quality specifications of the hedging instrument and those of the underlying exposure

put option Contract which gives the buyer the right, but not the obligation, to sell a given amount of an asset at a pre-determined price on or before a designated date

QP *see* quotation period

quanto options (quantos) In the money markets, options in which the strike price for the underlying is denominated in a second currency (eg a foreign currency Bund option)

quartation Process by which silver is separated from gold using nitric acid

quasi-American options These allow the option holder to exercise at agreed times other than maturity

quotation period (QP) The specified time period over which the pricing of a contract is fixed

random risk Risk that has no identifiable relationship with other market factors

range forward Forward contract in which, instead of an individual spot rate for exchange, a range is agreed, allowing for exchange at any rate prevailing within that range at maturity. If the spot rate at maturity is outside that range, the exchange takes place at the end of the range nearest that rate. The buyer of the contract fixes only one end of the range, the seller retaining the right to fix the other

reduced cost option Generic term for options for which there is a reduced premium, either because the buyer undertakes to forgo a percentage of any gain, or because he or she offsets the cost by writing other options (eg, minimax, range forward). *See also* zero-premium option and zero-cost collar

relative performance option Option whose value varies in line with the relative value of two assets

repo Agreement to buy (sell) a security while at the same time agreeing to sell (buy) the same security at a pre-determined future date

return on value-at-risk (ROVAR) An analysis conducted to determine the relative rates of return on different risks, allowing corporations to compare different risk capital allocations and structure capital decisions effectively

reversal The act of switching from a fixed to a floating basis in a swap, or vice versa

rho Measure used in the financial risk management industry to describe the change in value of an option in response to a given change in the discount rate

roller-coaster swap Swap in which a counterparty alternately pays a fixed then a floating rate

SEC The Securities and Exchange Commission (US regulatory body)

sensitivity (or scenario) analysis Analysis of the possible loss of future earnings, fair values or cashflows arising from selected hypothetical changes in market rates and prices

settlement date Date on which a contract must be "settled" (ie paid for and delivered) according to the terms of the contract. In some metals markets, for example, this may be two business days after the transaction date

settlement price On the futures exchanges, a price for each contract is agreed by an exchange committee at the end of each day based on that day's trading, and may be used by the exchange or its clearing house to assess open positions and to calculate variation margin calls, etc

SFA The Securities and Futures Authority

Sharpe ratio Measure of the attractiveness of the return on an asset, calculated by comparing how much risk premium the investor can expect to receive in return for the incremental risk (volatility) that the investment carries. It is the ratio of the risk premium over the volatility of the asset

short To short the market, or to establish a short position, is to sell an asset that the seller does not yet own (the opposite of going long)

SIB The Securities and Investment Board, which is the principal regulator of financial services in the UK

Simex Singapore International Monetary Exchange

SPAN *see* Standard Portfolio Analysis of Risk

spot price Price paid for metals and other commodities when they are offered for immediate payment and physical delivery

spread lock swap Swap with an option to fix the floating-rate payment at a given spread over a benchmark fixed rate, at some time or for some period in the future

SROs Self Regulatory Organisations regulate most institutions involved in investment activities in the UK, and are in turn watched over by the Securities and Investment Board

standard bar In the case of gold, a standard bar weighs approximately 400 ounces or 12.5kg and offers a minimum fineness of 995; in the case of silver, a standard bar weighs approximately 1,000 oz and offers a minimum fineness of 999.0

Standard Portfolio Analysis of Risk (SPAN) Methodology used in the calculation of margins on the London Metals Exchange and elsewhere

static hedging strategy Hedges that are put in place with the intention of leaving them to run their course are known as static hedges, in contrast to dynamic hedging (qv)

step-down swap Swap in which the fixed rate payment decreases over the life of the swap

step-up swap Swap in which the fixed rate payment increases over the life of the swap

stop loss order Pre-set instruction to sell or otherwise liquidate a position when the prevailing price drops below (or moves above) a designated threshold. The intention of a stop loss order is to make certain that losses from a given position or portfolio cannot exceed a level set when the strategy is embarked upon. However, institutions carrying out the order may not be able to guarantee that they will be able to execute the order at the given price if market conditions are difficult

straddle The sale of a put and a call with the same strike price on the same underlying and with the same expiry. The strike is normally set at the money. For purchasing two premiums, the purchaser benefits if the underlying moves enough either way. Straddles therefore enable the purchaser to hedge against an expected increase in volatility in the underlying. The seller of a straddle, on the other hand, assumes unlimited risk but benefits if the underlying does not move

strangle As with a straddle, the sale or purchase of a put option and a call option on the same instrument, with the same expiry, but at strike prices that are out-of-the-money. As both options are out-of-the-money, strangles cost a purchaser less to set up than straddles, but profits are only generated if the underlying moves dramatically. The seller of a strangle, on the other hand, makes money in the range between the two strike prices but loses if the price moves substantially outside the strike prices

stress testing Analysis that gives the value of a portfolio under a range of worst-case scenarios

strike price An option gives the holder the right, but not the obligation, to purchase the underlying (eg copper) at a predetermined price known as the "strike price". The strike price is set when the contract is agreed. The extent to which an option has value (is "in the money") is partly governed by how far the strike price is above/below the prevailing market price for the underlying commodity

structured note Structured notes are OTC products that bundle several disparate elements to create a single product, generally by embedding options in a debt instrument such as a medium-term note

swap The exchange of one sort of cashflow for another for a pre-determined length of time. Usually, swaps involve the exchange of a fixed price (determined when the swap is agreed) for a floating market price. *See also* asset swap, cancellable swap, commodity swap, swaption)

swaption Option to enter into a swap at a future date and pre-determined fixed rate. The terms "payer's option" and "receiver's option" indicate whether the owner has the right, but not the obligation, to pay or to receive fixed rate payments (*see also* cancellable swap)

synthetic option Replication of the payment profile of an option using cash or, more often, futures contracts

TAPOs *see* Traded Average Price Options

technical analysis Name given to the analysis of price behaviour in markets, often using charts and graphs of historical market data. The aim is to highlight patterns in the way prices change which can be used to predict (and thus profit from) the nature of price changes in the future. Technical analysis concentrates on short-term market movements and can be contrasted with fundamental analysis (qv)

term repo Sale and repurchase of a security at an agreed maturity

termination Cancellation of a swap agreement, with settlement based on the current value of the swap

theta Measure used in the financial risk management industry to describe a change in the value of an option for a given passage of time (ie the "time decay" of the option)

time basis The basis (qv) that arises when a hedge position is placed in a contract month which differs from the underlying exposure

total return swap Swap agreement in which the total return of bank loans or credit-sensitive securities are exchanged for some other cashflow, usually tied to Libor, or other loans, or credit-sensitive securities. It allows participants to effectively go long or short the credit risk of the underlying asset

Traded Average Price Options (TAPOs) Name given to the average price financially settled options traded on the London Metals Exchange (LME). Equivalent to the average price (rate) or Asian-style options traded in the OTC market

traded option Option that is listed on and cleared by an exchange, with standard terms and delivery months

translation risk Foreign currency assets and liabilities of a firm may have to be translated into the domestic currency at the end of the firm's financial year. Translation risk is the risk that this translation will dramatically affect the value of the company's assets and liabilities due to exchange rate fluctuations

trigger option *see* barrier option

tri-party repo Delivery of collateral to an agreed third party

tunnel option Set of collars, typically zero cost, covering a series of maturities from the current date. They might, for example, be for dates six, 12, 18 and 24 months ahead. The special feature of a tunnel is that the strike price on both sets of options, not just on the options bought, is constant

unallocated accounts In contrast to allocated accounts (qv), in these accounts specific bars of metal are not held separately for each customer. Unallocated accounts are the most usual and the cheapest way of holding metal, but the account holder is treated as an unsecured creditor

up-and-away option *see* up-and-out option

up-and-in option Type of barrier option (qv) which is activated if the value of the underlying goes above a pre-determined level (*see also* down-and-in option)

up-and-out option Type of barrier option (qv) that is extinguished if the value of the underlying goes above a pre-determined level (*see also* down-and-out option)

value-at-risk (VAR) Methodological approach to calculating the financial exposure represented by financial instruments and portfolios of financial instruments. Formally, the probabilistic bound of market losses over a given period of time (known as the holding period) expressed in terms of a specified degree of certainty (known as the confidence interval). Put more simply, the VAR number is the worst-case loss expected over the holding period within the probability set out by the confidence interval. Larger losses are possible but with a low probability. For instance, a portfolio whose VAR is $20 million over a one-day holding period, with a 95% confidence interval, would have only a 5% chance of suffering an overnight loss greater than $20 million

VAR *see* value-at-risk

variance/covariance methodology Methodology for calculating the value-at-risk (qv) of a portfolio as a function of the volatility of each asset or liability position in the portfolio and the correlation between the positions

variation margin Additional cash or collateral margin payable by an investor or hedger when an open position held by them on an exchange is affected adversely by movements in the underlying

vega (kappa) Measure used in the financial risk management industry to describe the change in value of an option in response to a change in volatility

volatility Measure of the degree of variability, but not the direction, of prices or rates

warehouse receipt Depository receipt, stating quantity and quality of the metal held, that is given out when delivery is taken on a futures exchange

warehousing Term used to describe how financial intermediaries (eg swap dealers) run books of derivatives without matching transaction for transaction. The object is to allow the management of a book as a whole rather than as a set of individual deals. In theory, all market makers should warehouse

warrant Certificate, often issued

as part of a package together with a bond, giving the purchaser the right, but not the obligation, to buy a specified amount of a given asset, such as the issuer's equity (equity warrants), bonds (debt warrants), currency, oil, gold or other commodity, at a specified price during the course of a given period of time

yield curve Graphical representation of the term structure of interest rates, usually depicted as spot yields on bonds with different maturities but with the same risk factors plotted against maturity

zero-cost collar Purchase of a put option at a desired strike price and the simultaneous sale of a call at a strike set so that the premium collected on the call matches the premium paid for the put. This results in a transaction with zero up-front costs

zero-cost option *see* zero premium option

zero premium option Generic term for options for which there is no premium, either because the buyer undertakes to forgo a percentage of any gain or because he or she offsets the cost by writing other options (*see also* reduced cost option)

INDEX